THE DUTY OF CARE IN NEGLIGENCE

This book aims to provide a detailed analysis and overview of the duty of care enquiry, drawing on both academic analyses and judicial experience in leading common law systems. A new structure through which duty problems can be analysed is also proposed. Given the vast number of issues currently dealt with in the duty enquiry, the book puts forward several original arguments that provide fresh and original insight into this core concept in tort law, both in academia and in practice. The main overall achievement is to provide clarity of the concept to the reader.

Volume 26 in the series Hart Studies in Private Law

The Duty of Care in Negligence

James Plunkett

·H A R T·
PUBLISHING

OXFORD AND PORTLAND, OREGON
2018

Hart Publishing

An imprint of Bloomsbury Publishing Plc

Hart Publishing Ltd
Kemp House
Chawley Park
Cumnor Hill
Oxford OX2 9PH
UK

Bloomsbury Publishing Plc
50 Bedford Square
London
WC1B 3DP
UK

www.hartpub.co.uk
www.bloomsbury.com

Published in North America (US and Canada) by
Hart Publishing
c/o International Specialized Book Services
920 NE 58th Avenue, Suite 300
Portland, OR 97213-3786
USA

www.isbs.com

HART PUBLISHING, the Hart/Stag logo, BLOOMSBURY and the
Diana logo are trademarks of Bloomsbury Publishing Plc

First published 2018

British Library Cataloguing-in-Publication Data
A catalogue record for this book is available from the British Library.

ISBN:	HB:	978-1-50991-484-5
	ePDF:	978-1-50991-485-2
	ePub:	978-1-50991-486-9

Library of Congress Cataloging-in-Publication Data

Names: Plunkett, James C. (James Christopher), 1982- author.

Title: The duty of care in negligence / James Plunkett.

Description: Oxford [UK] ; Portland, Oregon : Hart Publishing, 2018.

Identifiers: LCCN 2017048783 (print) | LCCN 2017052189 (ebook) |
ISBN 9781509914869 (Epub) | ISBN 9781509914845 (hardback : alk. paper)

Subjects: LCSH: Reasonable care (Law) | Negligence. | Torts.

Classification: LCC K938 (ebook) | LCC K938 .P58 2018 (print) | DDC 346.03/2—dc23

LC record available at https://lccn.loc.gov/2017048783

Typeset by Compuscript Ltd, Shannon

To find out more about our authors and books visit www.hartpublishing.co.uk. Here you will find extracts,
author information, details of forthcoming events and the option to sign up for our newsletters.

ACKNOWLEDGEMENTS

This book is based largely on a doctoral thesis that I completed at the University of Oxford. First and foremost, I would therefore like to thank my DPhil supervisor, Donal Nolan, for his tremendous support and guidance both during the DPhil and beyond. I could not have hoped for a better supervisor and his contribution to this book has been invaluable.

I am also greatly indebted to those who have been generous enough to provide me with comments on earlier drafts, including Roderick Bagshaw, Angus Johnston, Ken Oliphant, Mark Lunney, James Goudkamp, Eric Descheemaeker, Andrew Robertson, and two anonymous reviewers.

I am also immensely grateful to the team at Hart Publishing, and in particular, Bill Asquith, Anne Fiegel, Linda Staniford, and Claire Banyard. I am also grateful to the *Cambridge Law Journal* for allowing me to reprint parts of a prior publication in Chapter Six, and to the *Monash Law Review* for allowing me to reprint a prior publication as chapter two.

Finally, my greatest thanks must go to my family, and in particular, mum, dad, Allison, and Clara, to whom I dedicate this book.

TABLE OF CONTENTS

LIST OF ABBREVIATIONS

B&M   Baker JH, *Baker and Milsom Sources of English Legal History: Private Law to 1750*, 2nd edn (OUP, 2010)
SS   Selden Society
OUP   Oxford University Press

LIST OF DIAGRAMS AND TABLES

TABLE OF CASES

Canada

Ireland

United Kingdom

United States

TABLE OF STATUTES

1

Introduction

A man is entitled to be as negligent as he pleases towards the whole world if he owes no duty to them.

Lord Esher, *Le Lievre v Gould* [1893] 1 QB 491, 497.

I. What is the Duty of Care?

The majority of the nominate torts offer only very narrowly defined levels of protection; that is, they protect only certain interests from interference caused by certain types of conduct. The law of private nuisance, for example, protects our interest in the peaceful use and enjoyment of our land from interference caused by others' use of their land; defamation protects our interest in our reputations from interference caused by another's representations; whilst false imprisonment protects our interest in freedom of movement from interference caused by another's physical restraint. Outside of these narrowly defined limits, the torts offer no protection at all. Negligence, on the other hand, the most commonly litigated of all torts, is defined purely by reference to the quality of the defendant's conduct. On its face, it is therefore capable of providing a practically limitless level of protection, ostensibly extending to *any* affected interest, caused by *any* carelessly performed activity. Yet, as Fleming has noted:

> [T]o permit the imposition of liability for *any* loss suffered by *anyone* as the result of carelessness would … [impose] too severe and indiscriminate a restriction on individual freedom of action by exposing the actor to the prospect of unpredictable liability.[1]

Accordingly, the scope of the law of negligence does not extend quite so far, and does not impose liability for *all* carelessly caused harm; rather, the law of negligence only imposes liability in circumstances where the defendant owes the claimant a 'duty of care'. The duty of care therefore performs the central normative function within the law of negligence, demarcating the circumstances in which a defendant will be held liable for carelessly causing damage to another, from the

---

[1] JG Fleming, *The Law of Torts*, 9th edn (Law Book Co, 1998) 150.

circumstances in which he may do so with impunity. Howarth encapsulates the role of duty nicely:

> The essence of a duty of care issue, as opposed to a causation, fault, or remoteness issue, is that the defendants are arguing that even though they were at fault, even though that fault caused the harm, even though the type of harm was foreseeable, even though the plaintiff was a foreseeable plaintiff and even though there were no intervening acts or events or any other reason to say that the damage was not caused directly by the defendant's fault, nevertheless the defendant should not be held liable in negligence.[2]

In the absence of a duty of care, carelessly caused injury is therefore *damnum absque injuria*.

II. Making Sense of the Duty of Care

Despite its purpose being so simply stated, identifying a set of coherent principles that is capable of explaining why a duty is owed in one case and not another has proved to be stubbornly elusive. The difficulty has only increased as the 'staggering march'[3] of negligence has continued throughout the twentieth and twenty-first century, and the range of circumstances that give rise to a duty of care has grown larger and larger. Indeed, it seems that just about any problem concerning the limits of the law of negligence can now be framed in terms of the defendant's duty of care. In response to the ever-increasing list of matters dealt with under the duty rubric, many of which involve entirely separate issues, the tendency has been for the courts to explain the existence or non-existence of a duty by reference to increasingly vague concepts, such as 'neighbourhood', 'proximity', and what is 'fair, just, and reasonable'. Whilst such labels might have the benefit of reconciling the cases, they only do so in the most abstract way, and so offer little-to-no predictive value in individual fact scenarios. Where, by contrast, principles with some explanatory power have been identified, they have almost invariably proved to be highly controversial, or only capable of explaining a small subclass of cases. Foreseeability of harm to the claimant, for example, has formed an integral element of every general duty test since *Heaven v Pender*,[4] yet is frequently criticised for being superfluous. Assumptions of responsibility are also often relied upon to explain the existence of a duty in certain cases, yet this explanation, too, is often criticised as being artificial, and only of very limited application in any event. Perhaps the most controversial of all explanations, however, are those based on 'policy', which,

---

[2] David Howarth, 'Duty of Care' in Ken Oliphant (ed), *The Law of Tort*, 2nd edn (LexisNexis Butterworths, 2007) 12.1. The claim that the issue of the 'foreseeable plaintiff' should not be a part of duty enquiry is a controversial one and so is discussed further in ch 4.

[3] Tony Weir, 'The Staggering March of Negligence' in Peter Cane and Jane Stapleton (eds), *The Law of Obligations: Essays in Celebration of John Fleming* (OUP, 1999).

[4] (1883) 11 QB 503 (CA).

despite often appearing to offer concise and convincing justifications for why a duty should or should not exist, are thought by many to be highly inappropriate. There are also those who claim that the duty enquiry itself is little more than a 'fifth wheel on the coach', performing no function not capable of being performed elsewhere in the negligence enquiry; in their opinion, we would be altogether better off without it. The apparent lack of any coherent understanding of the duty enquiry is no doubt one of the principal reasons why Ibbetson feels confident in claiming, 'That the tort of negligence is in a mess goes almost without saying.'[5]

III. The Aim of this Book

The general aim of this book is to provide a detailed overview and analysis of the duty of care enquiry, drawing on both academic analyses and judicial experience in leading common law systems. A new structure through which duty problems can be analysed is also proposed.[6] It is, of course, true that much has been written on the duty of care enquiry in the past, including countless articles and book chapters,[7] a number of books on particular duty problems,[8] and two monographs.[9] The articles and book chapters, however, inevitably tend to be piecemeal, focussing only on narrow aspects of the duty enquiry, often making it difficult to see how they fit into the larger picture; the books on duty issues, whilst typically highly insightful, again only focus on narrow aspects of duty rather than on how those issues fit into a broader enquiry;[10] and the existing monographs, aside from now being decades old, have tended to focus exclusively on the content of the law rather than providing an analysis of it. There is, then, no detailed overview and analysis of the duty enquiry as a whole. This book aims to remedy that deficiency. In particular, it aims to: provide a detailed overview of the history of the duty of care; bring together the disparate and often ostensibly unrelated commentary into a framework that provides a coherent picture of the concept as a whole; isolate and articulate the discrete problems dealt with under the (typically) singular duty rubric; provide original commentary and analyses of some of the existing debates;

---

[5] David Ibbetson, 'How the Romans Did for Us: Ancient Roots of the Tort of Negligence' (2003) 26 UNSWLJ 475, 475.

[6] Or, at least, it is encouraged that an existing but largely ignored structure is explicitly recognised.

[7] Many of these are cited throughout the book.

[8] See, eg, Christian Witting, *Liability for Negligent Misstatements* (OUP, 2004); Cherie Booth and Daniel Squires, *The Negligence Liability of Public Authorities* (OUP, 2006); Peter Handford, *Tort Liability for Mental Harm*, 3rd edn (Lawbook Co, 2016); Claire McIvor, *Third Party Liability in Tort* (Hart, 2006).

[9] AJE Jaffey, *The Duty of Care* (Dartmouth, 1992); Norman A Katter, *Duty of Care in Australia* (LBC Information Services, 1999).

[10] This is in no way intended as a criticism, but merely to highlight that the aim of such books is entirely different to the aim of this one.

provide overviews and analyses of a number of often overlooked and under-analysed aspects of the duty enquiry; articulate a more structured approach to resolving duty problems; and, finally, explore whether there are any practical differences in how the courts in different jurisdictions approach the duty problem. Ideally, we will then be able to see how we got into this 'mess', and how we might be able to get out of it.

IV. The Structure of this Book

The book consists of eight chapters in total; an introduction (chapter one), six substantive chapters (chapters two to seven), and a conclusion (chapter eight). Chapter two provides a historical introduction to the duty concept, beginning with an overview of how 'duty' first came to be an element of the negligence enquiry, and then moving on to the important period between the late-nineteenth and early-twentieth century, during which a general conception of the duty of care was sought and eventually articulated. Chapter three then provides an overview of the various methods through which the existence of a duty of care has subsequently been determined, starting with the 'neighbour principle', and then moving through to the *Anns* two-stage test, the *Caparo* three-stage test, the salient features test, and the pockets approach. An analysis of the benefits and difficulties of the various approaches is also provided. Chapter four turns to the anatomy of the duty concept, and it is argued that duty is best understood as consisting of two discrete parts: factual duty and notional duty. It is then suggested that the factual aspect of the duty enquiry is superfluous and that things would be simpler without it. Chapter five explores the general principles of the notional aspect of the duty enquiry, which, it is suggested, is best understood as consisting of two separate types of determinations: those that relate to broad situations, and those based on assumptions of responsibility. Both of these types of notional duty determinations are explored in detail, as is how they interact with each other. A method for resolving notional duty problems without the use of a singular general duty test is then proposed. Chapter six then considers some of the more theoretical aspects of the notional duty enquiry, including the propriety of basing notional duty determinations (relating to situations) on considerations of policy, as well as whether a notional duty enquiry is necessary at all. Chapter seven changes focus again, moving to an empirical study of ultimate appellate court duty decisions, and explores whether the understanding of duty provided in the previous chapters is actually reflected in judicial decisions, and the extent to which it differs among three leading jurisdictions. The six substantive chapters can therefore be best understood as approaching the duty concept from four primary perspectives: the historical development of the duty concept (chapters two and three), the anatomy of the duty concept (chapters four and five), theoretical issues involved in the duty concept (chapter six), and an empirical analysis of the duty concept (chapter seven).

V. Scope and Terminology

The analysis presented in this book is not intended to be jurisdiction specific, although the principal focus is on Commonwealth legal systems, and, in particular, the common law of Australia, Canada, and the UK. Sources from these jurisdictions therefore tend to be more frequently used than sources from other jurisdictions, though sources from South Africa, New Zealand, and the United States are also referred to. Chapter two, however, which explores an overview of the history of the duty of care, inevitably relies almost exclusively on English sources. Given the differences in the different jurisdictions' terminology for the parties before the court, the neutral 'claimant' and 'defendant' will be adopted when speaking in the abstract, but 'plaintiff', 'pursuer', 'claimant', 'defendant' and 'defender' will be used as appropriate when referring to specific parties. The 'plaintiff' terminology will also be used when discussing English cases decided prior to 26 April 1999, being the commencement date of the Civil Procedure Rules 1998. The book is also an exclusively *common law* analysis, and so the effect of any relevant legislation is not considered. For the avoidance of doubt, the common law of England and Wales, Northern Ireland and Scotland will be referred to collectively as the law of the UK.[11] The terms 'duty' and 'duty of care' are used interchangeably to avoid the latter term becoming monotonous.

---

[11] Indeed, as Stevens notes: 'In most, if not all, respects the law of torts as administered by the House of Lords is the law of the United Kingdom. This is so even if the body of law is given a different label (delict) north of the border. English and Scottish law have converged as a result of the House of Lords tying the two systems together in this area. Many of our leading torts cases come from Scotland, including, of course, the most well-known of all': Robert Stevens, 'Torts' in Louis Blom-Cooper, Gavin Drewry and Brice Dickson (eds), *The Judicial House of Lords: 1876–2009* (OUP, 2009) 629–30 (footnotes omitted).

2

The Historical Foundations
of the Duty of Care

Gaius speaks of the need to get back to the beginning of things, and every good lawyer knows that to understand a topic in the law of one time, you need to begin from the preceding period. New solutions are always developed from old ones, and in the process ideas get pulled out. Legal history is indispensable.

Peter Birks, 'The Roman Law Concept of Dominium and the Idea of Absolute Ownership' [1985] Acta Juridica 1, 3.

I. Introduction

Liability for carelessly caused damage has existed since at least the fourteenth century.[1] The duty of care, however, which plays the important role of specifying the circumstances in which that carelessly caused damage will be actionable, is a relatively modern invention, only emerging as recently as the early nineteenth century. This is not to say, of course, that prior to this point *all* carelessly caused damage was actionable; this has never been the position of the common law and limits on recoverability have always existed. It is the aim of this chapter to explore how those limits came to be determined via the idea of a 'duty of care', as well as how the existence of a duty of care subsequently came to be determined via a general test. In particular, the first part of the chapter brings together existing commentary to provide an overview of how the duty of care first came to be an element of the negligence enquiry. The second part of the chapter moves on to the important period between the late-nineteenth and early-twentieth century, about which surprisingly little has been written at all, during which a general conception of the duty of care, with which we are familiar today, was sought, and eventually achieved.

---

[1] In particular, liability for negligence under 'trespass on the case,' which has existed since the fourteenth century (see, eg, *Bukton v Tounesende* (1348) B&M 399, better known as the *Humber Ferry Case*), appears to have been fault based from the beginning (see David Ibbetson, 'How the Romans Did for Us: Ancient Roots of the Tort of Negligence' (2003) 26 UNSWLJ 475 501), however it is arguable that early liability under trespass *vi et armis*, which has existed since the thirteenth century, *also* required that the harm was caused carelessly (JH Baker, *An Introduction to English Legal History*, 4th edn (OUP, 2007) 403). See also the comments in fn 9.

II. The Beginnings of the Duty of Care

The term 'duty' has been used for centuries, and it is not unusual to find obligations described as 'duties' in medieval cases. A 'duty' to keep one's fire safely, for example, can be traced back to the early fifteenth century.[2] However, prior to the emergence of an independent action for negligence, 'duty' was little more than a word, and played no analytical role in the determination of questions of liability. Indeed, 'negligence', too, was little more than a word under the early common law, merely being a way in which a number of discrete wrongs could be committed; a pleader's adverb[3] rather than a wrong in itself. For example, actions were available for: the negligent mis-performance of an undertaking;[4] the negligent non-performance of an undertaking;[5] the negligent loss of control of dangerous forces, such as fires[6] animals,[7] or water;[8] and the negligent causing of harm through the application of force to the plaintiff's land, goods, or person.[9] Without any suggestion that negligence itself gave rise to liability outside of these discrete situations, a duty of care type device was hardly needed, as the discrete situations in which negligence was an ingredient served precisely the same purpose as the modern duty of care: to identify those circumstances in which the law imposed an obligation to avoid negligently causing damage to another.

By the end of the seventeenth century, however, negligence was coming to be seen as the basis for an independent wrong in itself, based on the defendant's

---

[2] *Beaulieu v Finglam* (1401) B&M 610.

[3] Vernon Palmer, 'Why Privity Entered Tort—an Historical Examination of *Winterbottom v Wright*' (1983) 27 Am J Legal Hist 85, 87. In addition to 'negligently', adverbs such as 'improvidently', 'unskilfully', 'carelessly' were also used to describe the defendant's conduct: see JH Baker, 'Trespass, Case and the Common Law of Negligence 1500–1700' in Schrage EJH (ed), *Negligence The Comparative Legal History of the Law of Torts (Comparative Studies in Continental and Anglo-American Legal History; CSC 22)* (Duncker & Humblot, 2001) 53.

[4] *Bukton v Tounesende* (1348) B&M 399.

[5] *Somerton v Colles* (1433) B&M 427; *Shipton v Dogge (no 2)* (1442) B&M 434 (also known as *Doige's Case*).

[6] *Beaulieu v Finglam* (1401) B&M 610; *Critoft v Emson and Nicols* (1506) CP 40/978 m 320, B&M 619 (fn 41); *Anon* (1582) B&M 624; *Turberville v Stampe* (1697) 12 Mod 152, 88 ER 1228.

[7] *Beneyt v Brokkere* (1358) cited in Robert C Palmer, *English Law in the Age of the Black Death: 1348–1381* (University of North Carolina Press 1993) 239, 371; *Mason v Keeling* (1700) 1 Ld Raym 606, 91 ER 1305. The action, known as *scienter* (knowingly), was used where the claimant had knowingly retained an animal with dangerous propensities.

[8] *Stapleton v Snayth* (1354) YB Pas 19, 32b–33a, [49] cited in ibid 398 and AKR Kiralfy, *The Action on the Case* (Sweet & Maxwell, 1951), 210; *Guybon v Palmer* (1516) cited in Baker, 'Trespass, Case and the Common Law of Negligence 1500–1700' (n 3) 62 (fn 66); *Abbot of Stratford v Hubbulthorn* (1529) cited in ibid.

[9] Whilst it is true that the action trespass *vi et armis* had no *formal* requirement of fault, and cases such as *Hulle v Orynge* (1466) B&M 369, 370–71 ('*The Case of Thorns*') (Choke J) and *Weaver v Ward* (1616) B&M 375, 376 (Hobart CJ) *appear to* impose strict liability, the action nevertheless does not seem to have been actionable in the absence of negligence: Baker, 'Trespass, Case and the Common Law of Negligence 1500–1700' (n 3) 65, and DJ Ibbetson, *A Historical Introduction to the Law of Obligations* (OUP, 1999) 61.

failure to take reasonable care.[10] Indeed, by 1700 plaintiffs were arguing that 'a man shall be answerable for all mischief proceeding from his neglect or his actions, unless they were of unavoidable necessity,'[11] and by the middle of the century, a chapter of the influential textbook *An Institute of the Law Relative to Trials at Nisi Prius* was titled 'Of Injuries Arising from Negligence or Folly,'[12] which suggested that:

> Every man ought to take reasonable care that he does not injure his Neighbour; therefore wherever a Man receives any Hurt through the Default of another, though the same were not wilful, yet if it be occasioned by Negligence or Folly, the law gives him an Action to recover Damages for the injury so sustained.[13]

This conceptual shift from discrete actions in which negligence was an ingredient to a single action based on negligence alone, however, presented a potentially major problem: whilst other wrongs were confined to the invasion of a particular interest,[14] there were no obvious confines on liability for the potentially limitless consequences of negligent behaviour. To modern eyes this might seem to have provided the ideal catalyst for the development of a duty type control device on the otherwise unbounded action for negligence. Yet, this was not the case at all, as notwithstanding its potential, the early actions for negligence were not common,[15] and tended to be confined to directly caused personal injuries and property damage in any event. There was therefore no immediate need to limit its scope. On the contrary, the idea of duty first emerged not as a way to limit liability for negligence, but to *expand* it, by allowing claims that would fail in contract to be converted to claims that could succeed in tort.

A. Duty Enters Relationship Negligence: From Contract to Tort and the Elevation of Duty

At around the same time that negligence was emerging as an independent wrong, so, too, were 'contract' and 'tort' emerging as distinct legal entities: the former based on obligations arising from private agreements and the latter concerning obligations arising from the law.[16] Generally this distinction was unproblematic,

---

[10] Many credit this shift as commencing with *Mitchell v Allestry* (1676) 1 Vent 295, 86 ER 190; (1675) 3 Keb 650, 84 ER 392 (though, the exact spelling of the parties' names varies). See, eg: Baker, *An Introduction to English Legal History* (n 1) 411; SFC Milsom, *Historical Foundations of the Common Law*, 2nd edn (Butterworths, 1981); Ibbetson (n 1) 501–02.

[11] *Mason v Keeling* (1700) 1 Ld Raym 606, 607; 91 ER 1305, 1306.

[12] Francis Buller, *An Institute of the Law Relative to Trials at Nisi Prius* (Dublin, 1768).

[13] ibid 35.

[14] Private nuisance, for example, was confined to interference with real property.

[15] Baker, *An Introduction to English Legal History* (n 1) 411–12: 'The means were now in place for the development of a distinct tort of negligence; but it did not happen suddenly. By modern standards there appears to have been remarkably little accident litigation.'

[16] ibid 317–18; 401.

as actions based on non-performance of an undertaking were clearly contractual, and actions based on the negligent causation of harm independent of any prior relationship were clearly tortious. But what about actions based on the negligent mis-performance of an undertaking, which were clearly ambiguous: should they be based on the breach of an implied promise to perform the undertaking with care or on the negligent performance itself?[17] This was particularly problematic in actions for negligence that arose from a prior relationship, including those against lawyers, surgeons, carriers, etc:[18] were they based in contract or tort? It took the courts over 100 years to answer this question, and they did so in the context of the liability of the 'common carrier,'[19] which straddled the tort/contract divide almost perfectly.

At the start of the eighteenth century the liability of common carriers was grounded in the so-called 'custom of the realm', the medieval action that imposed strict liability on innkeepers[20] and, later, carriers.[21] Over time, however, the custom of the realm came to be seen as nothing but part of the common law and not to be specifically pleaded,[22] so plaintiffs 'dropped the statement of the custom from the declaration and confined themselves to describing the defendant as a common carrier without more.'[23] By the middle of the century, however, actions against carriers for lost goods were being classified as contractual. In *Dale v Hall*,[24] for example, the court held that a 'promise to carry safely, is a promise to keep safely.'[25] The same conclusion was reached more explicitly in *Gibbon v Paynton*:[26] 'the true principle of a carrier's being answerable is the reward.' By the later part of the century, however, the contractual basis of the carrier's liability was put in doubt, when it was said in *Forward v Pittard*:[27]

> It appears from all the cases for 100 years back, that there are events for which the carrier is liable independent of his contract. By the nature of his contract, he is liable for all due

---

[17] DJ Ibbetson, 'The Tort of Negligence in the Common Law in the Nineteenth and Twentieth Centuries' in EJH Schrage (ed), *Negligence The Comparative Legal History of the Law of Torts (Comparative Studies in Continental and Anglo-American Legal History; CSC 22)* (Duncker & Humblot, 2001) 237. Prior to the tort-contract distinction, both the mis-performance and non-performance of an undertaking fell under the action on the case for *assumpsit* (which can be translated as 'he has undertaken'): Baker, *An Introduction to English Legal History* (n 1) 338.

[18] MJ Prichard, *Scott v Shepherd (1773) and the Emergence of the Tort of Negligence* (SS, 1976) 24–25. Of course, where the plaintiff had a special agreement with the defendant he would obviously sue in contract, but often this was not the case.

[19] ibid 25.

[20] *Navenby v Lasseks* (1368) B&M 603 (also known as *Navenby v Lascells* (1368); see Baker, *An Introduction to English Legal History* (n 1) 408).

[21] *Rich v Kneeland* (1613) B&M 614–15. See also, William Selwyn, *Abridgement of the Law of Nisi Prius*, vol II, 4th edn (Stevens and Sons, 1817) 378–80.

[22] Prichard (n 18) 26.

[23] ibid.

[24] (1750) 1 Wils KB 281, 95 ER 619.

[25] ibid 282, 620 (Lee CJ). See also James Oldham, *The Mansfield Manuscripts and the Growth of English Law in the Eighteenth Century*, vol II (University of North Carolina Press, 1992) 1118.

[26] (1769) 4 Burr 2298, 2302; 98 ER 199, 201.

[27] (1785) 1 TR 27, 99 ER 953.

care and diligence; and for any negligence he is suable on his contract. But there is a
further degree of responsibility by the custom of the realm, that is, by the common law;
a carrier is in the nature of an insurer.[28]

Despite the courts' wavering about the proper basis of the carrier's liability, as long
as plaintiffs suffered no procedural advantage in either tort or contract, the source
of liability was not of paramount importance.

By the start of the nineteenth century, however, procedural differences between
contract and tort were emerging. Perhaps most significantly, the rules of joinder
were favourable to plaintiffs who sued in tort; in particular, whilst liability in tort
was severable, and so a plaintiff could sue any of a group of defendant carriers,
liability in contract was joint, meaning all parties to the simple contract of carriage had to be discovered and listed before they could be sued,[29] and the acquittal
of *any* of the co-defendants would be fatal to the plaintiff's claim.[30] Actions in
tort also had a potentially longer limitation period,[31] and were thought to entitle
a plaintiff to higher damages.[32] To avoid the procedural disadvantages associated
with contract, plaintiffs who had suffered an injury in the course of the negligent
mis-performance of a contract therefore began to formulate their declarations
in tort. But on what basis could they justify this? How did plaintiffs distinguish
between a claim in tort and a claim in contract? They could not base their claim
on the older action on the case for *assumpsit*, as *assumpsit* had recently come to
be identified with consideration, and so was too closely connected to the promise
itself. They could also not base their claim on the custom of the realm as it was no
longer being pleaded.[33] Instead, plaintiffs focussed on the source of the defendant's 'duty'. As Ibbetson explains:

> The nineteenth century witnessed an increasing recognition that the main division within
> the law of obligations was that between contract and tort ... Given this division, some
> distinguishing criterion was essential, but ... none could be found within the earlier com-
> mon law. Moreover, since it was well established that in a wide range of cases a tortious
> action could be brought for the negligent breach of a contractual duty it was no solution
> to say that an action was contractual whenever there was a relevant contract between
> the parties. The most straightforward test was to analyse both contractual and tortious
> obligations as arising out of breaches of duties, and say that the duty in contract arose out
> of the agreement of the parties while the duty in tort arose by operation of law.[34]

---

[28] ibid 33, 956.

[29] Prichard (n 18) 27; Ibbetson, *A Historical Introduction to the Law of Obligations* (n 9) 171–72.

[30] Prichard (n 18) 27; Ibbetson, *A Historical Introduction to the Law of Obligations* (n 9) 171–72.

[31] In contractual actions the limitation period commenced at the point of the breach, whereas in
tort it commenced at the time of the injury. See *Battley v Faulkner* (1820) 3 B & Ald 288, 106 ER 668;
Dyster v Battye (1820) 3 B & Ald 448, 106 ER 727; *Fraser v Swansea Canal Navigation Co* (1834) 1 Ad
& El 354, 110 ER 1241. See also Ibbetson, *A Historical Introduction to the Law of Obligations* (n 9) 172.

[32] Palmer (n 3) 89.

[33] According to Prichard, it was also 'too cumberous an allegation to develop into any kind of
generalised test': Prichard (n 18) 31.

[34] David Ibbetson, '"The Law of Business Rome": Foundations of the Anglo-American Tort of Negligence' (1999) 52 CLP 74, 88. See also Percy Winfield, 'Duty in Tortious Negligence' (1934) Colum L

Unsurprisingly, plaintiffs' attempts to use 'duty' as a tool by which they could circumvent the formalities of a claim in contract were contested by defendants. Initially, the courts sided with the defendants and insisted that, despite the plaintiff's allegations of a 'duty' in tort, the cause of action against a common carrier was always contractual.[35] Yet in *Govett v Radnidge*,[36] where the defendant carrier negligently staved a hogshead of treacle as they were loading it, the King's Bench held that the plaintiff was entitled to sue in tort:

> What inconvenience is there in suffering the party to allege his gravamen, if he please, as consisting in a breach of duty arising out of an employment for hire, and to consider that breach of duty as tortious negligence, instead of considering the same circumstances as forming a breach of promise implied from the same consideration of hire.[37]

The court affirmed its position in *Ansell v Waterhouse*,[38] a case in which a stage-coach proprietor received the plaintiff's wife to be carried safely 'yet the defendant not regarding his duty in this behalf conducted himself so carelessly, negligently and unskillfully …' that the coach was overturned and the plaintiff's wife 'was greatly injured &c.'[39] Despite the defendant arguing that the plaintiff was required to sue in contract, and so locate and join all 16 other proprietors of the stage coach as co-defendants, the plea was rejected and the plaintiff was permitted to proceed in tort.[40] In *Bretherton v Wood*[41] the Court of Exchequer Chamber affirmed that an action against a common carrier could be grounded purely in tort: 'a breach of this duty is a breach of the law, and for this breach an action lies founded on the common law, which action wants not the aid of contract to support it.'[42]

In the following years, other cases of negligence arising from a prior relationship also came to be grounded in tort.[43] In *Boorman v Brown*,[44] for example, the Court of Exchequer held that a broker owed a duty to his client because 'the principle … would seem to be that the contract creates a duty, and the neglect to perform that duty, or the nonfeasance, is a ground of action upon a tort.'[45] And so by the end of

---

Rev 41, 65: 'In the first half of the nineteenth century contract and tort were slowly being disentangled, and negligence had gradually come into existence as an independent tort (in addition to retaining its old meaning of a mode in which a wrongful act might possibly be committed). In the process of separating contract from tort and in the development of the tort of negligence, a confused notion about assumpsit became the germ of the duty idea. It was thought that, as assumpsit in contract always showed an "undertaking" of liability, therefore liability in tort must show something equivalent to it, ie "duty" …'.

[35] Prichard (n 18) 27–28.
[36] (1802) 3 East 62, 102 ER 520.
[37] ibid 70, 523 (Lord Ellenborough CJ).
[38] (1817) 6 M&S 385, 105 ER 1286.
[39] Ibid.
[40] ibid. See also Prichard (n 18) 28.
[41] (1821) 3 Brod & Bing 54, 129 ER 1203.
[42] ibid 62, 1206. See also Ibbetson, *A Historical Introduction to the Law of Obligations* (n 9) 172.
[43] Prichard (n 18) 28.
[44] (1842) 3 QB 511, 114 ER 603.
[45] ibid 526, 609 (CJ Tindall). This sweeping statement, 'open to the objection that it made every breach of contract into a tort', was soon scaled down: Palmer (n 3) 91.

the first quarter of the nineteenth century actions for negligence against those in prior relationships were able to be based in tort and rested upon the defendant's 'duty' arising from law.

B. Duty Enters Non-Relationship Negligence

The start of the nineteenth century saw a significant increase in the number of negligence claims brought before the courts. Winfield attributes the rise to '… industrial machinery. Early railroad trains, in particular, were notable neither for speed nor safety. They killed any object from a Minister of State to a wandering cow, and this naturally reacted on the law.'[46] Whatever the cause, the increase in claims forced the courts to offer further guidance as to the proper scope and limits of negligence actions. Although negligence actions arising from prior relationships had come to rest on the idea of the negligent breach of a tortious duty, duty did not yet play an explicit role in the determination of liability for negligence in non-relationship cases. This, however, soon began to change as the language of duty eventually permeated actions for non-relationship negligence.

As had been the case with relationship negligence, initially the language of 'duty' was only used by plaintiffs. In *Daniels v Potter*,[47] for example, the plaintiff was injured when he was struck by the defendants' cellar flap as he was walking in the street. In his declaration the plaintiff alleged that:

> [I]t was the duty of the defendants so to place the cellar flap as to not injure any of the king's subjects passing along the highway; and they, not regarding their duty, so negligently, carelessly, and improperly placed it, that, by reason of their negligence, it fell upon him.[48]

Shortly thereafter, in *Luxford v Large*,[49] a plaintiff sued a defendant ship-owner for negligently sailing his steam ship in such a way that it created a large swell in the River Thames, which filled and sank the plaintiff's boat. Again, the plaintiff

---

[46] Percy Winfield, 'The History of Negligence in the Law of Torts' (1926) 42 LQR 184, 195. For a more detailed overview of the societal background see: WR Cornish and GdN Clark, *Law and Society in England 1750–1950* (Sweet & Maxwell 1989) 483–84: 'Transport provided the most dramatic evidence of increasing risk. The improvement of eighteenth century roads through turnpike trusts and new techniques of construction brought a growth of road traffic that constantly threatened the very advances. Yet speeds increased: 4–5 m.p.h. in mid-century to 10–14 m.p.h. by the 1830s'; D Nolan, 'The Fatal Accidents Act 1846' in TT Arvind and J Steele (ed), *Tort Law and the Legislature: Common Law, Statute and the Dynamics of Legal Change* (Hart, 2012) 135–37. See also Baker, *An Introduction to English Legal History* (n 1) 412, who notes that 'The apparent explosion in the number of negligence cases … is in part an illusion caused by the beginning of nisi prius reporting in the 1790s. Nevertheless, there does appear to have been an increase in the number of cases.' For a detailed history of traffic liability in England and Wales, see: R Bagshaw, 'The Development of Traffic Liability in England and Wales' in Wolfgang Ernst (ed), *The Development of Traffic Liability* (Cambridge University Press, 2010).

[47] (1830) 4 C&P 262, 172 ER 697.

[48] ibid 265, 698 (Wilde Sergt).

[49] (1833) 5 C&P 421, 172 ER 1036.

described the defendant's negligence as consisting of a breach of duty ('not regarding his duty, &c.'[50]). Then, in *Drew v New River Co*,[51] the plaintiff alleged that by reason of the defendants being about to:

> perform certain works respecting certain water-pipes of theirs under the pavement of a public footway … thereupon it became *the duty of the defendants*, by their workmen and servants, to use due and proper care and precaution in performing the said work, and laying and depositing the said stones, &c., so that the King's subjects might not be injured thereby …[52]

The year 1837, however, marked a 'turning point',[53] as both defendants and judges, rather than just plaintiffs, also began to adopt the language of duty, with judges even using the idea of duty to determine questions of liability. The first such case appears to be the well-known *Vaughan v Menlove*,[54] where the defendant's carelessly constructed hay rick had caught fire and burned down the plaintiff's nearby house. In response to the plaintiff's declaration that the defendant had not been 'regarding his duty',[55] the defendant denied liability using the same language as the plaintiff:

> [T]here was no duty imposed on the Defendant, as there is on carriers or other bailees, under an implied contract, to be responsible for the exercise of any given degree of prudence: the Defendant had a right to place his stack as near to the extremity of his own land as he pleased …[56]

Vaughan J, however, rejected the defendant's submission on the basis that 'every one takes upon himself the duty of so dealing with his own property as not to injure the property of others.'[57]

Later the same year was the case of *Langridge v Levy*.[58] The defendant had sold a gun to the father of the plaintiff, and falsely represented that the gun was 'good, safe and secure'.[59] However, after the father gave the gun to his son, the plaintiff discharged it and was injured when the gun 'burst and exploded' in his hands.[60] As the plaintiff could not argue that he was a party to the contract of sale it was instead argued that liability arose by reason of a breach of the defendant's duty: 'the law imposes on all persons who deal in dangerous commodities or instruments, an obligation that they should use reasonable care …'[61] The defendant,

---

[50] ibid 422, 1036.
[51] (1834) 6 C&P 754, 172 ER 1449.
[52] ibid 422, 1036 (emphasis added). See also Prichard (n 18) 42.
[53] Winfield, 'Duty in Tortious Negligence' (n 34) 51.
[54] (1837) 3 Bing NC 468, 132 ER 490.
[55] ibid 469, 491.
[56] ibid 472, 492.
[57] ibid 477, 494.
[58] (1837) 2 M&W 519, 150 ER 863.
[59] The court held that it was, in fact, a 'bad, unsafe, ill-manufactured and dangerous gun': ibid 519, 863.
[60] ibid.
[61] ibid 525, 865.

however, disputed this: 'no duty could result out of a mere private contract, the defendant being clothed with no official or professional character out of which a known duty could arise.'[62] The court agreed with the defendant, as to uphold the widely expressed duty formulated by the plaintiff would:

> lead to that indefinite extent of liability ... [and] would be an authority for any action against the vendors, even of such instruments and articles as are dangerous in themselves, at the suit of *any person* whomsoever into whose hands they might happen to pass, and who should be injured thereby.[63]

Notwithstanding the court's rejection of the plaintiff's submissions on duty, it nevertheless found for him on the grounds of deceit: the defendant had warranted the gun to be safe, which it was not, and this was fraudulent misrepresentation.[64]

Duty was again the determining factor in the famous and much-discussed case of *Winterbottom v Wright*.[65] The Postmaster General had contracted with the defendant to provide a mail coach, and, separately, with the plaintiff's employer to horse the coach and to provide a driver. The plaintiff, who was employed to drive the coach, was injured when he was thrown from the coach after its wheel fell off, the result of the defendant failing to maintain the coach as he was required to do under his contract with the Postmaster General. As the carriage had been provided by the defendant under contract to the Postmaster General, there was no contract between the plaintiff and the defendant. The plaintiff therefore alleged that the defendant owed him a 'duty' by virtue of his contract with the Postmaster General to 'keep and maintain the said mail-coach in a fit, proper, safe, and secure state and condition for the purpose aforesaid.'[66] The court, however, found that no such duty existed, as to allow the plaintiff to be owed a duty based on a contract to which he was not a party:

> [M]ight be the means of letting in upon us an infinity of actions ... [and] Unless we confine the operation of such contracts as this to the parties who entered into them, the most absurd and outrageous consequences, to which I can see no limit, would ensue.[67]

Although the basis for the denial of a duty has been the subject of much discussion,[68] it was nevertheless the lack of a relevant duty that determined the question of liability.

By the middle of the nineteenth century, then, the idea of duty was being used to explain liability in cases of both relationship and non-relationship negligence alike. Nevertheless, there was no sudden assertion of a duty in *every* negligence

---

[62] ibid 521, 864.
[63] ibid 530, 868.
[64] ibid 532, 868–69. See also Winfield, 'Duty in Tortious Negligence' (n 34) 53.
[65] (1842) 10 M&W 109, 152 ER 402.
[66] ibid 109, 403.
[67] ibid 114, 405 (Lord Abinger CB).
[68] Palmer (n 3).

claim or any dramatic change in the style of pleadings;[69] duty was still only being used in an ad hoc manner to bolster claims, rather than because it was required. However, now that the language of duty had become commonplace, it was only 'a very short step from this to say that negligence is not actionable *unless* there is a duty to take care.'[70]

C. Duty as an Element of the Action for Negligence

Despite the language of duty being used in relationship negligence since the very early nineteenth century and non-relationship negligence since the 1830s, it was not until the second half of the century that judges began to insist that a duty of care was a *necessary* ingredient in cases of negligence. One of the earliest such cases appears to have been *Degg v Midland Railway Company*,[71] where Bramwell B held, 'There is no absolute or intrinsic negligence; it is always relative to some circumstances of time, place, or person ... there can be no action except in respect of a duty infringed ...'[72] The position was forcefully affirmed in 1860 by Erle CJ in *Marfell v The South Wales Railway Co*:[73]

> The undefined latitude of meaning in which the word 'negligence' has been used, appears to me to have introduced the evil of uncertain law to a pernicious extent; and I think it essential to ascertain that there was a legal duty, and a breach thereof, before a party is made liable by reason of negligence.[74]

And in 1862 Wilde B insisted in *Swan v North British Australasian Co*[75] that, 'The action for negligence proceeds from the idea of an obligation towards the plaintiff to use care, and a breach of that obligation to the plaintiff's injury.'[76] The insistence on a duty was soon seen in other cases,[77] and Wilde B's definition was incorporated into Addison's 1864 edition of *A Treatise on the Law of Torts*.[78] What, however, was the motivation for this significant change? It seems that the elevation

---

[69] Prichard (n 18) 33.

[70] Winfield, 'Duty in Tortious Negligence' (n 34) 54.

[71] (1857) 1 H&N 773, 156 ER 1413.

[72] ibid 781–82, 1416.

[73] (1860) 8 CB NS 525, 141 ER 1271.

[74] ibid 534, 1275.

[75] (1862) 7 H&N 603, 158 ER 611.

[76] ibid 636, 625.

[77] See, eg, *Cox v Burbidge* (1863) 13 CB NS 431, 436; 143 ER 171, 173 (Erle CJ) ('[there had to be] some affirmative proof of negligence in the defendant in respect of a duty owing to the plaintiff'); *Grill v General Iron Screw Colliery Co* (1866) 1 CP 600 (CP), 612 (Willes J) ('[negligence is] really the absence of such care as it was the duty of the defendant to use'). See also WR Cornish and others, *The Oxford History of the Laws of England*, vol XII: 1820–1914 Private Law (OUP, 2010) 923.

[78] CG Addison, *Wrongs and their Remedies, Being a Treatise on the Law of Torts*, 2nd edn (V and R Stevens, Sons and Haynes, 1864) 15.

of the importance of duty of care in liability for negligence was the result of a number of factors.[79]

As we have already seen, the concept of duty allowed courts to distinguish between the basis of contractual and tortious obligations. As Ibbetson explains:

> [T]he most straightforward test was to analyse both contractual and tortious obligations as arising out of breaches of duties, and to say that the obligation in contract arose out of the agreement of the parties while the duty in tort arose by operation of law ... [and] More importantly for the present investigation, it provided a further stimulation to conceive of liability in tort in general as deriving from the breach of a legal duty, and liability in negligence in particular as deriving from the breach of a duty of care.[80]

Ibbetson also points to the tendency in the nineteenth century to equate negligence with neglect, such that doing something badly (misfeasance) was seen as a different type of wrong to neglecting to do something that was required (negligence). The analysis of liability in terms of a neglect or breach of a duty, however, explained liability for acts as well as omissions:[81] negligence was the omission to do something you had a duty to do or the doing of something you had a duty not to do.

The duty/breach structure was also convenient as it not only mirrored the historic twofold structure of the action on the case, which required the plaintiff to set out the facts of their action that gave rise to the defendant's particular obligation as well as the way in which the obligation had wrongfully been breached,[82] but also provided a simple way to explain why liability attached to some types of negligent conduct but not others; in the former there was a duty to take care and in the latter there was not.[83] The shift also appears to have been influenced, albeit on a higher level of generality, by the passing of the Common Law Procedure Act 1852, which abolished the forms of action and thereby prompted a more 'scientific treatment of principles'[84] of the common law.

---

[79] Ibbetson, *A Historical Introduction to the Law of Obligations* (n 9) 170–74; Ibbetson, 'The Tort of Negligence in the Common Law in the Nineteenth and Twentieth Centuries' (n 17) 235–41.

[80] Ibbetson, 'The Tort of Negligence in the Common Law in the Nineteenth and Twentieth Centuries' (n 17) 238.

[81] Ibbetson, '"The Law of Business Rome": Foundations of the Anglo-American Tort of Negligence' (n 34) 87–88; Ibbetson, 'The Tort of Negligence in the Common Law in the Nineteenth and Twentieth Centuries' (n 17) 236.

[82] The older writs generally adopted the syntactical structure 'whereas X, nevertheless, Y'. As Birks explains, 'The whereas clauses thus supplied the relevant background and, in particular, advanced some basis for the defendant's being under a legal duty to the plaintiff to behave differently from the dreadful way in which the 'nevertheless' sentence then reveals that he did behave': Peter Birks, 'Negligence in the Eighteenth Century Common Law' in EJH Schrage (ed), *Negligence The Comparative Legal History of the Law of Torts (Comparative Studies in Continental and Anglo-American Legal History; CSC 22)* (Duncker & Humblot, 2001) 186. See also Ibbetson, 'How the Romans Did for Us: Ancient Roots of the Tort of Negligence' (n 1) 511–12.

[83] Ibbetson, *A Historical Introduction to the Law of Obligations* (n 9) 171.

[84] Frederick Pollock, *The Law of Torts: A Treatise on the Principles of Obligations Arising from Civil Wrongs in the Common Law*, 1st edn (Stevens and Sons, 1887) vii.

However, perhaps the most significant reason for the adoption of an analysis of liability based on the breach of a duty was that it allowed judges to have more control over the open-endedness of the early law of negligence. In particular, without any limitation on recoverability for carelessly caused harm, there was a considerable expansion in claims for negligence in the first half of the nineteenth century,[85] and judges soon became concerned about the 'fact that juries were willing to give damages on the merest suggestion that the defendants—particularly railway companies—were negligent.'[86] In *Wilkinson v Fairrie*,[87] for example, although the defendant directed the plaintiff into an unlit passage where he fell down an open stairwell, the plaintiff's claim was abruptly rejected on the basis that 'if he could see his way, the accident was the result of his own negligence; if he could not ... he ought not to have proceeded without a light.'[88] By insisting on the existence of a duty, and then formulating that duty as they saw fit, judges were able to exercise far greater control over questions of liability.[89] Indeed, the more precisely the judges formulated the duties, the more control they had, as they could remove cases from juries altogether if they determined that the relevant duty did not exist. In *Collis v Selden*,[90] for example, a plaintiff was injured when a chandelier, negligently hung by the defendant, fell on him. Rather than find that a general duty existed and leave the question of fault to the jury, the judge determined the matter himself by holding that no relevant duty existed in the first place, because:

> There would be no end of actions if we were to hold that a person having once done a piece of work carelessly, should, independently of honesty of purpose, be fixed with liability in this way by reason of bad materials or insufficient fastening.[91]

As a result of the courts' tendency to define duties of care in such great detail, there soon emerged a long list of specific instance duties. This is evident in Beven's *Principles of the Law of Negligence*,[92] in which he devoted 700 pages to the multitude of individual duty situations. This approach to duty later came to be known as the 'multifarious' duty approach.

Of course, it was one thing to say that a duty was necessary, but another to explain why a duty existed in one case and not another. What, then, was the test for the existence of a duty? It seems that the earliest duties were simply based on the old 'forms of action' and earlier common law:

> A duty to ensure passenger safety was recognised, which was analogous to contractual duties, or to duties imposed by those exercising a 'common calling'. The duty to take

---

[85] Cornish and others (n 77) 921–22.

[86] ibid 923.

[87] (1862) 1 H&C 633, 158 ER 1038.

[88] ibid 634, 1038 (Pollock CB following Bramwell B in the court below).

[89] JC Smith, 'Clarification of Duty—Remoteness Probems through a New Physiology of Negligence: Economic Loss, a Test Case' (1974) 9 UBC LawRev 213 221; Ibbetson, *A Historical Introduction to the Law of Obligations* (n 9) 173.

[90] (1868) 3 CP 495.

[91] ibid 497–98 (Willes J). See also Cornish and others (n 77) 944.

[92] Thomas Beven, *Principles of the Law of Negligence* (Stevens and Haynes, 1889).

care to avoid collisions was seen as analogous to the interests protected by the action of trespass. A duty not to leave a hazardous item in public places was recognised, and analogised to nuisance. A duty not to sell dangerous goods was recognised, which was a version of the duty not to deceive.[93]

Indeed, in Beven's *Principles of the Law of Negligence* we find many 'duties' that are said to arise from cases that occurred sometimes hundreds of years before negligence gave rise to an independent cause of action, let alone any conception of duty.[94] Later duties, on the other hand, appear to have developed incrementally, 'whereby the plaintiff was expected to demonstrate the existence of a duty by showing that the case fell within an already recognised duty situation or was very closely analogous to one.'[95] When there was no existing authority a duty was therefore unlikely to be recognised. Courts were also quick to deny the existence of a duty where they felt it would lead to a significant extension in liability. In *Morgan v The Vale of Neath Railway Co*,[96] for example, Pollock CB denied that a master owed a duty to a servant who had been injured by the negligence of another servant, because: 'It appears to me that we should be letting in a flood of litigation, were we to decide the present case in favour of the plaintiff.'[97] In some sense, then, the law of negligence was again beginning to resemble a long list of discrete torts in which negligence was in ingredient rather than a conceptually unified whole. This, however, was soon about to change.

III. Towards a General Conception

Whilst the multifarious approach to duties gave the judiciary the control they sought, at a time when academics such as Austin, Wendell Holmes and Pollock were looking for more philosophical foundations of negligence and tort law, much of which was based around the language of duty,[98] the unprincipled and 'uncultivated wilderness' of single instance duty situations of which the law consisted seemed unsatisfactory.[99] Was there a test for the existence of a duty of care that could be based on something more abstract, with the result that a more general rule could be formulated? Was there a principled explanation as to *why* a duty

---

[93] Cornish and others (n 77) 923–24.

[94] Many of which were mere jurisdictional artefacts, having evolved from the early courts' jurisdictional limits into substantive law: see, eg, Milsom (n 10) 286–87.

[95] Ibbetson, *A Historical Introduction to the Law of Obligations* (n 9) 190.

[96] (1865) 1 QB 149 (Ex).

[97] ibid 155 (Pollock CB). See also *Stubley v The London and North Western Railway Co* (1876) 1 Ex 13 (Ex), 18 (Bramwell B): 'If such a precaution is necessary here, it must also be used elsewhere; and the argument would shew that on every road, every canal, every railway in the kingdom, means must be taken to warn people against the consequences of their own folly. It would cost too much to provide such a machinery of precaution.'

[98] Cornish and others (n 77) 890–91, 941.

[99] 'The Duty of Care Towards One's Neighbour' (1883) 18 LJ 618, 619.

existed in one situation and not another, of which the existing cases were just instances?

Without any theoretical framework, the existing single instance duties were far from conceptually uniform and varied in both scope (to whom it was owed) and content (what the duty entailed): some duties were owed to the world at large whilst others were only owed to a certain class of persons; some duties were a duty to take reasonable care whilst others were a duty to do a particular thing.[100]

The tortious duty of a manufacturer to a consumer, for example, although at one time arguably not existing at all,[101] came to be owed only to those particular consumers whom the manufacturer subjectively knew had planned to use their goods.[102] The duty was first described in *George v Skivington*.[103] Here, a chemist compounded and then sold a bottle of hair shampoo to the plaintiff for the use of his wife. The shampoo turned out to have been negligently compounded and when used by the plaintiff's wife caused her hair to fall out. It was held that:

> [W]here an article of this description is purchased by A for the use of B, and it is alleged and stated at the time of the purchase and sale, to have been so purchased, and therefore becomes *known* to the defendant, who is the seller of the article—the duty arises upon the part of the seller of the article, that it shall be reasonably fit for the purpose.[104]

The court was quick to note, however, that 'The case, no doubt, would have been very different if the declaration had not alleged that the defendant knew for whom the compound was intended.'[105]

The duty of property owners, meanwhile, whilst extending to all entrants, varied in content depending on the status of the entrant.[106] The duty to an invitee, for example, was 'the exercise of reasonable care ... to prevent damage from unusual danger of which the occupier knows or ought to know';[107] the duty to a licensee was to refrain from laying traps and wilful deceit;[108] whilst the duty to a trespasser, if it could be described as a 'duty' at all, was merely to abstain from the intentional infliction of harm.[109]

---

[100] EK Teh, 'Reasonable Foreseeability in Negligence (1833–1882)' (1975–1977) 5 UTasLR 45, 50–62.

[101] *Winterbottom v Wright* (1842) 10 M&W 109, 109 ER 402.

[102] Though, a duty would also exist if the seller fraudulently misrepresented that the product was safe (*Langridge v Levy* (1837) 2 M&W 519, 150 ER 863) or the product was dangerous *per se* (RFV Heuston, 'Donoghue v Stevenson in Retrospect' (1957) 20 MLR 1, 11).

[103] (1869) 5 LR Ex 1, 39 LJ Ex 8.

[104] 39 LJ Ex 8, 9 (Kelly CB) (emphasis added).

[105] 5 LR Ex 1, 4 (Pigott B). See also *Blakemore v Bristol & Exeter Railway* (1858) 8 E&B 1035, 120 ER 385; Michael L Richmond, 'The Development of Duty: *Langridge* to *Palsgraf*' (1986–1987) 31 St Louis ULJ 903, 905–10.

[106] Norman S Marsh, 'History and Comparative Law of Invitees, Licensees and Trespassers' (1953) 69 LQR 182. Up to seven categories of entrant eventually existed, before being replaced with a common duty of care in the Occupiers Liability Act 1957. See also Cornish and Clark (n 46) 505–07.

[107] *Indermaur v Dames* (1866) 1 CP 274 (CP), 287 (Willes J). Willes J's judgment was later affirmed in the Court of Exchequer: *Indermaur v Dames* (1866–67) 2 CP 311 (Ex).

[108] *Gautret v Egerton* (1867) 2 CP 371, 374 (Willes J). See also *Indermaur v Dames* (1866) 1 CP 274 (CP) (Willes J).

[109] *Deane v Clayton* (1817) 7 Taunt 489, 521; 129 ER 196, 209 (Dallas J). The line between 'intend' to inflict and 'negligently' inflict, however, was not clear: Marsh (n 106) 188.

In traffic cases, both on roads and on the water, however, a duty was effectively owed to the whole world, and its content was simply to take reasonable care: '[the] duty which the law casts upon those in charge of a carriage on land, or a ship or a float of timber on water, [is] to take reasonable care and use reasonable skill to prevent it from doing injury.'[110]

Duties could also be very specific, as in a duty to do or refrain from doing a particular thing, hardly going beyond the facts of the particular case. In *Farrant v Barnes*,[111] for example, the defendant delivered a carboy of nitric acid to the plaintiff's master. The plaintiff, not being warned that the acid was dangerous, carried the carboy on his back and was injured when it burst. On the question of duty Willes J said:

> I am of the opinion that persons employing others to carry dangerous articles are bound to give reasonable notice of the character of such articles, and are liable, if they do not do so, for the probable consequences of such neglect of duty.[112]

In *Jackson v Metropolitan Railway Co*,[113] the duty was also formulated narrowly:

> I take it to be part of the duty of a railway company which invites persons to resort to its stations and to travel by its trains (inter alia) to provide two things: first, sufficient accommodation to meet the ordinary requirements of the traffic; secondly, a sufficient staff to maintain order and prevent irregularity and confusion, and to protect passengers from annoyance, inconvenience, or injury from travellers who set not only the regulations of the company but also decency and order at defiance.[114]

The existing law therefore offered little guidance in the way of a generalised duty test. Duties of different content and scope, whilst seemingly appropriate for the cases they were designed for, had little general application: a duty based on the defendant's knowledge of the identity of the plaintiff, for example, would all but eliminate liability for traffic accidents,[115] whilst any general duty to take care, if owed to the whole world, would render the entire duty enquiry meaningless.

---

[110] *River Wear Commissioners v Adamson* (1877) 2 AC 743 (HL), 767 (Lord Blackburn).
[111] (1862) 31 LJCP 137.
[112] ibid 140. See also Teh (n 100) 60.
[113] (1877) 2 CP 125.
[114] ibid 141 (Cockburn CJ). See also Teh (n 100) 60–61.
[115] Another limitation of basing the duty on the defendant's knowledge of the consumer was identified in *MacPherson v Buick Motor Co* 111 NE 1050 (NY 1916). The plaintiff purchased a motor vehicle from a car dealership which, in turn, had purchased the vehicle from the defendant manufacturer. The plaintiff was later injured as he was driving the vehicle due to a defect in one of the vehicle's wheel spokes. The defendant denied the existence of a duty as they had no contract with the plaintiff—indeed, they had never met nor even knew of his existence. Yet, as Cardozo CJ pointed out, the plaintiff, as the final consumer, despite his identity not being known to the defendants, was just about the *only* person the defendant could be sure would be affected by their negligence, and the car dealership, to whom the defendants admitted a duty, were 'the one person of whom it might be said with some approach to certainty that by him the car would not be used' (at 1053).

A. *Heaven v Pender*

The absence of any clear conceptual unity among the duty cases is hardly surprising; the duty cases did not emerge from any *a priori* general principles, but, rather, general principles only later emerged from the duty cases. As Buckland and McNair observed, in the formative periods, common lawyers, much like Roman lawyers, were not great theorists and simply decided cases on their facts, rather than from first principles; it was only when they looked back that general principles emerged.[116]

The first person to attempt to extrapolate a principle from the many duty cases was Sir William Brett, the Master of the Rolls. The central feature of Brett MR's duty formulation was the idea of 'foreseeability'. Brett MR first introduced the idea of foreseeability into the duty realm in 1870: 'I am of the opinion that no reasonable man could have foreseen [the damage] ... [therefore] It seems to me that no duty was cast upon the defendants ...'[117] In 1883 he attempted a more general formulation still, feeling that a duty *should* be owed:

> [W]henever the circumstances disclosed are such that, if the person charged with negligence thought of what he was about to do, or omit to do, he must see that, unless he used reasonable care, there must be at least a great probability of injury to the person charging negligence against him, either to his person or property, then there is a duty shown to use reasonable care.[118]

However, Brett MR's most famous formulation came later that same year in the case of *Heaven v Pender*,[119] where he explicitly acknowledged that he was attempting to formulate a duty formula that applied to *all* cases of negligence:

> When two drivers or two ships are approaching each other, such a relation arises between them when they are approaching each other in such a manner that, unless they use ordinary care and skill to avoid it, there will be danger of an injurious collision between them. This relation is established in such circumstances between them, not only if it be proved that they actually know and think of this danger, but whether such proof be made or not ... In the case of a railway company carrying a passenger with whom it has not entered into the contract of carriage the law implies the duty, because it must be obvious that unless ordinary care and skill be used the personal safety of the passenger must be endangered. With regard to the condition in which an owner or occupier leaves his house or property other phraseology has been used ... it seems to me, that there must be some larger proposition ... The proposition which these recognised cases suggest, and which is, therefore, to be deduced from them, is that whenever one person is by circumstances placed in such a position with regard to another that every one of ordinary sense who

---

[116] WW Buckland, AD McNair and FH Lawson, *Roman Law and Common Law*, 2nd edn (Cambridge University Press, 1965) 11.

[117] *Smith v London and South Western Railway Co* (1870) 5 CP 98 (CP), 103.

[118] *Cunnington v The Great Northern Railway Co* (1883) 49 LT 392 (QB), 393.

[119] (1883) 11 QB 503 (CA).

did think would at once recognise that if he did not use ordinary care and skill in his own conduct with regard to those circumstances he would cause danger to the person or property of the other, a duty arises to use ordinary care and skill to avoid such danger.[120]

Brett MR's formulation was significant for two reasons. First, it described the content of the duty as simply a duty to use care, rather than a duty to do or not to do a particular thing. Second, Brett MR's test transcended the traditional categories of duty by relying on a common theme. In essence, the existence of a duty, which was a duty to take care, depended on 'foreseeability'.[121]

The other two members of the court, Lord Justices Cotton and Bowen, although also finding for the plaintiff (on the narrower ground that they were invitees[122]), were 'unwilling to concur with the Master of the Rolls in laying down unnecessarily the larger principle which he entertains.'[123] However, as early as 1885 Brett MR's formulation was nevertheless being advocated by plaintiffs,[124] and in 1888 Hawkins J of the Queen's Bench division said of Brett MR's formula: 'That, in my opinion, is a correct statement of the law.'[125] Brett MR, too, continued to use his wide formulation in subsequent cases.[126]

Other judges, however, felt that Brett MR's formulation was too wide and preferred the narrower approach of Lord Justices Cotton and Bowen. In *Caledonian Railway v Mulholland*,[127] for example, the brakes failed in the defendant's freight car and killed an employee of the purchaser of the car's load. Although it was clearly foreseeable that a negligently maintained freight car could injure its intended users (indeed, this was put forward by the respondents), Lord Herschell found that 'if we were to hold that such an obligation existed, some very strange consequences would ensue—consequences so unreasonable, it seems to me, as to shew that the duty cannot exist.'[128]

---

[120] ibid 509.

[121] James P Murphy, 'Evolution of the Duty of Care: Some Thoughts' (1980–1981) 30 DePaul L Rev 147, 147 ('This rationale was that duty hinges on foreseeability, nothing more and nothing less'); Teh (n 100) 67 ('What proposition did "these recognised cases suggest"? In *Heaven v Pender* the proposition was reasonable foreseeability'); Leon Green, 'The Duty Problem in Negligence Cases' (1928) 28 Colum L Rev 1014, 1029 ('Upon analysis it is clear that this formula is identical with the "foreseeability" or "anticipation of harm" formula').

[122] Richmond (n 105) 921.

[123] *Heaven v Pender* (1883) 11 QB 503 (CA), 516 (Cotton LJ, with whom Bowen LJ concurred).

[124] *Hurst v Taylor* (1885) 14 QB 918 (QB), 919: 'The defendants' obligation comes within the terms of the proposition enunciated by Brett, MR, in *Heaven v Pender*'.

[125] *Thrussell v Handyside & Co* (1888) 20 QB 359 (QB), 363.

[126] See, eg, *Thomas v Quartermaine* (1887) 18 QB 685 (CA), 688 ('you are bound not to do anything negligently so as to hurt a person near you, and the whole duty arises from the knowledge of that proximity'); *Coventry, Sheppard & Co v The Great Eastern Railway Co* (1883) 11 QB 776 (CA), 780 ('the documents have a certain mercantile meaning attached to them and therefore the defendants owed a duty to merchants and persons likely to deal with them'); *Seton, Laing & Co v Lafone* (1887) 19 QB 68 (CA), 72 ('if a man in the course of business volunteers to make a statement on which it is probable that in the course of business another will act ... there is a duty to take reasonable care that the statement shall be correct'). See also Cornish and others (n 77) 947.

[127] (1898) AC 216 (HL).

[128] ibid 226 (Lord Herschell).

Outside of the courts, academic descriptions of Brett MR's generalised formula ranged from 'the true rule'[129] to 'dangerously wide'.[130] Others dismissed his quest for a general formula entirely: 'Perhaps [lists of specific instance duties] cannot be avoided, as the world has not, in the matter of wrongs, agreed upon any wide principle such as "perform your promises," which is at the bottom of the law of contracts.'[131] And Pollock later observed that whilst *Heaven v Pender* 'may now be regarded as based on a conception sound in principle ... The precision of a neat draftsman has never been counted among [Brett MR's] accomplishments.'[132]

Perhaps in response to the mixed reactions to his to his duty formulation, Brett MR, who had by that stage become Lord Esher, later stated that he 'detest[ed] the attempt to fetter the law by maxims. They are almost invariable misleading: they are for the most part so large and general in their language that they always include something which really is not intended to be included in them.'[133] Shortly thereafter, following some confusion over the extent to which his duty formula created liability for negligent misstatements,[134] Lord Esher also took the opportunity to clarify, and arguably narrow, his previous formulation to make it clear that it was never intended to apply to negligent statements, but only negligent *acts*:

> The case of *Heaven v Pender* ... established that, under certain circumstances, one may owe a duty to another, even if though there is no contract between them. If one man is near to another, or is near to the property of another, a duty lies upon him not to do that which may cause personal injury to that other, or may injure his property.[135]

The existence of a duty, then, depended on not only foreseeability but on physical 'nearness', or proximity. By the close of the nineteenth century, however, Lord Esher appeared to have retreated from his generalised formula even further,[136] stating that liability in negligence is the neglect of 'some duty' and giving specific instances of such duties, thereby seemingly embracing the traditional multifarious approach:

> [A] person cannot be held liable for negligence unless he owed some duty to the plaintiff and that duty was neglected. There are many circumstances that give rise to such a duty, as, for instance, in the case of two persons using a highway, where proximity imposes a duty on each to take reasonable care not to interfere with the other. So if a person has a house near a highway, a duty is imposed on him towards persons using the highway; and similarly there is a duty to an adjoining owner or occupier; and, if by the negligent management of his house he causes injury, in either of these cases he is liable.[137]

---

[129] Horace Smith, *A Treatise on the Law of Negligence*, 2nd edn (Philadelphia: The Blackstone Publishing Company, 1884) 8.

[130] 'Duty Not to be Negligent: Towards Whom and Under what Circumstances it Arises' (1883) 27 Sol J 778, 778–79.

[131] 'The Duty of Care Towards One's Neighbour' (n 99) 619.

[132] Frederick Pollock, 'The Snail in the Bottle and Thereafter' (1933) 49 LQR 22, 25.

[133] *Yarmouth v France* (1887) 19 QB 647 (CA), 653.

[134] *Derry v Peek* (1889) 14 AC 337 (HL); cf *Cann v Wilson* (1888) 39 ChD 39.

[135] *Le Lievre v Gould* [1893] 1 QB 491 (CA), 497. Arguably, however, this was already clear from his existing formula's limitation to 'injury to the person or property of another'.

[136] Cornish and others (n 77) 949.

[137] *Lane v Cox* [1897] 1 QB 415 (CA), 417.

Textbooks of the time also seem to approve of the multifarious approach to duty. In Salmond's *The Law of Torts*, for example, the existence or absence of a duty of care is said to pertain to a 'detailed exposition of the law' and not on 'general principles of liability',[138] whilst Pollock describes the 'modern way of regarding legal duties' as not being a 'general duty not to do harm'.[139] By the end of the nineteenth century, then, after Brett MR's brief flirtation with the idea of a generalised test, the law again returned to the single instances approach to the duty of care.[140]

B. The Twentieth Century and the Ever-Changing Role of Foreseeability

Following Brett MR's failure to achieve a generally accepted duty formula, the Courts of the early twentieth century were notable for their absence of any critical discussion of duty. As Richmond later observed:

> The neatness and consistency which had characterised the development of the law in Great Britain seemed lost. Exceptions began to proliferate in the law, because judges could find precedent for almost any proposition by carefully writing their opinion in the proper terms.[141]

As late as 1928, almost 50 years after *Heaven v Pender*, Leon Green of Yale Law School lamented the lack of any judicial guidance on the question of duty:

> Where shall he find the source of duties? Do judges find them already made? Do they assume them? Do they create them, and if so, do they create them in wholesale, or must each court create a particular duty which fits the particular case then before it? So far as I have been able to discover, the common law courts have stumbled through the whole of the period of their existence without committing themselves on this enquiry. Perhaps it is a subject which is not to be talked about.[142]

Green then described Brett MR's judgment of *Heaven v Pender* as 'the most impressive attempt to answer this puzzling question' of when a duty of care will 'be imposed upon affirmative conduct and to what extent.'[143] The position of

---

[138] John William Salmond, *The Law of Torts* (1907) 22 (a similar quote appears in all subsequent editions prior to 1932).

[139] Pollock, *The Law of Torts: A Treatise on the Principles of Obligations Arising from Civil Wrongs in the Common Law* (n 84) 22 (more or less the exact same quote is found in all 14 editions of Pollock's textbooks). See also CG Addison, *A Treatise on the Law of Torts, or, Wrongs and their Remedies*, 8th edn (Stevens and Sons, 1906) 13 ('The circumstances, under which such a duty may arise are so multifarious that the subject will be dealt with in detail later').

[140] Ibbetson, 'The Tort of Negligence in the Common Law in the Nineteenth and Twentieth Centuries' (n 17) 243.

[141] Richmond (n 105) 924.

[142] Green (n 121) 1024.

[143] ibid 1028.

the time was also succinctly summed up, albeit retrospectively, by Asquith LJ in *Candler v Crane, Christmas & Co*:[144]

> Certain classes owed duties of care to certain other classes: road users to other road users; bailees to persons entrusting property to them; doctors and surgeons (and originally barbers) to persons entrusting their bodies to them; occupiers of premises to persons whom they invite or permit to come on the premises; and so on. These categories attracting the duty had been added to and subtracted from time to time. But no attempt had been made in the past to rationalize them; to find a common denominator between road users, bailees, surgeons, occupiers, and so on, which would explain why they should be bound to a duty of care and some other classes who might be expected equally to be so bound should be exempt—no attempt, that is, save that of Lord Esher, MR (from which his colleagues dissociated themselves) in *Heaven v Pender*.

Nevertheless, although it may not have been obvious at the time, a generalised test of duty continued to develop quietly in the background, and the test centred around the idea introduced by Lord Esher: foreseeability.

Although Lord Esher was responsible for introducing foreseeability as a test for the existence of a duty, he was not the first to advocate its role in determining questions of liability. Indeed, as far back as the Romans, liability for damage to goods (under the *Lex Aquilia*) depended on some idea of foreseeability.[145] Within the common law, however, foreseeability first emerged as a question of the remoteness of the damage.[146] Although such questions were traditionally the sole responsibility of the jury, by the middle of the nineteenth century judges were beginning to remove cases from juries, and make a finding of no liability, where they believed the damage was not sufficiently 'proximate' or was too 'remote':[147] after all, there were cases where the breach of a conventional duty might directly cause unforeseeable damage for which the court did not believe the defendant should be held liable. Judges were therefore using remoteness—in much the same way that they were using the emerging concept of duty—as a method of limiting the liability of defendants.[148] Although the idea that a defendant was only responsible for the 'proximate' consequences of his conduct dated back to Francis Bacon in the sixteenth century[149] and, in the case of liability for negligence, to Buller's

---

[144] [1951] 2 KB 164 (CA), 188.

[145] Paul, Sabinus, book 10: D.9.2.31: '*Culpam autem esse, quod cum a diligente prouideri poterit, non esset prouisum*' (there is fault when what could have been foreseen by a diligent man was not foreseen).

[146] At the time, 'remoteness' encompassed what we would today describe as 'factual causation' and the broad meaning of 'legal causation' (*novus actus interveniens* and remoteness/proximate cause); that is, it concerned whether the damage could be broadly said to be attributable to the behaviour of the defendant. Factual and legal causation do not appear to have become distinct concepts until around the 1960s.

[147] Ibbetson, 'The Tort of Negligence in the Common Law in the Nineteenth and Twentieth Centuries' (n 17) 246.

[148] Cornish and others (n 77) 928. See also JG Fleming, 'Remoteness and Duty: The Control Devices in Liability for Negligence' (1953) 31 Can Bar Rev 471.

[149] Francis Bacon, *Maxims of the Law* (London, 1598): '*Regula I: In iure non remota causa, sed proxima spectatur*' (Rule 1: In law the proximate cause is looked to, not the remote one). See also Cornish and others (n 77) 928; Ibbetson, 'The Tort of Negligence in the Common Law in the Nineteenth and Twentieth Centuries' (n 17) 246.

Nisi Prius,[150] it was not until 1850 that the idea was formally adopted by the courts:[151]

> I entertain considerable doubt whether a person who is guilty of negligence is respon-
> sible for all the consequences which may under any circumstances arise, and in respect
> of mischief which could by no possibility have been foreseen, and which no reasonable
> person would have anticipated.[152]

The idea was further expanded upon by Frederick Pollock in his first edition of *The Law of Torts:*

> Those consequences, and those only, are deemed 'immediate', 'proximate', or, to
> anticipate a little, 'natural and probable', which a person of average competence and
> knowledge, being in the like case with the person whose conduct is complained of, and
> having the like opportunities of observation, might be expected to foresee as likely to
> follow upon such conduct.'[153]

Soon, however, questions of foreseeability were no longer being considered as determinative of the remoteness of the damage, but of whether the act had been negligent in the first place. In *Blyth v Birmingham Waterworks,*[154] for example, an unusually severe frost froze the defendant's fire hydrants which subsequently caused water to escape from the mains and flood the plaintiff's house. All members of the court agreed that the accident was unforeseeable, yet did not even consider the question of remoteness, instead holding that because the accident was unforeseeable there was insufficient evidence of negligence for the matter to be left to the jury.[155] The same conclusion was reached more explicitly by Channel B in *Smith v London and South Western Railway Co:*[156]

> Where there is no direct evidence of negligence, the question what a reasonable man
> might foresee is of importance in considering the question whether there is evidence for
> the jury of negligence or not ... but when it has been determined that there is evidence of
> negligence, the person guilty of it is equally liable for its consequences, whether he could
> foresee them or not.[157]

---

[150] Buller (n 12) 36: 'it is proper in such cases to prove that the injury was such, as would probably follow from the act done'.

[151] Courts had previously refused to impose liability on the basis that the harm was not the 'natural consequence' of the defendant's act, but as Cornish notes, these tended to involve harm caused by third parties rather than harm that was unforeseeable: Cornish and others (n 77) 928–34.

[152] *Greenland v Chaplain* (1850) 5 Ex 243, 248; 155 ER 104, 106 (Pollock CB). Pollock CB made similar remarks in *Rigby v Hewitt* (1850) 5 Ex 240, 243; 155 ER 103, 104: 'of this I am quite clear, that every person who does a wrong, is at least responsible for all the mischievous consequences that may reasonably be expected to result'. In both cases, Pollock CB was alone in his views, the rest of the court preferring a 'natural consequences' test.

[153] Pollock, *The Law of Torts: A Treatise on the Principles of Obligations Arising from Civil Wrongs in the Common Law* (n 84) 28.

[154] (1856) 11 Ex 781; 156 ER 1047.

[155] 11 Ex 780, 785 (Bramwell B) ('it appears to me that it would be monstrous to hold the defendants responsible because they did not foresee and prevent an accident'); 2 Jur NS 333, 334 (Alderson B) ('The whole thing was an accident occasioned by frost, which was utterly unforeseen ... That cannot be called negligence').

[156] (1870) 6 CP 14 ('*Smith*').

[157] ibid 21 (Channel B).

The implications of *Smith* were potentially very far-reaching, as once it was established that the defendant's conduct was negligent, liability ensued for *all* consequences, whether they were foreseeable or not. It is therefore not surprising that in the years that followed, Brett MR attempted, albeit unsuccessfully, to bring questions of foreseeability into the determination of duty.[158]

Notwithstanding *Smith*, however, foreseeability was soon again being considered as a question of remoteness. In *Victorian Railways Commission v Coultas*,[159] a crossing guard negligently invited a woman and her husband to drive their buggy across a railway track crossing into the path of an oncoming train, thereby placing them 'in imminent peril of being killed.' Although the woman and her husband were not physically injured, the wife suffered severe shock and so sued the crossing guard's employer. The Privy Council found for the defendants on the grounds that the damage suffered by the wife was 'too remote', as the plaintiff's injury could not 'be considered a consequence which, in the ordinary course of things, would flow from the negligence of the [defendant]'.[160]

By the start of the twentieth century, however, the appropriate place for foreseeability in the negligence enquiry was *again* being questioned. In *Dulieu v White & Sons*,[161] the defendant lost control of a horse-drawn carriage and crashed into the public house in which the pregnant plaintiff was working. As a result of the collision the plaintiff suffered severe shock and gave birth prematurely. Kennedy J implied that matters concerning foreseeability ought to be dealt with under duty rather than remoteness. In particular, after discussing a recent unreported case that had been decided on the grounds that the harm was too remote, he stated:

> I should myself, as I have already indicated, have been inclined to go a step further, and to hold upon the facts ... [that] as the defendant neither intended to affect the plaintiff nor did anything which could reasonably or naturally be expected to affect him injuriously, there was no evidence of a breach of legal duty.[162]

Although Kennedy J's quote could be interpreted as doubting either the existence of a duty or any evidence of a breach, the fact that he had only just given a construction of the case based on duty ('as I have already indicated') suggests that the former interpretation is the correct one. What could 'reasonably or naturally be expected' (that is, what was reasonably foreseeable), was again playing a role in the determination of a duty.

There was, therefore, no consensus on the role that foreseeability was to play in the determination of liability: the authorities suggested it could be applied at

---

[158] Though note the comments of Beven, who suggests that foreseeability applies *only* 'in determining what is negligence [and] not in limiting the consequences flowing from it when once established': T Beven, *Negligence in Law*, 2nd edn (Stevens and Haynes, 1895) 105–06. cf F Pollock, *The Law of Torts*, 7th edn (Stevens and Sons, 1904) 40 (fn g).

[159] (1888) 13 AC 222 (PC).

[160] ibid 225 (Couch).

[161] [1901] 2 KB 669 (KB).

[162] ibid 675 (Kennedy J).

the duty, breach or remoteness stages. Additionally, the vagueness of the language used in cases provided little guidance on what, exactly, it was that needed to be foreseeable; *Smith*, as we have seen, unhelpfully said that 'the question what a reasonable man might foresee is of importance' without more.

The turning point appears to have come in 1921 following the case of *Re Polemis and Furness, Withy & Co Ltd*[163] which held that, whilst foreseeability of damage is relevant in determining whether an act is negligent, once the defendant's act is deemed to be negligent, 'the fact that the damage it in fact causes is not the exact kind of damage one would expect is immaterial, so long as the damage is in fact directly traceable to the negligent act ...'[164] Although *Re Polemis* was silent on the issue of duty, it had nevertheless clarified and defined the role of foreseeability at the fault and remoteness stages of the negligence enquiry: at the fault stage the question was the whether *some* damage was foreseeable,[165] whilst at the remoteness stage foreseeability of the *exact kind of damage actually suffered* was irrelevant.[166]

With the role of foreseeability in the fault and remoteness stages now rigidly defined, duty was the obvious vehicle for expanding or limiting liability on the basis of foreseeability: but if not foreseeability of some damage, or foreseeability of the kind of damage actually suffered, then foreseeability of what? It was not long until this question was answered. In *Hambrook v Stokes Brothers*[167] the defendant failed to secure their parked lorry, causing it to roll down a hill by itself. When the plaintiff's wife, who was accompanying her children to school, saw the out-of-control lorry, she became very worried for the safety of her children, who had turned the corner in front of her and so were out of her sight. Although she did not see the ensuing collision, she suffered severe anxiety and shock, which eventually led to her death, when she heard that a child answering the description of her daughter had been injured. Clearly there was no issue of fault, as some damage was surely foreseeable, and *Re Polemis* ensured that the question of remoteness was not in issue. There still, however, had to be a duty in the first place, yet *Dulieu v White & Sons* had earlier confined the duty in cases of psychiatric harm to 'shock which arises from a reasonable fear of immediate personal injury to *oneself*.'[168] The plaintiff's wife, however, suffered shock from a fear of immediate personal injury to her *children*. If the plaintiff were to succeed, a new duty would need to be recognised, and Bankes LJ did this on the basis that harm to the *actual plaintiff* was foreseeable. In particular, after finding that the authorities established that

---

[163] [1921] 3 KB 560 (CA) ('*Re Polemis*').

[164] *Re Polemis*, 577 (Scrutton LJ).

[165] In that a reasonable person would not engage in certain behaviour if it created a foreseeable risk of *some* harm, and the fact that that the harm that *actually* occurs is of a different kind to that foreseen does not make the unreasonable behaviour retrospectively reasonable.

[166] The wide test was subsequently subject to much criticism, but, as noted by Davies, 'A wide remoteness test [the 'directness' test] was unexceptional when duty was narrowly conceived': Martin Davies, 'The Road From Morocco: Polemis Through Donoghue to No-Fault' (1982) 45 MLR 534, 541.

[167] [1925] 1 KB 141 (CA).

[168] *Dulieu v White & Sons* [1901] 2 KB 669 (CA), 675 (Kennedy J) (emphasis added).

'what a man ought to have anticipated is material when considering the extent of his duty'[169] he employed a simple syllogism:

(1) A man owes a duty where he ought to foresee that his negligence might cause mental shock to a mother occasioned by fearing for her own safety.
(2) From the perspective of the defendant, there is no difference between a mother fearing for her own safety and a mother fearing for her child's safety.
(3) A man therefore owes a duty where he ought to foresee that his negligence might cause mental shock to a mother who suffers mental shock occasioned by fearing for her child's safety.

Forty years after *Heaven v Pender,* then, duty was again coming to be based on the question of foreseeability; in particular, whether the defendant ought to have anticipated, or foreseen, harm to a person in the position of the plaintiff.[170]

Of course, even though the role of foreseeability in the duty enquiry had now been articulated, foreseeability of harm to the particular plaintiff could not be the *only* requirement for a duty to exist; such a rule, although narrower than Brett MR's formulation, would nevertheless remain open to similar objections. Other than foreseeability of harm to the plaintiff, then, what else was required? To this question *Hambrook v Stokes Brothers* offered little guidance, yet an attempt to do exactly that was just around the corner, and it was instigated by a snail in a bottle of ginger beer.

C. *Donoghue v Stevenson*

The duty issue was addressed again in the famous Scottish case of *Donoghue v Stevenson.*[171] According to the pleadings, the pursuer suffered gastro-enteritis and mental depression, *inter alia,* after drinking from a bottle of 'snail-infected

---

[169] *Hambrook v Stokes Brothers* [1925] 1 KB 141 (CA), 151 (Bankes J). Whilst Atkin LJ acknowledged that the 'question appears to be as to the extent of the duty, and not as to remoteness of damage' (at 158) he was less explicit than Bankes LJ in his reasons for expanding the existing duty to include the plaintiff.

[170] Whilst this construction was later famously adopted by Cardozo CJ in the in the New York Appeals Court case *Palsgraf v Long Island Railway Co* (1928) (248 NY 339; 162 NE 99), and by Lord Wright in *Bourhill v Young* ([1943] AC 92 (HL)), it was not entirely new. As early as *Langridge v Levy* (1837) 2 M&W 519, 150 ER 863 the court specifically rejected the theory that 'wherever a duty is imposed on a person by contract or otherwise, and that duty is violated, *anyone* who is injured by the violation of it may have a remedy against the wrong-doer' (emphasis added): *Langridge v Levy* (1837) 2 M&W 519, 530; 150 ER 863, 868 (Parke B). Goodhart, on the other hand, attributes the origins of the idea to Brett MR's comments in *Smith v London and South Western Railway Co* (1870) 5 CP 98, 103: 'Brett, J dissented on the ground that the defendant had not been negligent *in regard to this particular plaintiff*, although the act of leaving the inflammable heaps might have been negligent in relation to others' (emphasis added) (AL Goodhart, 'The Unforeseeable Consequences of a Negligent Act' (1928) 39 Yale LJ 449, 453). The idea that foreseeability of harm to a person in the position of the plaintiff is distinct from the questions of remoteness and fault will be further explored in ch 4.

[171] [1932] AC 562 (HL).

ginger beer' that had been purchased for her by a friend. As the ginger beer had not been purchased by the pursuer she could not sue in contract and so was forced to argue that liability arose by reason of a tortious duty of a manufacturer 'to the ultimate purchaser or consumer to take reasonable care that the article is free from defect likely to cause injury to health.'[172] Shortly after the pursuer's writ was lodged, the defender made an application for the writ to be struck out and, despite the application being dismissed in the Outer House of the Court of Session following a reclaiming motion, it was upheld in the Inner House of the Court of Session three to one. The pursuer appealed to the House of Lords.

Lord Atkin, like Brett MR, believed in a general conception of duty, and in 1931, prior to delivering his speech in *Donoghue v Stevenson,* said in a lecture delivered at King's College London, 'I doubt whether the whole of the law of tort could not be comprised in the golden maxim to do unto your neighbour as you would that he should do unto you.'[173] Lord Atkin believed it 'remarkable how difficult it is to find in the English authorities statements of general application defining the relations between parties that give rise to the duty,'[174] but also recognised that the attempt at a general formula 'made by Brett MR in *Heaven v Pender* ... [a]s framed ... was demonstrably too wide.' He nevertheless acknowledged that it appeared 'if properly limited, to be capable of affording a valuable practical guide.'[175] Lord Atkin's 'practical guide,' which famously became known as the 'neighbour dictum', was based on foreseeability, but, as suggested by Lord Esher in *Le Lievre v Gould,* limited by the notion of 'proximity':

[I]n English law there must be, and is, some general conception of relations giving rise to a duty of care, of which the particular cases found in the books are but instances ... The rule that you are to love your neighbour becomes in law, you must not injure your neighbour; and the lawyer's question, Who is my neighbour? receives a restricted reply. You must take reasonable care to avoid acts or omissions which you can reasonably foresee would be likely to injure your neighbour. Who, then, in law is my neighbour? The answer seems to be—persons who are so closely and directly affected by my act that I ought reasonably to have them in contemplation as being so affected when I am directing my mind to the acts or omissions which are called in question. This appears to me to be the doctrine of *Heaven v Pender* (1), as laid down by Lord Esher (then Brett MR) when

---

[172] ibid 578–79 (Lord Atkin).

[173] Lord Atkin 'Law as an Educational Subject' [1932] JSPTL 27, 30. Lord Atkin, however, seems to have taken the idea from Pollock, who had said in his 1895 edition of *The Law of Torts*: '"Thou shalt do no hurt to thy neighbour." Our law of torts, with all its irregularities, has for its main purpose nothing else but development of this precept' (Frederick Pollock, *The Law of Torts*, 4th edn (Stevens & Sons, 1895) 12). A similar statement was made in Pollock's 1887 1st edition: 'all members of a civilized commonwealth are under a general duty towards their neighbours to do them no hurt without lawful cause or excuse' (Pollock, *The Law of Torts: A Treatise on the Principles of Obligations Arising from Civil Wrongs in the Common Law* (n 84) 3); though, as Hepple later noted, 'as a proposition of law this was certainly wrong in 1887' (B Hepple, 'Negligence: The Search for Coherence' (1997) 50 CLP 69, 76).

[174] *Donoghue v Stevenson* [1932] AC 562 (HL), 589.

[175] ibid 580.

it is limited by the notion of proximity introduced by Lord Esher himself and AL Smith LJ in *Le Lievre v Gould* …[176]

Lord Atkin ultimately held that the impossibility of intermediate inspection satisfied the proximity requirement and that the defender therefore owed the pursuer a duty of care. Two of the other four Law Lords also found for the pursuer, although in separate speeches, and the matter was relisted for proof. Following the defender's death from appendicitis shortly after the case was heard, the case was settled for a reported amount of £200.[177] There was never a hearing of evidence, and Mrs Donoghue never proved that there was really a snail in the bottle of ginger beer.[178]

In light of the five individual speeches, identifying a clear ratio decidendi from *Donoghue v Stevenson* was no simple task and there has been much discussion as to what, exactly, it was.[179] At its narrowest, it had merely overruled *Winterbottom v Wright* and stood for nothing more than that a manufacturer now owed a duty to consumers. Indeed, this was the interpretation favoured by most commentators,[180] including the law reporter who authored the 'somewhat conservatively worded headnote.'[181] Then there was the view that it had simply approved the multifarious approach to duties, which could be extended only by close analogy to existing duties. This appeared to be the view of Lord Macmillan, who based his finding for the pursuer on the fact that 'the *categories* of negligence are never closed.'[182] The wider view, however, was a rejection of the multifarious approach to duties of care and the adoption of a test whereby duties of care were now owed to anyone who had suffered an injury to their 'life or property'[183] and could be considered one's 'neighbour,' as per Lord Atkin's formula. This is undeniably the popular view of the case.

Whatever the true ratio of the case, it could no longer be said that duties of care were 'a subject which is not to be talked about'.[184] On the contrary, 'The factors underlying the decision to recognise a new duty of care [were] now the subject of open analysis and discussion.'[185]

---

[176] ibid 580–81. Whether Lord Atkin's conception of proximity *actually* imposed any additional limitations on the foreseeability-based test is discussed further in ch 3.

[177] Martin R Taylor, 'Mrs Donoghue's Journey' in Burns (ed), *Donoghue v Stevenson and the Modern Law of Negligence: the Paisley Papers: the Proceedings of the Paisley Conference on the Law of Negligence* (1991) 33.

[178] William W McBryde, '*Donoghue v Stevenson*: The Story of the "Snail in the Bottle" Case' in AJ Gamble (ed), *Obligations in Context: Essays in Honour of Professor DM Walker* (W Green, 1990) 26.

[179] See, eg, Heuston (n 102) 5–10; Ibbetson, *A Historical Introduction to the Law of Obligations* (n 9) 190–91.

[180] See, eg: the case notes in (1932) Sol J 387; [1933] CLJ 116; (1932) 173 LT 411; (1932) 174 LT 399; (1932) 74 LJ 75; (1932) 10 Can Bar Rev 478. See also, Ibbetson, *A Historical Introduction to the Law of Obligations* (n 9) 190.

[181] *Candler v Crane, Christmas & Co* [1951] 2 KB 164 (CA), 189 (Asquith LJ).

[182] *Donoghue v Stevenson* [1932] AC 562 (HL), 619 (emphasis added).

[183] ibid 599 (Lord Atkin).

[184] Green (n 121) 1024.

[185] Heuston (n 102) 24.

IV. Conclusion

Prior to the emergence of negligence as an independent wrong, there was little need for a duty of care; the discrete nature of the wrongs in which negligence was required performed essentially the same function, limiting liability for negligence to a set of defined situations. As negligence developed into a wrong in its own right, however, its potential reach was practically limitless, yet few chose to make use of the emerging action, and so there was no immediate need to impose restrictions on its scope. On the contrary, duty was first employed as a way of *expanding* the scope of negligence, by reformulating breaches of contractual duties, which arose by reason of agreement, as breaches of tortious duties, which arose by reason of law. Over time, this terminology spread from relationship negligence to non-relationship negligence, and, eventually, negligence was no longer actionable without a duty. As the action for negligence expanded, however, the focus of duty changed from inclusionary to exclusionary. Yet this was not because duty was the *only* way to limit liability for negligence, but, as a result of the division of functions between judge and jury, because it was the most convenient.

By the last quarter of the nineteenth century, although duty was firmly established into the analysis of liability for negligence, the courts were yet to offer an adequate explanation for why a duty existed in one situation but not another. Brett MR was the first to make such an attempt and his explanation was that duties were of uniform content (duty to take care), and that their scope depended on the idea of foreseeability. Although Brett MR's explanation was eventually rejected, the idea that duty depended on some notion of foreseeability was not easily forgotten. The climax of this development was in 1932, when Lord Atkin pronounced his neighbour dictum: the duty, as Brett MR had suggested, was a duty to take care, and its existence depended on a modified version of Brett MR's foreseeability formula. Although judicial development of the duty test has continued over the last 80 years, the general position remains relatively unchanged: the question of when damage caused by another's careless conduct becomes actionable is determined by reference to a general duty test or principle.

Lord Atkin's neighbour principle is, however, only the beginning of the story, and so, in chapter three, we will explore the various other methods that have been used to determine the existence of a duty of care, both by past and modern courts.

IV. Conclusion

3

Methods for Determining
the Existence of a Duty of Care

The development of the tort of negligence since the seminal case of *Donoghue v Stevenson* has not been one of steady advance along a broad front. It has been a much more confused series of engagements with salients and beachheads, and retreats as well as advances. It has sometimes been only long after the event that it has been possible to assess the true significance of some clash of arms.

Lord Walker in *Customs and Excise Commissioners v Barclays Bank plc*
[2007] 1 AC 181, 209.

I. Introduction

The question 'Who, then, in law, is my neighbour?'[1] has caused courts, lawyers, and academics alike considerable consternation since it was first posed by Lord Atkin over 80 years ago. Despite the various attempts to answer it, usually in the form of general duty 'tests,' no simple method for determining the existence of a duty of care has emerged. Chapter three traces the development of these various methods, in addition to examining why they have generally been of limited success. In particular, we will see how Lord Atkin's neighbour dictum soon proved to be inadequate as a general duty criterion, leading, initially, to an apparent return to the multifarious approach, and, later, to a number of further attempts at an ostensibly all-encompassing generalised test. The common theme throughout is the difficulty the courts have faced in articulating a test that struck the right balance; one that was general enough to explain the existing duty cases, yet particular enough to offer useful guidance in fact-specific situations. We will also see how some methods reject the use of general tests altogether, preferring to instead determine the existence of a duty via narrower and more fact-specific principles.

---

[1] *Donoghue v Stevenson* [1932] AC 562 (HL) ('*Donoghue v Stevenson*').

II. The Aftermath of *Donoghue v Stevenson*

As discussed in chapter two, prior to *Donoghue v Stevenson* duties of care were imposed somewhat arbitrarily, rather than in accordance with any sort of general conception. Lord Atkin's neighbour dictum, however, was an attempt at such a general conception; one that encapsulated the entirety of the wide range of discrete duty situations. To some extent, his attempt initially proved quite influential, with a number of courts seizing upon his generalisation to justify the imposition of a duty of care in novel situations. For example, the neighbourhood test was relied on to impose a duty of care on the manufacturers of woollen-underpants,[2] independent lift contractors,[3] car-dealers,[4] and even tombstone makers.[5] Perhaps most significantly, however, in *Stennett v Hancock*,[6] the neighbour principle was relied on to justify the imposition of a duty of care on a vehicle repairer towards not only his client, but towards *any person* foreseeably physically injured as a result of their negligent repairs. Of course, as the neighbour dictum was a 'general conception of relations giving rise to a duty of care, of which the particular cases found in the books are but instances,'[7] it could be used to explain not only where a duty *did* exist but also where a duty did *not* exist. And so, in *Bourhill v Young*,[8] the neighbour dictum was relied on to deny that any duty was owed to a pregnant 'fishwife' who had suffered serious shock, leading to a stillborn child shortly thereafter, as a result of hearing, but not seeing, a motorcycle accident involving a stranger.[9]

Nevertheless, whilst some judges were happy to adopt the neighbour dictum as a general principle of duty, others were not. In particular, aside from doubts about whether the neighbour dictum formed part of the ratio of the case,[10] it was widely believed that the dictum required little more than foreseeability of harm

---

[2] *Grant v Australian Knitting Mills ltd* [1936] AC 562 (PC).

[3] *Haseldine v CA Daw & Son Ltd* [1941] 2 KB 343 (CA).

[4] *Herschtal v Stewart & Ardern Ltd* [1940] 1 KB 155 (KB); *Andrews v Hopkinson* [1957] 1 QB 229 (QB).

[5] *Brown v Cotterill* (1934) 51 TLR 21 (KB).

[6] [1939] 2 All ER 578 (KB).

[7] *Donoghue v Stevenson* 580.

[8] [1943] AC 92 (HL) ('*Bourhill*').

[9] ibid 102.

[10] Stone, for example, sardonically suggested that the decision could logically be confined to physical injury to Scots widows caused by the presence of dead snails in opaque bottles (J Stone, *The Province and Function of Law: Law as Logic, Justice and Social Control; a Study in Jurisprudence* (Stevens 1947) 187–88), whilst Cane has questioned whether it was just 'an ethical and aspirational statement of little or no legal value' (P Cane, *The Anatomy of Tort Law* (Hart, 1997) 7). See also: GBJB Hughes, *Jurisprudence* (Butterworth & Co, 1955) 232–34; RWM Dias, 'The Breach Problem and the Duty of Care' (1956) 30 TulLRev 377, 402 (fn 89); RFV Heuston, 'Donoghue v Stevenson in Retrospect' (1957) 20 MLR 1, 5–6. For more modern commentary, see DJ Ibbetson, *A Historical Introduction to the Law of Obligations* (OUP, 1999) 190–91; Keith Stanton, 'The Neighbour Principle in the 21st Century: Yesterday's Revolution' (2012) 20 Tort L Rev 61, 62; Simon Deakin, Angus Johnston and Basil Markesinis, *Markesinis and Deakin's Tort Law*, 7th edn (OUP, 2012) 109–110.

to be satisfied and so, much like Brett MR's earlier attempt at a duty formula in *Heaven v Pender*,[11] was too widely drawn to serve as a useful statement as to when one party owes another a duty of care.[12] There was, of course, the fact that Lord Atkin had explicitly stated that a duty test based on foreseeability alone (that is, Brett MR's formulation in *Heaven v Pender*[13]) was 'demonstrably too wide',[14] and that his 'neighbour dictum', whilst based primarily on reasonable foreseeability of harm, was '*limited by the notion of proximity*';[15] however, Lord Atkin's definition of 'proximity'[16] was generally seen to be synonymous with his neighbour dictum itself, such that 'neighbourhood', 'proximity' and 'reasonable foreseeability', were merely different ways of saying the same thing.[17] On the basis of this understanding, the existence of a duty of care continued to be denied in many circumstances that clearly satisfied Lord Atkin's test.

It was clearly foreseeable, for example, that making a negligent misstatement could cause a pecuniary loss to anyone who relied on that misstatement. Yet, in *Candler v Crane Christmas & Co*,[18] despite acknowledging that the circumstances of the case satisfied the neighbourhood principle,[19] the court denied that a duty could exist in the absence of a fiduciary relationship, a contract, or fraud.[20] Similarly, Lord Atkin's statement, 'You must take reasonable care to avoid acts *or omissions*

[11] (1883) 11 QB 503 (CA) ('*Heaven v Pender*').

[12] See, eg, Scrutton LJ in *Farr v Butters Bros* [1932] KB 606 (CA), 614: 'It is quite clear that the statement ... [of] Lord Atkin, needs qualification ... [T]he general proposition stated by Lord Atkin ... is wider than is necessary ...'

[13] *Heaven v Pender* 509.

[14] *Donoghue v Stevenson* 580.

[15] ibid 581 (emphasis added).

[16] 580–81 (footnotes omitted): 'This [the neighbour dictum] appears to me to be the doctrine of *Heaven v Pender* as laid down by Lord Esher (then Brett MR) when it is limited by the notion of proximity ... if proximity be not confined to mere physical proximity, but be used ... to extend to such close and direct relations that the act complained of directly affects a person whom the person alleged to be bound to take care would know would be directly affected by his careless act.'

[17] See, eg: WL Morison, 'A Re-Examination of the Duty of Care' (1948) 11 MLR 9, 24; JG Fleming and WL Morison, 'Duty of Care and Standard of Care' (1953) 1 SydLR 69, 71; MA Millner, *Negligence in Modern Law* (Butterworths, 1967) 13; Julius Stone, *Precedent and Law* (Butterworths, 1985) 265; JA Smillie, 'The Foundation of the Duty of Care in Negligence' (1989) 15 MonLR 302, 310, 314; AJE Jaffey, *The Duty of Care* (Dartmouth, 1992) 6, 11; JG Fleming, *The Law of Torts*, 9th edn (Law Book Co, 1998) 151; A Beever, *Rediscovering the Law of Negligence* (Hart, 2007) 184; McHugh J in *Tame v New South Wales; Annetts v Australian Stations Pty Limited* (2002) 211 CLR 317, 356; Lord Oliver in *Murphy v Brentwood DC* [1991] 1 AC 398 (HL), 486; Iacobucci J in *Odhavji Estate v Woodhouse* (2003) 233 DLR (4th) 193 [47]. Compare the views of Katter, who argues that Lord Atkin's notions of proximity and reasonable foreseeability were distinct: Norman Katter, 'Who Then in Law is My Neghbour?' (2004) 12 Tort L Rev 85, 90.

[18] [1951] 2 KB 164 (CA).

[19] ibid 195 (Asquith LJ); 200 (Cohen LJ). Indeed, Denning LJ found for the plaintiff on this basis in his dissent (at 177).

[20] ibid, following *Derry v Peek* (1889) 14 AC 337 (HL). See the judgments of Asquith and Cohen LJJ generally. Note also *Le Lievre v Gould* [1893] 1 QB 491 (CA), 502, where Bowen LJ said 'the law of England ... does not consider that what a man writes on paper is like a gun or other dangerous instrument ...'

which you can reasonably foresee would be likely to injure your neighbour,'[21] appeared to obviate the 'vital'[22] and 'fundamental'[23] distinction between acts and omissions. Yet, in *East Suffolk Rivers Catchment Board v Kent*,[24] it was confirmed that the neighbour dictum was not to be taken literally in such cases. The existing duty owed to trespassers, which conferred immunity on occupiers for all but the deliberate infliction of harm,[25] also ought to have been affected by Lord Atkin's test; it was clearly foreseeable that failing to take care of your property could injure those who foreseeably came on to it, whether as visitors or trespassers. Yet, in *Edwards v Railway Executive*,[26] the House of Lords held that the old law continued to apply.[27] Similarly, the rule that lessors of defective premises owed no duty, outside of contract, to their lessees, or their lessees' lawful guests, who were foreseeably injured as a result of those defective premises,[28] also ought to have been wiped out by the neighbour dictum, yet was upheld in both *Otto v Bolton*[29] and *Travers v Gloucester Corporation*.[30] Even in cases of defective products causing foreseeable injury to consumers the neighbour dictum did not apply unconditionally, and a duty of a care was often denied where the defect could have been discovered by intermediate examination prior to the injury.[31]

---

[21] *Donoghue v Stevenson* 580 (emphasis added).

[22] Dias (n 10) 402 (fn 89).

[23] JC Smith and Peter Burns, 'Donoghue v Stevenson—The Not So Golden Anniversary' (1983) 46 MLR 147, 154.

[24] [1941] AC 74 (HL).

[25] This had been most recently affirmed in *Robert Addie & Sons (Collieries) Ltd v Dumbreck* [1929] AC 358 (HL), 371 (Viscount Dunedin), affirming Hamilton LJ in *Latham v Johnson* [1913] 1 KB 398 (CA), 410, who had defined the duty of an occupier as nothing more than 'not to injure the trespasser wilfully ... otherwise a man trespasses at his own risk.'

[26] [1952] AC 737 (HL).

[27] See also *Cairns v St Marylebone BC* (1954) *The Times*, 8 December 1954 (QB), where, to counsel's suggestion that the neighbour dictum justified extending an occupier's duty of care to trespassers, Glyn-Jones J respond with an astonished 'My God!', and ultimately found the defendants 'clearly not liable': ibid 11.

[28] *Cavalier v Pope* [1906] AC 428 (HL). This was the rule Lord Buckmaster had in mind when he said, at *Donoghue v Stevenson* 577: 'If one step, why not fifty? Yet if a house be, as it sometimes is, negligently built, and in consequence of that negligence the ceiling falls and injures the occupier or anyone else, no action against the builder exists according to the English law, although I believe such a right did exist according to the laws of Babylon.'

[29] [1936] 2 KB 46 (KB).

[30] [1947] 1 KB 71 (KB).

[31] *Denny v Supplies & Transport Co* [1950] 2 KB 374 (CA); *Buckner v Ashby & Horner Ltd* [1941] 1 KB 321 (CA); *Haseldine v CA Daw & Son Ltd* [1941] 2 KB 343 (CA); *Dransfield v British Insulated Cables Ltd* [1937] 4 All ER 382 (KB); *London Graving Dock Co v Horton* [1951] AC 737 (HL). See also Heuston (n 10) 13–14, D Nolan, 'Product Liability' in K Oliphant (ed), *Common Law Series: The Law of Tort*, 3rd edn (LexisNexis, 2015) 19.32. The 'intermediate examination' exception was based on Lord Atkin's comments in *Donoghue v Stevenson* at 582–83: '[A] proximate relationship ... may be too remote where inspection even of the person using, certainly of an intermediate person, may reasonably be interposed.' For criticism of Lord Atkin for equating proximity in defective goods cases with the lack of an opportunity of intermediate examination/inspection, see, eg, G Williams, 'Negligent Contractors and Third Parties' (1942) 42 LJ 115, 124, FC Underhay, 'Manufacturers' Liability: Recent Developments Since Donoghue v Stevenson' (1936) 16 Can Bar Rev 283, 286.

Despite, then, the potentially wide reaching effects of Lord Atkin's test, it did *not* provide a 'general conception of relations giving rise to a duty of care, of which the particular cases found in the books are but instances.' Indeed, as noted by Wrottesley J in 1939, outside of cases involving 'negligence which results in danger to life, danger to limb, or danger to health,'[32] the neighbour dictum had little application; and even within such cases its application was not universal, given that foreseeable injuries to 'life, limb, or health' caused by goods with reasonably discoverable defects, injuries to trespassers, or injuries that arose as a result of defective premises, gave rise to no duty. As late as 1957, 25 years after *Donoghue v Stevenson* had been decided, Heuston therefore felt able to say:

> [The neighbour principle] cannot properly be treated as being, a general formula which will explain all conceivable cases of negligence. Even at a fairly high level of abstraction it needs considerable qualifications and reservations before it can be accepted.[33]

The limited effects of the neighbour principle, and the courts' continued reliance on pre-*Donoghue v Stevenson* 'exceptions' to the neighbour principle meant that, in practice, a duty of care was only recognised where it fell into one of the discrete categories recognised by the law, and so it was the multifarious approach to duty, which had been favoured by Lord Macmillan, that continued to dominate.[34]

III. The Staggering March of Negligence[35]

Much of the reluctance of the courts to depart from the multifarious approach to duty can be put down to the doctrine of precedent. Both trial judges and the Court of Appeal were bound by the existing authorities, whilst the House of Lords was, at the time, subject to the doctrine of self-binding precedent.[36] There was certainly also much sympathy for the view that 'the duty to be careful only exists where the wisdom of our ancestors has decreed that it should exist.'[37] Not everyone, however,

---

[32] *Old Gate Estates Ltd v Toplis & Harding & Russell* [1939] 3 All ER 209 (KB), 217.

[33] Heuston (n 10) 23.

[34] See, generally, ibid; Ibbetson (n 10) 191. See also Nicholas J McBride and Roderick Bagshaw, *Tort Law*, 4th edn (Pearson, 2012) 106: 'Lord Atkin's "neighbour principle" had very little impact in terms of being used by the courts after *Donoghue v Stevenson* to determine whether or not a defendant owed a claimant a duty of care.'

[35] For the 'Staggering March of Negligence' outside of the duty context, see: Tony Weir, 'The Staggering March of Negligence' in Peter Cane and Jane Stapleton (eds), *The Law of Obligations: Essays in Celebration of John Fleming* (1999).

[36] This is usually attributed to Lord Halsbury's decision in *London Street Tramways Co Ltd v London CC* [1898] AC 375 (HL), but can in fact be traced back to Lord Campbell in *Beamish v Beamish* (1861) 9 HL Cas 274, 338–9; 11 ER 735, 761. See Louis Jacques Blom-Cooper, '1966 and All That: The Story of the Practice Statement' in Louis Blom-Cooper, Gavin Drewry and Brice Dickson (eds), *The Judicial House of Lords: 1876–2009* (OUP, 2009) 129.

[37] PA Landon, 'Notes' (1941) 57 LQR 179, 183. See also Heuston (n 10) 4.

was prepared to allow legal history to dictate the progression of the common law, and by the middle of the twentieth century, more progressive views were beginning to emerge. As early as 1943, Lord Wright wrote that '[T]he instinct of inertia is as potent in judges as in other people … Precedents would still be precedents, though not coercive but merely persuasive',[38] and similar calls for change continued in the 1950s, many of which came from Lord Denning. In 1959, for example, Lord Denning wrote:

> It seems to me that when a particular precedent—even of your Lordships' House— comes into conflict with a fundamental principle, also of your Lordships' House, then the fundamental principle must prevail. This must at least be true when, on the one hand, the particular precedent leads to absurdity or injustice and, on the other hand, the fundamental principle leads to consistency and fairness. It would, I think, be a great mistake to cling too closely to particular precedent at the expense of fundamental principle.[39]

However, it was not until the 1960s that, at least in relation to the duty of care, these views began to be realised. As Mitchell explains:

> In 1963 the House of Lords as a judicial body was in transition. Throughout the 1950s, under the leadership of Viscount Simonds, the House had taken a very limited view of its role in developing the Common Law. Certainty and precedent were the dominant themes. By the 1960s, however, a more nuanced approach was beginning to appear. Bold creativity of the kind practiced by Lord Denning was still untypical, but there was an emerging sense that certain legal areas, at least, were suitable for judicial development.[40]

In particular, the courts were becoming more assertive and daring in their treatment of precedent,[41] and the constraints of legal history were loosening their grip. The method for determining the existence of a duty of care was therefore able to undergo a significant evolution, paving the way for the long list of exceptions to *Donoghue v Stevenson* to be eroded,[42] and alternative general tests to be explored.

One of the earliest changes came in the area of pure economic loss, in what was the most significant duty case since *Donoghue v Stevenson*, *Hedley Byrne & Co Ltd v Heller & Partners Ltd*.[43] The plaintiff was a firm of advertising agents who had purchased forward television and print advertisements on behalf of their clients. As was the practice of the time, the plaintiff became personally liable for the cost of the ads they purchased. After becoming concerned about a client's creditworthiness, the plaintiff asked their bankers to make appropriate enquiries about the client's financial position. The plaintiff's bankers, in turn, asked the defendant, being

---

[38] Lord Wright, 'Precedents' (1943) 8 CLJ 118, 144.

[39] *London Transport Executive v Betts* [1959] AC 213 (HL), 247. See also Denning LJ in *Candler v Crane, Christmas & Co* [1951] 2 KB 164 (CA), 178; and Blom-Cooper (n 36) 130.

[40] Paul Mitchell, '*Hedley Byrne & Co Ltd v Heller & Partners Ltd* (1963)' in Charles Mitchell and Paul Mitchell (eds), *Landmark Cases in the Law of Torts* (Hart, 2010) 181.

[41] ibid.

[42] JC Smith, 'Clarification of Duty—Remoteness Probems through a New Physiology of Negligence: Economic Loss, a Test Case' (1974) 9 UBCLawRev 213, 217.

[43] [1964] AC 465 (HL) ('*Hedley Byrne*').

the client's bankers, to provide a credit reference. The credit reference, despite being marked 'without responsibility on the part of the [defendant]', came back favourable,[44] and so the plaintiff purchased the advertising space on behalf of their client. Shortly thereafter, however, the client went into liquidation and the plaintiff lost £17,000. The plaintiff sued the defendant on the basis that they would not have purchased the advertisements if they had known the client's true financial position. Despite the common law's longstanding reluctance to impose a duty in relation to pure economic loss caused by negligent misstatements,[45] the House of Lords held that, in certain circumstances at least, a duty of care *could* exist.[46] Although a number of separate speeches were delivered, in order for a duty to exist the majority appear to have required that the defendant 'assumed responsibility' for the quality of their statement for the benefit of the plaintiff, and that the defendant knew or should have known that the plaintiff would rely on that statement.[47] Despite the Court's lengthy analysis of the law, considering that the statement had been made 'without responsibility', no duty was held to arise on the facts.[48] *Hedley Byrne* nevertheless represented a significant development in the way the courts approached the duty issue. In particular, it appeared to create a *new* test for the existence of a duty of care, being one that did *not* depend on Lord Atkin's neighbour principle,[49] and one that expanded the law of negligence into the realm of pure economic loss.

The reach of the duty of care was expanded elsewhere too. The minimal duty to trespassers, for example, had by the 1950s come to be seen as particularly harsh, especially as it applied to children.[50] The law's initial response was to find implied licences, so that trespassing children were transformed into lawful visitors.[51] Of course, this solution, which depended on a fiction, was clearly unsatisfactory,

---

[44] The client was described as a '[r]espectably constituted company, considered good for its ordinary business engagements.'

[45] *Simpson v Thompson* (1877) 3 AC 279 (HL); *Derry v Peek* (1889) 14 AC 337 (HL); *Le Lievre v Gould* [1893] 1 QB 491 (CA); *Old Gate Estates Ltd v Toplis & Harding & Russell* [1939] 3 All ER 209 (KB); *Candler v Crane Christmas & Co* [1951] 2 KB 164 (CA).

[46] Technically, the House of Lords did not overrule the still binding *Derry v Peek* (1889) 14 AC 337 (HL), as they continued to be bound by their prior decisions until 1966 (see the *Practice Statement (HL: Judicial Precedent)* [1966] 1 WLR 1234; [1966] 3 All ER 77). As Mitchell says, the better view is that they circumvented the still-binding authorities not by overruling them, but by 'reinterpreting' and 'distinguishing' them: Mitchell (n 40) 178.

[47] Lord Reid (486-87), Lord Morris (494, 503), Lord Hodson (514), and Lord Pearce (538).

[48] To which Honore commented that the court had gone 'to the village via the moon': A Honore, 'Hedley Byrne & Co Ltd v Heller & Partners Ltd' (1964–1965) 8 JSPTL 284, 291. Though even if the disclaimer had *not* been given, it seems that the court would have decided the same way: Mitchell (n 40) 177.

[49] This was made explicitly clear by Lord Reid (482), Lord Devlin (516, 525) and Lord Pearce (536). For further discussion, see McBride and Bagshaw (n 34) 106 (fn 19).

[50] See, eg, *Pearson v Lambeth LBC* [1950] 2 KB 353 (CA); *Williams v Cardiff Corp* [1950] 1 KB 514 (CA). See also Denning LJ's comments in *Videan v British Transport Commission* [1963] 2 QB 650 (CA), 663: 'This rule seems fair enough if you put all trespassers in the same bag as burglars or poachers and treat them all alike.'

[51] See *Cooke v Midland Great Western Railway of Ireland* [1909] AC 229 (HL) and *Lowery v Walker* [1911] AC 10 (HL). See also the discussion of Denning LJ in *Videan v British Transport Commission* [1963] 2 QB 650 (CA), 663–64.

and so in *Videan v British Transport Commission*[52] the Court of Appeal relied on Lord Atkin's neighbour dictum to extend an occupier's duty to trespassers whose presence was foreseeable,[53] and also found that the content of the duty was one of 'common humanity'.[54] This approach was later approved by the House of Lords in *British Railways Board v Herrington*.[55]

Liability for omissions also came to be considerably expanded. In *Dutton v Bognor Regis Urban DC*,[56] for example, the defendant council, in the course of a building inspection, failed to notice that a property's foundations did not comply with the relevant byelaws. Although the council had a statutory power to perform the inspection, they were under no public obligation to do so. A subsequent purchaser sued the council for negligence when subsidence occurred. The majority of the Court of Appeal found that the defendant owed a duty to the plaintiff on the basis that she was someone closely and directly affected by the inspector's negligence, and so fell within Lord Atkin's neighbour principle.[57]

Even the rule that manufacturers owed no duty to those injured by their defective products where there had been a reasonable opportunity of intermediate examination, at that point the primary obstacle to the neighbour principle providing a general rule for when a duty would be held to exist in relation to physical injuries,[58] was effectively abolished in *Griffiths v Arch Engineering Co Ltd*:[59]

> [T]he importance laid on the possibility—that is, the probability—of intermediate examination is merely one facet of the wider principle as it has now been formulated, namely, was there a reasonably foreseeable risk that the plaintiff in fact injured would sustain injury if no precautions were taken to guard against the risk.[60]

From then on, the possibility of intermediate examination was dealt with elsewhere in the negligence enquiry[61] (except insofar as the possibility of intermediate

---

[52] [1963] 2 QB 650 (CA).

[53] ibid 672–73 (Harman LJ); 665 (Denning LJ) ('at least in the case of activities taking place, opposed to doing nothing, in which case his liability is that of an occupier:' at 667); 679–80 (Pearson LJ). A similar decision had been handed down by the High Court of Australia several years prior: *Thompson v Bankstown Municipal Council* (1953) 87 CLR 619.

[54] ibid 680–81 (Pearson LJ).

[55] [1972] AC 877 (HL).

[56] [1972] 1 QB 373 (CA).

[57] ibid 400, 410–11. As the Court of Appeal could not overrule *East Suffolk Rivers Catchment Board v Kent* [1941] AC 74 (HL), a decision of the House of Lords, it instead distinguished it on the somewhat questionable grounds that failing to repair a dam wall within a reasonable time, as had been the case in *East Suffolk Rivers Catchment Board v Kent,* amounted to nonfeasance, whilst failing to detect a breach of the byelaws, as had been the case here, was misfeasance.

[58] The other obstacle, being the rule that lessors of defective premises owed no duty to take care of their lessees and their guests, discussed at (n 28), had earlier been abrogated by s4 of the Occupiers' Liability Act 1957 (later replaced by s4 of the Defective Premises Act 1972).

[59] [1968] 3 All ER 217 (Newport Assizes). For an overview of the rule's decline in the preceding years, see Heuston (n 10) 13–14.

[60] [1968] 3 All ER 217 (Newport Assizes), 222 (Chapman J).

[61] M Lunney and K Oliphant, *Tort Law: Text and Materials* (5th edn, OUP 2013) 117; Nolan (n 31) 19.32. Though note Lord Keith in *Murphy v Brentwood DC* [1991] 1 AC 398 (HL), 464, who commented that 'there may [nevertheless] be room for disputation.'

examination made it unforeseeable that the plaintiff would suffer any harm), and so, save for a *very* small number of exceptions,[62] conduct that created a foreseeable risk of *physical* harm to the plaintiff always attracted a duty of care.

Arguably, however, the most profound development in the test for the existence of a duty of care came in 1970. In *Home Office v Dorset Yacht Co Ltd*,[63] the Home Office was sued for failing to prevent seven inmates from escaping from a Borstal institution and damaging the plaintiffs' nearby yacht. As there was little authority on point, save for a County Court case that based the existence of a duty on foreseeability alone,[64] the House of Lords took the opportunity to clarify the law relating to the existence of a duty of care. Most significant was the judgment of Lord Reid:

> About the beginning of this century most eminent lawyers thought that there were a number of separate torts involving negligence, each with its own rules, and they were most unwilling to add more. They were of course aware from a number of leading cases that in the past the courts had from time to time recognised new duties and new grounds of action. But the heroic age was over; it was time to cultivate certainty and security in the law; the categories of negligence were virtually closed. The Attorney-General invited us to return to those halcyon days, but, attractive though it may be, I cannot accede to his invitation.

> In later years there has been a steady trend towards regarding the law of negligence as depending on principle so that, when a new point emerges, one should ask not whether it is covered by authority but whether recognised principles apply to it. *Donoghue v Stevenson* may be regarded as a milestone, and the well-known passage in Lord Atkin's speech should I think be regarded as a statement of principle. It is not to be treated as if it were a statutory definition. It will require qualification in new circumstances. But I think that the time has come when we can and should say that it ought to apply unless there is some justification or valid explanation for its exclusion.[65]

Lord Reid recognised that Atkin's neighbour dictum, whilst useful as a starting point, was too wide to explain *all* of the duty cases. Much like Lord Atkin had qualified Brett MR's test with his notion of proximity, Lord Reid qualified Lord Atkin's test with the proviso that it only applied where there was not some 'justification or valid explanation' why it ought not. This represented the first attempt at a general duty formulation since *Donoghue v Stevenson*.

Whilst Lord Reid's approach certainly appeared to explain the approach taken in the existing duty cases, his speech had nevertheless been given alone. It was to be another eight years before the House of Lords confirmed that Lord Reid's approach was, indeed, the correct one.

---

[62] See, eg, *Shaw Savilll & Albion Co Ltd v The Commonwealth* (1940) 66 CLR 344, concerning the so-called 'combat immunity.'

[63] [1970] AC 1004 (HL).

[64] *Greenwell v Prison Commissioners* (1951) 101 LJ 486 (CC).

[65] [1970] AC 1004 (HL), 1026–27.

IV. The Rise and Fall of *Anns v Merton*

In *Anns v Merton LBC*[66] the defendant local authority approved building plans for a block of flats which required the foundations to be three feet or deeper. The building contractors nevertheless only dug the foundations to a depth of two feet and six inches. Eight years later structural defects began to occur in the building, allegedly as a result of the shallow foundations. The plaintiffs, who at that point were lessees of the building, sued the defendant for their alleged negligence in failing to ensure that the builders complied with the approved plans. On the question of duty, Lord Wilberforce, with whom the rest of the House of Lords concurred, said:

> Through the trilogy of cases in this House, *Donoghue v Stevenson, Hedley Byrne & Co Ltd v Heller & Partners* Ltd and *Home Office v Dorset Yacht Co Ltd*, the position has now been reached that in order to establish that a duty of care arises in a particular situation, it is not necessary to bring the facts of that situation within those of previous situations in which a duty of care has been held to exist. Rather the question has to be approached in two stages. First one has to ask whether, as between the alleged wrongdoer and the person who has suffered damage there is a sufficient relationship of proximity or neighbourhood such that, in the reasonable contemplation of the former, carelessness on his part may be likely to cause damage to the latter, in which case a prima facie duty of care arises. Secondly, if the first question is answered affirmatively, it is necessary to consider whether there are any considerations which ought to negative, or to reduce or limit the scope of the duty or the class of person to whom it is owed or the damages to which a breach of it may give rise.[67]

This approach to duty, which became known as the 'two-stage' test, was effectively a restatement of the test proposed by Lord Reid in *Home Office v Dorset Yacht Co Ltd*; only now, it had the full support of the House of Lords. Significantly, just as Lord Atkin appeared to have done in *Donoghue v Stevenson*,[68] Lord Wilberforce, too, appeared to have used the term 'proximity' as a mere synonym for foreseeability.[69]

The two-stage test represented a significant change of focus. Whereas in the past the onus was on the *plaintiff* to establish why a duty ought to exist, now, provided that some foreseeable damage had been suffered by the plaintiff, the onus was on the *defendant* to provide some explanation why a duty ought *not* to exist and why

---

[66] [1978] AC 728 (HL).

[67] *Anns v Merton LBC* [1978] AC 728 (HL), 751–52 ('*Anns*').

[68] See discussion at (n 17).

[69] Richard Kidner, 'Resiling From the Anns Principle: The Variable Nature of Proximity in Negligence' (1987) 7 LS 319, 322, 327–28; *Sutherland Shire Council v Heyman* (1985) 157 CLR 424, 477–78 (Brennan J), 506 (Deane J); *Murphy v Brentwood DC* [1991] 1 AC 398 (HL), 487 (Lord Oliver). See also the comments of Lord Oliver in *Caparo Industries plc v Dickman* [1990] 2 AC 605 (HL), 645–47, and the detailed discussion of the first stage of *Anns* in JA Smillie, 'Principle, Policy and Negligence' (1984) 11 NZULR 111, 132, 136.

some exception ought to apply.[70] *All* foreseeable losses were therefore now subject to a prima facie duty of care and the multifarious approach to duty was well and truly a thing of the past. As Ibbetson explains, *Anns* confirmed that:

> [T]he law of negligence was beginning to be conceptualized in terms of an ocean of liability for carelessly causing foreseeable harm, dotted with islands of non-liability, rather than as a crowded archipelago of individual duty situations.[71]

The two-stage test was subsequently interpreted by some courts as an invitation to reconsider existing authority and overturn long-established areas of non-liability.[72] In *The Irene's Success*,[73] for example, Lloyd J held that cases involving pure economic loss had to be reconsidered in light of *Anns*, whilst in *Ross v Caunters*,[74] another case of pure economic loss, Megarry VC relied on the *Anns* test to circumvent the *Hedley Byrne* reliance requirement. However, the so called 'high-watermark' of the *Anns* approach occurred in *Junior Books Ltd v Veitchi Co Ltd*.[75] The defenders were engaged as sub-contractors to lay a floor in the pursuer's factory, but the defenders did a poor job and the floor soon began to crack. For reasons that are not clear, the pursuers sued the defenders, rather than the primary contractors, for the cost of replacing the defective floor: a purely economic loss. Whilst the existence of a duty of care could have conceivably been justified under the principle in *Hedley Byrne*,[76] the majority of the House of Lords instead relied on the two-stage *Anns* test, effectively denying any distinction between physical damage and pure economic loss. As Smith and Burns later commented, after *Junior Books*, 'The sorts of situations in which pure economic loss is now recoverable are so numerous that it would be difficult to state an exclusionary rule clearly.'[77]

The *Anns*-based expansion of the law of negligence, however, particularly in the area of pure economic loss, soon came to be seen as regrettable. Writing extra-judicially, Lord Oliver suggested that it had 'led to a spate of claims which had become more and more repugnant to common sense.'[78] *Anns* was simply too easy to satisfy, and 'the pendulum [had] now swung from over-particularisation to the

---

[70] See also: Smith and Burns (n 23) 150; JC Smith, 'The Mystery of Duty' in L Klar (ed), *Studies in Canadian Tort Law* (Butterworths, 1977) 6; Lord Goff in *Smith v Littlewoods Organisation Ltd* [1987] AC 241 (HL), 280.

[71] Ibbetson (n 10) 192–93.

[72] Lunney and Oliphant (n 61) 137; EW Peel and J Goudkamp, *Winfield and Jolowicz on Tort*, 19th edn (Sweet & Maxwell, 2014) 5-017; Smillie, 'The Foundation of the Duty of Care in Negligence' (n 17) 306.

[73] *Schiffahrt & Kohlen GMBH v Chelsea Maritime Ltd (The Irene's Success)* [1982] QB 481 (QB), 484 (Lloyd J). This was subsequently overruled by *Leigh and Sillavan Ltd v Aliakmon Shipping Co Ltd (The Aliakmon)* [1986] AC 785 (HL).

[74] [1980] Ch 297 (Ch), 310–11, 313–14.

[75] [1982] 1 AC 520 (HL) ('*Junior Books*').

[76] Indeed, this is generally how the case is rationalised today: *D&F Estates v Church Commissioners* [1989] 1 AC 177 (HL), 215 (Lord Oliver); *Murphy v Brentwood DC* [1991] 1 AC 398 (HL), 466 (Lord Keith), 481 (Lord Bridge). See also McBride and Bagshaw (n 34) 183, Lunney and Oliphant (n 61) 429–30.

[77] Smith and Burns (n 23) 152.

[78] Lord Oliver, 'Judicial Legislation' (1989) 2 LJIL 3, 16.

other extreme of over generalization ...'[79] As a result, any control the House of Lords had once had over setting the boundaries of the law of negligence was practically gone. The earliest sign of the retreat from *Anns* occurred in *Governors of the Peabody Donation Fund v Sir Lindsay Parkinson*,[80] where Lord Keith, the most vocal critic of *Anns*, said of the test:

> There has been a tendency in some recent cases to treat these passages as being themselves of a definitive character. This is a temptation which should be resisted. ... in determining whether or not a duty of care of particular scope was incumbent upon a defendant it is material to take into consideration whether it is just and reasonable that it *should* be so.[81]

Later cases confirmed the retreat,[82] and it soon became clear that *Anns* was not a licence to reconsider existing authority and only applied to novel cases,[83] and that foreseeability of harm alone was not enough to justify the imposition of a duty of care:

> It has been said almost too frequently to require repetition that foreseeability of likely harm is not in itself a sufficient test of liability in negligence. Some further ingredient is invariably needed to establish the requisite proximity of relationship between plaintiff and defendant, and all the circumstances of the case must be carefully considered and analysed in order to ascertain whether such an ingredient is present. The nature of the ingredient will be found to vary in a number of different categories of decided cases.[84]

At least insofar as it applied to the liability of local authorities for purely economic loss, *Anns* was eventually overruled in *Murphy v Brentwood DC*,[85] where the House of Lords unanimously declared that it had been wrongly decided—Lord Keith even going so far as to say that it was 'clear that *Anns* did not proceed upon any basis of established principle.'[86] Of the decision, Howarth said: '[W]hen the Law Lords, by 7–0, declare unsound a case that has been cited in 189 English cases in only 13 years (and until recently mostly with approval) we know something extraordinary has happened.'[87] Of course, given that *Anns* had been so completely emasculated

---

[79] Smith and Burns 162. Some attribute this shift to a Conservative government and change of Lordships. See, eg: David Howarth, 'Negligence After Murphy: Time to Re-Think' (1991) 50 CLJ 58, 59; Weir (n 35) 137 (fn 214). Compare John G Fleming, 'Requiem for Anns' (1990) 106 LQR 525 (who blames the 'ill-conceived decision in *Junior Books Ltd v Veitchi Co Ltd*'); and Robert Stevens, 'Torts' in Louis Blom-Cooper, Gavin Drewry and Brice Dickson (eds), *The Judicial House of Lords: 1876–2009* (OUP, 2009) 636 (who blames the conflation of *injuria* with *damnum*).

[80] [1985] AC 210 (HL).

[81] ibid 240–41 (emphasis added).

[82] *Yuen Kun Yeu v Attorney-General of Hong Kong* [1988] AC 175 (PC) 190–4 (Lord Keith); *Rowling v Takaro Properties Ltd* [1988] AC 473 (PC) 501 (Lord Keith). See also the comments of Lord Oliver in *Caparo Industries plc v Dickman* [1990] 2 AC 605 (HL), 647 (*Anns* was 'severely qualified by subsequent decisions'); and Lord Keith in *Murphy v Brentwood DC* [1991] 1 AC 398 (HL), 461.

[83] *Leigh and Sillavan Ltd v Aliakmon Shipping Co Ltd* (*The Aliakmon*) [1986] AC 785 (HL), 815 (Lord Brandon, with whom the rest of the court agreed).

[84] *Hill v Chief Constable of West Yorkshire* [1989] AC 53 (HL), 60 (Lord Keith).

[85] [1991] 1 AC 398 (HL) ('*Murphy v Brentwood DC*').

[86] ibid 471.

[87] Howarth (n 79) 58.

in the preceding years, its ultimate end, as general approach to duty questions, had occurred many years prior, and so, in that sense, *Murphy v Brentwood DC* was of little consequence; besides, the House of Lords had revisited the general duty issue in the landmark decision of *Caparo Industries plc v Dickman*,[88] less than six months earlier.

V. *Caparo*

In *Caparo*, the plaintiff company made a successful takeover bid for another company, Fidelity, in reliance on an audit report that had been prepared by the defendants. Although the audit report showed that Fidelity had made a pre-tax profit of £1.2m, they had in fact made a loss of £400,000. The plaintiff sued the defendants for the loss they had suffered by overpaying for the shares as a result of the audit report. After the claim was struck out by the trial judge, a decision that was later reversed by the Court of Appeal, the House of Lords were yet again faced with the task of providing guidance as to when a duty of care does or does not exist. Lord Bridge, in his leading judgment, was reluctant to attempt any complete duty formulation, noting Lord Atkin's earlier warning that 'To seek a complete logical definition of the general principle is probably to go beyond the function of the judge, for the more general the definition the more likely it is to omit essentials or to introduce non-essentials.'[89] Lord Bridge also highlighted the 'inability of any single general principle to provide a practical test which can be applied in every situation to determine whether a duty of care is owed ...'[90] Notwithstanding these warnings, Lord Bridge then noted that, what emerges from the cases is that:

> [I]n addition to the foreseeability of damage, necessary ingredients in any situation giving rise to a duty of care are that there should exist between the party owing the duty and the party to whom it is owed a relationship characterised by the law as one of "proximity" or "neighbourhood" and that the situation should be one in which the court considers it fair, just and reasonable that the law should impose a duty of a given scope upon the one party for the benefit of the other.[91]

Lord Bridge's dictum, which was almost a verbatim restatement of Bingham LJ's judgment in the Court of Appeal,[92] came to be known as the 'three-stage' test for the existence of a duty of care, as it required: (1) foreseeability; (2) proximity; and (3) that the imposition of a duty would be fair, just, and reasonable.

---

[88] [1990] 2 AC 605 ('*Caparo*').

[89] ibid 616, citing *Donoghue v Stevenson* 580.

[90] *Caparo* 617. See also Lord Oliver (at p633): 'I think that it has to be recognised that to search for any single formula which will serve as a general test of liability is to pursue a will-o'-the wisp.'

[91] ibid 617–18.

[92] *Caparo Industries plc v Dickman* [1989] QB 653 (CA) 678–79: 'The first is foreseeability ... The second is ... usually described as proximity ... The third requirement to be met before a duty of care will be held to be owed by A to B is that the court should find it just and reasonable to impose such a duty.'

Notwithstanding Lord Bridge's denial that any simple duty formula could possibly exist, the three-stage test has come to be regarded as the 'classic exposition of the modern approach to establishing a duty of care',[93] and continues to represent the UK's approach to duty questions today.[94]

A. Foreseeability

As we have already seen, since *Donoghue v Stevenson*, foreseeability of harm to the plaintiff has always been a necessary, but not sufficient,[95] requirement for a duty of care to exist. The rationale behind the requirement is that, in the eyes of the law, a defendant cannot be expected to exercise reasonable care towards the world at large, but only to those he can reasonably foresee could be affected by his actions; if the defendant cannot foresee that his actions will harm the claimant, then he cannot have a legal duty to take care to avoid harming them.[96] This is not to say, however, that harm to the *actual and specific* claimant must be foreseeable in order for a duty to be owed. Mr Stevenson, for example, could not have denied the existence of a duty to Mrs Donoghue because he could not foresee that *Mrs Donoghue in particular*, a person whom he had never met, would consume his product. Rather, the foreseeability requirement merely requires that the defendant's conduct might foreseeably affect a person in her position, *or a class of persons to which she belonged.*[97] The nature, and necessity, of the foreseeability requirement will be further explored in chapter four.

B. Proximity

'Proximity' has been used as a duty determinant since at least the late nineteenth century,[98] and, as we saw, was central to the idea of a general duty principle in both *Donoghue v Stevenson* and *Anns*. Yet, as we also saw, in both cases, 'proximity' appeared to be being used as little more than a synonym for foreseeability.[99]

---

[93] Lunney and Oliphant (n 61) 137.

[94] *Customs and Excise Commissioners v Barclays Bank* [2007] AC 181 (HL) ('*Customs and Excise Commissioners v Barclays Bank*').

[95] *cf* Beever (n 17) 120, who argues that foreseeability alone *is* sufficient.

[96] See, eg, A Robertson, 'Justice, Community Welfare and the Duty of Care' (2011) 127 LQR 370, 373; Christian Witting, 'The Three Stage Test Abandoned in Australia—Or Not?' (2002) 118 LQR 214, 218; J Stapleton, 'Duty of Care Factors: a Selection from the Judicial Menus' in Peter Cane and Jane Stapleton (eds), *The Law of Obligations: Essays in Celebration of John Fleming* (OUP, 1998) 61; JG Fleming, 'Remoteness and Duty: The Control Devices in Liability for Negligence' (1953) 31 Can Bar Rev 471, 486; NJ McBride and R Bagshaw, *Tort Law*, 3rd edn (Pearson Longman, 2008) 59.

[97] *Farrugia v Great Western Railway* [1947] 2 All ER 565 (CA).

[98] *Le Lievre v Gould* [1893] 1 QB 491, 504 (CA) (Smith LJ): 'The decision of *Heaven v Pender* was founded upon the principle, that a duty to take due care did arise when the person or property of one was in such *proximity* to the person or property of another that, if due care was not taken, damage might be done by the one to the other' (emphasis added).

[99] See (n 17) and (n 69).

By the 1980s, however, the foreseeability-based understanding of proximity was being challenged, and proximity appeared to be developing into an important legal concept in its own right. In *McLoughlin v O'Brian*,[100] for example, Lord Wilberforce retreated from the foreseeability-based understanding of proximity, indicating that, at least in secondary psychiatric injury cases, proximity required closeness in 'time and space'.[101] Similarly, in *Yuen Kun-Yeu v A-G of Hong Kong*,[102] Lord Keith held that proximity referred to the 'the whole concept of necessary relationship between plaintiff and defendant',[103] as 'Lord Atkin clearly had in contemplation that all the circumstances of the case, not only the foreseeability of harm, were appropriate to be taken into account in determining whether a duty of care arose'.[104] This was elaborated upon even further by Bingham LJ in the Court of Appeal's decision in *Caparo*:

> The approach will vary according to the particular facts of the case, as is reflected in the varied language used. But the focus of the inquiry is on the closeness and directness of the relationship between the parties. In determining this, foreseeability must, I think, play an important part: the more obvious it is that A's act or omission will cause harm to B, the less likely a court will be to hold that the relationship of A and B is insufficiently proximate to give rise to a duty of care.[105]

This new understanding of proximity clearly involved considerations beyond reasonable foreseeability, and, soon after *Caparo*, came to be relied on to justify the outcome of duty questions in a number of cases. In cases of negligent misstatements causing pure economic loss, for example, a *Hedley Byrne* type assumption of responsibility was typically understood as evidence of the requisite degree of proximity,[106] whilst in cases involving liability for the criminal conduct of third parties, sufficient proximity would exist where the claimant was at a 'special distinctive risk'.[107]

Of course, an assumption of responsibility or a claimant that was at a 'special distinctive risk' could not always be required in order to establish proximity, such as in cases involving directly caused physical injury, where the parties are typically complete strangers. Accordingly, in such cases, reasonable foreseeability alone was thought to be enough, as explained in *Canadian National Railway Co v Norsk Pacific Steamship*:[108] '[W]here there is physical injury or damage one posits

[100] [1983] 1 AC 410 (HL), 427.
[101] ibid 422.
[102] [1988] AC 175 (PC).
[103] ibid 191.
[104] ibid 192. See also Lord Keith's comments in *Governors of the Peabody Donation Fund v Sir Lindsay Parkinson* [1985] AC 210, 240 (HL).
[105] *Caparo Industries plc v Dickman* [1989] QB 653 (CA), 679. See also Deane J's comments in *Jaensch v Coffey* (1984) 155 CLR 549, 580.
[106] *Caparo Industries plc v Dickman* [1989] QB 653 (CA), 679 (Bingham LJ); *Sutherland Shire Council v Heyman* (1985) 157 CLR 424, 498 (Deane J): *Murphy v Brentwood DC* 486 (Lord Oliver). More recently, this appears to have been the view of Lords Hoffmann and Walker in *Customs and Excise Commissioners v Barclays Bank* (at 199 and 210 respectively), and Lord Kerr in *Michael v Chief Constable of South Wales Police* [2015] AC 1732 (HL), [158]–[159].
[107] *Hill v Chief Constable of West Yorkshire* [1989] AC 53 (HL), 62 (Lord Keith).
[108] (1992) 91 DLR (4th) 289.

proximity on the ground that if one is close enough to someone or something to do physical damage to it one is close enough to be held legally responsible for the consequences.'[109] What amounted to sufficient proximity between the parties, then, depended on the facts of the case. The obvious difficulty with this understanding of proximity is that it is not clear why an assumption of responsibility (or that the claimant be at some 'special distinctive risk,' etc) is required in some cases, whilst foreseeability of injury alone is enough in others. According to the courts at least, the reason was that what amounts to sufficient proximity in a particular case depends on what is fair, just, and reasonable in the circumstances. As Lord Nicholls explained in *Stovin v Wise*:[110]

> The *Caparo* tripartite test elevates proximity to the dignity of a separate heading. This formulation tends to suggest that proximity is a separate ingredient, distinct from fairness and reasonableness, and capable of being identified by some other criteria. This is not so. Proximity is a slippery word. Proximity is not legal shorthand for a concept with its own, objectively identifiable characteristics. Proximity is convenient shorthand for a relationship between two parties which makes it fair and reasonable one should owe the other a duty of care. This is only another way of saying that when assessing the requirements of fairness and reasonableness regard must be had to the relationship of the parties.[111]

Of course, if the existence of a duty of care depends on what is fair, just, and reasonable, and what amounts to sufficient proximity, too, depends on what is fair, just, and reasonable, then the proximity 'stage' would appear to be superfluous. Indeed, as McBride and Bagshaw state, it is 'hard to imagine' a court denying that there was a relationship of proximity if harm to the plaintiff was reasonably foreseeable and, in the opinion of the court, it was fair, just, and reasonable to impose a duty.[112]

For much the same reason, proximity has also been criticised for being devoid of any content, and little more than a label to attach to the conclusion that a duty of care exists. Dawson J, for example, wrote in *Hill v Van Erp*[113] that proximity was 'the result of a process of reasoning rather than the process itself,' whilst McHugh J, writing extra-judicially, has said 'The difficulty with proximity ... is that it is a legal rule without specific content and merely records the result of a finding reached on other grounds.'[114] More recently, Rogers has expressed the view that 'there is a

---

[109] ibid 1153 (McLachlin J).

[110] [1996] AC 923 (HL).

[111] ibid 932. See also: *Alcock v Chief Constable of South Yorkshire Police* [1992] 1 AC 310 (HL), 411 (Lord Oliver); and *Marc Rich & Co v Bishop Rock Marine Co Ltd* [1996] AC 211 (HL), 235 (Lord Steyn). For academic commentary to this effect, see: WVH Rogers, *Winfield and Jolowicz on Tort*, 18th edn (Sweet & Maxwell, 2010) 179; Tom Hickman, 'Negligence and Article 6: The Great Escape?' (2002) 61 CLJ 13, 14; and Kidner (n 69) 328.

[112] McBride and Bagshaw (n 96) 58. See also Jaffey (n 17) 18.

[113] (1997) 188 CLR 159, 178. See also Brennan J in *Hawkins v Clayton* (1988) 164 CLR 539, 555–56.

[114] MH McHugh, 'Neighbourhood, Proximity and Reliance' in PD Finn (ed), *Essays on Torts* (Law Book Co Ltd 1989) 36.

tenable view that [proximity] is really no more than a statement of the conclusion that there is or is not a duty.'[115]

Despite these criticisms, the concept of proximity continues to have its advocates.[116] Witting, for example, perhaps the concept's most vocal proponent, argues that much of the criticism of proximity is 'misguided',[117] as proximity was never intended to be a 'test'.[118] Similarly, Kramer believes that 'The critics of proximity who worry that proximity is not a simple formula are attacking a straw man. Proximity is a label for the enquiry ... not a rule or formula that encapsulates or replaces that enquiry.'[119] Indeed, even Lord Bridge conceded in *Caparo* that proximity was 'not susceptible of any such precise definition' and so amounted to little more than a 'convenient label' to attach to the features of a situation that gave rise to a duty of care.[120]

But if proximity is not a test or formula, what is it? According to Witting, proximity is best understood as concerning the features of the 'factual relationship between the parties' prior to the defendant's alleged carelessness occurring.[121] The greater the factual links, or 'causal pathways',[122] between the parties, the greater the potential for the defendant to (and increased likelihood that he or she will) cause the claimant harm, and so the easier we can say that the claimant's 'loss really is the product of the defendant's conduct and ... should be identified with him rather than with someone else.'[123] Similarly, Robertson argues that proximity concerns the 'closeness and directness'[124] of the effect of the claimant's conduct on the defendant, and is informed by factors such as the defendant's control over or role in creating the risk of harm that occurred as well as the antecedent relationship between the parties.[125] As to whether the 'closeness

---

[115] Rogers (n 111) 169. For further criticism of proximity, see: Stone (n 17) 264–68; K Barker, 'Unreliable Assumptions in the Modern Law of Negligence' (1993) 109 LQR 461, 461; Howarth (n 79) 60; Smillie, 'The Foundation of the Duty of Care in Negligence' (n 17) 312, 316; D Nolan, 'Deconstructing the Duty of Care' (2013) 129 LQR 559, 583–84, and *Canadian National Railway Co v Norsk Pacific Steamship* (1992) 91 DLR (4th) 289 [112] (Stevenson J).

[116] Christian Witting, 'Negligent Inspectors and Flying Machines' (2000) 59 CLJ 544; Christian Witting, 'Duty of Care: An Analytical Approach' (2005) 25 OJLS 33; Witting, 'The Three Stage Test Abandoned in Australia—Or Not?' (n 96); Adam Kramer, 'Proximity as Principles: Directness, Community Norms and the Tort of Negligence' (2003) 11 Tort L Rev 70; Robertson (n 96); A Robertson, 'Policy-Based Reasoning in Duty of Care Cases' (2012) 33 LS 119; A Robertson, 'Proximity: Divergence and Unity' in A Robertson and M Tilbury (eds), *Divergences in Private Law* (Hart, 2016).

[117] Witting, 'Negligent Inspectors and Flying Machines' (n 116) 216.

[118] ibid 216.

[119] Kramer (n 116) 75.

[120] *Caparo* 618. See also: Lord Oliver at 633 and 651 and Lord Roskill at 628; Bingham LJ in the Court of Appeal, at [1989] QB 653, 679; and Deane J in *Sutherland Shire Council v Heyman* (1985) 157 CLR 424, 497.

[121] C Witting, 'What are We Doing Here? The Relationship Between Negligence in General and Misstatements in English Law' in Kit Barker, Ross Grantham and Warren Swain (eds), *The Law of Misstatements: 50 Years on from Hedley Byrne v Heller* (Hart, 2015) 39.

[122] Witting, 'Duty of Care: An Analytical Approach' (n 116) 37, C Witting, 'The House that Dr Beever Built: Corrective Justice, Principle and the Law of Negligence' (2008) 71 MLR 621 632.

[123] Witting, 'Negligent Inspectors and Flying Machines' (n 116) 560.

[124] Robertson, 'Proximity: Divergence and Unity' (n 116) 10–11.

[125] ibid 11.

and directness' is sufficient to satisfy the proximity stage, Robertson believes this is ultimately an 'ought' question; in particular, whether, as a matter of interpersonal justice,[126] the circumstances dictate that the defendant *ought* to take account of the interests of the claimant.[127] According to its proponents, then, if we move away from an understanding of proximity as a test in itself, and instead towards a concept that focusses on the closeness of the relationship between the parties and the various features that give rise to that closeness, it is able to perform a 'distinct analytical function'.[128]

This narrower understanding of proximity certainly overcomes a number of the objections levelled against the more general conception. In particular, by making it clear that proximity is focussed on the closeness or directness of the relationship between the defendant and claimant, it has a more definable, and so less 'empty,' content. Similarly, by confining the focus of proximity to the facts of the case, it can no longer be said that it is synonymous with the third stage of the *Caparo* test and therefore superfluous; in particular, it only concerns what is fair, just, and reasonable in the *interpersonal justice* sense, whilst the third stage of *Caparo* tends to be more concerned with external 'policy' factors,[129] and so what is fair, just, and reasonable in the *community welfare* sense.

Nevertheless, both Witting and Robertson concede that determining whether there is sufficient proximity will ultimately require the consideration of different factors in different types of cases. Robertson is most explicit in this regard, noting that 'the concept of proximity does not provide a precise criterion or rigid formula that can be applied mechanically to a given situation ... considerations to be taken into account will vary across different classes of case, as will their relative weight ...'[130] So, for example, in cases of negligent misstatement causing pure economic loss, proximity might be evidenced by explicit knowledge of the defendant that the claimant was intending to rely on the statement and would likely suffer loss as a result.[131] In manufacturers' liability cases, on the other hand, proximity could be evidenced simply from the fact that conduct of the defendant might create a risk to consumers.[132]

Proximity therefore remains, even in its narrower sense, an extremely broad and highly variable concept, meaning one thing in one case and something else entirely in another case. And whilst its proponents argue that the different meanings can be reconciled by focussing on the number and nature of the 'causal pathways' to

---

[126] ibid (n 116) 11–12.

[127] ibid 10. Kramer, too, relies on the idea of 'directness': Kramer (n 116) 77.

[128] Witting, 'Duty of Care: An Analytical Approach' (n 116) 34. See also Kramer (n 116) 72 (proximity is a 'meaningful definitional element') and Robertson, 'Justice, Community Welfare and the Duty of Care' (n 96) 374 (proximity is 'a workable criterion').

[129] Witting, 'Duty of Care: An Analytical Approach' (n 116) 36-37; Robertson, 'Proximity: Divergence and Unity' (n 116) 14. The meaning of 'policy' is discussed in further detail below in Section V.C.

[130] Robertson, 'Proximity: Divergence and Unity' (n 116) 12.

[131] Witting, 'Negligent Inspectors and Flying Machines' (n 116) 559.

[132] Ibid 558. Witting is referring specifically to the facts of *Donoghue v Stevenson*.

harm, or on whether, as a matter of interpersonal justice, the defendant ought to have been mindful of the interest of the claimant affected, it is certainly debateable whether this provides sufficient clarity so as to make proximity a useful concept.

Also problematic is that, even if we adopt the narrow definition of proximity, and accept that it *is* meaningful and *does* perform a distinct analytical function, this does not appear to be how it is understood by the courts. Courts continue, for example, to endorse the view that proximity depends on, or is even synonymous with, considerations of policy, something that even proximity's proponents would likely reject.[133] In *Chandler v Cape*,[134] for example, Arden LJ held that the proximity and fair, just, and reasonable requirements of *Caparo* are 'directed to the essentially same question.'[135] Lord Kerr expressed a similar view in the more recent case of *Michael v Chief Constable of South Wales Police*:[136]

> Not only does the answer to the question, 'is there a proximate relationship' bear on the matter of what is fair etc, what is 'fair, just and reasonable' tends to blend with the concept of 'proximity'.

Similar comments have been made in both Australia[137] and Canada.[138] Yet, as we saw above, such an understanding not only makes the entire concept redundant, but also robs it of any analytical function at all. If, then, judges at even the highest level *still* use the term in a way that even proximity's advocates would not support, maybe it is time for the concept to be retired and replaced with something else less susceptible to confusion.

Views on the utility of proximity as a concept therefore vary considerably, with descriptions ranging from 'a label which embraces ... [no] definable concept'[139] to an 'integral element' of the duty enquiry.[140] Notwithstanding the controversy, however, there can be little doubt that the concept, at least in some form or another, continues to be relied upon by courts when making duty determinations.[141] Whether or not such a concept (as distinct from the factors that fall within it) is necessary is explored further in chapter five.

---

[133] Robertson, for example, explicitly rejects this: Robertson, 'Proximity: Divergence and Unity' (n 116) 14.

[134] *Chandler v Cape plc* [2012] 1 WLR 3111.

[135] ibid [62]. See also the comments of Lord Oliver in *Alcock v Chief Constable of South Yorkshire Police* [1992] 1 AC 310: 'no doubt "policy", if that is the right word, or perhaps more properly, the impracticability or unreasonableness of entertaining claims to the ultimate limits of the consequences of human activity, necessarily plays a part in the court's perception of what is sufficiently proximate.'

[136] [2015] AC 1732 (HL) [158]. Almost identical comments were made at ibid [156]. Lord Neuberger, writing extrajudicially, also recently stated that proximity involved a 'heavy dollop of policy': Lord Neuberger, 'Implications of Tort Law Decisions' (Address to Northern Ireland Personal Injury Bar's Inaugural Conference, County Down, 13 May 2017) www.supremecourt.uk/docs/speech-170513.pdf.

[137] See (n 231) to (n 235).

[138] See (n 169).

[139] *Caparo* 633 (Lord Oliver).

[140] Robertson, 'Proximity: Divergence and Unity' (above n 116) 14, 18.

[141] See, eg, Robertson, 'Proximity: Divergence and Unity' (above n 116) 14–16, and Section III(B) of ch 7.

C. Policy Considerations and What is Fair, Just, and Reasonable

Prima facie, the third stage of the *Caparo* test, whether it is fair, just, and reasonable to impose a duty, admits a potentially limitless range of considerations. Lord Nicholls, for example has called the third stage 'vague' and 'uncomfortably loose',[142] whilst Lunney and Oliphant believe that 'the third stage of the *Caparo* approach can be regarded as the general repository for a miscellaneous set of ... arguments, undefined in nature and unlimited in number, which are invoked haphazardly and in an ad hoc fashion ...'.[143] Of course, if the third stage were truly unlimited, it would all but render the first two stages of the *Caparo* test redundant, as it could easily be argued that it is not fair, just, and reasonable to impose a duty where the parties are not in a relationship of 'proximity',[144] or where harm to the claimant is not foreseeable. Accordingly, the third stage is usually understood in a narrower sense; in particular, as referring to considerations of 'policy'.[145]

The use of policy considerations to resolve private law disputes can be dated to at least 1414,[146] and to determine duty problems since 1842.[147] However, the idea of policy as an aspect of a *general* duty formulation, whilst being suggested by academics as early as the 1940s and 1950s,[148] did not gain traction in the courts until the 1960s. The earliest statement to this effect appears to be that of Lord Pearce, who stated in *Hedley Byrne* that the size of the 'sphere of the duty of care in negligence ... depends ultimately upon the courts' assessment of the demands of society for protection from the carelessness of others'.[149] This statement was later relied upon by Lord Denning in *Dorset Yacht Co Ltd v Home Office*,[150] who was far

---

[142] *Stovin v Wise* [1996] AC 923 (HL), 933 (Lord Nicholls).

[143] Lunney and Oliphant (n 61) 140. See also Nolan, who calls it a 'blatant tautology:' Nolan, 'Deconstructing the Duty of Care' (n 115) 582.

[144] See, eg, McBride and Bagshaw (n 96) 58.

[145] *Michael v Chief Constable of South Wales Police* [2015] AC 1732 (HL), [160] (Lord Kerr); *Customs and Excise Commissioners v Barclays Bank* 190 (Lord Bingham); *Perre v Apand Pty Ltd* (1999) 198 CLR 180 [259] (Kirby J); *Pyrenees Shire Council v Day* (1998) 192 CLR 330 [249] (Kirby J); Prue Vines, Peter Hanford and Carol Harlow, 'Duty of Care' in Carolyn Sappideen and Prue Vines (eds), *Fleming's The Law of Torts*, 10th edn (Thomson Reuters (Professional) Australia Limited, 2011) 155; J Stapleton, 'The Golden Thread at the Heart of Tort Law: Protection of the Vulnerable' (2003) 24 Aust Bar Rev 135, 137; J Murphy and C Witting, *Street on Torts*, 13th edn (OUP, 2012) 46; H Luntz, 'The Use of Policy in Negligence Cases in the High Court of Australia' in M Bryan (ed), *Private Law in Theory and Practice* (Routledge-Cavendish, 2007) 77. See also Deane J in *Sutherland Shire Council v Heyman* (1985) 157 CLR 424 [5], who, albeit prior to *Caparo*, equates 'notions of what is "fair and reasonable"' with 'considerations of public policy'.

[146] *Dyer's Case* (1414) YB Pas 2 Hen V, fo 5, pl 26. See also WSM Knight, 'Public Policy in English Law' (1922) 38 LQR 207, 207.

[147] *Winterbottom v Wright* (1842) 10 M&W 109, 152 ER 402. For why this decision was based on 'policy', see Vines, Hanford and Harlow (n 145) 156. *cf* Beever (n 17) 11.

[148] See, eg: FH Lawson, 'The Duty of Care in Negligence: A Comparative Study' (1947) 22 TulLRev 111, 113; RG McKerron, 'The Duty of Care in South African Law' (1952) 69 SALJ 189, 196; JG Fleming, 'The Action Per Quod Servitum Amisit' (1952) 26 ALJ 122, 127; F James, 'Scope of Duty in Negligence Cases' (1952) 47 NwULRev 778, 808; Fleming, 'Remoteness and Duty: The Control Devices in Liability for Negligence' (n 96) 485.

[149] *Hedley Byrne* (Lord Pearce) 536. Though, as Mitchell notes, this was 'very much the exception': Mitchell (n 40) 181–82.

[150] [1969] 2 QB 412.

more explicit, commenting that the determination of a duty of care was 'at bottom a matter of public policy which we, as judges, must resolve',[151] a comment that was later approved by Lord Diplock in the House of Lords.[152] It was not until *Anns*, however, that, under the second stage of the test,[153] policy considerations were officially declared to be central to any general duty formula.

There is, however, considerable uncertainty as to the proper scope and content of the term 'policy',[154] which has led MacCormick, for example, to conclude that the term is 'hideously inexact'.[155] In the duty context, however, it is generally understood that arguments based on policy tend to focus on whether, *taking into account the consequences that the imposition of a duty would have on the community*, it would be fair, just, and reasonable to impose a duty.[156] An argument that it would be unfair to impose a duty on a police officer towards those they are investigating because it may lead to 'detrimentally defensive' policing is an example of a policy-based argument.[157] Considerations of policy are typically contrasted with considerations of 'principle',[158] which focus on whether, *as between the parties before the court*, it is fair, just, and reasonable, to impose a duty.[159] An argument that a police officer should owe a duty to those they are investigating because of the close connection between the parties and the high probability that a carelessly conducted investigation will cause damage to the suspect, is an example of a principle-based argument (which, under the *Caparo* formulation, would be discussed at the proximity and foreseeability stages). Arguments based on policy, then, focus on considerations of *public* policy or community welfare, whilst arguments based on principle focus on considerations of interpersonal justice.[160]

Policy considerations are often thought to play an important part in determining the outcome of modern duty questions, particularly at the ultimate appellate

---

[151] ibid 426. See also Lord Denning MR's comments in *Spartan Steel & Alloys Ltd v Martin & Co (Contractors) Ltd* [1973] QB 27 (CA), 37.

[152] *Home Office v Dorset Yacht Co Ltd* [1970] AC 1004 (HL), 1058 (Lord Diplock).

[153] Although Lord Wilberforce did not use the term 'policy,' his dictum is widely considered to incorporate considerations of what we would today label as policy: *Yuen Kun-Yeu v A-G of Hong Kong* [1988] AC 175 (PC), 193 (Lord Keith); Stapleton, 'The Golden Thread at the Heart of Tort Law: Protection of the Vulnerable' (n 145) 137; Vines, Hanford and Harlow (n 145) 155.

[154] Robertson, 'Justice, Community Welfare and the Duty of Care' (n 96) 371. See, eg, the definition given by Bell, who defines policy in a way that would also render the first two stages of the *Caparo* test redundant: J Bell, *Policy Arguments in Judicial Decisions* (Clarendon Press, 1983) 23.

[155] N MacCormick, *Legal Reasoning and Legal Theory* (Clarendon Press, 1978) 263.

[156] Robertson, 'Justice, Community Welfare and the Duty of Care' (n 96) 371; R Dworkin, *Taking Rights Seriously* (Harvard University Press, 1978) 22, 82; R Stevens, *Torts and Rights* (OUP, 2007) 308;

[157] *Hill v Chief Constable of West Yorkshire* [1989] AC 53 (HL), 63 (Lord Keith).

[158] According to Stevens, the distinction can be traced back to *Egerton v Brownlow* (1853) 4 HL Cas 1, 123; 10 ER 359, 408–409, where Parke B distinguished between 'public policy' and 'the policy of the law': Stevens (n 156) 308.

[159] EJ Weinrib, 'The Disintegration of Duty' in M Stuart Madden (ed), *Exploring Tort Law* (Cambridge University Press, 2005) 157; Robertson, 'Justice, Community Welfare and the Duty of Care' (n 96) 371; Dworkin (n 156) 22, 82.

[160] For a more detailed discussion of the meaning of 'policy,' see James Plunkett, 'Principle and Policy in Private Law Reasoning' (2016) 75 CLJ 366.

level.[161] The permissibility of policy-based arguments in determining duty issues is, however, controversial. Why this is so is explored in chapter five.

VI. Canada and the 'Two Stage' Test

Despite *Anns* falling out of favour in the UK, and having only a limited effect in Australia,[162] it proved to be highly influential in Canada. After initially being adopted by the Supreme Court in *City of Kamloops v Nielsen*,[163] the two-stage test was met with much enthusiasm, and was repeatedly affirmed by the Supreme Court for almost two decades.[164] Over the course of time, however, as had been the case in the UK, the two-stage test led to a considerable expansion in liability for negligence, occasionally well beyond what would have been allowed in the UK or Australia.[165] Indeed, upon reflection, Neyers described the two-stage test as giving rise to an 'untrammelled expansion of negligence liability in the Canadian context.'[166]

The Supreme Court of Canada took the opportunity to revisit the duty question in the 2001 case, *Cooper v Hobart*.[167] After explaining that *Anns* continued to provide a 'useful framework in which to approach the question of whether a duty of care should be imposed in a new situation',[168] the court proceeded to set out a reformulated version of the two-stage test:

> In brief compass, we suggest that at this stage in the evolution of the law, both in Canada and abroad, the *Anns* analysis is best understood as follows. At the first stage of the *Anns* test, two questions arise: (1) was the harm that occurred the reasonably foreseeable consequence of the defendant's act? and (2) are there reasons, notwithstanding the proximity between the parties established in the first part of this test, that tort liability should not be recognized here? The proximity analysis involved at the first stage of the Anns test focuses on factors arising from the relationship between the plaintiff and the defendant. These factors include questions of policy, in the broad sense of that word. If foreseeability and proximity are established at the first stage, a prima facie duty of care arises. At the second stage of the *Anns* test, the question still remains whether there are

---

[161] Robertson, 'Policy-Based Reasoning in Duty of Care Cases' (n 116) 121, 128, 137. See also Jonathan Morgan, 'Policy Reasoning in Tort Law: The Courts, the Law Commission and the Critics' (2009) 125 LQR 215, 215. The extent to which this is the case is explored in ch 7, Section III(E).

[162] This was evident as early as *Seale v Perry* [1982] VR 193, and later made clear by the High Court in *Sutherland Shire Council v Heyman* (1985) 157 CLR 424, 481 (Brennan J), and 503–505, 507 (Deane J).

[163] (1984) 10 DLR (4th) 641.

[164] See, eg, *BDC Ltd v Hofstrand Farms Ltd* (1986) 26 DLR (4th) 1 (Estey J); *Rothfield v Manolakos* (1989) 63 DLR (4th) 449 (Cory J); *Canadian National Railway Co v Norsk Pacific Steamship* (1992) 91 DLR (4th) 289; *Dobson (Litigation Guardian of) v Dobson* (1999) 174 DLR (4th) 1.

[165] Compare, eg, *Canadian National Railway Co v Norsk Pacific Steamship* (1992) 91 DLR (4th) 289 with *Spartan Steel & Alloys Ltd v Martin & Co (Contractors) Ltd* [1973] QB 27 (CA).

[166] JW Neyers, 'Distilling Duty: the Supreme Court of Canada Amends Anns' (2002) 118 LQR 221, 224.

[167] (2001) 206 DLR (4th) 193 ('*Cooper*').

[168] ibid 202 [28] (McLachlin CJC and Major J).

residual policy considerations outside the relationship of the parties that may negative the imposition of a duty of care. It may be, as the Privy Council suggests in *Yuen Kun Yeu*, that such considerations will not often prevail. However, we think it useful expressly to ask, before imposing a new duty of care, whether despite foreseeability and proximity of relationship, there are other policy reasons why the duty should not be imposed.[169]

Despite the Court paying lip-service to *Anns*, and insisting that they were merely 'highlighting' and 'honing' the existing law,[170] *Cooper* nevertheless represented a substantial reformulation of the two-stage test,[171] a reformulation that ultimately led to an end of the expansion of the law of negligence in Canada that had occurred under the pre-*Cooper* two-stage test.[172]

On one view, *Cooper* had done little more than create a three-stage test, identical in substance, if not name, to the three-stage *Caparo* test. Indeed, this appeared to be the understanding of Iacobucci J, who, in *Odhavji Estate v Woodhouse*,[173] described the reformulated *Anns* test as consisting of three independent stages: foreseeability of harm, sufficient proximity between the parties, and an absence of policy reasons to negative a duty.[174] McLachlin CJ, however, quickly rejected this suggestion, denying that it was the correct understanding of *Cooper*, and that the two-stage test was instead to be understood as follows:

> [A]t stage one, foreseeability and factors going to the relationship between the parties must be considered with a view to determining whether a *prima facie* duty of care arises. At stage two, the issue is whether this duty is negated by other, broader policy considerations.[175]

In other words, the test did not consist of three independent stages, as is the case under *Caparo*, but two independent stages, one of which consisted of two related 'questions'.[176] It will be noticed that the first stage largely corresponds to what we

---

[169] ibid 202–203 [29] (McLachlin CJC and Major J). The reference to 'policy' as part of the first stage is, admittedly, bizarre, as it is not clear what, if any, difference there is between 'policy' considerations that are relevant to the first stage and 'policy' considerations that are relevant to the second stage. Klar, too, notes that the meaning of the term is 'not altogether clear': Lewis Klar, *Tort Law*, 5th edn (Carswell, 2012) (n 174) 187. See also, Robertson (n 106) 37. For examples of the Court using 'policy' considerations as part of the proximity enquiry, see: *D(B) v Children's Aid Society* (2007) 284 DLR (4th) 682; *Hill v Hamilton-Wentworth Regional Police Services Board* (2007) 285 DLR (4th) 620.

[170] ibid 196 [1] (McLachlin CJC and Major J).

[171] Neyers (n 166) 222; Stephen GA Pitel, 'Negligence: Canada Remakes the Anns Test' (2002) 61 CLJ 252, 253.

[172] Allen M Linden and Bruce Feldthusen, *Canadian Tort Law*, 9th edn (LexisNexis, 2011) 300.

[173] 233 DLR (4th) 193.

[174] 218 [52]. Klar and Pitel also seem to endorse this view: Klar (n 169) 178–79; Pitel (n 171) 254.

[175] *Childs v Desormeaux* (2006) 266 DLR (4th) 257, 263 [12]. Unsurprisingly, this largely echoes McLachlin CJ and Major J's comments on the first (*Cooper* 204 [34]) and second (*Cooper* 206 [37]) stages of the two-stage test in *Cooper*.

[176] It is also arguable that Canada's *Anns* test is different to *Caparo* on the basis that the second stage of *Anns* looks for reasons why a duty should *not* be imposed, whilst the equivalent (ie third) stage of *Caparo* looks for reasons why a duty *should* be imposed. However, as Robertson notes, this distinction is not reflected by what occurs in practice, as the majority of applications of *Caparo* focus exclusively on reasons why a duty should *not* be imposed in any event: Robertson, 'Policy-Based Reasoning in Duty of Care Cases' (n 116) 131. See also the comments in ch 7, Section III(E)(iii).

have seen is described as considerations of 'principle', and the second of which corresponds to what we have seen is described as considerations of 'community welfare'.[177] Notwithstanding, however, McLachlin CJ's insistence that the UK's three-stage approach and Canada's two-stage approach are distinct, there is no doubt that the competing tests for the existence of a duty of care are 'remarkably similar'.[178]

VII. Assumption of Responsibility and the 'Extended' *Hedley Byrne* Principle

We saw above that *Hedley Byrne* determined that a duty of care will be owed whenever a defendant assumes responsibility towards the claimant for the quality of their conduct. This was particularly significant in cases involving purely economic loss where, despite the developments elsewhere, and save for a small number of exceptions,[179] *Hedley Byrne* remained the preferred test for establishing the existence of a duty of care.[180] At least as initially understood, the assumption of responsibility test was interpreted and applied quite strictly, so that only explicit or relatively unequivocal assumptions of responsibility, and only those in relation to statements,[181] could satisfy the test. Indeed, at least according to Lord Devlin in *Hedley Byrne*, there could only be an assumption of responsibility where the relationship between the parties was 'equivalent to contract', meaning, 'in circumstances in which, but for the absence of consideration, there would be a contract'.[182] Given the narrow understanding of what it meant to 'assume a responsibility', the assumption of responsibility test was only capable of explaining the existence of a duty in a very limited set of circumstances. By the 1990s, however, what it meant to 'assume a responsibility' came to be understood in a much wider sense than 'equivalent to contract', leading to what became known as

---

[177] See Section V(C) above. See also Robertson, 'Justice, Community Welfare and the Duty of Care' (n 96), who proposes a two-stage duty test largely along these lines.

[178] Linden and Feldthusen (n 172) 299. Stevens even goes so far as to say that the two approaches are 'practically indistinguishable': R Stevens, 'The Divergence of the Australian and English Law of Torts' in Simone Degeling, J Edelman and J Goudkamp (eds), *Torts in Commercial Law* (Thomson Reuters, 2011) 40 (fn 11).

[179] See, eg, *Anns* and *Junior Books*.

[180] *Mutual Life & Citizens Assurance Co Ltd v Evatt* [1971] AC 793 (PC); *Smith v Eric S Bush* [1990] 1 AC 831 (HL); *Caparo*. Whilst *Hedley Byrne* tended to be confined to cases involving purely economic loss *in practice*, there is no indication in the speeches of the law lords that *Hedley Byrne* was intended to be understood in this way. Indeed, McBride and Bagshaw label the idea that the assumption of responsibility test was to be confined to cases involving purely economic loss as a 'common misconception': see McBride and Bagshaw (n 34) 187.

[181] That *Hedley Byrne* was not confined to statements was not *explicitly* recognised until *Henderson v Merrett Syndicates Ltd* [1995] 2 AC 145 (HL).

[182] *Hedley Byrne* 529.

the 'extended' *Hedley Byrne* principle, and considerable confusion surrounding the application of the test, including the extent to which it could be used as a general duty determinant that could explain *all* duty cases, and how such a test was to be reconciled with other general duty tests such as *Caparo*.

The extension of *Hedley Byrne* first became evident in *Smith v Eric S Bush*.[183] The defendant had provided a negligently prepared valuation of a property to the plaintiff's bank. The valuation was provided to and for the bank, and at no point did the defendant communicate directly with the plaintiff. The defendant also included a disclaimer of liability on the valuation stating that the valuation was supplied without any warranty as to its accuracy. The plaintiff subsequently purchased the property in reliance on the valuation, which had been provided to her by the bank, and suffered economic loss as a result. Notwithstanding that the defendant had not made any *actual* representation to the plaintiff, and had explicitly disclaimed any responsibility for the accuracy of the report, Lord Templeman nevertheless relied on *Hedley Byrne* to justify the imposition of a duty of care on the basis that, as the defendant knew or ought to have known that the plaintiff would rely on the report when deciding whether or not to buy the house, an assumption of responsibility could be inferred.[184] As for the disclaimer, it was held to be of no effect by virtue of section 2(2) of the Unfair Contract Terms Act (1977).[185]

A further expansion of the assumption of responsibility concept, giving rise to the so-called 'extended' *Hedley Byrne* principle, occurred in a trio of cases in 1995, led by the efforts of Lord Goff. The first of these cases, *Spring v Guardian Assurance plc*,[186] involved a plaintiff who was suing his former employer for the negligent preparation of an employment reference. The reference was so unfavourable that the plaintiff was unable to gain further employment in the industry. As the reference had been requested by the potential employer, and not the plaintiff, the defendant had not actually made any representation to the plaintiff at all. Lord Goff,[187] with whom Lord Lowry agreed,[188] nevertheless imposed a duty on the basis that an assumption of responsibility could be inferred. Lords Slynn and Woolf, also imposed a duty, but did so by relying on the tripartite test. Lord Keith dissented.

Later that same month, the Lords gave their speeches in *Henderson v Merrett Syndicates Ltd*,[189] where members of an unprofitable investment syndicate (the 'Names') sued those responsible for management of the syndicate. Due to the

---

[183] [1990] 1 AC 831 (HL) ('*Smith v Eric S Bush*').
[184] ibid 844.
[185] Whilst this explains why the term could not be relied on as a matter of contract, and so had no *contractual* effect, it fails to explain why it was nevertheless not sufficient evidence to establish that, as a matter of fact, responsibility in *tort* was not assumed.
[186] [1995] 2 AC 296 (HL) ('*Spring*').
[187] ibid 316–19.
[188] ibid 325.
[189] [1995] 2 AC 145 (HL) ('*Henderson v Merrett Syndicates Ltd*').

structure of the syndicate, many of the Names had had no contractual relationship or direct contact with the defendants. As far as Lord Goff was concerned, however, the fact that the parties had never communicated with each other was no reason to prevent the existence of a duty being based on an assumption of responsibility:

> [T]here is in my opinion plainly an assumption of responsibility in the relevant sense by the managing agents towards the Names in their syndicates. The managing agents have accepted the Names as members of a syndicate under their management. They obviously hold themselves out as possessing a special expertise to advise the Names on the suitability of risks to be underwritten; and on the circumstances in which, and the extent to which, reinsurance should be taken out and claims should be settled. The Names, as the managing agents well knew, placed implicit reliance on that expertise, in that they gave authority to the managing agents to bind them to contracts of insurance and reinsurance and to the settlement of claims. I can see no escape from the conclusion that, in these circumstances, prima facie a duty of care is owed in tort by the managing agents to such Names.[190]

This time, the rest of the court agreed with Lord Goff's analysis. *Henderson v Merrett Syndicates Ltd* was also significant because it clarified that *Hedley Byrne* applied not only in relation to statements, but also to the provision of services.[191]

Lastly, in *White v Jones*,[192] two intended beneficiaries under a will sued the testator's solicitor for negligently failing to include them in the will prior to the testator's death. Again, there had not been any representation whatsoever to the plaintiff, nor could it be said that there had been any reliance by the plaintiffs. Indeed, Lord Goff even acknowledged that 'the *Hedley Byrne* principle cannot, in the absence of special circumstances, give rise on ordinary principles to an assumption of responsibility by the testator's solicitor towards an intended beneficiary',[193] Nevertheless, Lord Goff also felt that, due to the 'impulse to do practical justice',[194] he was justified in *deeming* that there had been such an assumption:

> [Y]our Lordships' House should in cases such as these extend to the intended beneficiary a remedy under the *Hedley Byrne* principle by holding that the assumption of responsibility by the solicitor towards his client should be held in law to extend to the intended beneficiary who (as the solicitor can reasonably foresee) may, as a result of the solicitor's negligence, be deprived of his intended legacy in circumstances in which neither the testator nor his estate will have a remedy against the solicitor.[195]

Lord Browne-Wilkinson, agreeing with Lord Goff, also held that 'the defendant solicitors were under a duty of care to the plaintiffs arising from an extension of the principle of assumption of responsibility explored in *Hedley Byrne*'.[196]

---

[190] ibid 182.
[191] Though as McBride and Bagshaw note, certain dicta in *Hedley Byrne* suggests that this had always been the case: McBride and Bagshaw (n 34) 180.
[192] [1995] 2 AC 207 (HL) ('*White v Jones*'). Compare *Hill v Van Erp* (1997) 188 CLR 159.
[193] *White v Jones* 262.
[194] ibid 259.
[195] ibid 268.
[196] ibid 270. Compare the powerful dissenting speech of Lord Mustill.

What it meant to 'assume responsibility' therefore meant something well beyond undertakings 'equivalent to contract' as to the quality of a statement; in particular, it had come to include implied undertakings, including in cases where the parties had never even communicated, and extended to not only statements, but the provision of services also. That the undertaking did not have to be explicit was not, of course, objectionable *per se*; an offeree can consent to a contract on the basis of their conduct alone, without the need to explicitly state 'I accept the terms of the contract', and so there therefore seems no good reason why one cannot also assume a responsibility in tort on the basis of their conduct alone. But it is equally clear that the utility of the explanation as a duty determinant has limits. Nevertheless, following Lord Goff's lead, the more liberal understanding of assumption of responsibility was soon being used to describe the existence of a duty in a raft of situations that did not lend themselves to an analysis in terms of an assumption of responsibility at all. In *White v Jones*, for example, Lord Nolan suggested that the duty owed by the driver of a motor vehicle to other road users (not to directly cause them physical injury) was based on the assumption of responsibility test,[197] whilst in *Customs and Excise Commissioners v Barclays Bank plc*, Lord Hoffmann suggested that:

> [T]he arguments in *Henderson's* case were a rerun of *Donoghue v Stevenson* in a claim for economic loss ... To say that the managing agents assumed a responsibility to the Names to take care not to accept unreasonable risks is little different from saying that a manufacturer of ginger beer assumes a responsibility to consumers to take care to keep snails out of his bottles.[198]

Such comments essentially endorsed an understanding of assumption of responsibility that could explain *all* duty cases, and, contrary to the apparent intention of the Law Lords in *Hedley Byrne*, implied that the assumption of responsibility test could be used as a duty test of general application.

Extending the meaning of 'assumption of responsibility' so widely was not unproblematic. One difficulty was that it meant the phrase 'assumption of responsibility' became, much like 'proximity', meaningless, merely expressing a conclusion rather than providing a useful test. After all, in what sense can a driver assume a responsibility to another road user (indeed, *all* road users) whom he has never met or communicated with, directly or indirectly?[199] It would arguably be no more artificial to justify the liability of a driver to a road user on the basis of an implied contract. This difficulty did not go unnoticed. According to Lord Sylnn in *Phelps v Hillingdon London BC*,[200] for example, the phrase 'assumption of responsibility' had become 'misleading ... [and] means simply that the law recognises that there is a duty of care. It is not so much that responsibility is assumed as that it is

---

[197] *White v Jones* 293–94.
[198] *Customs and Excise Commissioners* [37].
[199] As Weir noted, such a broad understanding 'rob[bed] the idea of all utility': Tony Weir, *Tort Law*, 2nd edn (OUP, 2002) 36.
[200] [2001] 2 AC 619 (HL).

recognised or imposed by law.'[201] Similarly, in *Customs and Excise Commissioners v Barclays Bank*, Lord Rodger commented that there were a number of cases that:

> [D]o not readily yield to an analysis in terms of voluntary assumption of responsibility, but where liability has none the less been held to exist ... [but doing so produces a rule which] inevitably lead[s] to the concept of voluntary assumption of responsibility being stretched beyond its natural limits—which would in the long run undermine the very real value of the concept as a criterion of liability in the many cases where it is an appropriate guide.[202]

McBride and Bagshaw, too, argue that it is 'not possible' to explain many of the cases, including *Smith v Eric S Bush*, *Spring* and *White v Jones*, on the basis that the defendant assumed a responsibility towards the claimant,[203] whilst Lunney and Oliphant state that 'the concept—arguably—has been stretched to breaking point.'[204]

A second difficulty with the extended *Hedley Byrne* principle was that, now it was being understood by some as a general test in itself, it was no longer clear how it interacted with other general duty tests, particularly *Caparo*. As Lord Bingham stated in *Customs and Excise Commissioners v Barclays Bank plc*:

> The problem here is, as I see it, that the further this test is removed from the actions and intentions of the actual defendant, and the more notional the assumption of responsibility becomes, the less difference there is between this test and the threefold test.[205]

Some judges therefore dismissed the assumption of responsibility test as unhelpful and unnecessary, choosing instead to rely on *Caparo* rather than the presence or absence of ostensibly fictitious assumptions of responsibility.[206] This was particularly significant in cases involving purely economic loss where, despite the assumption of responsibility test historically being the *only* method for establishing the existence of a duty,[207] a duty could now be imposed absent any assumption of responsibility (fictitious or otherwise) at all. Others, however, tried to reconcile the competing approaches by explaining away assumptions of responsibility as

---

[201] ibid 654. See also: McBride and Bagshaw (n 34) 174–75 (regarding whether or not the concept is 'empty'); Barker (n 115) 462 (who argues, *inter alia*, that neither assumption of responsibility nor reliance 'has a useful role to play in the duty enquiry'); and Steve Hedley, 'Negligence—Pure Economic Loss—Goodbye Privity, Hello Contorts' (1995) 54 CLJ 27, 29 ('[assumption of responsibility is] a vague principle, and not a very useful one unless it can be sensibly applied by judges of far less eminence [than those in the House of Lords]').

[202] ibid 204.

[203] McBride and Bagshaw (n 34) 188–91.

[204] Lunney and Oliphant (n 61) 446.

[205] *Customs and Excise Commissioners* 191.

[206] See, eg, Lord Griffiths in *Smith v Eric S Bush*, who preferred a pre-*Caparo* version of the three-stage test as 'the phrase "assumption of responsibility" can only have any real meaning if it is understood as referring to the circumstances in which the law will deem the maker of the statement to have assumed responsibility to the person who acts upon the device'. (ibid 862. Lord Jauncey took a similar view: ibid 871). See also, Lords Slynn and Woolf in *Spring*, who also relied on *Caparo* rather than the assumption of responsibility test.

[207] Though, that *Hedley Byrne* actually ever stood for such a proposition has been labelled 'nonsense': McBride and Bagshaw (n 34) 188.

simply evidence of proximity.[208] Whilst the attempt at conceptual unification can be appreciated, not only did it further complicate the already problematic concept of proximity, but it was difficult to see why, where the defendant had explicitly assumed a responsibility towards the claimant, it still needed to be shown that it was fair, just, and reasonable for a duty to be imposed. As Lord Steyn put it in *Williams v Natural Life Health Foods Ltd*:[209]

> [O]nce a case is identified as falling within the extended *Hedley Byrne* principle, there is no need to embark upon any further enquiry whether it is 'fair, just and reasonable' to impose liability ...[210]

Other judges therefore maintained that they were indeed distinct tests. But in the absence of any guidance as to which test applied in which circumstances, they seemed to be legitimate alternatives, and this gave rise to the problem of which test should prevail in the event they produced inconsistent outcomes. Lower courts tended to circumvent this problem by insisting that both approaches should always lead to the same outcome.[211] Though, as Mitchell and Mitchell note, this was an 'utterly unconvincing basis for imposing liability' as the only way of ensuring that both approaches would lead to the same outcome was by 'manipulating the questions, so that each is effectively the same'.[212]

A third difficulty with the extended *Hedley Byrne* principle was that it was no longer clear what role was to be played by reliance. In particular, whereas earlier authority had tended to suggest that some form of reliance on the negligent representation was necessary for the existence of a duty,[213] such a requirement had come to be doubted following cases like *White v Jones*, where there appeared to be no reliance at all, and comments of Law Lords suggesting that reliance was instead merely a question of causation.[214]

---

[208] In *Caparo*, for example, Lord Bridge suggested that, far from a test in itself, an assumption of responsibility was simply an 'essential ingredient' in demonstrating proximity between the plaintiff and defendant: ibid 620–21. This seemed to have been influenced by Bingham LJ's similar comments in the Court of Appeal: see (n 106). See also Lord Bridge's comments at 623: 'I do not think that in the context of the present appeal anything turns upon the difference between these two approaches.'

[209] [1998] 1 WLR 830 (HL).

[210] ibid 834 (Lord Steyn, with whom the rest of the Lords agreed). These comments mimicked those of Lord Goff in *Henderson v Merrett Syndicates Ltd*, at 181.

[211] See, eg, *Merrett v Babb* [2001] QB 1174 (CA). See also Lunney and Oliphant (n 61) 440.

[212] Paul Mitchell and Charles Mitchell, 'Negligence Liability for Pure Economic Loss' (2005) 121 LQR 194, 199.

[213] *Hedley Byrne* 486–87 (Lord Reid), 497 (Lord Morris) 503 (Lord Morris) 514 (Lord Hodson), 538 (Lord Pearce); *Junior Books* 546–47 (Lord Roskill); *D&F Estates v Church Commissioners* [1989] 1 AC 177 (HL), 215 (Lord Oliver); *Murphy v Brentwood DC* 481 (Lord Bridge). See also Barker, 'Unreliable Assumptions in the Modern Law of Negligence' (n 115) at fn 52–53.

[214] See, eg, Lord Steyn in *Williams v Natural Life Health Foods Ltd* [1998] 1 WLR 830 (HL), 836 ('if reliance is not proved, it is not established that the assumption of reliance had any causative effect'); and Lord Goff in *Henderson v Merrett Syndicates Ltd* 180 ('[I]n the case of the provision of information and advice, reliance upon it by the other party will be necessary to establish a cause of action (because otherwise the negligence will have no causative effect) ...'). Though this comment is difficult to reconcile with his later comments in the same case that 'an assumption of responsibility *coupled with reliance by the plaintiff*' is required (at 186–87), and that 'an assumption of responsibility coupled with the concomitant reliance may give rise to a tortious duty of care' (at 194). Barker nevertheless describes

The role of assumptions of responsibility in duty analyses was eventually considered by the House of Lords in *Customs and Excise Commissioners v Barclays Bank*. The House of Lords was clear that the assumption of responsibility test did not provide the basis for a duty test of general application (that is, one capable of explaining *all* duty cases), and that *Caparo* remained the primary test for establishing the existence of a duty of care.[215] The existence of an assumption of responsibility did, however, continue to have a useful role to play when understood narrowly, as originally envisaged by Lord Devlin.[216] As Stanton explains:

> [T]he consensus is that [assumption of responsibility] is a test which is useful when a person has *expressly* indicated a willingness to undertake responsibility for the interests of another but that it fails to provide any useful assistance in the more common case where there is no such express undertaking. An implied assumption of responsibility merely begs the question as to what circumstances justify the implication being made. It is simpler to ask what circumstances justify the recognition of a duty of care than to ask what circumstances justify the implication of an assumption of responsibility which gives rise to a duty of care.[217]

Lord Goff's extended *Hedley Byrne* principle would therefore appear to be no more.

As to precisely what role was played by an assumption of responsibility *as understood in the narrow sense*, their Lordships were less clear, as the five separate speeches contained inconsistent, and occasionally self-contradictory, explanations. On the one hand, it was said that an assumption of responsibility was merely one factor to be taken into account when determining the existence of proximity;[218] *Caparo* still needed to be satisfied in its entirety. Yet, this was difficult to reconcile with further comments that an assumption of responsibility, whilst not necessary, would be sufficient to establish the existence of a duty,[219] suggesting that it *did* continue to operate as a distinct duty test in itself, albeit not an all-encompassing one.

Despite the evident confusion, in practical terms it appears that, notwithstanding its characterisation as merely evidence of proximity, an assumption of responsibility will continue to provide an independent method for establishing the existence of a duty of care, at least where the assumption of responsibility is sufficiently clear. Where there has not been an assumption of responsibility, however, it appears that the claimant may still try their luck under *Caparo*, as

---

the requirement, at least in Australia and the UK, as 'firmly embedded' in the duty rules: K Barker, 'Negligent Misstatement in Australia—Resolving the Uncertain Legacy of Esanda' in Kit Barker, Ross Grantham and Warren Swain (eds), *The Law of Misstatements: 50 Years on from Hedley Byrne v Heller* (Hart, 2015) 328.

[215] *Customs and Excise Commissioners v Barclays Bank* 191 (Lord Bingham), 199 (Lord Hoffmann), 204 (Lord Rodger), 2016 (Lord Mance).

[216] See, eg, ibid 190 (Lord Bingham), 199 (Lord Hoffmann).

[217] Stanton (n 10) 66. (emphasis added).

[218] *Customs and Excise Commissioners v Barclays Bank* 199 (Lord Hoffmann), 210 (Lord Walker).

[219] Ibid 190 (Lord Bingham), 199 (Lord Hoffmann), 204 (Lord Rodger), 216 (Lord Mance).

the claimant did in *Customs and Excise Commissioners v Barclays Bank*, though ultimately failing under both tests. The role of assumptions of responsibility in the duty enquiry is discussed further in chapter five.

VIII. Australia and the 'Salient Features' Test

For the first three-quarters of the twentieth century, Australian courts, much like Canadian courts, made only a very limited contribution to the development of duty jurisprudence, typically deferring to the UK courts entirely. However, following 1975 legislation abolishing appeals to the Privy Council,[220] the High Court of Australia was able to move away from the legalism that had characterised earlier courts, towards a more progressive court that was no longer reluctant to disagree with the Law Lords of the UK.[221] Although *Anns* was nevertheless followed initially,[222] its influence was short lived,[223] and it was soon replaced by the first uniquely Australian approach to duty: Deane J's proximity test.[224] Beginning in *Jaensch v Coffey*,[225] Deane J argued that proximity was a 'unifying concept', or 'touchstone', for determining the existence of a duty of care:

> [O]ne finds, in cases in the comparatively uncharted areas of the law of negligence, repeated reference to proximity as a touchstone for determining the existence and content of any common law duty of care to avoid reasonably foreseeable injury of the type sustained … The requirement of a relationship of 'proximity' in that broad sense should, in my view, be accepted as a continuing general limitation or control of the test of reasonable foreseeability as the determinant of a duty of care.[226]

Deane J's proximity test proved to be highly influential amongst the other judges of the High Court, and dominated the Australian approach to duty for much of

---

[220] Privy Council (Appeals from the High Court) Act 1975 (Cth). Appeals on federal and Constitutional law matters had been abolished eight years previously under the Privy Council (Limitation of Appeals) Act 1968 (Cth). Appeals from State Supreme Courts were later abolished in the Australia Acts of 1986. Theoretically, appeals to the Privy Council are still possible, if the High Court grants a certificate under the still operational section 74 of the Constitution, but it is extremely unlikely this will ever occur. See Tony Blackshield, 'Australia Acts 1986' in Michael Coper, Tony Blackshield and George Williams (eds), *Oxford Companion to the High Court of Australia* (OUP, 2001); Michael Coper, Tony Blackshield and George Williams, 'Privy Council, Judicial Committee of the' in Michael Coper, Tony Blackshield and George Williams (eds), *Oxford Companion to the High Court of Australia* (OUP, 2001).

[221] This was particularly evident under the leadership of Mason CJ. See Michelle Dillon and John Doyle, 'Mason Court' in Michael Coper, Tony Blackshield and George Williams (eds), *Oxford Companion to the High Court of Australia* (OUP, 2001).

[222] *Wyong Shire Council v Shirt* (1980) 146 CLR 40, 44 (Mason J); *Jaensch v Coffey* (1984) 155 CLR 549, 553 (Gibbs CJ).

[223] See (n 162).

[224] See, generally, Peter Handford, 'The Snail's Antipodean Adventures' in Joe Thomson (ed), *The Juridicial Review: Donoghue v Stevenson the Paisley Papers* (W Green, 2013) 321–26.

[225] (1984) 155 CLR 549.

[226] ibid 583–84.

the following decade.[227] It even seemed to exact some influence in the House of Lords, where a number of cases determined during Deane J's time on the High Court relied on *some* general concept of proximity to determine the existence of a duty.[228] Proximity was generally understood quite widely, concerning both notions of 'the relationship between the parties ... [and] the notion of nearness of closeness ... [in] space and time ...,'[229] *and* considerations of public policy. In *Jaensch v Coffey*,[230] for example, Deane J accepted that proximity should not be 'either ostensibly or actually divorced from considerations of public policy which underlie and enlighten it,'[231] whilst in *Gala v Preston*,[232] Brennan J held that 'proximity in its extended sense may also comprehend policy considerations'.[233] Similar statements were later made by the majority of the court (Mason CJ, Dean and Gaudron JJ) in *Bryan v Maloney*,[234] and by Dawson J in *Hill v Van Erp*.[235] Deane J's all-encompassing concept of proximity was therefore understood considerably more widely than it was in both the UK and Canada. In particular, whereas Deane J saw proximity as something capable of acting as a *comprehensive* duty determinant, and explaining the outcome of *all* duty cases, under both *Caparo* and Canada's approach to *Anns*, proximity was merely a *part* of the test—only one of *three* elements. As we also saw above, even at the best of times proximity is not an unproblematic concept, and only becomes more problematic when it begins to subsume concepts like public policy; indeed, as Handford comments, the increasing reliance on public policy within proximity 'was probably the beginning of the end. Perhaps, like Aesop's frog, it blew itself bigger and bigger until it burst.'[236] And so after Deane J left the High Court in November 1995, proximity soon fell out of favour. In *Hill v Van Erp*,[237] for example, the first duty case since the departure of Deane J, a number of judges expressed doubt about the utility of proximity as

---

[227] See, eg, *San Sebastian v Minister* (1986) 162 CLR 340, *Cook v Cook* (1986) 162 CLR 376, *Gala v Preston* (1991) 172 CLR 243, *Burnie Port Authority v General Jones* (1994) 179 CLR 520, and *Bryan v Maloney* (1995) 182 CLR 609. See also P Cane, 'Proximity' in Michael Coper, Tony Blackshield and George Williams (eds), *Oxford Companion to the High Court of Australia* (OUP, 2001).

[228] See, eg: *Alcock v Chief Constable of South Yorkshire Police* [1992] 1 AC 310 (HL), 396 (Lord Keith), 402 (Lord Ackner), 406 (Lord Oliver) and 420 (Lord Jauncey); *Smith v Eric S Bush* 856, 871–72 (Lord Jauncey); and *Caparo* passim (Lords Janucey and Oliver).

[229] *Jaensch v Coffey* (1984) 155 CLR 549, 584–85 (Deane J). Deane J made similar comments in *Hackshaw v Shaw* (1984) 155 CLR 614, *Sutherland Shire Council v Heyman* (1985) 157 CLR 424, and *Stevens v Brodribb Sawmilling Co Pty Ltd* (1986) 160 CLR 16.

[230] (1984) 155 CLR 549.

[231] ibid 585.

[232] (1991) 172 CLR 243.

[233] ibid 260.

[234] (1995) 182 CLR 609, 618: '[Policy considerations can be] legitimately taken into account in determining whether sufficient proximity exists in a novel category.'

[235] (1997) 188 CLR 159, 176: '[T]he identification of the requirements of proximity in developing areas of the law is not divorced from the considerations of public policy which underlie and enlighten the concept.' See also the discussion in Katter (n 109) 17–18.

[236] Handford (n 224) 325, citing Aesop, *Aesop's Fables* ('The Frog and the Ox'). See also the comments of Dawson J in *Hill v Van Erp* (1997) 188 CLR 159, 177.

[237] (1997) 188 CLR 159.

a duty determinant,[238] whilst by 1998, Kirby J felt able to state that 'it is tolerably clear that proximity's reign in this Court, at least as a universal identifier of the existence of a duty of care at common law, has come to an end.'[239] The 'demise of proximity as a unifying theme'[240] was echoed shortly thereafter in *Perre v Apand Pty Ltd*,[241] where McHugh J explained that 'this Court no longer sees proximity as the unifying criterion of duties of care.'[242]

Despite the High Court's unequivocal rejection of proximity, it nevertheless failed to make clear what the rejected test was to be replaced with. Whilst Kirby J argued for the adoption of the *Caparo* three stage-test,[243] the rest of the court were reluctant to commit to any kind of general formula.[244] The lack of clear guidance from the High Court on how duty questions were to be determined was described by one lower court judge as 'disgraceful',[245] whilst Witting has said it 'culminated in nothing less than doctrinal chaos'.[246] This confusion appeared to reach its climax in *Perre v Apand Pty Ltd*,[247] where, despite every member of the High Court concluding that a duty existed, they all did so for different reasons.

The High Court eventually clarified their position in *Sullivan v Moody*,[248] a case where the court had to determine whether a duty of care was owed by child protection authorities towards those being investigated for sexual abuse. In a rare joint judgment (at least for the time), the High Court clarified that the 'three stage approach ... does not represent the law in Australia.'[249] In particular, the High Court believed that, in light of the difficulties with proximity and the potential for the third stage to be 'misunderstood as an invitation to formulate policy rather than to search for principle',[250] the three stage approach had too much scope for duty determinations to be 'reduced to a discretionary judgment based upon a sense of what is fair, just and reasonable as an outcome in a particular case'.[251] Instead, the Court preferred an approach based on an 'evaluation of the factors which tend for and against a conclusion' that a duty does or does

---

[238] 176–78 (Dawson J); 188-90 (Toohey J); 210–11 (McHugh J); and 237–239 (Gummow J). Though, Deane J was not blind to the limits of proximity as a general determinant, as evidenced by his comments in *Sutherland Shire Council v Heyman* (1985) 157 CLR 424, 497, that: 'There is an incontestable element of truth in that statement in that the notion of proximity is obviously inadequate to provide an automatic or rigid formula for determining liability.'

[239] *Pyrenees Shire Council v Day* (1998) 192 CLR 330, 414.

[240] *Perre v Apand Pty Ltd* (1999) 198 CLR 180 [70].

[241] (1999) 198 CLR 180.

[242] ibid [74]. See also the comments of Gaudron J at [27].

[243] *Pyrenees Shire Council v Day* (1998) 192 CLR 330, 419-20; *Perre v Apand Pty Ltd* (1999) 198 CLR 180, 275.

[244] Handford (n 224) 325–26.

[245] *Metal Roofing & Cladding Pty Ltd v Eire Pty Ltd* (1999) 9 NTLR 82 (FC) (Bailey J) [24]. See also the discussion in Luntz (n 145) 76.

[246] Witting, 'The Three Stage Test Abandoned in Australia—Or Not?' (n 96) 214.

[247] (1999) 198 CLR 180.

[248] (2001) 207 CLR 562 ('*Sullivan*').

[249] ibid [49].

[250] ibid.

[251] ibid.

not exist.[252] 'Factors' of particular importance to the Court in *Sullivan* were that any recognised duty be coherent with other laws,[253] that it not be incompatible with other established duties,[254] and that the proposed duty would not give rise to indeterminate liability.[255]

This approach has subsequently come to be known as the 'salient features' test, based on the comments of Gummow J in *Perre v Apand*,[256] but has also come to be known as the 'multi-factorial' approach.[257] Within the High Court, Kirby J took the clear lead in developing and explaining the test, despite his personal preference for the three stage test.[258] Surprisingly, however, with the exception of Kirby J, who retired from the Court in February 2009, the High Court has offered almost no guidance on the salient features test whatsoever. Instead, the most authoritative statement on the salient features test has come from Allsop J in the New South Wales Court of Appeal decision of *Caltex Refineries (Qld) Pty Ltd v Stavar*,[259] who said that the salient features include:

(a)   the foreseeability of harm;
(b)   the nature of the harm alleged;
(c)   the degree and nature of control able to be exercised by the defendant to avoid harm;
(d)   the degree of vulnerability of the plaintiff to harm from the defendant's conduct, including the capacity and reasonable expectation of a plaintiff to take steps to protect itself;
(e)   the degree of reliance by the plaintiff upon the defendant;
(f)   any assumption of responsibility by the defendant;
(g)   the proximity or nearness in a physical, temporal or relational sense of the plaintiff to the defendant;
(h)   the existence or otherwise of a category of relationship between the defendant and the plaintiff or a person closely connected with the plaintiff;
(i)   the nature of the activity undertaken by the defendant;
(j)   the nature or the degree of the hazard or danger liable to be caused by the defendant's conduct or the activity or substance controlled by the defendant;
(k)   knowledge (either actual or constructive) by the defendant that the conduct will cause harm to the plaintiff;
(l)   any potential indeterminacy of liability;

---

[252] ibid [50].

[253] ibid 580–581 [53]–[54].

[254] ibid 581–582 [55]–[60].

[255] ibid 582–583 [61]–[63].

[256] (1999) 198 CLR 180 [198], [201]–[203]. Though Gummow J attributes the language to Stephen J in *Caltex Oil (Australia) Pty Ltd v The Dredge 'Willemstad'* (1976) 136 CLR 529, 576–77.

[257] See, eg, W Swain, 'Hedley Byrne v Heller in Australia: "Never Has There Been Such a Judicial Jamboree"' in Kit Barker, Ross Grantham and Warren Swain (eds), *The Law of Misstatements: 50 Years on from Hedley Byrne v Heller* (Hart, 2015) 41, 45.

[258] See, eg, his comments in *Graham Barclay Oysters Pty Ltd v Ryan* (2002) 211 CLR 540 [222], [236]–[243]; *Woolcock Street Investments Pty Ltd v CDG Pty Ltd* (2004) 216 CLR 515 [123], [158], [169]; and *Harriton v Stephens* (2006) 226 CLR 52 [64]–[65].

[259] (2009) 75 NSWLR 649.

(m) the nature and consequences of any action that can be taken to avoid the harm to the plaintiff;

(n) the extent of imposition on the autonomy or freedom of individuals, including the right to pursue one's own interests;

(o) the existence of conflicting duties arising from other principles of law or statute;

(p) consistency with the terms, scope and purpose of any statute relevant to the existence of a duty; and

(q) the desirability of, and in some circumstances, need for conformance and coherence in the structure and fabric of the common law.[260]

Allsop J added that the test 'should not ... be treated as a shopping list, all the items of which must have application in a particular case. Rather, it provides a list of considerations which should be considered, as potentially relevant, depending on the kind of case before the Court'.[261]

Like other duty tests, the salient features test is not without its problems. As noted by McHugh, for example:

> Left unchecked, this approach becomes nothing more than the exercise of a discretion— like the process of sentencing, where the final result is determined by the individual 'judge's instinctive synthesis of all the various aspects'. Different judges will apply different factors with different weightings. There will be no predictability or certainty in decision-making because each novel case will be decided by a selection of factors particular to itself. Because each factor is only one among many, few will be subject to rigorous scrutiny to determine whether they are in truth relevant or applicable.[262]

This criticism has been echoed by Robertson, who has said of the test, '[i]t lacks structure and ... it lacks focus ... [as it] does not provide a method by which the different considerations can be evaluated and weighed against one another.'[263] Arguably, then, the salient features test is not a 'test' at all, so much as a formalised label for the unrestricted consideration of any arguments that appeal to the court; indeed, Gummow J first discussed the idea of salient features as a duty determinant under the heading 'No general formula',[264] just as Lord Bridge's three-stage test followed his comments regarding the 'inability of any single general principle to provide a practical test which can be applied in every situation to determine whether a duty of care is owed ...'.[265] The extent to which the salient features test *actually* prevents 'discretionary judgment' is therefore far from clear.

---

[260] ibid [103].

[261] ibid [172].

[262] *Crimmins v Stevedoring Committee* (1999) 200 CLR 1 [77] (footnotes omitted). For further criticism, see ibid [71]–[78] generally, and Katter (n 17) 88.

[263] Robertson, 'Proximity: Divergence and Unity' (n 116) 33–34. A similar criticism is voiced by Barker in Barker, 'Negligent Misstatement in Australia—Resolving the Uncertain Legacy of Esanda' (n 214) 342.

[264] *Perre v Apand* (1999) 198 CLR 180, 242.

[265] *Caparo* 617. See also the judgment of Lord Oliver (at 633): 'I think that it has to be recognised that to search for any single formula which will serve as a general test of liability is to pursue a will-o'-the wisp.'

IX. Pockets

The focus of this chapter so far has been predominantly on *general* duty tests,[266] each of which we have seen, has been the subject of considerable criticism. There is, however, another method for determining the existence of a duty of care, one which allays some of the criticisms directed at general tests: the so-called 'pockets' approach. Under the pockets approach, cases are not decided by recourse to broad general tests or principles that are said to underlie *all* duty cases, but by recourse to the particular reasons or logic that are deemed to underlie the outcome of groups, or 'pockets', of cases involving similar fact scenarios. On this understanding, pockets are not merely examples of the application of general tests and principles, but indicators of duty in their own right.[267] Different principles therefore govern different types of cases. So, for example, there are independent sets of rules that govern the liability of police officers for failing to apprehend a suspect,[268] the liability of public authorities for omissions,[269] the liability for defective buildings causing purely economic loss,[270] and liability for secondary victims of psychiatric injury.[271]

There is considerable authority for the pockets approach. In *Caparo*, for example, immediately before detailing the three-stage test, Lord Bridge was explicit that:

> Whilst recognising, of course, the importance of the underlying general principles common to the whole field of negligence, I think the law has now moved in the direction of attaching greater significance to the more traditional categorisation of distinct and recognisable situations as guides to the existence, the scope and the limits of the varied duties of care which the law imposes.[272]

Similarly, Lord Roskill said:

> If this conclusion involves a return to the traditional categorisation of cases as pointing to the existence and scope of any duty of care, as my noble and learned friend Lord Bridge of Harwich, suggests, I think this is infinitely preferable to recourse to somewhat wide generalisations which leave their practical application matters of difficulty and uncertainty.[273]

According to the headnote writer at least, this, and not the three-stage test, was *the* basis of the case.[274] Both the High Court of Australia and Supreme Court of

---

[266] The principal exception to this being the assumption of responsibility test, which, as we have seen, only justifies the existence of a duty in *some* cases.

[267] Smillie, 'Principle, Policy and Negligence' (n 69) 120.

[268] *Hill v Chief Constable of West Yorkshire* [1989] AC 53 (HL).

[269] *Gorringe v Calderdale MBC* [2004] 1 WLR 1057 (HL).

[270] *D&F Estates v Church Commissioners* [1989] 1 AC 177 (HL).

[271] *Alcock v Chief Constable of South Yorkshire Police* [1992] 1 AC 310 (HL).

[272] *Caparo* 618.

[273] ibid 628.

[274] ibid 606–607.

Canada have also made it clear that the first step in any duty analysis is to look to the existing cases for guidance.[275]

The principal benefit of the pockets approach is the predictability it offers when compared to general tests. Indeed, it is undeniable that more reliable guidance is offered by reference to specific and identifiable arguments, as they apply to a particular fact scenario, than by reference to concepts of more general application, such as whether the parties are in a relationship of 'proximity' or whether the imposition of a duty would be 'fair, just, and reasonable'. It also prevents a fresh duty analysis needing to be undertaken in every case involving slightly different fact scenarios to those that have come before the courts already.

In the majority of cases, the facts will fit comfortably into an existing pocket and the pockets approach will essentially resemble an orthodox application of the principle of *stare decisis*, whereby *any* question of law is determined by reference to principles drawn from similar cases. As much was observed by McLachlin CJ in *Childs v Desormeaux*:[276]

> The reference to categories simply captures the basic notion of precedent: where a case is like another case where a duty has been recognized, one may usually infer that … a duty of care will arise.[277]

Despite its benefits, and ostensibly orthodox nature, the pockets approach has nevertheless been subjected to criticism. According to Witting, for example, without any underlying rationalisation for the discrete pockets, there can become 'a degree of arbitrariness in the way that cases are categorised and issues determined'.[278] The reason why a duty exists in one pocket, may therefore be entirely different to, and even contradict, the reason why a duty exists in another pocket. Whilst this may not be especially problematic in day-to-day cases, where the facts of the case fit neatly into a single pocket, it *can* be problematic where the facts of the case fall into multiple pockets. In particular, the selection of the relevant pocket will determine, at the outset, the types of reasons that can be relied upon in determining the outcome of the duty enquiry, and so potentially preclude consideration of otherwise relevant factors, a process which, according to Stapleton, can be 'akin to the tail wagging the dog'.[279] Stapleton cites *Smith v Eric S Bush* as an example of such a case, which, as we saw above, involved a plaintiff purchasing a defective property in reliance on a negligent misstatement and suffering purely economic loss as a result. The case was ultimately classified into the pocket of negligent misstatement

---

[275] See, eg, *Perre v Apand* (1999) 198 CLR 180, 217 (McHugh J); *Crimmins v Stevedoring Industry Finance Committee* (1999) 200 CLR 1 [61] (McHugh J); *Brookfield Multiplex Ltd v Owners Corporation Strata Plan 61288* (2014) 254 CLR 185 [169] (Gageler J); *Cooper* [41] (McLachlin J); *Childs v Desormeaux* (2006) 266 DLR (4th) 257 [15] (McLachlin CJ).

[276] (2004) 239 DLR (4th) 61.

[277] ibid [15]. The same observation is made in Prue Vines, 'The Needle in the Haystack: Principle in the Duty of Care in Negligence' (2000) 23 UNSWLJ 35, 35.

[278] Witting, 'Negligent Inspectors and Flying Machines' (n 116) 552. See also, Stanton (n 10) 71.

[279] Jane Stapleton, 'Duty of Care and Economic Loss: A Wider Agenda' (1991) 107 LQR 249, 284–85.

cases, where a duty could be, and was, held to exist on the basis of the reasons given in *Hedley Byrne*. According to Stapleton, however, if the case had been classified into the pocket of defective building cases, the logic would have pointed towards a duty being denied.[280] Stapleton argues that the pockets approach should therefore be abandoned, and that courts should instead focus on 'convincing' and 'unconvincing' factors that point for and against the existence of a duty. In this way 'pockets would be the natural end product of the analysis, not its dictator'.[281] This criticism of the pockets approach could, however, be mitigated to a large extent, or possibly even overcome entirely, with more careful classification of the pockets, and the reasons they rely upon, so as to avoid overlap and contradictory logic; and even if it could not be, it is nevertheless arguable that such a limitation is outweighed by the benefits of the pockets approach, namely, the added certainty in predicting outcomes due to the restricted number of reasons in play and limiting the number of occasions on which the courts need to undergo fresh duty analyses.

A more fundamental limitation of the pockets approach concerns how it applies to novel cases. In particular, a strict application of the pockets approach would require that novel cases *never* give rise to a duty of care, as, by definition, novel cases do not fall into an existing pocket of case law upon which a duty could be based. Whilst such an approach has the benefit of avoiding the need for reliance on vague general duty principles or tests, and preserves the predictability of the law,[282] it would also keep the law static and unable to evolve, a situation that few would agree should be the case. To remedy this deficiency, some jurisdictions have therefore reserved the pockets approach for cases that already fall into existing pockets, whilst dealing with novel cases via general principles; this appears to be the position in Canada, for example.[283] Of course, whilst such an approach is able to deal with novel cases in a manner that allows the law to evolve, it only does so by reintroducing the problems the pockets approach is trying to overcome, being the problems associated with determining the existence of a duty by reference to vague general principles.

As a compromise, a related method has developed, whereby the pockets approach determines the majority of cases, but novel cases are dealt with, not via general tests, but by incremental extensions of existing pockets. In this way, the vagaries of general tests are avoided, but the law is still able to develop over time and deal with novel cases without the need to artificially force them into the strict confines of the existing pockets or simply denying a duty altogether. This approach is known as 'incrementalism.'

---

[280] Ibid 277–83. The basis for the denial of a duty in such a pocket being *D&F Estates v Church Commissioners* [1989] 1 AC 177 (HL)). This conclusion is questionable, however, as, given the finding that there had been an assumption of responsibility, it is doubtful that the logic of *D&F Estates v Church Commissioners* would have applied.

[281] Ibid (n 279) 285. See also Jane Stapleton, 'In Restraint of Tort' in Peter Birks (ed), *Frontiers of Liability*, vol 2 (OUP, 1994), and Stapleton, 'Duty of Care Factors: a Selection from the Judicial Menus' (n 96).

[282] Assuming the problem of overlapping pockets could be dealt with via better classification.

[283] *Cooper* [42] (McLachlin J); *Childs v Desormeaux* (2006) 266 DLR (4th) 257 [15] (McLachlin CJ).

X. Incrementalism

Incrementalism is usually associated with the following passage of Brennan J's judgment in *Sutherland Shire Council v Heyman*:[284]

> It is preferable, in my view, that the law should develop novel categories of negligence incrementally and by analogy with established categories, rather than by a massive extension of a prima facie duty of care restrained only by indefinable 'considerations which ought to negative, or to reduce or limit the scope of the duty or the class of person to whom it is owed.'[285]

Incrementalism, then, working from the basis of existing pockets, determines the existence of a duty on the grounds that the facts of the case either fit into an existing pocket, or into a new pocket that is an incremental extension of an existing pocket. Accordingly, like the pockets approach, incrementalism 'rejects'[286] any reliance on general duty formulations or principles, but, unlike the pockets approach, entails a more flexible approach to resolving the existence of a duty in circumstances that do not fit neatly into existing pockets.

Although the incremental approach never managed to achieve much popularity in Brennan J's native Australia, it was enthusiastically embraced by the Supreme Court of Canada in *Canadian National Railway Co v Norsk Pacific Steamship Co*[287] (at least in relation to claims for purely economic loss), and by the House of Lords in *Caparo*, where Lord Bridge famously said:

> Whilst recognising, of course, the importance of the underlying general principles common to the whole field of negligence, I think the law has now moved in the direction of attaching greater significance to the more traditional categorisation of distinct and recognisable situations as guides to the existence, the scope and the limits of the varied duties of care which the law imposes. We must now, I think, recognise the wisdom of the words of Brennan J in the High Court of Australia in *Sutherland Shire Council v Heyman* ...[288]

The 'wisdom' of Brennan J's words was approved by Lord Keith in *Murphy v Brentwood DC*[289] shortly thereafter and so, at least in the UK, soon went from 'relative obscurity, to a position of prominence ... central to the methodology'

---

[284] (1985) 157 CLR 424.

[285] ibid 481. Brennan J's dicta appears to be based on his earlier comments in *Jaensch v Coffey* (1984) 155 CLR 459, 575. For a later statement of Brennan J's understanding of incrementalism, see *Bryan v Maloney* (1995) 182 CLR 609, 652–55.

[286] Keith Stanton, 'Professional Negligence: Duty of Care Methodology in the Twenty First Century' (2006) 22 PN 134, 141; Keith Stanton, 'Incremental Approaches to the Duty of Care' in Nicholas J Mullany (ed), *Torts in the Nineties* (LBC Information Services, 1997) 38. See also the comments of McHugh J in *Crimmins v Stevedoring Committee* (1999) 200 CLR 1 [73]: 'The policy of developing novel cases incrementally by reference to analogous cases acknowledges that there is no general test for determining whether a duty of care exists.'

[287] (1992) 91 DLR (4th) 289 (McLachlin CJ). See especially [40]–[41].

[288] *Caparo* 618. See also Lord Roskill at 628.

[289] *Murphy v Brentwood DC* 461.

used to determine duty cases.[290] In *White v Jones*, for example, Lord Browne-Wilkinson clearly adopted an incremental approach in determining the existence of a duty of care, stating that 'although the present case is not directly covered by the decided cases, it is legitimate to extend the law to the limited extent proposed using the incremental approach by way of analogy ...'.[291] He then proceeded to extend the principle in *Hedley Byrne* to cover the facts of the case, explaining that 'this is a case where such development should take place since there is a close analogy with existing categories of special relationship giving rise to a duty of care to prevent economic loss.'[292] The incremental approach was also relied on in *Gorham v British Telecommunications plc*,[293] *Punjab National Bank v de Boinville*,[294] and *Goodwill v British Pregnancy Advisory Service*.[295]

The increasing reliance on incrementalism (and the pockets approach) is typically seen as a response to the massive expansion in the reach of the law of negligence that had occurred under the general duty principle outlined in *Anns*.[296] Incrementalism, it was thought, would give the appellate courts far greater control over the future development and expansion of the law of negligence than general tests, thereby forestalling any potential for massive expansions in the future. As Stapleton explains:

> [C]oncerning the retreat to incrementalism ... it is fairly clear that it was motivated principally by concern that recovery in negligence for economic loss was threatening to get out of hand ... The complaint seemed to be that if the analysis of duty was generalised ... into some sort of principle or 'test' it was doomed to generate far too much liability in the hands of lower courts who needed more restraining guidelines. Better to eschew this 'modern' approach and return to the incremental approach.[297]

Despite its express approval by the House of Lords and Supreme Court of Canada, incrementalism has nevertheless been subjected to considerable criticism. Perhaps the principal criticism is directed at the vagueness of the term 'incremental'. In particular, it is objected that it is not clear at which point the facts of a case are sufficiently analogous to established categories to allow incremental extensions; are the facts required to be almost identical, or is it sufficient that they are broadly similar?[298] According to Toohey J in *Bryan v Maloney*,[299] for example, 'the very term "incremental" invites enquiry because what is incremental is in the eyes of the beholder.' In other words, what one judge considers analogous, another might consider wildly dissimilar; what

---

[290] Stanton, 'Incremental Approaches to the Duty of Care' (n 286) 38.

[291] *White v Jones* 270.

[292] ibid 275.

[293] [2000] 1 WLR 2129 (CA), 2144 (Schiemann LJ), and 2141 (Pill LJ).

[294] [1992] 1 WLR 1138 (CA).

[295] [1996] 1 WLR 1397 (CA) (Gibson LJ).

[296] Stanton, 'Professional Negligence: Duty of Care Methodology in the Twenty First Century' (n 286) 141.

[297] Stapleton, 'In Restraint of Tort' (n 281) 85.

[298] See, eg, McBride and Bagshaw (n 96) 69.

[299] (1995) 182 CLR 609, 661.

one judge considers a small step, another might consider a giant leap.[300] Of course, whilst the precise meaning of incrementalism is undeniably vague, this is not a problem unique to incrementalism; indeed, as we have seen, the terms 'proximity', 'fair, just, and reasonable', and 'assumption of responsibility' are subject to precisely the same criticism. Further, as Nolan points out, '"incrementalism" is nothing more than the analogical reasoning employed in a common law system to decide *any* novel question of law.'[301] McLachlin J has made a similar observation, noting that incrementalism is 'consistent with the incremental character of the common law'.[302] Any criticism on this basis would therefore appear to be misguided.

A more fundamental criticism of incrementalism relates to its rejection of general duty principles. In particular, in the absence of any underlying principles, the existence of a duty of care has been said to rest on illusory foundations. According to Howarth, for example:

> It should be noted what an extraordinarily weak argument the argument from authority is in this context. If the only justification for saying that a situation was a duty-situation is that it had been declared to be such on a previous occasion, the question arises as to what justified the decision to treat the situation as a duty-situation the first time that it arose. By definition, the first time that it arose, there was no specific authority for the decision 'on those precise facts', and if such authority is the only justification for a decision that a duty exists, the first case must therefore have been wrongly decided.[303]

Incrementalism has also been said to be unable to handle 'truly novel' cases, being those that do not fit into existing pockets or incremental extensions of existing pockets, other than with the 'unhelpful response' that the claimant must lose.[304] Such criticisms are not, however, likely to be of great concern to advocates of incrementalism, given that the rejection of any reliance on underlying theories, and the inability of 'truly novel' cases to attract a duty and thereby give rise to massive extensions in the law, are viewed as incrementalism's primary benefits.

In any event, modern courts do not seem to be prepared to abandon the idea that *some* general principle underlies all duty cases, and so incrementalism is seen

---

[300] See, eg, Rogers (n 111) 162: '[The incremental approach] gives no indication of where the increments should stop—one might simply reach a radically different in three steps rather than one leap.' See also Stanton, 'Incremental Approaches to the Duty of Care' (n 286) 46.

[301] Nolan, 'Deconstructing the Duty of Care' (n 115) 583.

[302] *Canadian National Railway Co v Norsk Pacific Steamship* (1992) 91 DLR (4th) 289 [41] (McLachlin J).

[303] Howarth (n 79) 70–71. See also: Gummow J in *Perre v Apand Pty Ltd* (1999) 198 CLR 180, 253–54 ('[T]he making of a new precedent will not be determined merely by seeking the comfort of an earlier decision of which the case at bar may be seen as an incremental development, with an analogy to an established category. Such a proposition, in terms used by McCarthy J in the Irish Supreme Court, "suffers from a temporal defect—that rights should be determined by the accident of birth"', quoting *Ward v McMaster* [1988] IR 337, 347); and Hayne J in *Brodie v Singleton Shire Council* (2001) 206 CLR 512, 631 ('recovery becomes an accident of history dependent upon when, in the development of the common law, the claim falls for consideration').

[304] Stanton, 'Professional Negligence: Duty of Care Methodology in the Twenty First Century' (n 286) 145. Though note McBride and Bagshaw, who argue that it is difficult to conceive of a situation about which the decided cases have nothing to say: McBride and Bagshaw (n 96) 56.

to be 'of little value as a test in itself'.[305] Incrementalism is, however, thought to play a valuable secondary or 'complementary'[306] role in determining the existence of a duty in novel cases. In particular, whilst general tests continue to act as the ultimate determinant of duty questions, incrementalism acts as a *limit* on their *application*, so as to prevent those general principles being used to justify the massive expansion that occurred under *Anns*. Indeed, this seems to have been the understanding that was recently approved by Lady Hale in *Woodland v Swimming Teachers Association*:[307]

> The common law is a dynamic instrument. It develops and adapts to meet new situations as they arise. Therein lies its strength. But therein also lies a danger, the danger of unbridled and unprincipled growth to match what the court perceives to be the merits of the particular case. So it must proceed with caution, incrementally by analogy with existing categories, and consistently with some underlying principle.

Given, however, that incrementalism is built on a rejection of the validity of general tests, assigning it a secondary role surely undermines its primary benefit.[308]

XI. Conclusion

Since *Donoghue v Stevenson* was handed down in 1932, the courts have endured a continual struggle in their attempts to articulate a precise formula that can be used to determine when a duty of care does or does not exist; in particular, a formula that is wide enough to capture the existing duties, but not so wide as to permit recovery in a raft of previously unrecognised situations; narrow enough to explain the no-duty cases, but not so narrow as to prevent the recognition of a duty in deserving cases. The vast range of duty situations has made this task extremely difficult, as different types of cases pull in different directions; a test that explains why a duty exists in cases of physical injuries (such as foreseeability alone), will typically be too wide for cases of purely economic loss; whilst a duty test that explains why a duty exists in cases of purely economic loss (such as an assumption of responsibility), will typically be too difficult to satisfy in cases of

---

[305] *Customs and Excise Commissioners v Barclays Bank* 192 (Lord Bingham).

[306] Stanton, 'Incremental Approaches to the Duty of Care' (n 286) 50. See also Lord Mance, at ibid 213, who appeared to agree: '[C]aution and analogical reasoning are generally valuable accompaniments to judicial activity, and this is particularly true in the present area.' This largely accords with the views of Mitchell and Mitchell (n 212) 199: 'Factual analogies and distinctions are not helpful in themselves; they are only helpful when used in combination with a test or principle which identifies the legally significant features of the situation.') Ironically, this is not considerably dissimilar to the role originally assigned to the incremental approach by Lord Bridge in *Caparo*.

[307] [2014] AC 537 (UKSC), 586.

[308] For further discussion on this point, see Stanton, 'Incremental Approaches to the Duty of Care' (n 286) 46.

physical injuries. Modern courts appear to believe the best way to achieve this balance is by taking refuge in increasingly vague terms, such as 'proximity' and 'fairness', or by requiring the presence of unspecified number of 'salient features' from an indeterminately long list. As Kirby J has noted, 'we seem to have returned to the fundamental test for imposing a duty of care, which arguably explains all the attempts made so far. That is, a duty of care will be imposed when it is reasonable in all the circumstances to do so'.[309] Whilst this certainly gives the courts the flexibility required to explain the existing law, and develop it as they see fit, it hardly gives lower courts and practitioners the certainty and predictability required of the law in practice.[310] Indeed, the courts' present general duty formulations are so vague and abstract that they are, arguably, not 'tests' in any meaningful sense at all. As much is explicitly conceded by the courts,[311] leading to the paradoxical position whereby the courts have 'declared (whether boldly or despairingly) that the elements of the [duty] test ... have no content, yet at the same time, they continue to be talked about and apparently applied'.[312] Stapleton even goes so far as to say that given the diverse range of 'complex concerns' that judges face in duty analyses, there *is* no duty test, nor *can* there be a duty test,[313] whilst Nolan, too, argues that the search for a general duty test merely 'obscures and confuses'.[314]

It is therefore perhaps unsurprising that, whilst the courts continue to pay lip service to these generalised tests, in the majority of day-to-day cases the tests are largely ignored in favour of a 'pockets' approach, whereby a range of different principles apply to a range of different factual situations. The pockets approach provides specific guidance for specific types of problems, and is therefore of considerably more use for low-level courts and practitioners. Whilst a strict application of the pockets approach has trouble dealing with novel cases, when used in conjunction with incrementalism it manages to overcome those problems as well as many of the criticisms directed at the vagaries of general tests, which are thought to only give the *illusion* of providing any workable underlying theory. Ironically, however, its independence of any all-encompassing general formula is the source of its main criticism; that it is not reducible to any general principle.

The courts therefore seem to be seeking an all-encompassing formula; one that is general enough to explain *all* duty cases, yet particular enough to offer useful

---

[309] *Graham Barclay Oysters Pty Ltd v Ryan* 211 CLR 540, para 244.

[310] McHugh J, for example, believes that a duty test should provide 'a conceptual framework that will promote predictability and continuity and at the same time facilitate change when it is needed': *Perre v Apand Pty Ltd* (1999) 8 CLR 180 [93].

[311] See, eg, *Caparo* 618 (Lord Bridge): 'the concepts of proximity and fairness ... are not susceptible of any such precise definition as would be necessary to give them utility as practical tests, but amount in effect to little more than convenient labels to attach to the features of different specific situations which, on a detailed examination of all the circumstances, the law recognises pragmatically as giving rise to a duty of care of a given scope.' See also *Caparo* 633 (Lord Oliver) 628 (Lord Roskill), *Customs and Excise Commissioners v Barclays Bank*, 189–92 (Lord Bingham); Jaffey (n 17) 18–19.

[312] Jenny Steele, 'Scepticism and the Law of Negligence' (1993) 52 CLJ 437, 445.

[313] Stapleton, 'Duty of Care Factors: a Selection from the Judicial Menus' (n 96) 60.

[314] Nolan, 'Deconstructing the Duty of Care' (n 115) 581–82.

guidance in fact-specific situations. Yet *no* formula can possibly accommodate such opposing tensions. It should therefore come as no surprise when Ibbetson says: 'That the tort of negligence is in a mess goes almost without saying';[315] and, as was suggested in chapter one, the courts' approach to the duty enquiry seems to be a principal reason for this. Of course, whilst the courts may have made a mess of duty, it does not follow that the concept itself is inherently problematic, just that the courts' present treatment of it is. In the next chapter we will therefore examine the function and anatomy of the duty enquiry in further detail, as, only when we understand what, exactly, it does, and how it does it, can we have any hope of articulating a reliable method for determining when a duty does or does not exist.

---

[315] David Ibbetson, 'How the Romans Did for Us: Ancient Roots of the Tort of Negligence' (2003) 26 UNSWLJ 475, 475.

4

Factual Duty

Who, then, in law, is my neighbour? The answer seems to be—persons who are so closely and directly affected by my act that I ought reasonably to have them in contemplation as being so affected when I am directing my mind to the acts or omissions which are called in question

Lord Atkin in *Donoghue v Stevenson* [1932] AC 562, 580.

I. Introduction

We saw in chapter three that an ever-increasing number of discrete issues are being dealt with under the duty rubric, with the result that explanations as to why a duty does or does not exist in a particular case are becoming more and more vague. In this chapter, we therefore try to isolate and better articulate some of these discrete issues in the hope of both simplifying the enquiry, at least to some degree, and providing guidance for future decisions. In particular, in the first part of this chapter we will see that the duty enquiry, in fact, involves both factual *and* notional elements. In the second part of this chapter we will explore the factual element in further detail and see that its presence in the negligence enquiry is unnecessary. The notional element of the duty enquiry will be explored in chapters five and six.

II. The Dual Function of Duty

A. The Attack on Duty

Lord Atkin's neighbour dictum provided that a duty was owed to all persons 'so closely and directly affected by my act that I ought reasonably to have them in contemplation as being so affected when I am directing my mind to the acts or omissions which are called in question.'[1] As we saw in chapter three, this was widely seen to provide a test for the existence of a duty based on foreseeability alone.[2]

---

[1] *Donoghue v Stevenson* [1932] AC 562 (HL) 580 ('*Donoghue v Stevenson*').
[2] See the discussion in Section II of ch 3.

Whilst many objected that such a duty test, based on foreseeability alone, cast the duty net too wide, others had a more fundamental objection: that such an understanding of duty rendered the enquiry completely unnecessary. According to Winfield, for example, the duty concept, on this understanding, was 'superfluous',[3] 'unnecessary',[4] and 'in theory ... might well be eliminated from the tort of negligence'.[5] Similarly, Buckland famously described the duty of care as 'an unnecessary fifth wheel on the coach, incapable of sound analysis and possibly productive of injustice'.[6] The basis of these criticisms was, essentially, that the function of the duty of care, which the critics saw as being to prevent liability in negligence extending to those who were not foreseeably affected by the defendant's conduct, was able to be satisfactorily performed at other stages of the negligence enquiry. As Stone explained:

> A duty towards the plaintiff then means that the defendant ought reasonably to have him in contemplation as likely to be affected by the conduct in question; in short, the defendant ought reasonably have anticipated injury to him. But is not that in any case one essential element of what is meant by the requirement of 'negligence' itself?[7]

The duty requirement was said to therefore be 'tautologous', or 'circuitous', with the 'negligence' (that is, 'fault', 'breach', or 'standard of care'[8]) requirement.[9] Similarly, if the focus were shifted from the foreseeability of some harm, a question of fault, to the foreseeability of the actual harm that materialised,[10] then, at least according to Buckland[11] and Price,[12] it became a question of remoteness, which already provided rules relating to a defendant's liability where 'the exact kind of damage' suffered by the claimant was unforeseeable.[13] According to the critics, then, *every* case decided on the grounds of duty could just as easily be decided on

---

[3] Percy Winfield, 'Duty in Tortious Negligence' (1934) Colum L Rev 41, 43, 66.

[4] ibid 59.

[5] ibid 66.

[6] WW Buckland, 'The Duty to Take Care' (1935) 51 LQR 637, 639.

[7] Stone, quite generously, attributes the idea to Holmes: J Stone, *The Province and Function of Law: Law as Logic, Justice and Social Control; a Study in Jurisprudence* (Stevens 1947) 182, citing OW Holmes, 'The Path of the Law' (1897) 10 Harv L Rev 457, 472. Prior to Stone, Green made exactly the same criticism in relation to Brett MR's duty formula: (Leon Green, 'The Duty Problem in Negligence Cases' (1928) 28 Colum L Rev 1014, 1029.) See also HT Terry, 'Negligence' (1915) 29 Harv L Rev 40; Winfield (n 3) 61–64.

[8] For reasons explained below, the 'fault' terminology is to be preferred to the 'breach' and 'standard' terminology, and so is used throughout this book.

[9] Stone (n 7) 182, 181. See also WL Morison, 'A Re-Examination of the Duty of Care' (1948) 11 MLR 9, 14, 15(22); and TW Price, 'The Conception of the 'Duty of Care' in the *Actio Legis Aquiliae*' (1949) 66 SALJ 171, 180.

[10] See, eg, *Smith v London and South Western Railway Co* (1870) 5 CP 98 (CP), 103; *Palsgraf v Long Island Railway Co* (1928) 248 NY 339; 162 NE 99; *Chester v Waverly Corp* (1939) 62 CLR 1; and *Bourhill v Young* [1943] AC 92 (HL).

[11] Buckland (n 6) 644.

[12] Price (n 9) 185–86, 288. Price even goes so far as to claim that despite what was said by the court, *Bourhill v Young* [1943] AC 92 (HL) was, in fact, a case of remoteness.

[13] *Re Polemis and Furness, Withy & Co Ltd* [1921] 3 KB 560 (CA).

some other ground not depending on duty at all,[14] and so duty had little role to play, performing no function not already performed elsewhere in the negligence enquiry.

Many also pointed to the fact that there was no equivalent of a duty of care outside of the common law, and so argued if other legal systems could operate without a duty of care, surely the common law could live without it too. Winfield, for example, described the duty requirement as 'wholly alien to Roman Law and of which there is no trace in the modern Continental systems'.[15] Similarly, Stallybrass, the normally 'conservative'[16] editor of *Salmond's Law of Torts*, argued that the Roman method 'provided a simpler and better solution of the problems involved than English law with its reliance upon a duty to take care'.[17] Buckland, too, pointed to the fact that there was no mention of 'duty' in the definition of negligence provided in section 165 of the draft US *Restatement of Torts*,[18] whilst Price, who described the duty enquiry as 'manifestly undesirable',[19] a 'fetish',[20] 'totally unnecessary',[21] and a 'will-o-the wisp',[22] maintained that it was yet to make its way into the Roman-Dutch law of South Africa.[23]

A number of commentators therefore believed that the duty concept performed *no* valuable function at all, and that this was why no equivalent concept had developed outside the common law. Its only saving grace, according to Winfield, was that, despite having no 'practical value ... it is now too deeply embedded in English law to remove it. It has been recognised by the House of Lords, and nothing but legislation can eradicate it.'[24] Of course, it is hard to believe that this could have been the only reason. Could the duty of care really have lasted so long if it were entirely superfluous, particularly at a time when juries had effectively been abolished in civil trials[25] and so the duty of care was no longer needed to

---

[14] Winfield (n 3) 64. It could, of course, be objected that *Re Polemis* did not, in fact, permit the materialisation of unforeseeable risks to be deemed too remote, but this is more of an objection to the law of remoteness than to the materialisation of unforeseeable risks being an issue of remoteness, and therefore *able to be* dealt with on grounds not depending on duty. This is discussed in further detail in Section IV below.

[15] ibid 58.

[16] RG McKerron, 'The Duty of Care in South African Law' (1952) 69 SALJ 189, 189–90.

[17] JW Salmond and WTS Stallybrass, *Salmond's Law of Torts*, 10th edn (Sweet & Maxwell, 1945) 431.

[18] Buckland (n 6) 644–45. The definition of negligence was eventually moved to §281 of the *Restatement of Torts* (1934).

[19] Price (n 9) 274.

[20] ibid 270.

[21] ibid 271.

[22] ibid. This characterisation of duty, or at least the search for a general duty formula, was later famously used by Lord Oliver in *Caparo Industries Plc v Dickman* [1990] 2 AC 605 (HL), 633 ('*Caparo*').

[23] ibid 275. *cf* McKerron (n 16) 189: 'It is clear, however, that the [duty] doctrine is just as firmly established in South African law as it is in English law.' Despite the subsequent commentary, as detailed below, Price's views remained unchanged 10 years later: TW Price, 'Aquilian Liability and the 'Duty of Care': A Return to the Charge' [1959] Acta Juridica 120.

[24] Winfield (n 3) 58. For a criticism of this rationale see: R Dale Gibson, 'A New Alphabet of Negligence' in Allen M Linden (ed), *Studies in Canadian Tort Law* (Butterworths, 1968) 215.

[25] DJ Ibbetson, *A Historical Introduction to the Law of Obligations* (OUP, 1999) 188–89.

distinguish between the respective roles of judges and juries? Much of the criticism of 'duty' was also, in fact, attacking a straw man in the form of Lord Atkin's foreseeability-based neighbour dictum, which, as we saw in chapter three, was not an entirely accurate representation of the law; indeed, there were many cases that satisfied the neighbour dictum but did not give rise to a duty of care.[26] How did the critics explain these cases? By the late 1940s, it was therefore being objected that the foregoing critiques were fundamentally flawed. In particular, it was being argued that the duty enquiry, in fact, performed *two* functions, and that the critics of the duty concept focussed only on the first of these functions, and either overlooked or simply ignored the second function entirely.[27]

B. Factual and Notional Duty

The first person to explicitly suggest that the duty enquiry had a dual function appears to have been Lawson.[28] According to Lawson, the duty enquiry served two 'entirely separate purposes':[29]

> [First,] to decide whether the plaintiff was or was not too remote from the reasonable contemplation of the defendant for damage done to the former to be imputable to the latter, and, secondly, to mark off from each other the situations where a person is required to advert to the possibility of damage to other persons from those where he may act without any regard for others, except, perhaps, that he must not deliberately do them harm.[30]

In other words, the function of the duty of care was to determine whether harm to the plaintiff was a reasonably foreseeable consequence of the defendant's conduct, *and* whether the broad circumstances in which the plaintiff suffered the injury *ought* to be subject to the laws of negligence. Around the same time, Stone, too, made the comment that by reason of the apparent tautology between negligence and duty, 'it must be obvious again that there is some determinant of the actual decision other than can be drawn by deductive logic from the category ostensibly used',[31] which he later explained to be a reference to the existence of a second aspect of the duty enquiry not expressed in Lord Atkin's (foreseeability based) test.[32]

---

[26] For example, there was no liability for negligently causing injury to trespassers, for pure economic loss resulting from negligent misstatements, etc. See Section II of ch 3 for further detail.

[27] FH Lawson, 'The Duty of Care in Negligence: A Comparative Study' (1947) 22 TulLRev 111; McKerron (n 16) 193; RWM Dias, 'The Breach Problem and the Duty of Care' (1956) 30 TulLRev 377, 404.

[28] Lawson (n 27).

[29] FH Lawson, *Negligence in the Civil Law* (Clarendon Press, 1950) 34.

[30] ibid. This, in fact, was Lawson's later description of the dual role. In his original description of the separate purposes, the second function was confined to 'determining the *kinds* of injury which can be brought within the action of negligence ...,' rather than the broad '*situations*' that come within the action for negligence: Lawson, 'The Duty of Care in Negligence: A Comparative Study' (n 27) 112. Lawson's later, and broader, description, however, is much more in line with the modern understanding of the second function of duty ('notional duty'), which is discussed in greater detail in ch 5, Section II.

[31] Stone (n 7) 182.

[32] Morison (n 9) 13 (fn 11), where Morison cites a personal note written to him by Stone.

McKerron[33] and Morison[34] made similar observations shortly thereafter. Dias later explained the distinction on the basis that the duty of care involved both a 'factual' question, since whether or not something is foreseeable will depend on the actual facts of the case,[35] and a question of law, or a 'notional' question, because whether or not the situation is one that falls within the law of negligence will depend on what has been decided in previous cases,[36] thereby coining the terminology of 'factual' and 'notional' duty. The 'notional' duty terminology in particular has since been criticised as unhelpful,[37] and arguably 'legal duty' would be more appropriate. Notwithstanding this, however, so as to avoid the introduction of new and potentially confusing terminology, the notional duty label will continue to be used.[38]

The criticisms of duty, then, focussed exclusively on the factual aspect, and ignored the notional aspect altogether. Indeed, the criticisms did not apply to the notional aspect at all: the notional aspect was in no way 'tautologous' with the fault or remoteness elements; nor was it 'wholly alien' to other systems of law, as the restriction of liability for negligence to a particular set of prescribed situations was present in both Roman law and other modern civil law systems.[39] Notional duty even explained the cases that satisfied Lord Atkin's neighbour dictum, but did not give rise to a duty of care; in particular, pecuniary loss caused by negligent misstatements, injuries suffered by trespassers, damage caused by omissions, etc, were irrecoverable not because the harm was not foreseeable, but because the law was not prepared to extend the law of negligence to permit recovery in those types of situations. In other words, there was a factual duty but no notional duty. Whilst, then, factual duty continued to be subject to the foregoing criticisms, and so widely believed to be a 'fifth wheel on the coach', notional duty soon came to be seen as obviously 'necessary',[40] 'indispensable',[41] and performing the 'primary function of the duty of care'.[42]

---

[33] McKerron (n 16) 190.

[34] Morison (n 9) 24.

[35] RWM Dias, 'The Duty Problem in Negligence' [1955] CLJ 198, 204.

[36] ibid 204. He refers to the second question as one of 'notional duty' at ibid 205.

[37] See, eg, (n 44).

[38] Indeed, the same could be said about the 'duty of care', which, as is explained below and in the following chapter, is not a helpful label at all. However, given it is well-known, it will continue to be used.

[39] For a detailed comparison see Lawson, who argues that that 'a comparison with Roman law and a number of systems largely derived from or strongly influenced by Roman law proves that such a duty of care, or some other requirement substantially identical with it, is hardly to be avoided …': Lawson, 'The Duty of Care in Negligence: A Comparative Study' (n 27) 113. See also WW Buckland, AD McNair and FH Lawson, *Roman Law and Common Law*, 2nd edn (Cambridge University Press, 1965) 367–70. A similar conclusion can be seen in Winfield's analysis of liability for carelessness in the medieval law of trespass: 'The question was not "Is there a duty?" but, "Was the defendant in fact a bailee, common carrier, or the like and, if so, what excuse has he to offer for the harm that has occurred' (Winfield (n 3) 49). A more detailed comparison with other legal systems is contained in Section III(C) of ch 6.

[40] Lawson, 'The Duty of Care in Negligence: A Comparative Study' (n 27) 112.

[41] Dias, 'The Duty Problem in Negligence' (n 35) 204.

[42] Lawson, *Negligence in the Civil Law* (n 29) 35. See also the discussion in MA Millner, *Negligence in Modern Law* (Butterworths, 1967) 230.

Despite the widespread criticism of factual duty, it nevertheless today remains an orthodox part of the negligence enquiry,[43] and, although the 'factual'/'notional' terminology is no longer popular,[44] the distinction continues to be widely recognised.[45] Nolan and Davies, for example, recently explained the distinction as follows:

> First, it answers the general question whether there can in principle be a right not to be subjected to damage by carelessness in the kind of situation to which the particular facts belong. Secondly, it addresses the question whether on the particular facts the defendant did indeed owe a duty to the claimant.[46]

Given the underlying importance of the factual/notional distinction to the structure of the duty enquiry, both factual and notional duty will be examined in further detail. Although there is a strong argument that the notional aspect of the duty enquiry is 'logically prior' to the factual aspect, as 'We must first ask whether the defendant could possibly owe a duty to anyone, and only if we answer this question in the affirmative can we ask the further question whether he owed a duty of care to this particular plaintiff,'[47] it is nevertheless convenient to examine the factual aspect first. We will therefore examine the factual aspect for the remainder of chapter four, and the notional aspect in chapters five and six.

III. Factual Duty, Fault, and Remoteness

Whether the defendant owed the claimant a factual duty, or a duty 'on the particular facts' of the case, is determined by asking whether harm to the claimant, *as opposed to harm to someone else*, was a reasonably foreseeable consequence of the defendant's conduct. A defendant is only liable for damage that results from

---

[43] See, eg: Prue Vines, Peter Hanford and Carol Harlow, 'Duty of Care' in Carolyn Sappideen and Prue Vines (eds), *Fleming's The Law of Torts*, 10th edn (Thomson Reuters (Professional) Australia Limited, 2011) 160; H Luntz and others, *Torts: Cases and Commentary*, 7th edn (Lexis Nexis, 2013) 120; M Lunney and K Oliphant, *Tort Law: Text and Materials*, 5th edn (OUP, 2013) 126; EW Peel and J Goudkamp, *Winfield and Jolowicz on Tort*, 19th edn (Sweet & Maxwell, 2014) 5-010; AM Dugdale, M Simpson and MA Jones, *Clerk & Lindsell on Torts*, 21st edn (Sweet & Maxwell, 2014) 8-07; Simon Deakin, Angus Johnston and Basil Markesinis, *Markesinis and Deakin's Tort Law*, 7th edn (OUP, 2012) 104–105; D Nolan and J Davies, 'Torts and Equitable Wrongs' in AS Burrows (ed), *English Private Law*, 3rd edn (OUP, 2013) 17.35–17.38; Lewis Klar, *Tort Law*, 5th edn (Carswell, 2012) 179; David Howarth, 'Duty of Care' in Ken Oliphant (ed), *The Law of Tort*, 2nd edn (LexisNexis Butterworths, 2007) 12.12–12.14; and D Nolan, 'Deconstructing the Duty of Care' (2013) 129 LQR 559.

[44] See, eg, WVH Rogers, *Winfield and Jolowicz on Tort*, 18th edn (Sweet & Maxwell, 2010) 5-5 (fn 40). Though it continues to be used in some major works, most notably Dugdale, Simpson and Jones (n 43) 8-06, 8-07, M Lunney, D Nolan and K Oliphant, *Tort Law: Text and Materials* (6th edn, OUP 2017) 126, and academic commentary (eg Nolan (n 43)).

[45] Peel and Goudkamp (n 43) 5-010; Lunney and Oliphant (n 43) 134–35 (though notional duty is termed 'the legal aspect of the duty of care'); Deakin, Johnston and Markesinis (n 43) 104–105; Dugdale, Simpson and Jones (n 43) 8-06, 8-07; Klar (n 43) 169; Nolan and Davies (n 43) 17.26.

[46] Nolan and Davies (n 43) 17.26. See also Peel and Goudkamp (n 43) 5-010.

[47] Lawson, *Negligence in the Civil Law* (n 29) 34.

a breach of duty *to the claimant,* and not damage that results from the breach of duty to another. Lord Atkin's neighbour dictum, with its focus on foreseeability, is the classic formulation of the factual duty enquiry. As we have seen, early commentators were highly critical of the factual aspect of the duty enquiry (even if they thought it was the *only* aspect of the duty enquiry), believing it to be superfluous, on the basis that its function was already performed elsewhere in the negligence enquiry. Notwithstanding this, however, factual duty continues to remain an orthodox part of the duty enquiry.[48] Indeed, Dorfman recently wrote of the 'impossibility of a duty purged of any requirement of foreseeability',[49] whilst Robertson has noted that, based on a survey of 92 recent duty cases:

> [A]pproximately 10 percent of the decisions in which duties were denied were based on a lack of foreseeability. A lack of foreseeability operated as a basis for denying duties of care in a wide range of case cases including, for example, cases involving psychiatric injury to an employee, physical injury caused indirectly or by the criminal act of a third party, property damage caused indirectly, and pure economic loss caused by a third party.[50]

If the early critics were right, and factual duty *is* superfluous, then this would be very curious. Accordingly, in this section we will examine this criticism of factual duty in further detail; in particular, whether the fault and remoteness stages *really* perform the same function as the factual duty enquiry. In the next section we will examine whether, even if they do perform the same function, there is nevertheless some other justification for retaining it.

A. Factual Duty and Fault

The fault stage of the negligence enquiry requires that the defendant's conduct unreasonably created a risk of harm to another. In determining what was 'reasonable,' the court will rely on the 'reasonable person' test; that is, if the defendant did something the reasonable person would not have done, or did not do something the reasonable person would have done, they are deemed to have behaved unreasonably.[51] Like the factual duty enquiry, the fault enquiry therefore involves an element of foreseeability, as the reasonable person's behaviour will depend on what he or she can foresee. Where, then, the defendant's conduct does not create a foreseeable risk of harm to anyone (that is, *no* harm is a foreseeable consequence of the defendant's behaviour), not only will there be no factual duty, as a defendant does not owe a duty to those he cannot foresee will be affected by his actions, there will also be no fault, as the reasonable person will take no precautions against the

---

[48] See (n 43).

[49] Avihay Dorfman, 'Foreseeability as Re-Cognition' (2014) 59 Am J Juris 163, 167.

[50] A Robertson, 'Policy-Based Reasoning in Duty of Care Cases' (2012) 33 LS 119, 133–34 (footnotes omitted). For details of the study, see ibid 129–30.

[51] *Blyth v Birmingham Waterworks* (1856) 11 Ex 781, 784; 156 ER 1047, 1049 (Alderson B).

materialisation of risks he or she cannot foresee. As Howarth puts it 'If there was no foreseeable risk at the time the defendant acted, it is impossible for the defendant to have been at fault and therefore impossible for the defendant to be liable.'[52] The question of liability is therefore determined at the fault stage, and the factual duty enquiry adds nothing.[53] Where, on the other hand, the defendant's behaviour does create a foreseeable risk of harm to the claimant, *and that risk materialises*, whilst there will clearly be a factual duty, as the defendant owes a duty to those he can foresee will be affected by his conduct, this is of little consequence, as liability will ultimately depend on whether the defendant's failure to take further steps to prevent the risk from materialising amounted to carelessness.[54] Where, then, the defendant's conduct creates no foreseeable risk of injury to anyone, or does create a foreseeable risk of harm to the claimant and that risk materialises, the ultimate question of liability is determined at the fault stage, and the factual duty enquiry is superfluous.

More problematic, however, is conduct that creates foreseeable risk A, but unforeseeable risk B materialises, such as in the case of the 'unforeseeable plaintiff'.[55] Clearly, in such a situation, there will be no factual duty owed to the plaintiff, as harm to the plaintiff (that is, risk B) was not a foreseeable consequence of the defendant's conduct. Equally clearly, the defendant has been at fault, as the reasonable person does not engage in behaviour that unreasonably creates a foreseeable risk of *any* harm; whether or not it is that harm or some other harm that materialises is irrelevant.[56] Of course, if there can be a situation in which the fault element is satisfied, and the factual duty enquiry is not, then it is wrong to say that factual duty is 'tautologous' with the fault enquiry.[57] However, before concluding that factual duty is therefore necessary, we must first examine the remoteness enquiry, which, like the factual duty enquiry, considers the extent to which a defendant will be held liable for the unforeseeable consequences of their otherwise careless behaviour.

---

[52] David Howarth, 'Many Duties of Care—Or A Duty of Care? Notes from the Underground' (2006) 26 OJLS 449, 458.

[53] A similar conclusion is reached in JC Smith, 'Clarification of Duty—Remoteness Probems through a New Physiology of Negligence: Economic Loss, a Test Case' (1974) 9 UBCLawRev 213, 218, 222; Jonathan Morgan, 'The Rise and Fall of the General Duty of Care' (2006) 22 PN 206, 209–10; Howarth, 'Many Duties of Care—Or A Duty of Care? Notes from the Underground' (n 52) 458; W Jonathan Cardi, 'Purging Foreseeability' (2005) 58 VandLR 739, 744–47; W Jonathan Cardi, 'Reconstructing Foreseeability' (2005) 46 BCLRev 921; and Howarth, 'Duty of Care' (n 43) 12.12–12.14.

[54] See, eg, *Bolton v Stone* [1951] AC 850 (HL); *Paris v Stepney BC* [1951] AC 367 (HL); *Latimer v AEC Ltd* [1953] AC 643 (HL); *Watt v Hertfordshire CC* [1954] 1 WLR 835 (CA); *Tomlinson v Congleton BC* [2004] 1 AC 46 (HL).

[55] 'Unforeseeable plaintiff', rather than 'unforeseeable claimant' or 'unforeseeable pursuer,' etc, appears to be the preferred terminology, and so will be used throughout this book.

[56] To put it another way, if it is unreasonable to engage in certain behaviour on the basis that it creates foreseeable risk of harm A to person P, such behaviour will not retrospectively become reasonable on the basis that it actually (and unforeseeably) causes harm B to person Q.

[57] See (n 9).

B. Factual Duty and Remoteness

The present law of remoteness was outlined in the landmark 1961 Privy Council decision of *Overseas Tankship (UK) Ltd v Morts Dock and Engineering Co Ltd*,[58] better known as '*The Wagon Mound (No 1)*'. The defendant ship owners had allowed oil to be discharged from their ship, the Wagon Mound, which was moored in Sydney harbour. The oil then drifted along the water towards the plaintiff's wharf, some 600 feet away. The plaintiffs were carrying on welding work at the time, which they determined to continue, after being advised that the oil could not reach flash point (170°F) and ignite whilst on the water from errant sparks alone. It seems, however, that one of the sparks nevertheless managed to ignite a rag or some cotton waste beneath the surface oil which acted as a wick, thereby allowing the oil to ignite and start a fire that eventually burned down the plaintiff's wharf. It was accepted in court that whilst the defendant could have foreseen the risk of damage to the wharf by fouling, and that the discharge of oil was careless in relation to that risk, they could *not* have foreseen the risk of damage to the wharf by fire. As the defendant was careless in relation to *a* risk, even if not the risk that materialised, the fault element of the negligence enquiry was therefore satisfied. On the question of remoteness, however, the court held:

> [I]t does not seem consonant with current ideas of justice or morality that for an act of negligence, however slight or venial ... the actor should be liable for all consequences however unforeseeable and however grave ...[59]

> [I]f it would be wrong that a man should be held liable for damage unpredictable by a reasonable man ... equally it would be wrong that he should escape liability ... if he foresaw or could reasonably foresee the intervening events which led to its being done ... Thus foreseeability becomes the effective test.[60]

As the actual consequences of the defendant's conduct were unforeseeable, the defendant therefore escaped liability.

Lord Hoffmann has described this enquiry as 'limit[ing] liability to those consequences which are attributable to that which made the act wrongful.'[61] Similarly, Clark and Nolan argue:

> [W]hat makes the defendant's act wrongful is the fact that it creates unreasonable risks, and it follows that in general negligence liability is imposed only where the consequence in question was the materialization of one of the risks which made the defendant's conduct negligent in the first place.[62]

---

[58] [1961] AC 388 (PC) ('*The Wagon Mound (No 1)*').
[59] ibid 422–23.
[60] ibid 426.
[61] *South Australia Asset Management Corp v York Montague Ltd* [1997] AC 191 (HL), 213.
[62] T Clark and D Nolan, 'A Critique of *Chester v Afshar*' (2014) 34 OJLS 659, 664.

Accordingly, if the risk that materialised was unforeseeable, being the risk that the particular plaintiff would suffer the particular kind of harm they in fact suffered, then the damage is too remote.[63]

The remoteness enquiry therefore encompasses the factual duty enquiry entirely, as the suffering of harm by an unforeseeable plaintiff is simply the materialisation of an unforeseeable risk. Where, then, the there is no factual duty, the harm suffered will necessarily also be too remote.[64] As Cardi notes:

> Whether a court considers the defendant-plaintiff nexus in the context of proximate cause [i.e. remoteness]—'was this plaintiff within the scope of the risk created by the defendant's breach?' ... or as a matter of duty—'did the defendant owe a duty to this plaintiff?' ... the underlying issue is the same: '[S]hould the court hold the defendant liable to this plaintiff?' ... the inquiry is identical.[65]

This observation is hardly new, and Nolan describes it as 'academic orthodoxy'.[66] Lord Denning, for example, has said that remoteness and duty are simply 'different ways of looking at one and the same question which is this: Is the consequence fairly to be regarded as within the risk created by the negligence',[67] whilst Oliver LJ has stated, 'Speaking for myself, I think that the question of the existence of a duty and that of whether the damage ... is too remote are simply two facets of the same problem.'[68] Numerous cases have also reached the same outcome via the two different paths; some judges deeming the damage too remote, others finding an absence of a duty.[69] Within academe, Weinrib describes the two issues as 'frequently interchangeable',[70] Beever says they are 'virtually identical',[71] whilst Prosser wonders whether remoteness is nothing more than duty 'under another name',[72]

---

[63] This is known as the 'risk theory of remoteness.' For more on the 'risk theory,' see: G Williams, 'The Risk Principle' (1961) 77 LQR 179; and M Stauch, 'Risk and Remoteness of Damage in Negligence' (2001) 64 MLR 191. As Hart and Honoré note, however, the risk theory of remoteness has difficulty explaining certain aspects of the law, including recovery where neither the extent of the harm nor the way it occurred was foreseeable, and recovery by those who were injured rescuing primary victims of the defendant's negligence (see, eg, *Chapman v Hearse* (1961) 106 CLR 112): HLA Hart and Tony Honoré, *Causation in the Law*, 2nd edn (Clarendon Press, 1985) 263–64. Such difficulties, however, apply equally to factual duty and so, notwithstanding that they pose problems for the risk theory of remoteness, do not affect the overall argument here that the remoteness enquiry encompasses the factual duty enquiry. See also (n 143).

[64] Compare the comments of Glass JA in *Minister Administering the Environmental Planning and Assessment Act 1979 v San Sebastian Pty Ltd* [1983] 2 NSWLR 268, 295–96, Vines, Hanford and Harlow (n 43) 152, and Rachael Mulheron, *Principles of Tort Law* (Cambridge University Press, 2016) 50, who argue that the foreseeability enquiry at the duty and remoteness stages raise different issues, the former being an abstract enquiry, the latter, more particular. Though see the response to this claim in Luntz and others (n 43) 118–19.

[65] Cardi, 'Purging Foreseeability' (n 53) 757 (footnotes omitted).

[66] Nolan (n 43) 572.

[67] *Roe v Minister of Health* [1954] 2 QB 66 (CA), 85 (Denning LJ). See also: Denning LJ's discussion of the difference between duty and remoteness in *King v Phillips* [1953] 1 QB 429 (CA) at 441–42. (Note that although Denning LJ is speaking of 'duty,' he is clearly referring to the factual aspect of duty.)

[68] *P Perl (Exporters) Ltd v Camden LBC* [1984] QB 342 (CA), 353 (Oliver LJ).

[69] See, eg, *Woods v Duncan* [1946] AC 401 (HL), *Dovuro Pty Ltd v Wilkins* (2003) 201 ALR 139, and *P Perl (Exporters) Ltd v Camden LBC* [1984] QB 342 (CA).

[70] EJ Weinrib, *The Idea of Private Law* (rev edn, OUP, 2012) 158.

[71] A Beever, *A Theory of Tort Liability* (Hart, 2016) 190.

[72] W Prosser, 'Palsgraf Revisited' (1952) 52 MichLRev 1, 12.

such that the only difference between findings of no duty and findings that the damage suffered was too remote is merely 'one of terminology'.[73] It should therefore be unsurprising that in the United States, section 6 of the second discussion draft of the *Restatement (Third) of Torts: General Principles* confines the duty enquiry to notional questions only,[74] whilst section 7 of the *Restatement (Third) of Torts: Liability for Emotional and Physical Harm* explicitly states that questions of foreseeability of the risk that materialised are *not* matters for duty, but matters for proximate cause (that is, remoteness).[75]

Where, then, the defendant's conduct creates a foreseeable risk, but an unforeseeable risk materialises, the matter is able to be resolved as a question of remoteness, and so the factual duty enquiry is, again, superfluous.

IV. Factual Duty and the Problem of the Unforeseeable Plaintiff

It seems, then, that factual duty is superfluous, performing no function not already able to be performed by either the fault or remoteness enquiries. Despite this, however, there is an argument that factual duty nevertheless remains necessary in order to deal with the problem of the unforeseeable plaintiff. In particular, notwithstanding that the same *outcome* can be achieved by dealing with the problem of the unforeseeable plaintiff as part of the remoteness enquiry, it can be argued that it must nevertheless be dealt with in the factual duty enquiry because, first, causing harm to an unforeseeable plaintiff does not amount to a 'wrong,' and, second, the 'wrong' in the law of negligence is the breach of a duty of care, rather than the breach of a duty of care which causes damage that is not too remote. If both of these premises are accepted, then the problem of the unforeseeable plaintiff *cannot* be dealt with at the remoteness stage and so factual duty *is* necessary after all.

---

[73] ibid (fn 48). See also Smith (n 53) 225; Howarth, 'Many Duties of Care—Or A Duty of Care? Notes from the Underground' (n 52) 458; D Howarth, *Textbook on Tort* (LexisNexis UK, 1995) 116; Deakin, Johnston and Markesinis (n 43) 104.

[74] *Restatement (Third) of Torts: General Principles, Discussion Draft No 2* (2000) section 6: 'Findings of no duty ... are based on judicial recognition of special problems of principle and policy that justify the withholding of liability.'

[75] *Restatement (Third) of Torts: Liability for Physical and Emotional Harm* (2010) section 7, Comment j: 'Despite widespread use of foreseeability in no-duty determinations, this Restatement disapproves that practice ...' For more on the US approach to duty, see: Cardi, 'Purging Foreseeability' (n 53); Cardi, 'Reconstructing Foreseeability' (n 53); W Jonathan Cardi and Michael D Green, 'Duty Wars' (2007) SCalLRev 671; D Owen, 'Duty Rules' (2001) 54 VandLRev 767; John CP Goldberg and Benjamin C Zipursky, 'The Moral of McPherson' (1998) 146 UPaLRev 1733; and John CP Goldberg and Benjamin C Zipursky, 'The Restatement (Third) and the Place of Duty in Negligence Law' (2001) 54 VandLRev 657; B Zipursky, 'Foreseeability in Breach, Duty and Proximate Cause' (2009) 44 Wake Forrest L Rev 1247.

This argument first arose in the context of two famous cases, *Palsgraf v Long Island Railway Co*[76] and *Bourhill v Young*,[77] both of which involved the issue of how to deal with the problem of the unforeseeable plaintiff in light of the law of remoteness of the time, which was governed by another famous case, *Re Polemis*.[78] The argument is not straightforward, and so it is worthwhile examining these cases in order to better understand it.

A. *Palsgraf*, *Bourhill* and *Re Polemis*

Although the problem of the unforeseeable plaintiff had first been alluded to by Parke B in *Langridge v Levy*,[79] and later by Brett J in the trial decision of *Smith*,[80] it was first dealt with explicitly by Cardozo CJ in the famous New York case of *Palsgraf*, 'a law professor's dream of an examination question'.[81] Two train guards were assisting a passenger onto the defendant's train as it was pulling away from the station when they carelessly dislodged an innocuous-looking package from the passenger's arms. The package turned out to contain fireworks, which exploded upon falling onto the tracks and thereby caused some scales on the other side of the platform to fall on and injure the plaintiff. In his leading judgment, Cardozo CJ found for the defendant on the grounds that no duty had been owed to the plaintiff by the defendant's guard: 'The conduct of the defendant's guard, if a wrong in its relation to the holder of the package, was not a wrong in its relation to the plaintiff, standing far away. Relatively to her it was not negligence at all.'[82] In other words, causing harm to an unforeseeable plaintiff was not a 'wrong'. The UK courts had to wait another 15 years before they were forced to confront the problem of the unforeseeable plaintiff, but eventually did so in *Bourhill*. The pursuer, a pregnant 'fishwife', suffered a serious shock after hearing, but not seeing, the defender negligently crash his motorcycle into oncoming traffic some 45 feet away. As a result of

---

[76] (1928) 248 NY 339; 162 NE 99 ('*Palsgraf*').

[77] [1943] AC 92. ('*Bourhill*').

[78] *Re Polemis and Furness, Withy & Co Ltd* [1921] 3 KB 560 (CA) ('*Re Polemis*').

[79] (1837) 2 M&W 519, 530; 150 ER 863, 868: (rejecting the view that 'wherever a duty is imposed on a person by contract or otherwise, and that duty is violated, anyone who is injured by the violation of it may have a remedy against the wrong-doer').

[80] *Smith v London and South Western Railway Co* (1870) 5 CP 98 (Brett J): 'But I am of opinion that no reasonable man could have foreseen ... [damage] to *the plaintiff's* cottage ... [Therefore] It seems to me that no duty was cast upon the defendants, in relation to *the plaintiff's* property ...' (emphasis added). See also AL Goodhart, 'The Unforeseeable Consequences of a Negligent Act' (1928) 39 Yale LJ 449, 453 (later reprinted as 'Chapter VII: The Palsgraf Case' in Arthur L Goodhart, *Essays in Jurisprudence and the Common Law* (Cambridge University Press, 1931) ('Brett, J dissented on the ground that the defendant had not been negligent in regard to this particular plaintiff, although the act of leaving the inflammable heaps might have been negligent in relation to others'); and JW Salmond, *The Law of Torts*, 6th edn (Sweet & Maxwell, 1924) 24 ('there is no negligence unless there is in the particular case a legal duty to take care, and this duty must be one which is owed to the plaintiff himself and not merely to others.').

[81] William Prosser, *The Law of Torts*, 4th edn (West Publishing Co, 1971) 254.

[82] *Palsgraf* 341.

the shock, the pursuer suffered a stillborn child shortly thereafter. As the New York Court of Appeals had done in *Palsgraf*, the House of Lords denied the existence of a duty of care on the basis that, whilst the defender had been negligent in relation to someone, they had not been negligent in relation to the plaintiff:

> Thus, in the present case John Young [the defendant] was certainly negligent in an issue between himself and the owner of the car which he ran into, but it is another question whether he was negligent vis-a-vis the appellant. In such cases terms like 'derivative' and 'original' and 'primary' and 'secondary' have been applied to define and distinguish the type of the negligence. If, however, the appellant has a cause of action it is because of a wrong to herself. She cannot build on a wrong to someone else.[83]

Palsgraf and *Bourhill* essentially boil down to the idea that 'Proof of negligence in the air, so to speak, will not do;'[84] that is, negligence is not an abstract enquiry, and the question of whether certain behaviour is negligent cannot be considered in isolation from its consequences. The *same* behaviour may therefore be negligent (and so a 'wrong') in relation to one consequence (such as foreseeable harm to person A), but not negligent (and so not a 'wrong') in relation to another consequence (such as unforeseeable harm to person B).

But this all looks very familiar. To say that negligence in the air will not do is simply to say that the defendant can only be responsible for the materialisation of foreseeable risks, which, as we saw above, is able to be dealt with as a matter of remoteness. The immediate difficulty with classifying the unforeseeable plaintiff as a matter of remoteness, however, was *Re Polemis*, the leading case on remoteness at the time. In *Re Polemis* the defendant's employees negligently dropped a plank of wood into the hold of the plaintiff's ship as they were loading cargo. The dropped plank somehow created a spark which ignited petrol vapour in the hold, causing an explosion and the eventual destruction of the ship. In relation to the defendant's liability the court held:

> To determine whether an act is negligent, it is relevant to determine whether any reasonable man would foresee that the act would cause damage; if he could not, the act is not negligent. But if the act would or might probably cause damage, the fact that the damage it actually causes is not the exact kind of damage one would expect is immaterial, so long as the damage is in fact directly traceable to the negligent act …[85]

Defendants were therefore liable for *all* the direct consequences of their negligence, whether those consequences had been foreseeable or not. If, then, the unforeseeable plaintiff were a matter for remoteness, on no sensible interpretation of *Re Polemis* could a defendant escape liability on the basis that the harm (directly)

---

[83] *Bourhill* 108 (Lord Wright). Lord Russell made similar comments at 102: 'Can it be said that [the defendant] could reasonably have anticipated that a person, situated as was the appellant, would be affected by his proceeding towards [the town of] Colinton at the speed at which he was travelling? I think not … In my opinion, he owed no duty to the appellant, and was, therefore, not guilty of any negligence in relation to her.'

[84] F Pollock, *The Law of Torts*, 11th edn (Stevens, 1920) 455.

[85] *Re Polemis* 577 (Scrutton LJ).

caused by their negligence was suffered by an unforeseeable plaintiff. Negligence therefore *would* be an abstract enquiry.

But this alone was hardly a sufficient reason to justify dealing with the problem of the unforeseeable plaintiff at the duty stage; if the court felt that *Re Polemis* implied that the law of negligence *was* an abstract enquiry, the obvious solution was surely to overrule the extremely unpopular[86] case, and to replace it with a remoteness test based on foreseeability. The defendant would therefore only be liable for the foreseeable consequences of their negligence, harm to an unforeseeable plaintiff would not be a wrong, and negligence would not be an abstract concept. The problem with this solution, however, at least according to the courts, was that remoteness merely concerned the measure of damages payable as a result of the defendant's 'wrong,' whilst duty concerned whether the defendant had committed a 'wrong' in the first place; that is, remoteness went to compensation rather than culpability.[87] As Cardozo CJ stated in *Palsgraf*:

> The law of causation, remote or proximate [ie remoteness], is thus foreign to the case before us. The question of liability is always anterior to the question of the measure of the consequences that go with liability. If there is no tort to be redressed, there is no occasion to consider what damage might be recovered if there were a finding of a tort.[88]

Lord Wright made similar comments in *Bourhill*: 'The question of liability is anterior to the question of the measure of the consequences which go with the liability ... What is now being considered is the question of liability.'[89] In other words, the 'wrong' in the law of negligence was the breach of the duty of care *only*. Issues of causation, remoteness, and damage, on the other hand, were relevant to determining the *remedy* (or compensation) that was available as a result of the wrong. This reasoning has received considerable support elsewhere.[90]

Accordingly, if the problem of the unforeseeable plaintiff was relevant to the 'wrong' rather than the remedy, and the wrong was the breach of the duty of care only, then the problem of the unforeseeable plaintiff *did* have to be dealt with as part of the duty rather than remoteness enquiry. Factual duty was therefore necessary after all.

---

[86] Davies, eg, said that 'It is no exaggeration to say that during its 40-year life *Re Polemis* became one of the most unpopular cases in the legal world.' Martin Davies, 'The Road From Morocco: Polemis Through Donoghue to No-Fault' (1982) 45 MLR 534, 534. See also JG Fleming, 'Remoteness and Duty: The Control Devices in Liability for Negligence' (1953) 31 Can Bar Rev 471, 481: 'Criticism of the decision *In re Polemis* has been more vocal and persuasive than its defence.'

[87] This is based on the famous wording of Lord Sumner in *Weld-Blundell v Stephens* [1920] AC 956 (HL), 984: 'What a defendant ought to have anticipated as a reasonable man is material when the question is whether or not he was guilty of negligence ... This, however, goes to culpability, not to compensation.'

[88] *Palsgraf* 346.

[89] *Bourhill* 110. See also Lord Wright's comments in Wright, 'Re Polemis' (1951) 14 MLR 393, 399.

[90] See eg: *Bourhill* 101 (Lord Russell); *Woods v Duncan* [1946] AC 401 (HL), 437 (Lord Porter); OW Holmes and F Pollock, *Holmes-Pollock letters: the Correspondence of Mr Justice Holmes and Sir Frederick Pollock, 1874–1932*, vol II (M De Wolfe Howe ed, Harvard University Press, 1941) 83 (per Holmes); JF Wilson and CJ Slade, 'A Re-Examination of Remoteness' (1952) 15 MLR 458, 467.

To summarise, then, the argument that factual duty is *not* superfluous, went something like this:

(1)   as negligence is not an abstract enquiry, negligently causing harm to an unforeseeable plaintiff does not constitute a 'wrong';
(2)   the 'wrong' in the law of negligence is the breach of a duty of care, rather than the breach of a duty of care that causes damage that is not too remote;
(3)   the problem of the unforeseeable plaintiff therefore *must* be a matter for duty rather than remoteness.

Although *Re Polemis* no longer represents the law, and so, as we have seen, this argument is now of little *practical* effect, if the syllogism is nevertheless valid, the factual duty element must nevertheless be a jurisprudentially necessary element of the negligence enquiry after all. Before we accept this conclusion, however, we will first explore the premises of the syllogism in further detail. It is most convenient to consider the second premise first.

B. Is the Duty of Care a 'Real' Duty?

The second premise of the claim that factual duty is necessary, is that the 'wrong' in the law of negligence is the breach of a duty of care, rather than the breach of a duty of care causing damage that is not too remote. In modern terms, this is said to mean that the duty of care is a 'real' duty. This belief stems from the idea that *all* civil 'wrongs' are based on breaches of a legal 'duty',[91] an idea that can be traced back to the Roman lawyer, Gaius.[92] So, for example, the 'wrong' in breach of contract cases is the breach of the 'duty' to perform the contract, and the 'wrong' in the law of nuisance is the breach of the 'duty' to not use one's land in a way that interferes with another's use and enjoyment of their land. In the same way, the 'wrong' in the law of negligence is said to be the breach of the 'duty' to take care.

That the 'wrong' in the law of negligence is the breach of the duty to take care *only*, is crucial to the claim that factual duty is necessary. If the 'wrong' were, instead, the breach of a duty to take care *to avoid causing damage that was not too remote*, then the problem of the unforeseeable plaintiff could simply be dealt with at the remoteness stage and so factual duty would *not* be needed to ensure that harm to an unforeseeable plaintiff did not amount to a 'wrong'.

On what basis, however, is it said that the wrong in the law of negligence is the breach of a duty to take care rather than the breach of a duty to take care to not cause damage that is not too remote? Despite the claim being crucial to the outcome in both *Palsgraf* and *Bourhill*, surprisingly, neither case offers any *actual* support for the proposition at all. Indeed, in a case note written on *Palsgraf*,

---

[91] P Birks, 'The Concept of a Civil Wrong' in D Owen (ed), *Philosophical Foundations of Tort Law* (Clarendon Press, 1995) 33; R Stevens, *Torts and Rights* (OUP, 2007) 2.
[92] Gaius, Institutes, 3.88.

Prosser said of the reasoning: 'with due respect to the superlative style in which [the judgment is written] ... [It] beg[s] the question shamelessly, stating dogmatic propositions without reason or explanation'.[93] More recently however, considerable support for the proposition has been offered by McBride. According to McBride, duties of care are indeed 'real' duties, and so the 'wrong' in the law of negligence is the breach of the duty to take care rather than the breach of a duty to take care not to cause damage that is not too remote, because if it were not the case we would encounter four problems. First, it would mean that, 'paradoxically', the law of negligence only protected claimants from defendants' carelessness *after* they had been harmed, effectively allowing defendants to behave as carelessly as they pleased prior to then.[94] Secondly, as the deliberate breach of a duty of care would not be a wrong, we could not explain why exemplary damages are routinely awarded against defendants for such breaches.[95] Thirdly, there would be no reason for the courts to ever award injunctions to prevent future carelessness if that carelessness were not a wrong in the absence of damage, yet there are cases, at least in the United States, where courts have done precisely this.[96] Fourthly, we would be unable to explain why the courts distort the law on causation, in cases such as *Reeves v Commissioner of Police of the Metropolis*[97] and *McGhee v National Coal Board*,[98] to impose liability on defendants who have not, on orthodox views, caused any harm.[99] In light of these problems, McBride concludes that the view that duties of care must be real duties is therefore the preferable one.[100]

The claim that duties of care are real duties is not, however, unproblematic. The biggest difficulty with the claim is that it deems a legal wrong to have been committed under the law of negligence without the claimant having suffered any actionable damage. Yet we know that this is simply not the law. In particular, whilst behaving in a manner that creates a risk of injury to another might be able to be legitimately described as a *moral* or *criminal* 'wrong', insofar as the law of negligence is concerned, provided that the 'wrongdoer' is fortunate enough to avoid injuring anyone, he has committed no 'wrong' at all. As Buckland explains:

> If I drive down Piccadilly at sixty miles an hour I am certainly careless, but if I get through without damaging anyone in any way I am under no liability at civil law to anyone. I may be a criminal, but that is another matter ... So far as civil law is concerned my carelessness is without any legal result whatsoever.[101]

---

[93] Prosser (n 72) 7.
[94] N McBride, 'Duties of Care: Do They Really Exist?' (2004) 24 OJLS 417, 425.
[95] ibid 426.
[96] ibid 427.
[97] [2000] 1 AC 360 (HL).
[98] [1973] 1 WLR 1 (HL).
[99] McBride (n 94) 430.
[100] ibid 441. For general criticisms of McBride's argument, see Howarth, 'Many Duties of Care—Or A Duty of Care? Notes from the Underground' (n 52); and Dan Priel, 'Tort Law for Cynics' (2014) 75 MLR 703.
[101] WW Buckland, *Some Reflections on Jurisprudence* (Cambridge University Press, 1945) 114. See also Lawson, 'The Duty of Care in Negligence: A Comparative Study' (n 27) 112; Birks (n 91) 37; and Morison in JG Fleming and WL Morison, 'Duty of Care and Standard of Care' (1953) 1 SydLR 69, 70–71.

Indeed, that damage is an 'essential ingredient'[102] of the cause of action in negligence, rather than merely a requirement of recoverability, is 'not in doubt'.[103] As Fleming explains:

> Actual damage or injury is a necessary element (the gist) of tort liability for negligence. Unlike assault and battery or defamation, where violation of a mere dignitary interest like personal integrity or reputation is deemed sufficiently heinous to warrant redress, negligence is not actionable unless and until it results in damage to the plaintiff.[104]

Brennan J, too, has noted that, a 'duty of care is a thing written on the wind unless damage is caused by the breach of that duty',[105] whilst Lord Hoffman has been similarly clear that 'Proof of damage is an essential element in a claim in negligence'.[106] If, then, the tort of negligence requires actionable damage to be complete, then the breach of a duty of care *alone* cannot amount to a legal wrong, and the claim that the 'duty' in the law of negligence is the duty to take care, must be wrong.

Other difficulties with the claim are highlighted by Nolan:

> First, a 'duty' of care is normatively unconvincing, since a right not to be exposed to risk is both counter-intuitive (do we really believe that a motorist who careers down Piccadilly at 60 miles an hour has violated the rights of all those he could have hit?) and philosophically problematic. Secondly, examples can be given which show that the duty of care cannot be a duty owed to others, at least if we accept the Hohfeldian correlation of such duties with claim rights. Suppose that A, a baby of six months, falls ill after eating a tin of baby food negligently manufactured by B eighteen months previously. A has a claim in negligence against B in such a case, but how could B have breached a duty he owed A, and how could A's rights therefore have been violated, before A had even been conceived? Thirdly, there are cases which indirectly demonstrate that duties of care are not really duties. In *Spartan Steel and Alloys Ltd v Martin & Co. (Contractors) Ltd*, for example, the same act of negligence by B caused A both property damage and pure economic loss. Had the wrong in the case been the act of negligence itself, then all the loss A suffered as a result of that act should have been recoverable, but as it was the Court of Appeal allowed A to recover only for the property damage, and not the pure economic loss.[107]

---

[102] *Leigh and Sillavan Ltd v Aliakmon Shipping Co Ltd* [1985] QB 350 (CA), 375 (Oliver LJ). See also Nolan (n 43) 561.

[103] D Nolan, 'New Forms of Damage in Negligence' (2007) 70 MLR 59, 59. See also: J Stapleton, 'The Gist of Negligence, Part 1: Minimum Actionable Damage' (1988) 104 LQR 213; J Stapleton, 'The Gist of Negligence, Part 2: The Relationship Between "Damage" and Causation' (1988) 104 LQR 389.

[104] JG Fleming, *The Law of Torts*, 9th edn (Law Book Co, 1998) 216. An almost identical quote is reproduced in Margaret Beazley, 'Damage' in Carolyn Sappideen and Prue Vines (eds), *Fleming's The Law of Torts*, 10th edn (Thomson Reuters (Professional) Australia Limited, 2011) 225.

[105] *John Pfeiffer Pty Ltd v Canny* (1981) 148 CLR 218, 241. See also, *Harriton v Stephens* (2006) 226 CLR 52, 115 (Crennan J); *Brookfield Multiplex v Owners—Strata Plan No 61288* (2014) 254 CLR 185 [124] (Bell and Keane JJ).

[106] *Rothwell v Chemical & Insulating Co Ltd* [2008] AC 281 (HL), [2]. See also the comments of Lord Hope in ibid at [47]: 'In strict legal theory a wrong has been done whenever a breach of the duty of care results in a demonstrable physical injury.'

[107] Nolan, 'Deconstructing the Duty of Care' (n 43) 561-62 (footnotes omitted).

As Nolan notes, the evidence against the proposition that duties of care are real duties is 'overwhelming'.[108] Similar sentiments have been expressed by both Lawson[109] and Zipursky.[110] The second premise underlying the claim that factual duty is necessary is therefore flawed. The duty of care is not a 'real' duty at all (in the sense that a breach of it does not amount to a legal 'wrong'), but merely a label for an element of the negligent enquiry. The 'real' duty is the breach of a duty of care that causes damage which is not too remote, and the problem of the unforeseeable plaintiff can therefore be dealt with at the remoteness stage without implying that causing harm to an unforeseeable plaintiff is a wrong.

It also follows from this conclusion that the element of negligence enquiry typically known as the 'breach', or 'breach of duty', element is a misnomer, as there is no 'duty' being 'breached'. A more appropriate name for the stage is therefore the 'fault' or 'standard of care' stage, the former of which has been adopted in this book.

C. Is the Problem of the Unforeseeable Plaintiff Relevant to the Wrong or the Remedy?

If the argument above, that the duty of care is *not* a 'real' duty, is accepted, then the claim that factual duty is necessary must fail. However, if the argument is rejected, then the claim is still dependent on the validity of first premise, being that that the problem of the unforeseeable plaintiff is relevant to the 'wrong' rather than to the extent of the liability for the wrong; or alternatively, to wrong rather than the remedy.

Importantly, the claim that foreseeability of harm to the plaintiff is relevant to the wrong is not, *in itself*, overly problematic; after all, if it were otherwise, the question of negligence *would* be divorced from its consequences, and negligence in the air *would* be an abstract concept, which few seem to agree should be the case. What *is* problematic, however, is what it implies: that, whereas foreseeability of harm to the plaintiff is relevant to the wrong (and so need be dealt with as part of the duty enquiry), foreseeability of the *other* consequences of the defendant's carelessness is relevant *only* to the question of the extent of liability for the wrong (and so need be dealt with as part of the remoteness enquiry). The reason this implication is problematic is because, not only is it unclear how the

---

[108] ibid 562.

[109] Lawson, 'The Duty of Care in Negligence: A Comparative Study' (n 27) 112: 'the formulation of the doctrine [as a duty *to take care*] is objectionable on analytical grounds, and ... it would be better to say that the duty is to avoid damaging the plaintiff by failing to take the requisite care rather than to take care to avoid damaging him.'

[110] Zipursky, 1272: 'The legal wrong in negligence is the negligent injuring of the plaintiff, not the failure of the defendant to conform his conduct to a standard of reasonable risk taking.'

different consequences of the defendant's carelessness are able to be isolated from one another and treated independently, but the basis for allocating the relevance of some of those consequences (that is, the foreseeability of harm to the plaintiff) to the question of the wrong and the relevance of others (that is, the foreseeability of everything else) to the question of the extent of liability for the wrong, is similarly unclear—such picking and choosing must have some rational basis underlying it.

One could, of course, object that the above implication is unnecessary, and that the problem can be overcome by accepting that the foreseeability of the kind of harm, the extent of the harm, and the way the harm occurred, are *also* relevant to the wrong, such that no distinction between the different consequences of the defendant's behaviour need be drawn, and all are treated in the same way. Such a response, however, would amount to little more than a relabelling of the 'remoteness' enquiry as 'factual duty', thereby contradicting the second premise and conceding that remoteness is relevant to the definition of the 'wrong' after all. Accordingly, if the claim that factual duty is necessary is to be maintained, there must be some justifiable distinction between foreseeability of harm to the plaintiff and foreseeability of the other consequences of the defendant's careless conduct, *and* some reason why the former is necessarily relevant to the wrong (and so a question of duty) whilst the rest are relevant to the remedy only (and so dealt with at the remoteness enquiry). There are, however, three reasons why this cannot be the case: the distinction is arbitrary, foreseeability of harm to the plaintiff and foreseeability of the kind of harm cannot be treated in isolation from one another, and it requires us to simultaneously adopt contradictory rationales.

i. The Distinction is Arbitrary

The first difficulty with treating foreseeability of harm to the plaintiff as relevant to the wrong, and foreseeability of the other consequences of the carelessness as relevant to the remedy only, is that it relies on an entirely arbitrary distinction. This is clearest in the case of foreseeability of harm to the plaintiff and foreseeability of the *kind* of harm suffered. Consider, for example, *Thorogood v Van Den Berghs and Jurgens Ltd*,[111] in which the plaintiff suffered an injury to his hand after it became caught in the revolving blades of a fan that had been placed on the ground for testing. It was found at trial that, whilst it was *not* foreseeable that a trained man standing nearby would suffer physical injury by allowing his hand to come in contact with the fan, as the plaintiff did, it *was* foreseeable that a trained man standing nearby would be at risk of suffering physical injury by having *his necktie* caught in the blades. In other words, *some* kind of injury to the particular plaintiff was foreseeable (that is, the 'necktie' kind), even though the kind actually suffered (the 'injured hand' kind) was not. Working from the basis that only foreseeability of harm to the plaintiff was relevant to the question of the wrong,

---

[111] [1952] 2 KB 537 (CA) ('*Thorogood's Case*').

Asquith LJ held the defendant liable for the damage, notwithstanding that it was unforeseeable:

> The foreseeability of the damage actually sustained is wholly irrelevant ... The actual damage may be wholly different in character, magnitude, or the detailed manner of its incidence, from anything which could have reasonably be anticipated.[112]

It is completely unclear, however, why foresight of the kind of damage is 'wholly irrelevant' to the wrong, whilst foresight of risk to the actual plaintiff is, apparently, essential. Prosser described the position as 'a fundamental and foolish inconsistency',[113] whilst Goodhart objected:

> [I]f we once reject the idea that an act has a general quality of wrongfulness where different persons are concerned, it would seem to follow logically that we must also reject the idea that an act has a general quality of wrongfulness where different consequences are concerned ...[If] A cannot be negligent to B 'in the air' [then] To hold A, who has been negligent to B in relation to certain foreseeable consequences, liable to B for unforeseeable consequences is no more reasonable than to hold A liable for such consequences if they happen to C.[114]

Fleming, too, objected that that such a distinction:

> introduces in to the law of negligence an element of stress which is difficult to justify on rational grounds. Both are aspects of the same problem of limitation of responsibility and cannot be divorced from each other by the verbal distinction between culpability on the one hand and compensation on the other.[115]

Accordingly, the claim that foreseeability of harm to the plaintiff is relevant to the wrong, whilst foreseeability of the other consequences of the defendant's carelessness are relevant to the remedy only, relies on an entirely arbitrary distinction and so has little normative attraction. If the distinction between the two is arbitrary, there can therefore be no good reason for treating one as relevant to duty, and the others as relevant to remoteness.

ii. Foreseeability of Harm to the Plaintiff and Foreseeability of the Kind of Harm cannot be Considered in Isolation from One Another

The second difficulty with treating foreseeability of harm to the plaintiff as relevant to the wrong, and the foreseeability of the other consequences of the defendant's

---

[112] *Thorogood's Case* 690.

[113] Prosser (n 72) 23.

[114] Goodhart (n 80) 465. See also Goodhart's comments in ALG, 'Obituary: Re Polemis' (1961) 77 LQR 175, 177: 'such a distinction [cannot] be supported on any obviously rational principle.'

[115] Fleming, 'Remoteness and Duty: The Control Devices in Liability for Negligence' (n 86) 496. See also ibid: 'It is, of course, pragmatically possible to maintain both the duty approach and the *Polemis* rule, and indeed interpret the latter in terms of a duty to protect others against unforeseeable consequences of negligent acts, but the essential inconsistency remains holding that one who can foresee harm to A is liable for unforeseen consequences to A and refusing to hold him liable for unforeseen harm to B. Whether the unforeseen harm is suffered by A or B is entirely fortuitous. The difficulty is fundamental ...'

carelessness as relevant to the remedy only, is that it requires them to be distinguished and treated in isolation from one another. This cannot, however, be done, as the problem of the unforeseeable plaintiff is less concerned with foresight of *some harm* to the particular plaintiff, than foresight of *the particular kind of* harm to the particular plaintiff. Why this is so is best illustrated by an example. Assume that the facts of *Palsgraf* and *Bourhill* were slightly different, and that the package of fireworks had belonged to Mrs Palsgraf, and the car with which Mr Young collided had belonged to Mrs Bourhill. In both examples, the plaintiffs would undoubtedly have been able to recover for the damage caused to their property by the carelessness of the defendants. Yet, if this is the case, *some* injury to the particular plaintiff *would* have been a foreseeable consequence of the defendant's carelessness, and so the defendant *would* have been negligent 'vis-a-vis' the plaintiff. Would it therefore follow that the plaintiffs could recover for their personal injuries as well? Surely not, or the actual results of *Palsgraf* and *Bourhill,* and the inability of the plaintiffs to recover for their personal injuries, would rest on the fortuitous and surely irrelevant fact that Mrs Palsgraf did not own the fireworks and Mrs Bourhill did not own the (presumably) damaged car.[116] But if that is not the explanation, then what is? Obviously, the results rest on the basis that it was unforeseeable that the particular plaintiff would suffer the particular 'kind' of injury; that is, whilst it may have been foreseeable on the hypothesised facts that the plaintiffs would suffer *property* damage, it remained unforeseeable that they would suffer *physical* injury. The result, then, is that the basis of the denial of the duty was not that harm to the particular plaintiff was unforeseeable, but that the particular *kind* of harm suffered by the particular plaintiff was unforeseeable. The problem of the unforeseeable plaintiff is therefore a misnomer; the *real* problem is the unforeseeability of the exact *kind* of harm to the plaintiff.

Of course, if it is not injury to the particular plaintiff that needs to be foreseeable, but injury of the particular *kind* suffered by the particular plaintiff that needs to be foreseeable, then, not only do *Palsgraf* and *Bourhill* appear to directly contradict *Re Polemis*, which had explicitly stated that the exact 'kind' of damage was *not* required to be foreseeable for that damage to be recoverable, but we are now very close to saying the remoteness of the damage is relevant to the wrong after all, thereby contradicting the first premise and so establishing that factual duty is unnecessary.

---

[116] Fleming describes such a result as 'capricious': JG Fleming, 'The Passing of Polemis' (1961) 39 Can Bar Rev 489, 497. The same 'capriciousness' can be illustrated by imagining that the cargo on the steamship Thrasyvoulos had belonged to a third party. As the defendant's carelessness only created a foreseeable risk of harm to the *ship*, and not the *cargo*, the defendant would therefore only be liable to the owner of the ship; that is, the 'wrong' was to the owner of the ship, not to the owner of the cargo. Now imagine that both the ship *and* the cargo belonged to the same party. Here, the defendant would be liable for the damage to the ship *and* the cargo; the 'wrong' was to the owner of the ship and so the defendant was liable for *all* direct consequences of that wrong. The defendant's liability for the cargo therefore seems to depend on who happens to own it. Goodhart (Goodhart (n 80) 466) and Dias (Dias, 'The Breach Problem and the Duty of Care' (n 27) 386) both argue that such an explanation is unsatisfactory, whilst Prosser describes it as 'utter nonsense' (Prosser (n 72) 23).

Although Cardozo,[117] Lord Wright[118] and others[119] recognised the difficulties involved with isolating foresight of harm to the plaintiff from foresight of the kind of harm suffered, the first person to tackle them in detail was E Anthony Machin. Machin accepted that factual duty required more than foresight of *any* injury to the particular plaintiff; however, it was not foresight of the 'kind' of injury that was also required, but foresight of injury to the particular plaintiff's affected 'interest',[120] such as plaintiff's 'interest' in freedom from physical bodily injury, 'interest' in freedom from injury to chattels, 'interest' in freedom from injury to land, and 'interest' in freedom from nervous shock.[121] As Machin explains:

> [I]t is difficult to accept that reasonable foresight of injury to the one interest should be sufficient to ground an action in respect of actual injury to the other, any injury to which being *ex hypothesi* unforeseeable ... [I]f I know that little Tommy's mother is watching him from a second-floor window as he plays in the street, and I nevertheless drive my motor-car at a reckless speed towards him and thereby kill him under her eyes, and she suffers shock, I am surely liable to her in respect of it because shock is foreseeable. Now suppose that little Tommy, unknown to me, has a stick of dynamite in his pocket which explodes and physically injures his mother. I can foresee no physical injury to the mother whatsoever. Upon what principle should I pay for such physical injury, when all I could reasonably foresee was injury to a different interest of hers? A person standing in the street a quarter of a mile away who was hit by a fragment thrown out by the explosion would clearly have no cause of action of any kind against me. Why should the mother be placed in any better position, so far as recovery for unforeseeable physical injury is concerned, because she already has a right to recover in respect of shock?[122]

Machin's 'interest theory' certainly addressed the difficulties highlighted above. Distinguishing 'kind of harm' from 'interests', reconciled the seeming conflict between *Palsgraf* / *Bourhill* and *Re Polemis* and explained the seeming overlap between the roles of factual duty and remoteness; factual duty required foresight of injury to the particular plaintiff's affected 'interest', and once that duty had been breached, remoteness permitted recovery for all directly caused 'kinds' of harm whether they were foreseeable or not. The reason, then, that Mrs Palsgraf could not have recovered for her personal injury even if she had owned the package of

---

[117] *Palsgraf* 347: 'There is room for argument that a distinction is to be drawn according to the diversity of interests invaded by the act, as where conduct negligent in that it threatens an insignificant invasion of an interest in property results in an unforeseeable invasion of an interest of another order, as, eg, one of bodily security. Perhaps other distinctions may be necessary. We do not go into the question now.'

[118] *Bourhill* 108 ('Her interest, which was in her own bodily security, was of a different order from the interest of the owner of the car'); ibid 110 ('[*Re Polemis*] must be understood to be limited ... to "direct" consequences to the *particular interest of the plaintiff* which is affected.').

[119] See, eg: J Smith, 'Legal Cause in Actions of Tort' in Harvard Law Review Association (ed), *Selected Essays on the Law of Torts* (Harvard Law Review Association, 1924) 649; Leon Green, 'The Palsgraf Case' (1930) 30 Colum L Rev 789, 790; F James, 'Scope of Duty in Negligence Cases' (1952) 47 NwULRev 778, 783.

[120] EA Machin, 'Negligence and Interest' (1954) 17 MLR 405, 410.

[121] ibid 418.

[122] ibid 410.

fireworks is because there would have only been foresight of injury to her 'chattel-interest', and not her 'body-interest'. For the same reason Mrs Bourhill could not have recovered for her personal injuries even if she had owned the car.[123]

The interest theory, however, is not unproblematic. First, it created even *more* arbitrary distinctions, now that the affected 'interest' was required to be foreseeable, whilst the 'kind' of harm, extent of harm, etc, inexplicably, were not.[124] Secondly, Machin's justification for requiring that damage to the affected *interest* be foreseeable, equally justified requiring that the *kind* of damage suffered be foreseeable, the exact proposition he was trying to disprove. In particular, how is the argument that 'it is difficult to accept that reasonable foresight of injury to the one interest should be sufficient to ground an action in respect of actual injury to the other, any injury to which being *ex hypothesi* unforeseeable',[125] any different to 'it is difficult to accept that reasonable foresight of one *kind of harm* should be sufficient to ground an action in respect of actual injury to another *kind of harm*, that was *ex hypothesi* unforeseeable'?[126] It is, therefore, perhaps unsurprising that the stated aim of Machin's 'interest theory' was nothing more than 'a means to an end',[127] and motivated more by pragmatism than logic; that is, Machin was *not* attempting to justify the necessity of factual duty requirement, but was merely attempting to provide an interpretation of *Palsgraf* and *Bourhill* that was reconcilable with *Re Polemis*: 'a compromise between the theory which requires foreseeability as a criterion both of duty and remoteness, and the theory which regards all direct damage as actionable provided some damage was foreseeable'.[128] Whilst Machin may, indeed, have achieved this, he only did so by making the duty enquiry even more confusing than it was in the first place.

There was, however, a rationale for the interest theory that had not been advanced by Machin, a rationale that was, arguably, more convincing than any of his explanations: that the interest theory eschewed any reliance on the problematic concept of 'kind' of damage. After all, what was a 'kind' of damage? Was, for example, damage to an eye the same 'kind' of damage as damage to a foot?[129]

---

[123] Similarly, in the *Re Polemis* example above, *neither* party could recover for the damage to the cargo, as different chattels involve different interests, so the interest in the cargo would have been different to the interest in the ship.

[124] AL Goodhart, 'The Imaginary Necktie and the Rule in *Re Polemis*' (1952) 68 LQR 514, 515 (fn 7).

[125] Machin (n 120) 412.

[126] Similarly, Machin's 'little Tommy' example, quoted above, could equally be used to justify foresight of the same 'kind' of harm: 'Upon what principle should I pay for such physical injury [or damage of one 'kind'], when all I could reasonably foresee was injury to a different interest [or of a different kind] of hers.'

[127] Machin (n 120) 418.

[128] ibid 419. That this was the only way to reconcile the cases, was often put forward as a reason in favour of such an interpretation: See, eg, Wilson and Slade (n 90) 468; RWM Dias, 'Trouble on Oiled Waters: Problems of *The Wagon Mound (No 2)*' (1967) 25 CLJ 62 (n 23) 179. Of course, the fact that two cases *can* be interpreted consistently, says nothing about whether the cases were correctly decided in the first place.

[129] Williams (n 63) 181; Prosser (n 72) 23; Goodhart, 'The Unforeseeable Consequences of a Negligent Act' (n 80) 467.

Similarly, how broad or narrow was a 'kind' of damage meant to be? On the one hand, if the level of abstraction is set low enough, then almost no kind of damage will be foreseeable (that is, the more specific the risk the less likely it will be foreseeable), whilst, on the other hand, vague generalisations of 'kinds' of harm will cover almost anything, and so every 'kind' of harm will be foreseeable.[130] Depending on the level of abstraction, both everything and nothing is foreseeable. Stevens sums up the problem as follows: 'there is no necessarily right answer to the question of what counts as the same [kind][131] of damage, and no criterion by which it can be determined. The [kind] is wholly dependent on the level of generality with which the damage is described ...'[132]

In contrast to the comparatively fixed idea of 'interests,' the 'kind' of harm concept seemed wildly imprecise and problematic. Requiring foreseeability of harm to the plaintiff's particular 'interest' therefore seemed a preferable and more stable option to foreseeability of the exact 'kind' of harm. But was this actually so? Consider, for example, *Smith*. The defendant train company had allowed dried grass cuttings to pile up close to its railway lines which were set alight by sparks from a passing locomotive. Wind carried the fire across an adjoining stubble field to the plaintiff's cottage over 200m away. The plaintiff's cottage was destroyed by the fire. Physical damage to the land adjoining the railway track was no doubt foreseeable, and so, according to the interest theory, the defendant was negligent vis-à-vis the owner of the stubble field's property interest in the stubble field. Damage to the plaintiff's cottage, however, being so far away, was not a foreseeable consequence of the defendant's actions, meaning that, per the interest theory, the defendant had not been negligent vis-à-vis the plaintiff's property interest in his cottage. So far, so good. The difficulty, however, comes when we hypothesise that the scrub field had belonged to the plaintiff.[133] Under the interest theory, this modification to the facts would mean that damage to the property interest of the plaintiff *would* have been foreseeable and so the plaintiff would have recovered for the damage to his cottage. The plaintiff's case, therefore, depended on who owned the adjoining scrub field. Such a capricious result, however, is clearly unsatisfactory. Whilst one might reply that the scrub field was on a separate title to the house, and so the subject of a separate property interest, this would imply that liability ought to depend on the nature of the property title, an equally capricious result.

One solution might be to define interests more narrowly, such that the interest in the scrub field is different to the interest in the house. But how narrow do we go?

---

[130] G Fridman and J Williams, 'The Atomic Theory of Negligence' (1971) 45 ALJ 117, 122. See also Fleming, 'The Passing of Polemis' (n 116) 520; Goodhart, 'The Imaginary Necktie and the Rule in *Re Polemis*' (n 124) 534.

[131] Stevens uses the word 'type', but this can be used interchangeably with 'kind'.

[132] Stevens (n 91) 155. See also ibid 156: 'Distinctions of this kind, based on an unstable concept, with no demonstrably correct result one way or the other, do no credit to our law.'

[133] The example is further discussed in: Williams (n 63) 185–86; and Fleming, 'The Passing of Polemis' (n 116) 525–27.

Is the interest in a house, for example, the same as the interest in an adjacent garage, and would it matter whether they were adjoined or detached? Would the interest in a house extend to the chattels inside the house, such as a painting, or even outside the house, such as a car in the driveway? And would the interest in a painting extend to the interest in the frame, or the paint on the canvas?[134] Clearly, a line needs to be drawn somewhere. On the one hand, 'interests' cannot be defined too broadly (adjoining land involves the same interest), or we will be left with capricious results, and a hopelessly undemanding test for foreseeably endangering an 'interest.' On the other hand, 'interests' cannot be defined too narrowly (the interest in a painting's canvas is separate to the interest in the paint on the canvas), or it will become extremely difficult to show that harm to a particular interest was ever foreseeable. Where, exactly, to draw the line clearly cannot be 'supported by any obviously rational principle',[135] and so will necessarily involve some degree of flexibility. Of course, the moment we start relying on discretion and flexibility to distinguish between different interests, we are back to where we started, and any meaningful distinction between 'kinds' of harm and 'interests' ceases to exist. The interest theory is therefore subject to the same problems it was trying to overcome. Indeed, even Machin conceded that when interests start being treated flexibly, and subdivided further, it would 'lead ultimately to a requirement of foreseeability of the very kind of damage which in fact occurred [and] [t]his would be incompatible with *Re Polemis*'.[136] Requiring foreseeability of damage to a particular 'interest' of the plaintiff is therefore just as problematic as requiring foreseeability of the same 'kind' of damage, and so does not provide a convincing way for distinguishing between foreseeability of harm to the plaintiff and foreseeability of the kind of harm suffered, nor can it provide a way for *Palsgraf* and *Bourhill* to be read consistently with *Re Polemis*.

If foreseeability of harm to the plaintiff and foreseeability of the kind of harm suffered cannot be distinguished, then the existence of a factual duty must, in fact, require foreseeability of the particular kind of harm suffered by the particular plaintiff. Of course, if the *kind* of harm suffered by the particular plaintiff needs to be foreseeable, then the first premise, that causing harm to an unforeseeable plaintiff does not constitute a wrong, is, in fact: 'causing *an unforeseeable kind of* harm to a particular plaintiff is not a wrong', or, in other words, causing harm that is too remote is not a wrong. Remoteness, then, *is* relevant to the wrong, and so the second premise contradicts the first premise. Factual duty is therefore not needed after all.

---

[134] The same difficulties arise in cases of the interest in bodily safety. Negligently exposing someone to spinning fan blades would surely give rise to liability for foreseeable physical maiming, but what if the plaintiff instead unforeseeably caught a chill. And would it matter if the chill was viral or bacterial? See Goodhart, 'The Imaginary Necktie and the Rule in *Re Polemis*' (n 124) 516.

[135] ALG (n 114) 177.

[136] Machin (n 120) 418.

iii. We Must Simultaneously Accept Contradictory Rationales

The third difficulty with treating foreseeability of harm to the plaintiff as relevant to the wrong, and the rest of the consequences as relevant to the remedy only, is that it relies on a rationale that contradicts the rationale underlying the second premise. In particular, the claim that foreseeability of harm to the claimant is relevant to the wrong rather than the remedy is based principally on an objection to the idea that negligence is an abstract enquiry, and that liability for carelessness can be determined without regard to the foreseeability of its consequences. The rationale underlying the second premise, however, being that the wrong in the law of negligence is the breach of a duty of care *only*, is based on the idea that the consequences of the defendant's carelessness are *completely irrelevant to* the wrong. Indeed, according to the second premise, the breach of the real 'duty' occurs at the moment of the carelessness, regardless of the consequences that follow: negligence in the air therefore *is* enough. Accordingly, if we accept the first premise we must reject the second premise, and if we accept the second premise, we must reject the first premise. The claim that the wrong in negligence is the breach of the duty of care only, *and* that foreseeability of harm to the plaintiff is relevant to the wrong whilst the rest of the consequences of the carelessness are relevant to the remedy only, is therefore inherently contradictory. Again, the claim that factual duty is necessary, can therefore not be justified.

V. Why Factual Duty Entered the Duty Enquiry and Why it Remains

Factual duty would therefore seem to be both theoretically and practically unnecessary; not only can the exact same outcome be achieved via the fault and remoteness enquiries, but the idea that it is nevertheless necessary to ensure that causing harm to an unforeseeable plaintiff did not amount to a 'wrong' is unconvincing. Given these problems, one may therefore ask, why the courts in *Palsgraf* and *Bourhill* introduced the problematic factual duty concept at all, when, as we have seen, the same result could have been achieved, and the above-mentioned difficulties avoided, if *Re Polemis* had simply been overruled and the problem of the unforeseeable plaintiff dealt with as a matter for remoteness? Whilst *Palsgraf* can conceivably be explained on the basis that the court did not want to leave the issue of the unforeseeable plaintiff to the jury (given the question of duty was one for the court whilst the issue of remoteness was for the jury), it does not explain the result of *Bourhill* given that, in the UK, juries were no longer being used in civil trials.[137] The answer, then, at least in the UK, must surely be that the reliance on

---

[137] See (n 25).

factual duty was nothing more than an artifice for the purpose of circumventing the well-established rule in *Re Polemis*. What other explanation can there be? Why create so many analytical difficulties in such an important cause of action when they could have all been avoided by overruling a single case? A reluctance to over-rule *Re Polemis* is surely the answer.

Even if, however, this explains the results of *Bourhill* and (possibly) *Palsgraf*, it does not explain why factual duty has endured. Indeed, after the Privy Council handed down the judgment in *The Wagon Mound (No 1)*, there was no longer any good reason for factual duty to remain; not only was it no longer necessary to ensure that *Re Polemis* remained good law, but, as we have seen, the foreseeability-based test of remoteness rendered the factual duty enquiry functionally superfluous.[138] Additionally, the reasoning relied on in *Palsgraf* and *Bourhill*, that justified the existence of the factual duty in the first place, was expressly disapproved. In particular, as to the claim that the breach of the duty of care was the 'wrong', whilst remoteness merely went to the measure of consequences that go with the 'wrong', the court said:

> [In relation to the proposition] 'This, however, goes to culpability not to compensation'. It is with the greatest respect to that very learned judge and to those who have echoed his words, that their Lordships find themselves bound to state their view that this proposition is fundamentally false.
>
> It is, no doubt, proper when considering tortious liability for negligence to analyse its elements and to say that the plaintiff must prove a duty owed to him by the defendant, a breach of that duty by the defendant, and consequent damage. But there can be no liability until the damage has been done. It is not the act but the consequences on which tortious liability is founded. Just as (as it has been said) there is no such thing as negligence in the air, so there is no such thing as liability in the air ... It is vain to isolate the liability from its context and to say that B is or is not liable, and then to ask for what damage he is liable. For his liability is in respect of that damage and no other.[139]

Remoteness, in other words, was *not* foreign to the 'wrong', and so there was no reason for the unforeseeable plaintiff to be dealt with as a matter of duty rather than a matter for remoteness to avoid negligence becoming an abstract enquiry. The court also disapproved of any meaningful distinction between foreseeability of harm to the plaintiff and foreseeability of the kind of harm suffered:

> [I]f it is supposed that similar unforeseeable damage is suffered by A and C but other foreseeable damage, for which B is liable, by A only. A system of law which would hold B

---

[138] Although *The Wagon Mound (No 1)*, a Privy Council decision, did not technically overrule *Re Polemis*, it was soon expressly approved by English courts: *Smith v Leech Brain & Co* [1962] 2 QB 405 (QB); *Hughes v Lord Advocate* [1963] AC 837 (HL). Though note (n 143).

[139] ibid 425. For a more recent statement of this position, see Lord Hoffmann in *Kuwait Airways Corp v Iraq Airways Co* (No 6) [2002] 2 AC 883 (HL), 1106: 'One cannot separate questions of liability from questions of causation. They are inseparably connected. One is never simply liable; one is always liable for something and the rules which determine what one is liable for are as much part of the substantive law as the rules which determine which acts give rise to liability.'

liable to A but not to C for the similar damage suffered by each of them could not easily be defended. Fortunately, the attempt is not necessary ... It is irrelevant to the question whether B is liable for unforeseeable damage that he is liable for foreseeable damage, as irrelevant as would the fact that he had trespassed on Whiteacre be to the question whether he has trespassed on Blackacre.[140]

In other words, remoteness was a question of the foreseeability of the *risk*,[141] requiring that both harm to the plaintiff *and* the kind of harm suffered by the plaintiff be foreseeable. There was, therefore, little point asking the same question at the duty stage.

Following *The Wagon Mound (No 1)*, it was abundantly clear that there was no longer any good reason for factual duty to remain a part of the duty enquiry. Notwithstanding this, however, more than 50 years later, factual duty remains alive and well, an orthodox part of the duty enquiry that is relied on in higher courts regularly,[142] despite the remoteness enquiry remaining largely the same.[143] What, however, explains this? If factual duty is so clearly superfluous, why has it not been consigned to the annals of legal history? It seems there are two reasons. First is the persistent belief that if we are to avoid imposing a 'duty' to take care to avoid causing unforeseeable harm, the duty *of care* stage must have a foreseeability requirement. Indeed, as we saw in chapter three, the belief that a defendant cannot be expected to exercise reasonable care towards the world at large, but only to those he can reasonably foresee could be affected by his actions, is the principal modern justification for retaining the foreseeability requirement.[144] Though, as we have also seen, such a justification is based on the mistaken belief that a 'duty' of care is a *real* duty rather than a mere label for an element of the negligence enquiry. The confusion has led Nolan to state that the 'duty' label is nothing more than a 'confusing and inappropriate ... misnomer.'[145] Secondly, is the reluctance among courts to discard well-established authority. In particular, much like the judges in

---

[140] ibid 425–26.

[141] JC Smith, 'The Mystery of Duty' in L Klar (ed), *Studies in Canadian Tort Law* (Butterworths, 1977) 33.

[142] See (n 50).

[143] There have been, however, a number of changes to the remoteness enquiry, which arguably undo the effect of *The Wagon Mound (No 1)*. In particular, the eggshell-skull rule (that the defendant is responsible for the full extent of a plaintiff's injury, even though it was unforeseeable due to some unusual sensitivity of the plaintiff) and unusual value rule (that a defendant is responsible for negligently caused damage, even where its degree is unforeseeably high, such as dropping a Ming vase that appeared to be a fake, or running over a millionaire in the belief they were a vagrant) potentially make a defendant liable for damages beyond those that were reasonably foreseeable. For criticism of the rules, see: Stevens (n 91) 155–58; A Beever, *Rediscovering the Law of Negligence* (Hart, 2007) 162–66. For defences of the rules, see: Williams (n 63) 193–98. Stauch (n 63) 207–214. See also the discussions in RWM Dias, 'Remoteness of Liability and Legal Policy' (1962) 20 CLJ 178, 186; Smith, 'Clarification of Duty—Remoteness Probems through a New Physiology of Negligence: Economic Loss, a Test Case' (n 53) 240, 243; Smith, 'The Mystery of Duty' (n 141) 33-34; Gibson (n 24) 208–209; Wilson and Slade (n 90) 469.

[144] See Section V(A).

[145] Nolan, 'Deconstructing the Duty of Care' (n 43) 563. See also Gibson (n 24) 191; Fleming and Morison (n 101) 70–71.

Palsgraf and *Bourhill* were reluctant to overrule the well-established *Re Polemis*, and so brought factual duty into existence in the first place, modern judges seem similarly reluctant to discard the now well-established enquiry. Although such reluctance could be justified on the grounds that 'it would also be foolish and mischievous [to discard such a well-established rule], because [to do so] would inflict much too great a shock on ingrained habits of legal thought',[146] as Gibson notes, 'fallacious or superfluous concepts must not be preserved in the law simply because they provide members of the legal profession with mementoes of their youth'.[147] It seems, then, that this is just another one of those times, in the long history of the common law, where the rationale for a case has been decisively rejected, yet the rule it created has survived.

VI. Why Does it Matter?

Even if the preceding argument is accepted in its entirety, one might still wonder, 'does it *really* matter'? Just because the same conclusion can be reached via two different paths does not mean that one of the paths is necessarily 'superfluous' and should be removed.[148] According to Lord Steyn in *Rees v Darlington Memorial Hospital NHS Trust*,[149] for example, provided that the same result is achieved, the 'the difference in method is not of great importance.'[150] One may even go so far as to argue that the 'right' result is more likely to be reached when two paths lead there rather than just the one. Whilst this might be an attractive argument, there are nevertheless a number of benefits to removing factual duty from the negligence enquiry and confining the duty stage to notional duty questions only. First, it would prevent the unhelpful confusion between notional and factual issues.[151] This would promote greater transparency in judicial reasoning, as decisions based on notional considerations would need to expressly articulate why those notional considerations were relevant and warranted a particular conclusion, rather than, as is often believed to be the case,[152] being disguised as factual issues. Secondly,

---

[146] Winfield (n 3) 58.

[147] Gibson (n 24) 215.

[148] See, eg, James (n 119) 784–85. Though, compare the position in the United States, where the allocation of an issue to duty or remoteness will determine whether it is an issue for the judge or an issue for the jury: Cardi, 'Purging Foreseeability' (n 53) 794–804.

[149] [2004] 1 AC 309 (HL) [30].

[150] ibid [30]. Lord Steyn was, in fact, talking about the distinction between duty of care and actionable damage, but the point remains. See also the comments of Sir Murray Stuart-Smith in *Vellino v CC of Greater Manchester* [2002] 1 WLR 218 (CA) [62].

[151] See also the discussion in Nolan, 'Deconstructing the Duty of Care' (n 43) 579–81.

[152] It has been suggested that *Bourhill*, for example, was a notional decision disguised as a factual decision: '[the] finding that the claimant was unforeseeable masked [notional] concerns which militated against imposing a duty of care. Was the decision that Mrs Bourhill was owed no duty of care really attributable to the fact that she was not a reasonably foreseeable victim of John Young's negligent

determining when a duty of care does or does not exist would be greatly simplified, as there would no longer be a need to formulate tests that accommodate both
factual and notional considerations.[153] Thirdly, the negligence enquiry would be
more coherent, as each stage of the enquiry would deal with a discrete issue: duty
would deal with whether the situation ought to be subject to the laws of negligence, the fault stage would deal with the quality of the defendant's behaviour,
causation would deal with whether the harm was attributable, as a matter of fact,
to the defendant's conduct, and remoteness would deal with whether the defendant had been careless in relation to the risk that materialised. Until the duty stage is
confined to notional questions only, the law will continue to be indecisive, inconsistent, and unpredictable.[154]

VII. Conclusion

As well as encouraging courts to think about duty in terms of general principles, Lord Atkin's neighbour principle also encouraged academics to think about
what the duty enquiry was really doing. Although early commentary dismissed
the duty concept as little more than a 'fifth wheel on the coach', closer analysis
of the concept itself, rather than just Lord Atkin's foreseeability-based formula,
soon revealed that it in fact performed a dual function, involving both factual and
notional elements. The focus of the factual duty enquiry is, like Lord Atkin's neighbour dictum, on whether harm to the claimant was a foreseeable consequence of
the defendant's carelessness, whilst the focus of the notional enquiry is on whether
the law of negligence ought to apply to the broad situation to which the particular facts belong. Whilst the notional aspect of the duty enquiry is 'invaluable', the
factual aspect would appear to be entirely unnecessary, or, as Buckland would say,
a 'fifth wheel on the coach'. In particular, it will necessarily be present where the
other elements of the negligence enquiry have been satisfied, and will only ever be
absent where either the fault or remoteness elements are absent also. *Palsgraf* and
Bourhill, however, argued that, even if the same result could be achieved at the
remoteness stage, factual duty is nevertheless required, as harming an unforeseeable plaintiff does not constitute a 'wrong', and the wrong in the law of negligence

---

driving? There seems little doubt that the reason consideration which motivated the House of Lords
was the fact that the damage suffered by the claimant was shock-induced' (Lunney and Oliphant (n 43)
134). See also: Richard Kidner, 'Resiling From the Anns Principle: The Variable Nature of Proximity in
Negligence' (1987) 7 LS 319, 325; Jenny Steele, 'Scepticism and the Law of Negligence' (1993) 52 CLJ
437, 453; RFV Heuston, 'Donoghue v Stevenson in Retrospect' (1957) 20 MLR 1, 17; Fleming, 'Remoteness and Duty: The Control Devices in Liability for Negligence' (n 86) 491–93; Beever, *Rediscovering
the Law of Negligence* (n 143) 408.

[153] See also: Nolan, 'Deconstructing the Duty of Care' (n 43) 582–85.

[154] Comments to this effect are also made in Smith, 'Clarification of Duty—Remoteness Probems
through a New Physiology of Negligence: Economic Loss, a Test Case' (n 53) 231.

is the breach of a duty of care, not the breach of a duty of care causing damage that is not too remote. However, this argument both relied on a problematic understanding of the meaning of 'wrong', as well as required arbitrary and problematic distinctions between the various consequences of the defendant's careless behaviour to be drawn. Despite these problems, factual duty remains an orthodox part of the duty enquiry, most likely for the same reason it entered the law in the first place; a reluctance to overrule existing authority. Whilst such reluctance might be understandable prior to the Practice Statement of 1966, the presence of factual duty today is actively harmful, and should be removed from the negligence enquiry. The duty enquiry, then, is best understood as a purely notional question, which will now be further examined in chapters five and six.

5

Notional Duty I: General Principles

[T]he more general issue of how far the principles of liability for negligence should be extended is a familiar one, and one with which this Court and others have repeatedly grappled since Lord Atkin enunciated the negligence principle in *McAlister (Donoghue) v Stevenson*, almost 70 years ago. That case introduced the principle that a person could be held liable only for reasonably foreseeable harm. But it also anticipated that not all reasonably foreseeable harm might be caught. This posed the issue with which courts still struggle today: to what situations does the law of negligence extend?

McLachlin CJC and Major J in *Cooper v Hobart* (2001) 206 DLR (4th) 193 [21].

[T]he court must ask in every case: Is this a situation in which the law requires, or is going now to require, the defendant to exercise care in the interests of the plaintiff, or is it a situation in which the defendant may unreasonably create risks for the plaintiff with impunity?

Morison W, 'Duty of Care and Standard of Care' (1953) 1 Sydney Law Review 69, 70.

I. Introduction

Whether or not we accept that factual duty is superfluous, there can be little doubt that the bulk of duty jurisprudence relates to the notional duty enquiry, which, as we have seen, determines whether the law of negligence applies to the 'situation' to which the facts of the case belong. Absent a notional duty, the defendant may carelessly cause harm to the claimant with impunity. Ultimately, the existence of a notional duty is a 'normative'[1] question, and the issue for the court is whether the law of negligence *ought* to apply to the particular situation. Notional duty explains why, for example, a defendant is generally legally responsible for carelessly causing the claimant to suffer physical injury or property damage, but is not, without more, legally responsible for carelessly failing to provide the claimant with a benefit (that is, causing harm through an omission), or carelessly causing harm

---

[1] Christian Witting, 'Duty of Care: An Analytical Approach' (2005) 25 OJLS 33, 37; David Howarth, 'Duty of Care' in K Oliphant (ed), *Common Law Series: The Law of Tort*, 3rd edn (LexisNexis, 2015) 12.10; P Cane, 'Another Failed Sterilisation' (2004) 120 LQR 189, 192.

that is purely economic in nature. As Lord Rodger explained in *D v East Berkshire Community Health NHS Trust*[2]

> [T]he world is full of harm for which the law furnishes no remedy. For instance, a trader owes no duty of care to avoid injuring his rivals by destroying their long-established businesses. If he does so and, as a result, one of his competitors descends into a clinical depression and his family are reduced to penury, in the eyes of the law they suffer no wrong and the law will provide no redress … A young man whose fiancée deserts him for his best friend may become clinically depressed as a result, but in the circumstances the fiancée owes him no duty of care to avoid causing this suffering … The same goes for a middle-aged woman whose husband runs off with a younger woman … However badly one of them may have treated the other, the law does not get involved in awarding damages.[3]

Identifying which situations do and do not attract a notional duty is, of course, relatively straightforward; one need only consult a tort law textbook to see whether the situation is subject to a notional duty or not. In this chapter, however, we are not so much interested in identifying the exact black letter boundaries of the law of negligence, as in what properties those determinations have, and the general method by which those boundaries are determined. In particular, we will examine the 'categorical' nature of notional duty, the relevance of assumptions of responsibility to the notional duty enquiry, and a proposed method for determining notional duty categories that does not depend on a general test at all.

II. The 'Categorical' Nature of Notional Duty

Aside from their being normative in nature, perhaps the other principal feature of notional duty determinations is that, save for those that depend on an assumption of responsibility,[4] they relate to 'situations', or 'categories of case'.[5] In particular, notional duty determinations, unlike factual duty determinations, 'transcend the particular dispute'[6] to establish a rule that applies to a broad type of situation, rather than just being 'tickets good only for a single ride'.[7] It is this generality that gives notional duty decisions their precedential value. As Nolan explains:

> [N]otional duty determinations are binding precedents, so that through decisions on duty appellate courts can exercise effective control over the boundaries of negligence

---

[2] [2005] 2 AC 373 (HL).
[3] ibid 410.
[4] See Section III below.
[5] Nothing seems to turn on the distinction between the two terms, and so they will be used interchangeably.
[6] EW Peel and J Goudkamp, *Winfield and Jolowicz on Tort*, 19th edn (Sweet & Maxwell, 2014) 5–10.
[7] W Jonathan Cardi and Michael D Green, 'Duty Wars' (2007) SCalLRev 671, 732.

liability and provide litigants, trial lawyers and lower court judges with clear guidance as to where those boundaries lie.[8]

In *Hill v Chief Constable of West Yorkshire*,[9] for example, the plaintiff, acting on behalf of her daughter's estate, sued the police for their failure to apprehend the Yorkshire Ripper before he murdered her daughter. The question for the court was not simply 'whether *the* defendant owed *the* plaintiff a duty of care', but whether the general *situation* could give rise to a claim in negligence; in particular:

> [W]hether the individual members of a police force, in the course of carrying out their functions of controlling and keeping down the incidence of crime, owe a duty of care to individual members of the public who may suffer injury to person or property through the activities of criminals ...[10]

Similarly, in *White v Jones*,[11] the plaintiffs, who were intended beneficiaries under a will, sued the testator's solicitor for carelessly failing to include them in the will prior to the testator's death. Again, the relevant question was not 'whether *the* defendant owed *the* plaintiffs a duty of care', but whether, in principle, 'solicitors are liable to the intended beneficiaries who, as a result of their negligence, have failed to receive a benefit which the testator intended they receive'.[12]

By 'transcending' the particular facts of the case, categorical determinations provide clear guidance to future courts when faced with similar fact scenarios. In particular, future courts do not need to ask 'was the harm foreseeable?' or 'was there sufficient proximity?' but simply, 'do the facts of the case come within an existing notional duty situation?'

The categorical nature of notional duty undoubtedly bears a strong resemblance to the pockets approach to duty. Indeed, when courts speak of duty as relating to different 'categories of cases,' it is often not clear whether they are endorsing the pockets approach or the categorical nature of duty determinations.[13] However, it is important to realise that they are nevertheless separate ideas; the categorical nature of notional duty is simply a reference to how notional duty determinations should be *expressed*, whilst the pockets approach, like the two and three stage tests, refers to a particular *method* by which the court can determine whether a notional duty situation should or should not be subject to the laws of negligence. The categorical nature of notional duty determinations is therefore not subject to

---

[8] D Nolan, 'Deconstructing the Duty of Care' (2013) 129 LQR 559, 568. See also 'comment j: The proper role for foreseeability' in section 7 of the *Restatement (Third) of Torts: Liability for Emotional and Physical Harm*: 'Determinations of no duty are categorical while foreseeability cannot be determined on a categorical basis. Foreseeability necessarily depends on the specific facts of the case and hence is appropriately addressed as part of the negligence determination.'

[9] [1989] AC 53 (HL).

[10] ibid 59B (Lord Keith).

[11] [1995] 2 AC 207 (HL).

[12] ibid 252 (Lord Goff).

[13] See, eg, *Cooper v Hobart* (2001) 206 DLR (4th) 193 [41] (McLachlin CJC and Major J); *Design Services Ltd v Canada* (2008) 293 DLR (4th) 437 [28] (Rothstein J); *Perre v Apand Pty Ltd* (1999) 198 CLR 180, 217 (McHugh J).

the objections that have been made to the pockets approach; in particular, unlike the pockets approach, the categorical nature of notional duty does not entail a rejection of general duty tests, nor does it have anything to say about how novel fact-scenarios are determined. Despite their similarity, then, the categorical nature of notional duty should *not* be equated with nor seen as an endorsement of the pockets approach, nor should it be seen as subject to the same objections. Accordingly, whether one supports the pockets approach to duty or not, duty determinations, howsoever resolved, should be expressed categorically.

Despite the importance of expressing notional duty determinations categorically, or as relating to certain situations, this aspect of the duty enquiry is underexplored. In this section we will therefore examine the idea of notional duty 'situations' and 'categories' further.

A. Notional Duty Situations are both Inclusionary and Exclusionary

It is commonly claimed that the role of notional duty is to identify the situations that should *not* be subjected to the laws of negligence rather than the situations that *should*; in other words, that notional duty is exclusionary in nature. According to Lord Goff in *Smith v Littlewoods Organisation Ltd*,[14] for example:

> [W]e have nowadays to appreciate that the broad general principle of liability for foreseeable damage is so widely applicable that the function of the duty of care is not so much to identify cases where liability is imposed as to identify those where it is not.[15]

Similarly, both Stevens and Ibbetson have described the role of notional duty under the present law as to identify the islands of non-liability within an ocean of liability;[16] again the implication being that notional duty determinations identify the situations where liability should *not* exist only. On this understanding, *all* situations are inclusionary, unless they are explicitly identified as exclusionary. It is in this sense that notional duty is often referred to as a 'control device'; in particular, working from the assumption that *all* carelessly caused harm gives rise to liability, notional duty, by identifying the various situations in which carelessly caused harm does not give rise to liability, 'controls' the boundaries of liability for negligence and so 'prevent[s] the incidence of liability from getting out of hand'.[17] The 'control device' view of notional duty is usually contrasted to the 'rights-based'

---

[14] [1987] AC 241 (HL).

[15] ibid 280 (Lord Goff).

[16] DJ Ibbetson, *A Historical Introduction to the Law of Obligations* (OUP, 1999) 192–93; R Stevens, *Torts and Rights* (OUP, 2007) 21.

[17] Prue Vines, Peter Hanford and Carol Harlow, 'Duty of Care' in Carolyn Sappideen and Prue Vines (eds), *Fleming's The Law of Torts*, 10th edn (Thomson Reuters (Professional) Australia Limited, 2011) 151–52. See also JG Fleming, 'Remoteness and Duty: The Control Devices in Liability for Negligence' (1953) 31 Can Bar Rev 471, 473–74.

view of notional duty, whereby all situations are *ex*clusionary, unless there is some good reason why they should be *in*clusionary.[18]

However, the claim that notional duty is about identifying no-liability situations only, whilst conceivable in theory, does not seem to reflect what occurs in practice. In particular, when a court is faced with a notional duty problem, although a determination that the situation does *not* give rise to a notional duty clearly creates an *exclusionary* situation, a determination that the situation *does* give rise to a notional duty clearly equally creates an *inclusionary* situation.[19] If it were otherwise, and notional duty determinations were exclusionary only, then only exclusionary determinations would create precedent, whilst inclusionary determinations would merely represent a drop in the abyss of the ocean of liability, and this simply not does not describe the precedential value of pro-duty determinations.[20]

Similarly, problematic is the assumption that the starting point in the law of negligence is that *all* carelessly caused harm is compensable (that is, that there is an ocean of liability), which provides the foundation for the claim that notional duty is exclusionary in nature. Again, whilst such a position seems conceivable in theory, there seems to be little case law to support it. Indeed, it is almost impossible to find a decision where the existence of a notional duty was based on the relevant starting point; that is, in the absence of *any* arguments one way or the other, the existence of a notional duty was determined *solely* on the basis that harm was suffered by the claimant.

Yet, notional duty is more than an 'uncultivated wilderness'[21] of discrete inclusionary and exclusionary situations. On the contrary, notional duty is best understood as consisting of a small number of broad inclusionary and exclusionary situations that are subject to a larger number of narrow exclusionary and inclusionary situations.[22] Carelessly caused physical injury, for example, gives rise to a broad inclusionary situation. Though, this is subject to a number of narrow exclusionary situations, including where the physical injury occurs in the course of armed conflict,[23] or as a result of the carelessness of the claimant's mother whilst

---

[18] See, eg, EJ Weinrib, 'The Disintegration of Duty' in M Stuart Madden (ed), *Exploring Tort Law* (Cambridge University Press, 2005) 158: 'Being harmed is merely a fact—that he or she is now less advantageously situated than before—that in itself has no correlative normative significance ... Harm matters only inasmuch as it stands under a right, for only when the duty breached by the defendant is correlative to the plaintiff's right do the parties occupy correlative normative positions. Accordingly, if the loss of which the plaintiff is complaining is not the subject matter of a right ... then the defendant is not under a duty of care to the plaintiff. In the old language of the law, harm is then mere *damnum absque injuria.*' See also A Beever, *Rediscovering the Law of Negligence* (Hart, 2007) 10.

[19] Though note (n 35).

[20] A clear example of such an inclusionary situation is *White v Jones* [1995] 2 AC 20 (HL).

[21] 'The Duty of Care Towards One's Neighbour' (1883) 18 LJ 618, 619.

[22] The same point is made in Nolan (n 8) fn 32.

[23] See, eg, *Shaw Savilll & Albion Co Ltd v The Commonwealth* (1940) 66 CLR 344, 361–62; *Mulcahy v Ministry of Defence* [1996] QB 732 (CA); *Smith v Ministry of Defence* [2014] 1 AC 52 (HL). Note that in Australia the immunity does not extend to injuries sustained in peacetime accidents: *Groves v The Commonwealth* (1982) 165 CLR 113.

the claimant was in utero.[24] Carelessly caused property damage also gives rise to a broad inclusionary situation,[25] as does carelessly caused psychiatric injury,[26] the latter of which is subject to an exclusion where the claimant's injury is a result of the tortfeasor injuring themselves,[27] and, at least in the UK, a *partial* exclusion where the claimant was a 'secondary victim'.[28] Carelessly caused pure economic loss, however, gives rise to a broad *exclusionary* situation, which is subject to a number of narrow *inclusionary* situations, including where the purely economic loss resulted from a solicitor's failure to include the claimant as a beneficiary in a will,[29] a damaging reference letter,[30] and, in Canada at least, the purchase of a defective building.[31] Damage that is the result of careless omissions, which includes the failure to prevent harm caused by third parties,[32] also gives rise to a broad exclusionary situation; again, one that it subject to narrower inclusionary situations, including, *inter alia*, certain omissions of prisons[33] and emergency services.[34] These are, of course, only a small number of the many exceptions, some narrower than others, that exist to the main broad inclusionary and exclusionary situations. It is therefore perhaps better to conceive of the law of negligence as consisting of a small number of seas (rather than oceans), some of liability, others of non-liability, subject to a number of islets (rather than islands) of non-liability or liability depending on the nature sea. Admittedly, it is not as simple, nor as catchy, as the ocean/island analogy, but it nevertheless seems to be a much more accurate, and helpful, representation of the law.[35] It is important to note that

---

[24] See, eg, *Dobson v Dobson* [1999] 2 SCR 753, Congenital Disabilities (Civil Liability) Act 1976, s 1(1). A duty will be imposed, however, in both in Australia and the UK, where the negligence is in relation to the driving of a motor vehicle; the justification being that the mother would be indemnified by compulsory insurance: *Lynch v Lynch (by her tutor Lynch)* (1991) NSWLR 411 (CA); Congenital Disabilities (Civil Liability) Act 1976, s 2. As to the adequacy of this reasoning, see I Malkin, 'A Mother's Duty of Care to her Foetus While Driving: A Comment on Dobson v Dobson (and Lynch v Lynch)' (2001) 9 TLJ 109.

[25] Arguably there is an exclusionary exception where the damage was caused by the conduct of a third party, but this 'exception' is better understood as resulting from an omission, and so an exclusionary situation to begin with.

[26] See, eg, *Page v Smith* [1996] 1 AC 155 (HL); *Tame v New South Wales, Annetts v Australian Stations Pty Ltd* (2002) 211 CLR 317.

[27] *Greatorex v Greatorex* [2000] 1 WLR 1970 (CA), *Homsi v Homsi* [2016] VSC 354.

[28] *Alcock v Chief Constable of South Yorkshire* [1992] AC 310 (HL). The exclusion is 'partial' because secondary victims can nevertheless recover where additional criteria are met.

[29] See, eg, *White v Jones* [1995] 2 AC 20 (HL), *Hill v Van Erp* (1997) 188 CLR 159.

[30] See, eg, *Spring v Guardian Assurance plc* [1995] 2 AC 296 (HL).

[31] See, eg, *Winnipeg Condominium Corp No 36 v Bird Construction Co* (1995) 121 DLR (4th) 193.

[32] So as to avoid overlap between the broad inclusionary categories, carelessly 'caused' physical injury, property damage, and psychiatric injury means harm that was *not* the result of an omission. Although pure economic loss and omissions can also overlap, as both are broad exclusionary situations, narrow situations that fall into both will need to be justified as inclusionary in any event; such situations therefore seem to be able to be dealt with in either category without difficulty.

[33] See, eg, *Home Office v Dorset Yacht Co Ltd* [1970] AC 1004 (HL).

[34] See, eg, *Kent v Griffiths (No3)* [2001] QB 36 (CA).

[35] It might be objected that, on this understanding, pro-duty decisions in seas of liability *do* represent little more than drops rather than recognising specific inclusionary situations. Though this

assumptions of responsibility also provide an important basis for overcoming exclusionary situations (mostly to broad exclusionary situations, but arguably also to the narrower exceptional exclusionary situations), and so are discussed further in Section III below.

B. The 'Relationship' and 'Interest' Views of Notional Duty

It has thus far been suggested that the categorical nature of notional duty relates to particular 'situations'. The term 'situation' is used as it has the benefit of allowing a broad range of circumstances to be taken into account when explaining the precise limits of notional duty determinations. There are, however, two competing views that argue that notional duty determinations can, in fact, be explained in much narrower terms: the 'relationship view' of notional duty, which claims that notional duty situations, in fact, relate to different categories of 'relationships', and the 'interest view' of notional duty, which claims that they, in fact, relate to a variety of protected 'interests'.

According to the relationship view, notional duty is about identifying which relationships ought to be subject to the laws of negligence. Examples of such relationships are manufacturer and consumer, teacher and student, occupier and entrant, driver and passenger/other road user, doctor and patient, police and prisoner, employer and employee, solicitor and client, etc. The relationship view of notional duty has attracted considerable support. According to Fleming, for example, 'everyone agrees that a duty must arise out of some "relation" ... between the parties',[36] whilst according to Hepple, notional duty concerns 'the question of which relationships ought to be protected [by the law of negligence]'.[37] Smillie, too, has suggested that the notional duty enquiry is simply about 'the categories of relationships which attract a duty of care'.[38] The relationship view of notional duty has been similarly influential in the courts, with both the High Court

does indeed often appear to be the case. See, eg, the opinion of Lord Toulson in *Michael v The Chief Constable of South Wales Police* [2015] AC 1732, concerning whether there can be a notional duty in relation to individual members of the public who suffer personal injury through the activities of criminals the police have failed to apprehend. Lord Toulson held, at [116], 'The question is ... not whether the police should have a special immunity, but whether an exception should be made to the ordinary application of common law principles [ie that liability does not ordinarily exist in relation to omissions] which would cover the facts of the present case.' In other words, the issue was whether an *exception* to the general exclusionary rule should be made rather than whether the particular situation ought to be inclusionary in the first place. A similar position appears to exist in relation to the broad inclusionary situations, where courts are generally reluctant to recognise exceptions. In any event, it is not clear why a decision that confirms a narrow situation *is* a drop in the ocean could not create precedent.

[36] JG Fleming, *The Law of Torts*, 9th edn (Law Book Co, 1998) 151. Though his use of scare quotes, and his subsequent qualification 'but what that relation is no one has ever succeeded in capturing a precise formula', would suggest that he did not endorse the view himself.
[37] B Hepple, 'Negligence: The Search for Coherence' (1997) 50 CLP 69, 81.
[38] JA Smillie, 'Principle, Policy and Negligence' (1984) 11 NZULR 111, 111.

of Australia[39] and Supreme Court of Canada[40] having repeatedly suggested that the existence of a duty depends on the category of relationship in question. Arguably, the relationship view of notional duty is even implicit in Lord Atkin's neighbour dictum, which was based on the idea that 'in English law there must be, and is, some general conception of *relations* giving rise to a duty of care, of which the particular cases found in the books are but instances'.[41]

Despite its popularity, however, the relationship view of notional duty is highly problematic. Whilst it is indeed true that certain relationships are *usually* the subject of a duty of care, it is equally true that the category of relationship is *not* the reason that the duty arises. This is evident for two reasons. First, the same relationship can give rise to a duty in one situation and not another. In *Spartan Steel & Alloys Ltd v Martin & Co (Contractors) Ltd,*[42] for example, the defendant carelessly cut off the electricity supply to the plaintiff's factory. As a result, the plaintiff suffered both purely economic loss and property damage. Despite the 'relationship' between the plaintiff and defendant being identical in relation to both kinds of damage, the court held that the defendant owed a duty in respect of the property damage only. Under the relationship view, the result cannot be explained. A second problem with the relationship view of notional duty is that it stretches the term 'relationship' beyond all meaning. As Howarth notes:

> Most defendants have had no relationship at all with their claimants. The driver of a car who carelessly runs down a pedestrian is hardly likely to have met the pedestrian on a previous occasion, and is certainly not allowed to escape liability by saying, 'Never seen him before in my life'. To describe the act of hitting someone as a 'relationship' is simply perverse. The usual explanation is that the parties are 'fellow road users'. But that is a relationship hardly different from 'fellow inhabitant of the country' or even 'fellow human being'…
>
> The relational view of negligence claims that the reason we have a duty of care is some relationship, or relation, that we have with our potential victims. The objection to

---

[39] *Jaensch v Coffey* (1984) 155 CLR 549, 578 (Deane J); *Crimmins v Stevedoring Industry Finance Committee* (1999) 200 CLR 1 [61] (McHugh J); *Modbury Triangle Shopping Centre Pty Ltd v Anzil* (2000) 205 CLR 254 [13] (Gleeson CJ); *Sullivan v Moody* (2001) 207 CLR 562 [47] (Gleeson CJ, Gaudon, McHugh, Hayne and Callinan JJ); *Vairy v Wyong Shire Council* [2005] 223 CLR 422 [27] (McHugh J), 443 (Gummow J); *Kuhl v Zurich Financial Services Australia Ltd* (2011) 243 CLR 361 [22] (French CJ and Gummow J)

[40] *Cooper v Hobart* (2001) 206 DLR (4th) 193 [31]–[32] (McLachlin CJC and Major J); *Odhavji Estate v Woodhouse* (2003) 233 DLR (4th) 193 [47] (Iacobucci J); *Hill v Hamilton-Wentworth Regional Police Services Board* (2007) 285 DLR (4th) 620 [21] (McLachlin CJC).

[41] *Donoghue v Stevenson* [1932] AC 562 (HL), 580 (Lord Atkin) (emphasis added). See also the comments in Norman A Katter, *Duty of Care in Australia* (LBC Information Services 1999) 29: 'The conclusion which may be drawn at this point is that Lord Atkin considers the underlying principle of general application giving rise to a duty if care is based on the relationship between the parties.' Though, as we saw in ch 3, it could be argued that Lord Atkin's comments were confined to 'relationships' in the factual duty sense only.

[42] [1973] QB 27 (CA), 37 ('*Spartan Steel*').

that view is that it entails either a perverse or a superfluous view of what counts as a relationship.[43]

The claim that the existence of a notional duty depends on the particular category of 'relationship' in question is therefore unconvincing.

Perhaps in light of the difficulties with the relationship view of notional duty, a second view emerged which claimed that the focus of notional duty is to determine which 'interests,' or 'kinds of harm,'[44] are worthy of protection.[45] So, for example, the interest in personal property and bodily safety are interests the law deems should be protected, and so are subject to a notional duty, whereas the interest in not suffering purely economic loss and the interest in receiving a benefit (that is, not suffering loss through an omission) are interests the law deems should not be protected, and so are not subject to a notional duty.[46] The interest view of notional duty is attractive, as it not only appears to explain many of the cases, including *Spartan Steel*, but it also provides an understanding of the law of negligence that is much more in line with many of the nominate torts, which are also often understood as protecting against the invasion of specified interests.[47] The interest view of notional duty has therefore gained considerable support. Fleming, for example, has argued that the 'Recognition of a duty of care is the outcome of a value judgment that the plaintiff's *interest*, which has been invaded, is deemed worthy of legal protection against negligent interference by conduct of the kind alleged against the defendant.'[48] Millner has also argued that the notional duty enquiry 'is to do with the range of interests which the law sees fit to protect against

---

[43] David Howarth, 'Many Duties of Care—Or A Duty of Care? Notes from the Underground' (2006) 26 OJLS 449, 464. See also David Howarth, 'Duty of Care' in Ken Oliphant (ed), *The Law of Tort*, 2nd edn (LexisNexis Butterworths, 2007) 12.36, where Howarth describes the use of the term 'relationship' in this sense as 'apt to lead to enormous artificiality, if not absurdity ... [and] doing violence to the English language.' Arguably even more 'absurd' is that, whilst a driver and pedestrian *are* in a 'relationship', a mother and her unborn child are *not* in a 'relationship': see (n 24).

[44] 'Interests' and 'kinds of harm' are typically equated. See, eg, Nolan (n 8) 583, and Gerhard Wagner, 'Comparative Tort Law' in Mathias Reimann and Reinhard Zimmermann (eds), *The Oxford Handbook of Comparative Law* (OUP, 2008) 1013–15.

[45] The interest view of *notional* duty should not be conflated with the interest view of *factual* duty (the 'interest theory'), explored in ch 4, as they ask entirely different questions: the former asks whether the type of interest *ought* to be protected, the latter asks whether the particular interest was *foreseeably* infringed.

[46] For examples of other non-protected interests, see: MA Millner, *Negligence in Modern Law* (Butterworths, 1967) 35–45; F James, 'Scope of Duty in Negligence Cases' (1952) 47 NwULRev 778, 786–87; 789–90; 798.

[47] Defamation, for example, protects one's interest in reputation, whilst private nuisance protects one's interest in the use and enjoyment of their land. See also, Fleming, 'Remoteness and Duty: The Control Devices in Liability for Negligence' (n 17) 473–74; AM Dugdale, M Simpson and MA Jones, *Clerk & Lindsell on Torts*, 21st edn (Sweet & Maxwell, 2014) 1–25 et seq. *cf* R Stevens, 'Rights and Other Things' in D; Nolan and A Robertson (eds), *Rights and Private Law* (Hart, 2012) 133–38.

[48] Fleming, 'Remoteness and Duty: The Control Devices in Liability for Negligence' (n 17) 486 (emphasis added). See also JG Fleming, 'The Action Per Quod Servitum Amisit' (1952) 26 ALJ 122, 127: '[T]he central problem of [duty is] whether the plaintiff's interest is worthy of legal protection ...'

negligent violation.'[49] The interest view of duty has also been influential in the courts.[50] As Nolan explains:

> Traditionally, the core of the notional duty question has been the issue of protected interests: which human interests are given general protection by the law of negligence, which limited protection, and which no protection at all. This issue is accommodated within the duty framework by formulating the duty in terms of the nature of the interest invaded, and so considering the existence of a duty separately in respect of each kind of damage suffered by the claimant. It follows that a finding that the defendant owed the claimant a duty of care in respect of one kind of damage does not entail that there was a duty in respect of a different kind of damage, which explains why in the *Spartan Steel* case the claimant company was unable to recover for its pure economic loss, even though the defendants' negligence also caused it actionable property damage.[51]

Like the relationship view of duty, however, the interest view is not unproblematic, and frequently has difficulty explaining the law. The interest in bodily safety, for example, whilst protected against most negligent invasions, is *not*, as we saw above, protected where the invasion occurs in the course of armed conflict,[52] or by the carelessness of the claimant's mother whilst the claimant was in utero.[53] Similarly, whilst there is no general protection against suffering purely economic loss, protection *is* afforded where the loss resulted from a negligently prepared employment reference letter,[54] or where it is the result of a solicitor's failure to include an intended beneficiary in a will.[55] The same interest is therefore protected against negligent interference in some situations but not others. Indeed, the interest view of duty only seems to be able to account for the existence or absence of a notional duty in the *broad* inclusionary and exclusionary situations, but is unable to account for the exclusionary and inclusionary exceptions; in other words, it explains the seas (or, as Nolan says, the 'core' of the notional duty question[56]), but not the islets. Accordingly, the claim that notional duty is about identifying which interests ought to be protected, whilst accurate in broad terms, fails to (and indeed is *unable* to) account for any of the narrow exceptional situations, as in such cases, the interest is simply not the focus of the analysis. Again, it is therefore unconvincing as an explanation of what the notional duty 'situations' represent.

Accordingly, the wide variety of circumstances that are taken into account in notional duty determinations simply cannot be explained in terms of protected 'relationships' or 'interests', or any other similarly narrow concept *alone*. On the contrary, notional duty determinations need to be defined across a number of

---

[49] Millner (n 46) 27.
[50] See, eg, *Tame v New South Wales; Annetts v Australian Stations Pty Limited* (2002) 211 CLR 317, 374–75 (Kirby J); *Harriton v Stephens* (2006) 226 CLR 52, 118 (Crennan J).
[51] Nolan (n 8) 569–70 (footnotes omitted).
[52] See (n 23).
[53] See (n 24).
[54] *Spring v Guardian Assurance plc* [1995] 2 AC 296 (HL).
[55] *White v Jones* [1995] 2 AC 207 (HL).
[56] See (n 51).

dimensions, including the kind of damage suffered by the claimant[57] (that is, was the harm physical, psychiatric, or purely economic?), *and* the way the harm occurred (that is, was it a direct consequence of the defendant's conduct or merely a consequence of their failure to act or prevent the harm?), *and*, potentially, the nature of the relationship between the parties[58] (that is, was the defendant a judicial figure, barrister, or public authority, or was the claimant an unborn child or rescuer?). The position is almost perfectly encapsulated by Gageler J in *Brookfield Multiplex Ltd v Owners Corporation Strata Plan 61288*:[59]

> A duty of care at common law is a duty of a specified person, or a person within a specified class, to exercise reasonable care within a specified area of responsibility to avoid specified loss to another specified person, or to a person within another specified class.

Only a term as broad as 'situation' can possibly take into account such a variety of aspects and allow the existing law to be explained.

C. The Level of Generality of the Notional Duty Situation

Even where notional duty situations are defined in terms of the kind of damage, the way it occurred, and the status of the relationship between the parties, there still remains the problem of the level of generality with which the situation should be formulated. Consider, for example, a publican who fails to prevent an intoxicated patron from leaving the local tavern, and the patron is killed in a motor vehicle accident, as a result of their intoxication, shortly thereafter. Is the issue for the court whether *anyone* can be legally responsible for failing to prevent another from injuring themselves as a result of their own inebriation, or something narrower, such as whether a *publican* can be legally responsible for failing to prevent an intoxicated patron injuring themselves as a result of their own inebriation?[60] Similarly, where a visitor suffers physical injury after tripping on the uneven concrete surface of a driveway whilst visiting a garage sale,[61] is the issue for the court whether a notional duty ought to exist in relation to physical injury caused to a visitor by reason of

---

[57] Or, alternatively, the relevant 'interest' of the claimant.

[58] Arguably the relevant factor is the *status of one of the parties* (ie that the defendant is a judge, barrister, or mother) rather than the *relationship between the parties*, but given that the status is only significant within particular relationships (ie the status of a barrister is only important when the claimant is a client, judicial status is only important when the claimant is a party to proceedings, and the status of a mother is only important when the claimant is the mother's unborn child), the later view seems to be the better one.

[59] (2014) 254 CLR 185 [169].

[60] See *CAL No 14 Pty Ltd v Motor Accidents Insurance Board* (2009) 239 CLR 390. Both situations essentially concern whether an inclusionary exception ought to be made to the general exclusionary nature of harm caused by omissions.

[61] See *Neindorf v Junkovic* (2005) 222 ALR 631. As above, both situations concern whether an inclusionary exception ought to be made to the general exclusionary nature of harm caused by omissions.

the state of the occupier's *driveway*, or whether a notional duty ought to exist in relation to physical injury caused to a visitor by reason of the state of the occupier's *property in general*? Despite the 'extraordinary malleability'[62] of the notional duty situation, the way it is formulated is of considerable importance. This is true not only for the case that is before the court, as it will determine the sorts of reasons that will need to be advanced in support of and against the existence of the formulated duty (that is, narrower propositions are usually easier to establish), but for future cases too, as how the situation is formulated determines the precedential value of the case (that is, broader propositions are of greater precedential value). Surprisingly, however, the courts have offered little guidance on the topic, save for vague-to-the-point-of-meaningless comments such as, 'The appropriate level of specificity when formulating the scope and content of the duty will necessarily depend on the circumstances of the case.'[63] Whilst there is, of course, no 'right' level of generality, there are nevertheless a number of important considerations that ought to be borne in mind.

On the one hand, courts should be careful not to formulate notional duty situations too broadly. In particular, where an *inclusionary* category is too broad, it is likely that the decision will ultimately extend to situations that were not originally envisaged, thereby forcing the decision to be quickly reconsidered, or for liability in those categories of case to be artificially limited at other stages of the negligence enquiry. For example, a determination that *all* drivers owed a notional duty to *all* road users, whilst unproblematic in relation to carelessly caused physical injury, *would* be problematic in relation to carelessly caused damage that was purely economic.[64] Indeed, as we saw above, this is precisely the problem with the relationship view of notional duty; it is simply too broad. Where an *exclusionary* category is too broad, there is a danger that the determination could lead to harsh results, again, requiring the decision to be overturned or artificially extended elsewhere.[65] The old exclusionary rule for *all* purely economic loss, for example, was departed from, at least partly it seems, on the basis of the injustice it created.[66]

On the other hand, overly narrow categories are similarly problematic, principally because they have limited precedential value. It is clear, for example, that a determination that 'an occupier has a duty to take care that visitors are not physically injured by reason of the state of the occupier's property' has far greater precedential force than a determination that 'occupiers of residential property

---

[62] Nolan (n 8) 581. For examples of the varying levels of generality, see ibid 580–81.

[63] *Kuhl v Zurich Financial Services Australia Ltd* (2011) 243 CLR 361, 372 (French CJ and Gummow J). See also Dawson J in *Northern Sandblasting Pty Ltd v Harris* (1997) 188 CLR 313, at 343: '[T]he nature and extent of the duty in the particular instance depends upon the circumstances of the case.'

[64] For example, where a driver carelessly breaks down on the motorway and thereby causes other road users to be delayed in getting to work, miss important meetings, wages, overtime pay, etc.

[65] And as we saw in ch 4, in the case of *Palsgraf v Long Island Railway Co* (1928) 248 NY 339; 162 NE 99 and *Bourhill v Young* [1943] AC 92 (HL), it is often better for courts to overrule a problematic decision than to try to circumvent it.

[66] See *Hedley Byrne & Co Ltd v Heller & Partners Ltd* [1964] AC 465 (HL).

have a duty to take care that visitors are not physically injured by reason of the state of their concrete driveway.' Indeed, in *Neindorf v Junkovic*,[67] a case involving this precise issue, Kirby J advocated the wider formulation:

> [I]in deciding whether or not a duty of care exists, it is necessary to ask what the scope of the purported duty is. However, by and large, the relevant inquiries in this regard are conducted at a relatively general level of abstraction ... It is firmly established that an occupier owes a duty of care to entrants in respect of risks of physical injury arising out of the condition of the occupier's premises. There is no need for the scope of this duty to be defined with any greater precision than this in the instant case.[68]

Not only are wider formulations more helpful in clarifying the law for future courts and lawyers, but it is also questionable whether experienced courts, particularly at the ultimate appellate level, should be spending their limited time and resources debating the existence of a duty in a situation that is so narrow that it barely transcends the facts of the case.[69]

Getting the right balance between overly broad and overly narrow notional duty formulations is therefore important. Ideally, the situation should be defined as broadly as possible, so as to maximise the precedential value of the determination, but not so broad as to open the doors too wide or rule out otherwise justifiable claims. When formulating the relevant notional duty situation, courts should bear this tension in mind, and so take considerable care when articulating the situation under consideration.

D. Notional Duty Situations and Questions of Fault

As Kirby J has noted, it is becoming 'all too common'[70] in recent times, for notional duty situations to be framed in terms of the behaviour of the defendant that is alleged to have been careless. That is, the court approaches the notional duty enquiry on the basis of whether or not there was a 'duty to do X'. For example, rather than asking whether there should be a notional duty in relation to physical injury caused to a passenger (or pedestrian, or other road user) by a driver's careless driving, the court might instead ask whether there was a 'duty' to drive at a reasonable speed, or a 'duty' to drive at a reasonable distance from the car in front. Formulations of notional duty in terms of the allegedly careless behaviour, like overly narrow notional duty formulations, tend to have little (and, in the case of the former, often *no*) precedential value. More problematic, however, is that the

---

[67] (2005) 222 ALR 631. Here, Mrs Junkovic tripped on a 10–12mm gap in the concrete driveway of Mrs Neindorf's home, where a garage sale was being held.

[68] ibid [50], [56].

[69] Though, this is not to say that decisions that recognise narrow categories cannot have other precedential value. *Anns v Merton LBC* [1978] AC 728 (HL), for example, whilst only applying to public body omissions in a *categorical* sense, also created a rule with ostensibly universal application.

[70] *Neindorf v Junkovic* (2005) 222 ALR 631 [52].

former type of formulation conflates issues of law (whether a duty should exist in this situation) with issues of fact (whether the behaviour was careless).[71] The point is well made by McHugh J, who has noted that using such formulations:

> Create[s] the risk that they will be treated as stating legal propositions and convert what is a question of fact into a question of law. Hence, their use invites error in analysis, particularly the analysis of judicial precedents ... The common law has no need to—and does not—categorise the cases in which the defendant was held to have breached a standard of care.[72]

The 'well known phenomenon'[73] of subsuming questions of fault into the notional duty formulation is especially common in the High Court of Australia.[74] In *Vairy v Wyong Shire Council*,[75] for example, the plaintiff suffered serious spinal injuries after diving into shallow water on land controlled by the defendant local authority. The issue for the court was whether the defendant was liable for failing to erect any signs prohibiting diving or warning of the dangers of doing so. On the question of duty, Gummow J said, 'The essential issue on the *Vairy* appeal [is] the content of the duty of care, namely, the alleged requirement of a warning or a prohibition by the Council.'[76] In other words, the issue for the court was whether the defendant had a 'duty' to put up a sign warning the plaintiff of the dangers of diving into the water. Ultimately, Gummow J found that no such 'duty' existed. Despite clearly conflating issues of duty and fault, confusingly, Gummow J then went on to conclude that:

> The trial judge erred in merging the question of the scope or content of the conceded duty of care and the question of breach. The content of the duty did not include, whatever else it may have included, an obligation to warn (still less to prohibit) of the kind contended for by the plaintiff.[77]

Gummow J adopted a similar approach to the duty question in *Mulligan v Coffs Harbour CC*.[78] On almost identical facts to *Vairy*, again Gummow J argued that the relevant issue for the court was whether the 'scope of the duty ... include[d] an obligation to warn the plaintiff about the risk of diving in the creek by reason of its variable depth.'[79] Again, he concluded that the 'scope' of the duty did not extend so far.

Formulations of notional duty situations in terms of the allegedly careless conduct, by conflating issues of law with issues of fact,[80] give rise to three

---

[71] Though, framing the notional duty situation broadly avoids both problems.
[72] *Vairy v Wyong Shire Council* (2005) 223 CLR 422, 433–34.
[73] Nolan (n 8) 578.
[74] Though it is not confined to them. See, eg: *Sam v Atkins* [2005] EWCA Civ 1452, and the discussion in Tony Weir, *An Introduction to Tort Law*, 2nd edn (OUP, 2006) 33.
[75] (2005) 223 CLR 422 ('*Vairy*').
[76] ibid 442.
[77] ibid 454.
[78] (2005) 223 CLR 486 ('*Mulligan*').
[79] ibid 497. See Gummow J's approval of this formulation at ibid 499.
[80] Which, as Kirby J notes, should still be 'properly quarantined': *Neindorf v Junkovic* [2005] 222 ALR 631 [54].

interrelated difficulties. First, they conflate the issue of whether a notional duty exists with the separate question of whether the defendant's behaviour was reasonable, discrete issues which require an evaluation of entirely independent considerations. In particular, whether a notional duty exists is, as we have seen repeatedly, a normative question, and the issue for the court is whether, *assuming the defendant was careless*, liability in negligence *ought* to apply to the particular situation. Such an enquiry invites consideration of factors that have nothing to do with the reasonableness of the defendant's conduct. So, for example, harm caused by omissions is generally not recoverable, even where the defendant had been careless, because, *inter alia*, permitting such claims would cause too great an interference with an individual's freedom of action.[81] Whether the defendant has been careless, however, involves an assessment of the particular facts of the case *only*. When the notional duty situation is formulated in terms of the allegedly careless conduct, the focus of the analysis therefore shifts from whether liability should exist, assuming the conduct *was* careless, to whether the conduct was careless in the first place. In *Kuhl v Zurich Financial Services Australia Ltd*,[82] for example, the plaintiff was injured when his arm was sucked into an industrial-strength vacuum hose that was passed to him by an employee of the defendant. As to whether a duty existed, according to French CJ and Gummow J, the relevant issue was whether the 'scope of the duty' included 'a duty to take additional reasonable precautions with respect to the passing of the hose so as to avoid causing injury to those receiving the hose'.[83] Unsurprisingly, as to whether a 'duty' was owed, the court focussed on the particular facts of the case, including whether it was foreseeable that an injury could occur through the passing, opposed to the use, of the hose.[84] Clearly, however, whether the injury was a foreseeable consequence of the defendants conduct relates to the reasonableness of the conduct, and not whether, assuming the passing of the hose *was* careless, the situation could, in principle, give rise to liability in negligence in the first place; a question which, considering directly caused physical injury is *the* archetypal notional duty situation, would surely have been answered in the affirmative. The same approach was adopted by Gummow J in *Mulligan*, discussed above, when he held that in determining the relevant 'scope' of the duty, it was appropriate to examine the issue by reference to 'considerations, albeit not propositions of law, touching on the readily apparent danger of [the] activity …;'[85] again, considerations more relevant to the question of fault than to whether liability *should* exist in the first place.

---

[81] See, eg, Lord Hoffmann in *Stovin v Wise* [1996] AC 923 (HL), 946.

[82] (2011) 243 CLR 361.

[83] ibid 374.

[84] ibid [31]: 'If it was not reasonably foreseeable that the passing of the hose exposed the receiver of the hose to any greater risk than when it was used for its intended purpose, there is no occasion for the scope of the duty to extend beyond that already owed to the user of the hose.' Again, this formulation presupposes that the normal risk does not give rise to any duty, which can only be on the basis that exposing the plaintiff to the risk involved when the hose is used 'for its intended purpose' was not careless.

[85] ibid 499.

The problem is evident in lower courts too. In *McPhersons Ltd v Eaton & Ors*,[86] the defendant hardware store sold asbestos sheeting to the plaintiff's employer. The plaintiff later developed mesothelioma as a result of working with and inhaling fibres from the asbestos sheeting. On the issue of duty, Ipp JA held that the relationship of vendor and purchaser, or vendor and end consumer, does not *automatically* give rise to a duty of care (even in relation to carelessly caused physical injury): 'something more' was required,[87] as '[w]ithout the requirement of some additional factor, a retailer would continuously be at risk if it did not investigate hazardous characteristics of all products sold by it.'[88] According to Ipp JA, that 'something more' was evidence that the defendant 'ought to' have known of the dangers of the asbestos. In other words, the existence of a 'duty' depended on whether the defendant was at fault, not on whether, *assuming the vendor was careless and therefore ought to have known of the dangers of the asbestos*, vendors ought to be liable for any physical harm that results to the ultimate consumer of the dangerous products they have carelessly sold, a question that since *Donoghue v Stevenson*[89] was decided in 1932 has consistently and unhesitatingly been answered in the affirmative.

A second problem with formulating notional duty situations in terms of the allegedly negligent conduct, being a 'duty to do X', is that it pre-empts questions of fault. In particular, if the court finds there is a 'duty to do X', the fault enquiry simply becomes, whether or not the defendant did 'X'; whereas if the courts finds there is no 'duty to do X', the fault enquiry is not even enlivened. As Howarth explains:

> [If] the duty of care is capable of being characterised as a duty to refrain from doing precisely what it was that the defendant did, or as a duty to do no more than precisely what the defendant did, the investigation of whether there has been a breach becomes superfluous. In the former case, there is always liability, and in the latter case there can never be liability.[90]

A particularly clear example of the notional duty formulation pre-empting the fault stage occurred in Gaudron J's judgment in *Romeo v Conservation Commission (NT)*.[91] The plaintiff, whilst heavily intoxicated, suffered serious injuries after falling from the top of a 6.5m cliff on a nature reserve under the control of the local council. As the area was a designated tourist area, the plaintiff argued that the defendant council was negligent for failing to install a fence or other barrier along the cliff. On the 'central issue ... [of] the content of the duty of care owed by the [defendant],'[92] Gaudron J held that:

---

[86] [2005] NSWCA 435 ('*McPhersons*').
[87] *McPhersons* [82] (Ipp JA).
[88] ibid [83] (Ipp JA).
[89] [1932] AC 562.
[90] David Howarth, 'Negligence After Murphy: Time to Re-Think' (1991) 50 CLJ 58, 72. See also Howarth's comments in Howarth, 'Duty of Care' (n 1) para 12.8, and McHugh J in *Graham Barclay Oysters Pty Ltd v Ryan* (2002) 211 CLR 540 at [106].
[91] (1998) 192 CLR 431 ('*Romeo*').
[92] ibid 456.

The actions of the Commission in constructing the road and providing parking facilities were calculated to encourage people to visit the particular area from which the appellant fell. And it was foreseeable that at least some would leave their cars and walk towards the clifftop, perhaps to obtain a better view, perhaps, simply, to stretch their legs. And it was also foreseeable that not all would be astute to take care for their own safety. In that context, it seems to me unarguable that, having provided access and car parking facilities, *there was a duty of care to provide fencing along the clifftop in the area near the car park*, although not in areas not readily accessible from it. That duty was a duty to provide fencing of a kind that would prevent visitors from straying too near the clifftop, not a low log fence as the trial judge appears to have had in mind in holding that a fence would not have made any difference in this case.[93]

As to the question of fault, Gaudron J was open that, on her construction of the duty, the question was already answered:

> As the duty of care is, in my view, limited to the fencing of the clifftop in the vicinity of the car parking area, no question arises as to the reasonableness of that measure. More precisely, the Commission's argument as to the impracticability of fencing the entire clifftop is simply irrelevant. And as there was a duty to fence, the argument that the appellant was well acquainted with the area and aware of its terrain and dangers is irrelevant to the question whether there was a breach by the Commission of its duty of care.[94]

The third problem with 'dressing up'[95] issues of fault as issues of notional duty is that it can lead to procedural difficulties. First, it confuses the respective roles of judge and jury (at least in the remaining jurisdictions that still use juries for civil trials—the United States of America and Victoria, Australia, for example); it is for the judge to determine whether and in what broad circumstances a notional duty exists, and for the jury to determine whether, on the particular facts of the case, the defendant's conduct could be considered careless. Secondly, and more significantly, is that keeping issues of law and fact separate is important for a properly functioning appellate review process, given that permission to appeal is typically confined to questions of law; and, in any event, judges tend to be more reluctant to interfere with determinations of fact that determinations of law.[96]

Formulations of notional duty situations in terms of the behaviour that is alleged to have been negligent, or in terms of a 'duty to do X', are therefore objectionable on analytical grounds; they conflate separate issues and shift the focus from the normative issue of whether the law of negligence *ought* to apply to the particular situation to whether the defendant's behaviour was careless, they preempt questions of fault, and they give rise to a number of procedural difficulties. Whilst Fleming is relatively gentle in his criticism of such formulations, merely commenting that 'this method of expression is best avoided',[97] perhaps Nolan's

---

[93] ibid 459.
[94] ibid.
[95] Nolan (n 8) 578.
[96] See, eg, the discussion of Major J in *Galaske v O'Donnell* (1994) 112 DLR (4th) 109 [54]–[61].
[97] Fleming, *The Law of Torts* (n 36) 117–18.

criticism is more appropriate: '[T]he fault issue cannot legitimately be subsumed into notional duty, and the confusion of issues of fault and notional duty has rightly been condemned as an error.'[98]

E. The 'Scope' of the Duty

A number of the above examples illustrate that notional duty issues are occasionally referred to in terms of the 'scope' of the duty, or, alternatively, the 'content' or 'extent' of the duty. So, for example, a court might say the 'scope' of the duty owed by a driver to a passenger extends to directly caused physical injury, but does not extend to purely economic loss.[99] The scope of the duty language is especially popular in the High Court of Australia. Whilst the term 'scope of the duty' is often used, as the previous example illustrates, as a reference to the precise nature of the notional duty situation, it is also used in a number of competing and often confusing ways, and it is important to be aware of the varying meanings ascribed to the term so as to be clear when the court is referring to the notional duty situation, and when they are referring to something else entirely.

In its usual sense, the 'scope of the duty' is simply a synonym for the 'precise notional duty situation.' This understanding of the 'scope' of the duty was well illustrated by Gummow J, who said in *Road Traffic Authority of NSW v Dederer*[100] that '[d]uties of care are not owed in the abstract. Rather, they are obligations of a particular scope, and that scope may be more or less expansive depending on the relationship in question.'[101] Indeed, it would be meaningless to say, for example, that a driver owes a duty to his passenger without more; one would need to specify that a driver owes a duty to a passenger *with respect to physical injury caused by their careless driving*. In this sense, the 'scope' of the duty simply expresses the extent of the situation covered by the notional duty, and so is unobjectionable.

In a second sense, the 'scope of the duty' is often used to refer to the appropriate *standard* of care. For example, it might be said that the 'scope' or 'content' of the duty owed by a driver to a passenger is to drive carefully, without exceeding the speed limit, or driving too closely to the car in front. As we have just seen, this form of expression is often the result of the court conflating the notional duty and fault issues, such as in *Mulligan*, where Gummow J spoke of the 'duty ... to warn the plaintiff about the risk of diving in the creek by reason of its variable depth,'[102] or in *Romeo*, where Gaudron J spoke of a 'duty of care to provide fencing along the clifftop in the area near the car park.'[103] On other occasions, however, it

---

[98] Nolan (n 8) 579.

[99] Say, if the driver's careless driving caused the passenger to arrive at work late and so miss out on wages.

[100] (2007) 324 CLR 330.

[101] ibid [43]. See also Morison in JG Fleming and WL Morison, 'Duty of Care and Standard of Care' (1953) 1 SydLR 69, 69–70: 'The question is not simply Did the defendant owe a duty? but What kind of duty?'

[102] *Mulligan* 497.

[103] *Romeo* 459.

seems clear that, whilst the court has properly distinguished between the issues of notional duty and fault, the expression of the relevant standard of care in terms of the content of the duty is simply the result of a poor wording. For example, also in *Romeo*, Hayne J said:

> It was not (and could not be) seriously suggested that the respondent in this case owed no duty of care to members of the public that might go to areas which it manages. The real subject for debate was what that duty required of it, for it is only when the content or scope of the duty is identified that questions of breach and causation of damage can be considered. So, too, in *Nagle v Rottnest Island Authority* ... the central question was not whether the Board owed any duty of care to those visitors lawfully visiting the island, it was what that duty of care required it to do.[104]

Similarly, in *Jones v Bartlett*,[105] Gummow and Hayne JJ commented that:

> [I]t would be of no utility merely to conclude that the duty is to be expressed simply as one to take reasonable care to avoid a foreseeable risk of injury to a person in the situation of the [plaintiff]. That would leave unanswered the critical questions regarding the content of the terms 'reasonable' and hence the content of the duty of care, matters essential for the determination of this case, for without them the issue of breach cannot be decided.[106]

Speaking in terms of 'duty', when the court is, in fact, referring to the relevant standard of care, is, of course, unnecessarily confusing and a method of expression best avoided.

The scope of the duty is also occasionally used in a third sense, referring to an independent stage in the negligence enquiry that places limits on the circumstances in which an already imposed duty to take care applies. Indeed, there is considerable authority in the High Court of Australia explicitly suggesting that the enquiry into the *scope* of the duty is independent to the enquiry into the *existence* of a duty. In *Romeo*, for example, Kirby J stated that, as he understood the law, the 'standard questions' involved in the negligence enquiry were, 'The duty of care issue ... The scope of the duty issue ... The breach issue...[and] The causation issue.'[107] He re-affirmed this formulation in *Graham Barclay Oysters Ltd v Ryan*[108] and *Modbury Triangle Shopping Centre Pty Ltd v Anzil*.[109] Similarly, in *Cole v South Tweed Heads Rugby League Football Club Ltd*,[110] in determining whether the defendant football club owed a duty to a patron who became so intoxicated at the club's bar that she was struck by a motor vehicle shortly after leaving, Gleeson CJ said:

> In the circumstances of this case, it is of little assistance to consider issues of duty of care, breach, and damages, at a high level of abstraction, divorced from the concrete facts.

---

[104] ibid 487.

[105] (2000) 205 CLR 205.

[106] ibid [167].

[107] ibid 475 [115]. Though later dicta of Kirby J suggests that he did not necessarily agree with the construction. See especially: *Neindorf v Junkovic* [2005] 222 ALR 631 [51]–[55].

[108] (2002) 211 CLR 540, 622.

[109] (2000) 205 CLR 254, 274 ('*Modbury*').

[110] (2004) 217 CLR 469 ('*Cole*').

> In particular, to ask whether the respondent owed the appellant a duty of care does not advance the matter ... Of course the respondent owed [the appellant] a duty of care. There is, however, an issue concerning the nature and extent of the duty.[111]

To suggest that the existence of a duty and the scope of the duty are separate enquiries is, of course, wrong, as it completely misconstrues the role of the notional duty enquiry. As we have seen, a notional duty does not exist in the abstract and cannot be divorced from the broad circumstances in question; a finding that a notional duty exists must *already* dictate the circumstances in which the defendant is required to take care (that is, the 'situation') and so is *already* limited to a particular 'scope'. Indeed, to suggest that a separate enquiry is needed to impose such limits makes one wonder how the anterior question as to the existence of a duty is determined in the first place. In *Cole*, for example, Gleeson CJ presumably based the existence of a duty purely on the occupier/visitor relationship of the defendant and plaintiff; but, as we have seen, without reference to the kind of harm suffered by the plaintiff or the way it occurred, the mere fact that the plaintiff was a visitor is not enough to give rise to a notional duty. Understood in this sense, the scope of the duty is a completely superfluous concept, and any perceived need for it is due to a misunderstanding of the role of duty.

Finally, the scope of the duty is occasionally used in a fourth sense, as limiting the extent of the defendant's liability to the materialisation of only those risks that made their conduct careless in the first place. The most well-known example of this use of the 'scope of the duty' is Lord Hoffmann's speech in *South Australia Asset Management Corporation v York Montague Ltd,*[112] where the court had to determine whether the defendant was responsible for *all* the consequences of a negligence overvaluation of property that was proposed to be used as security for a loan, including a drop in the property market, or only those that resulted from the valuation being wrong, namely the claimant banks receiving less security for loans than they would have required had the valuation been correct. Speaking throughout in terms of the 'scope of the duty,' Lord Hoffmann stated that:

> [A] person under a duty to take reasonable care to provide information on which someone else will decide upon a course of action is, if negligent, not generally regarded as responsible for all the consequences of that course of action. He is responsible only for the consequences of the information being wrong.[113]

As Nolan points out, however, this sense of the scope of the duty is little more than an 'unhelpful and pointless reformulation of the remoteness issue'.[114] Indeed, as we saw in chapter four, the remoteness issue *already* confines the liability of

---

[111] ibid 472. See also Gleeson CJ's comments in *Modbury* 263.
[112] [1997] AC 191 (HL) ('*SAAMCO*').
[113] ibid 214.
[114] Nolan (n 8) 579.

defendant to the materialisation of those risks that made their conduct careless in the first place; and so, for the same reasons that there is no need for factual duty to perform the same task, there is also no need for it to be done under the 'scope of the duty' label, whether as a separate element of the negligence enquiry or as a synonym for factual duty. Writing extra-judicially, Lord Hoffmann even conceded that his use of the 'scope of the duty' label in *SAAMCO* was 'inappropriate' and that he would try to 'mend [his] language in the future'.[115]

If the scope of the duty language is to be used at all, it should be confined to the first use, referring to the precise details of the notional duty situation; the other three senses in which it is used are superfluous and apt to mislead.

III. Assumptions of Responsibility

Since *Hedley Byrne & Co Ltd v Heller & Partners Ltd*[116] was decided in 1963, the law has been clear that, even where the facts of the case fall into an exclusionary situation, a duty may nevertheless exist if the defendant 'assumed a responsibility' towards the claimant.[117] Although *Hedley Byrne* and assumptions of responsibility tend to be associated exclusively with cases involving purely economic loss, as McBride and Bagshaw note, this is a 'common misconception',[118] as there is no sign that the Law Lords in *Hedley Byrne* intended for their comments to be confined in such a way. Indeed, today assumptions of responsibility play a crucial role in establishing the existence of a duty in cases involving purely economic loss, *and* omissions/third party liability,[119] and it is even arguable that an assumption

---

[115] Lord Hoffmann, 'Causation' (2005) 121 LQR 592, 596. Though this does not seem to have been heeded, and in the most recent consideration of *SAAMCO* in the UKSC, Lord Sumption spoke in terms of the 'scope of the duty' throughout: *BPE Solicitors v Hughes-Holland* [2017] 2 WLR 1029.

[116] [1964] AC 465 (HL) ('*Hedley Byrne*').

[117] Arguably, an assumption of responsibility provided a justification for the existence of a notional duty even prior to *Hedley Byrne*. It has been argued, for example, that the existence of the duty in *Stansbie v Troman* [1948] 1 KB 48 (CA), a case decided more than a decade before *Hedley Byrne*, was based on an assumption of responsibility: *Smith v Littlewoods Organisation Ltd* [1987] AC 241 (HL), 272 (Lord Goff); and Nicholas J McBride and Roderick Bagshaw, *Tort Law*, 4th edn (Pearson, 2012) 187 (fn 194).

[118] ibid. Indeed, they go as far as labelling the claim 'nonsense'.

[119] See, eg: *Michael v The Chief Constable of South Wales Police* [2015] AC 1732 (HL) (Lord Toulson); *Mitchell v Glasgow City Council* [2009] 1 AC 87 (HL) (Lord Hope); *Watson v British Boxing Board of Control* [2001] QB 1134 (CA) (Lord Phillips MR); *Barrett v Ministry of Defence* [1995] 1 WLR 1217 (CA) (Bedlam LJ); and *Smith v Littlewoods Organisation Ltd* [1987] AC 241 (HL) (Lord Goff). Given the availability of a statutory remedy in Australia under s 18 of the Australian Consumer Law (formerly s 52 of the Trade Practices Act 1974 Cth), and the fact that cases involving purely economic loss in Canada are now resolved under the *Anns* two-stage approach (*Hercules Managements Ltd v Ernst & Young* (1997) 146 DLR (4th) 577), the vast majority of the jurisprudence relating to the assumption of responsibility test has developed in the UK.

of responsibility could provide the basis for a duty in *any* (that is, broad *or* exceptional) exclusionary category.[120]

A. A Distinctive Type of Justification?

As we saw in chapter three, there is much disagreement about the precise role of assumptions of responsibility in the duty enquiry. Whilst some believe it is merely one of many factors to be taken in to account when determining whether the claimant has satisfied a general duty test, others believe that assumptions of responsibility provide a distinctive and independent type of justification for the existence of a notional duty. In particular, they believe that the notional duty does not arise because 'this situation ought to be subject to the laws of negligence,' but because, 'even though this broad situation ought to *not* be subject to the laws of negligence, the defendant assumed a responsibility to the claimant and so ought to be bound by it.' Indeed, this was the understanding of Lord Devlin himself in *Hedley Byrne*:

> I do not understand any of your Lordships to hold that it is a responsibility imposed by law upon certain types of persons or in certain sorts of situations. It is a responsibility that is voluntarily accepted or undertaken ...[121]

Advocates of this view often explain the uniqueness of the assumption of responsibility type justification in terms of 'consent,' or the 'voluntariness' of the undertaking.[122] In particular, whereas in those situations where a notional duty is recognised whether we consent to it being recognised or not, our obligation to not carelessly cause damage is imposed *by the law*; where the notional duty is based on an assumption of responsibility, our obligation to not carelessly cause damage is based on 'the objective manifestation of consent for which we are responsible'.[123] The distinctiveness of the assumption of responsibility justification for the existence of a duty, and its reliance on ideas of voluntariness and consent, has even led to some claiming

---

[120] For example, although there does not seem to be any case on point, there seems to be no good reason why the combat immunity should not apply if an officer gave an explicit undertaking to a soldier that a particular mission would be safe, and, after participating in the mission in reliance on the undertaking, the soldier was injured as a result of the mission, in fact, being unsafe, as the arguments against liability in that situation *generally* would not answer the objection that the officer breached an explicit undertaking. Such situations are so rare, however, that the practical significance of this argument (ie whether an assumption of responsibility could impose a duty in a narrow exclusionary situation) is limited.

[121] *Hedley Byrne* 529.

[122] Stevens, *Torts and Rights* (n 16) 10, 12; Beever (n 18) 273. *cf* K Barker, 'Unreliable Assumptions in the Modern Law of Negligence' (1993) 109 LQR 461, 470–73; Andrew Robertson and Julia Wang, 'The Assumption of Responsibility' in Kit Barker, Ross Grantham and Warren Swain (eds), *The Law of Misstatements: 50 Years on from Hedley Byrne v Heller* (Hart, 2015) 55–57.

[123] Stevens, *Torts and Rights* (n 16) 12.

that it does not belong in the law of negligence,[124] or even the law of tort,[125] at all, as it more closely resembles an obligation that arises as a result of the law of contract.

B. Criticism

Justifying the existence of a notional duty on the basis that the defendant 'assumed a responsibility' towards the claimant has, however, been criticised on the basis that, far from providing an independent type of justification, an 'assumption of responsibility' is merely a label for the conclusion that a notional duty should be imposed.[126] In support of this claim, critics tend to point to cases such as *White v Jones*,[127] where the defendant was *deemed* to have assumed a responsibility to the claimant 'in law,'[128] despite the parties never having even communicated with each other, directly or indirectly, and *Smith v Eric S Bush*,[129] where the defendant was held to have assumed a responsibility towards the plaintiff, again, despite the parties never having met or communicated, and despite the defendant *expressly* disclaiming any responsibility.[130] It is undeniably difficult to see such uses of the concept of assumption of responsibility as anything but fictitious, and so critics are right to say that such cases do not support the notion that the obligation is voluntarily imposed.[131] However, it does not follow from the fact that *some* cases use the concept of assumption of responsibility fictitiously that the concept *itself* is meaningless. Indeed, those who claim assumptions of responsibility are a separate type of justification for the existence of a notional duty tend to *agree* that cases such as *White v Jones* and *Smith v Eric S Bush* are not helpful illustrations of what it means to assume a responsibility. According to McBride and Bagshaw, for example:

> Of course, the courts have in the past found that a defendant 'assumed a responsibility' to a claimant [fictitiously] ... but in those cases the courts were guilty of abusing the

[124] Beever (n 18) 273; A Beever, 'The Basis of the *Hedley Byrne* Action' in Kit Barker, Ross Grantham and Warren Swain (eds), *The Law of Misstatements: 50 Years on from Hedley Byrne v Heller* (Hart, 2015) (who says its inclusion in the law of negligence has been a 'disaster,' at p102); David Campbell, 'What Mischief does Hedley Byrne v Heller Correct?' in Kit Barker, Ross Grantham and Warren Swain (eds), *The Law of Misstatements: 50 Years on from Hedley Byrne v Heller* (Hart, 2015) (who says it should be 'abolished' entirely, at p112).

[125] M Gergen, 'Negligent Misrepresentation as Contract' (2013) 101 Cal L Rev. See also Paul Mitchell, '*Hedley Byrne & Co Ltd v Heller & Partners Ltd* (1963)' in Charles Mitchell and Paul Mitchell (eds), *Landmark Cases in the Law of Torts* (Hart, 2010) 187–88.

[126] See Section VII of ch 3.

[127] [1995] 2 AC 207 (HL) ('*White v Jones*').

[128] ibid 268 (Lord Goff).

[129] [1990] 1 AC 831 (HL) ('*Smith v Eric S Bush*'). The express disclaimer was held to be of no effect by virtue of section 2(2) of the Unfair Contract Terms Act (1977), and so could not provide a basis for the failure to assume a responsibility. Though, it was noted that, as far as the common law was concerned, the disclaimer *was* effective (Lord Griffith at 856), and that if the case had arisen prior to 1977 the disclaimer would have prevented the assumption of responsibility from arising (Lord Jauncey at 853).

[130] See, eg: Barker (n 122) 466–67; Robertson and Wang (n 122) 59–60, 65–67.

[131] For further examples of cases that are undeniably difficult to explain on the basis that there was a *voluntary* assumption of responsibility, see Barker (n 122) 466–67.

concept—in those cases the courts wanted to find that the defendant owed the claimant a duty of care for such-and-such a reason and they simply *said* that the defendant 'assumed a responsibility' to the claimant in order to provide themselves with some legal justification for their finding that the defendant owed the claimant a duty of care.[132]

Even in his speech in *White v Jones*, Lord Goff was explicitly clear that the existence of a duty was *not* based on the defendant assuming a responsibility to the claimant,[133] but on the basis of the 'impulse to do practical justice'.[134] To say that assumption of responsibility is a meaningless or artificial concept on the basis of such cases, is therefore misleading, as it relies on an understanding of assumptions of responsibility that few would endorse.

It is nevertheless true that if the concept of assumption of responsibility is to have any meaning, it must be understood more narrowly, referring only to circumstances where the defendant has clearly indicated that the claimant can rely on them in some respect, whether it be the performance of an activity, provision of services, or supply of information.[135] This certainly seemed to have been the original intention of Lord Devlin, who said in *Hedley Byrne* that an assumption of responsibility will only exist where the relationship between the parties is, 'in the words of Lord Shaw in *Nocton v Lord Ashburton* ... "equivalent to contract," that is, where there is an assumption of responsibility in circumstances in which, but for the absence of consideration, there would be a contract.'[136]

Yet, whilst a narrower understanding of what it means to assume a responsibility reduces the likelihood of the term being used fictitiously, it gives rise to other difficulties. In particular, short of requiring potential defendants to explicitly state 'I consent that I will take care in the performance of this task and accept responsibility for the consequences of my careless failure to do so,' determining when the defendant has indicated that the claimant can rely on them will not always be clear. Indeed, as noted by Lord Devlin in *Hedley Byrne*, 'Where there is an express under-

---

[132] McBride and Bagshaw (n 117) 175. McBride and Bagshaw then cite Lord Goff's speech in *White v Jones* as a particularly transparent example of this. See also Stevens, *Torts and Rights* (n 16) 35, 43; and Beever, *Rediscovering the Law of Negligence* (n 18) 305. Arguably, this is now even recognised by the courts, following the narrower formulation of what it means to assume a responsibility approved in *Customs and Excise Commissioners v Barclays Bank plc* [2007] 1 AC 181 (HL).

[133] *White v Jones* 262: '[T]he *Hedley Byrne* principle cannot, in the absence of special circumstances, give rise on ordinary principles to an assumption of responsibility by the testator's solicitor towards an intended beneficiary.'

[134] ibid 259. For judicial statements going further than this, see the comments of Lord Steyn in *Williams v Natural Life Health Foods* [1998] 1 WLR 830 (HL) at 837 ('There is nothing fictional about this species of liability in tort'), and Lord Bingham in *Customs and Excise Commissioners v Barclays Bank plc* [2007] 1 AC 181 (HL) ('there *are* cases in which one party can accurately be said to have assumed responsibility for what is said or done to another, the paradigm situation being a relationship having all the indicia of contract save consideration' (emphasis added)).

[135] This is not to suggest that the claimant must *actually* rely on the representation, just that the defendant has indicated that the claimant *may* rely on the representation. The distinction is significant and discussed in further detail below.

[136] *Hedley Byrne* 529.

taking, an express warranty as distinct from mere representation, there can be little difficulty. The difficulty arises in discerning those cases in which the undertaking is to be implied.'[137] It is for this reason that the question of whether the defendant has assumed a responsibility must be determined *objectively*.[138] So, for example, a hospital might assume responsibility to a patient who has just arrived in the emergency department by putting him or her on a stretcher and administering medical treatment. No verbal communication between the parties is even necessary; the conduct alone would be sufficient to manifest an *objective* indication that the hospital was assuming responsibility for the patient's physical wellbeing.[139]

But the objective understanding of what it means to assume a responsibility is criticised too; in particular, it is argued that, outside of the exceedingly rare cases where an assumption of responsibility is explicit, there is rarely *any* evidence from which one can conclude that responsibility to perform an activity, give advice, etc, with care has been objectively assumed, with the result that 'what is called an "objective test" almost inevitably becomes a question as to whether it is reasonable to impose the obligation on the defendant'.[140] As Wang and Robertson explain:

> The essential problem with this idea … is that the courts do not require that the defendant manifest *any* consent to the obligation in question, and the cases do not support the notion that there is any such requirement … a person who consents to do something does not thereby place himself or herself under a legal obligation, unless he or she makes a commitment and manifests an intention to be legally bound by that commitment. If the defendant only consented 'to do something,' and did not manifest any consent to the legal obligation that arises from that conduct, then there is nothing distinctive about this category of obligation. It is simply imposed by law on the basis of conduct that is potentially harmful.[141]

In other words, merely undertaking to do something *cannot* be understood as assuming a responsibility, or manifesting consent to an obligation (let alone a *legal* obligation), to do that something with care. If, then, merely doing something is deemed to give rise to a legal obligation to do that something with care, as such an obligation cannot be explained on the basis that it consented to, it must therefore be explained on the basis that the imposition of the obligation is thought to be reasonable. So, for example, Wang and Robertson would presumably argue that merely placing a patient onto a hospital stretcher and administering medical

---

[137] *Hedley Byrne* 529.

[138] *Smith v Eric S Bush* 862; *Henderson v Merrett Syndicates Ltd* [1995] 2 AC 145 (HL), 181; *Phelps v Hillingdon London Borough Council* [2001] 2 AC 619 (HL), 654.

[139] This is not to say a similar duty could not be formulated in categorical terms. Such a duty would, however, require a distinct justification, being that doctors *as a class* ought to be deemed responsible for hospital patients *as a class*, rather than on the basis that *the* doctor assumed a responsibility to *the* patient.

[140] Robertson and Wang (n 122) 57. See also C Witting, 'What are We Doing Here? The Relationship Between Negligence in General and Misstatements in English Law' in Kit Barker, Ross Grantham and Warren Swain (eds), *The Law of Misstatements: 50 Years on from Hedley Byrne v Heller* (Hart, 2015), and Barker (n 122).

[141] Robertson and Wang (n 122) 56–57 (emphasis added).

treatment could *not*, without more, be understood as an undertaking to provide that treatment with care, as nothing about such conduct suggests that not only will treatment be provided, but it will *also* be provided with care. The result of critics' strict interpretation of what it means to assume a responsibility is that the objective test will almost never be satisfied, and so fails to rescue the idea that assumptions of responsibility are a different type of justification for the existence of a notional duty; that is, notional duties based on assumptions of responsibility, like those based on the category of case, are *also* imposed by the law rather than voluntarily assumed or consented to.

There is certainly some merit to this criticism. Indeed, determining when conduct can be objectively understood as manifesting consent to an obligation to take care will rarely, if ever, be clear. It is suggested, however, that critics of the assumption of responsibility concept place the bar too high, and demand too much of the objective test. After all, the law of contract relies on an objective test to determine when an offer has been accepted,[142] apparently, without controversy. The law of contract also infers a manifestation of consent to an implied term, as well as the legal obligation to obey that term, not on the basis of actual consent to the term, but on the basis that an 'officious bystander' would think such a term is 'so obvious that it goes without saying.'[143] Yet, again, there appears to be no suggestion that the question of whether a term was implied inevitably becomes a question of whether the obligation imposed by the contractual term is reasonable. None of this is intended to deny that when responsibility can be said to be objectively assumed will rarely, if ever, lend itself to a simple answer; just that the position is hardly any different in contract law. As Feldthusen notes:

> Certainly, a duty may arise where the defendant in fact did not intend to assume responsibility for its advice or information, let alone indicate expressly that it intended to be legally bound. The issue is whether the defendant's conduct viewed objectively suggests that the defendant did assume such responsibility, that is, did intend the plaintiff to rely. I know of no judicial success in reading the minds of actors to determine subjective intention, so I fail to see how employing an objective test to determine a subjective intention undermines the quest for a subjective intention. Are contractual obligations assumed or imposed? How do we answer that question and why? What we really ought to care about is the impression created in the reasonable plaintiff's mind leading to detrimental reliance. This is the relevant wrong.[144]

It is therefore not clear why, if consent to a legal obligation can be determined by an objective test in the law of contract, consent to a legal obligation cannot be determined via an objective test in the law of tort.

---

[142] *Smith v Hughes* (1871) 6 QB 597, 607; Edwin Peel, *Treitel: The Law of Contract*, 14th edn (Sweet & Maxwell, 2015) 2-016.

[143] *Shirlaw v Southern Foundries (1926) Ltd* [1940] 2 KB 206, 227.

[144] Bruce Feldthusen, '*Hedley Byrne* and the Supreme Court of Canada' in Kit Barker, Ross Grantham and Warren Swain (eds), *The Law of Misstatements: 50 Years on from Hedley Byrne v Heller* (Hart, 2015) 276.

Critics of assumptions of responsibility have nevertheless objected that the situations in tort and contract are different. Barker, for example, has argued that 'the use of contractual analogies to justify negligence liability [in cases where the parties have never communicated] is nonsensical, because existing contractual principles do not imply promises between parties who have never directly communicated or met.'[145] Barker is surely right that an objective test cannot be applied more widely in tort than in contract, however, it is not clear why the analogy does not work otherwise; that is, for parties who *have* directly communicated and *have* met. So, for example, where a hospital places a patient on a stretcher and begins administering medical treatment, the hospital can be said to be manifesting consent to provide that treatment with care on the basis that an officious bystander would, presumably, think that the obligation to do so was so obvious it went without saying; indeed, if it were otherwise, the parties would likely have thought twice about proceeding with the treatment.[146] It also seems unrealistic and overly pedantic that a hospital could respond to an allegation of negligent mistreatment with, 'we only undertook to treat you, not to do it carefully.'[147] This may be contrasted with the case of a motorist who embarks on a road journey; not only has the motorist made no representation to other road users whatsoever, but, whereas a patient goes to a hospital primarily for the purpose receiving competent medical treatment, road users use the road primarily to get from A to B, *not* in order to get a benefit from other road users. They can therefore not be described as having given an undertaking to other road users at all. Similarly, where valuation advice is created for the purpose of compliance with corporate reporting requirements,[148] or so that a lender can determine whether the object being valued provides sufficient security for a loan to a third party,[149] it is difficult to see how the provision of the advice could *also* be understood as consisting of an undertaking as to its accuracy when used for *another* purpose.

Regardless of which view is ultimately preferred, the difference between the views of the advocates and critics of the assumption of responsibility concept should not be overstated: *both* agree that there are circumstances that can legitimately be described as manifesting consent to the imposition of a legal obligation to take care with the performance of an activity, etc, such that the concept *can* have some explanatory force;[150] and *both* agree that, at least for the most part, the

---

[145] Barker (n 122) 469.

[146] The argument that in an emergency situation the patient would very likely have proceeded with the treatment anyway, whilst highly relevant to the question of causation, is distinct from the question of whether there was an assumption of responsibility in the first place.

[147] Beever, 'The Basis of the *Hedley Byrne* Action' (n 124) 106.

[148] *Caparo Industries plc v Dickman* [1990] 2 AC 605 (HL).

[149] *Smith v Eric S Bush.*

[150] See, eg: Robertson and Wang's comments on *Williams v Natural Life Health Foods* [1998] 1 WLR 830 (HL) in Robertson and Wang (n 122) 56 (fn 59) and 59; Witting (n 140) 236; C Witting, 'Justifying Liability to Third Parties for Negligent Misstatements' (2000) 20 OJLS 615, 629; Barker (n 122) 465; and K Barker, 'Negligent Misstatement in Australia—Resolving the Uncertain Legacy of Esanda' in Kit Barker, Ross Grantham and Warren Swain (eds), *The Law of Misstatements: 50 Years on from Hedley Byrne v Heller* (Hart, 2015) 323 (fn 20).

(objective) requirement of consent to a legal obligation is not borne out in the cases. The main area of disagreement therefore relates to where, precisely, the line between assuming a responsibility and not assuming a responsibility should lie; in other words, the disagreement is not about whether the concept is useful in *theory*, but whether it is useful in *practice*.

Assumptions of responsibility therefore *do* seem to provide an independent type of justification for the imposition of a notional duty, at least where assumptions of responsibility are understood in sufficiently narrow terms, and as focussing on whether the defendant can be said to have objectively indicated that they can be relied upon in the performance of some activity, etc. Admittedly determining when someone has assumed a responsibility is not always straightforward, but it has been argued that it is no more difficult than determining when conduct alone can be understood as a manifestation of consent to a legal obligation in the law of contract. Assumptions of responsibility therefore play a different, but important role in notional duty determinations. Before looking at how the two independent justifications for the existence of a notional duty interact with one another, we will first briefly explore the role of reliance in assumptions of responsibility cases.

C. The Role of Reliance

What, then, is the role of reliance? As we saw in chapter three, its role under the current law is not entirely clear: some cases suggest that for an assumption of responsibility to give rise to a duty the assumption must *also* have been relied upon, whilst others suggest that the existence of the duty depends on the assumption of responsibility alone, and that if reliance plays any role at all it is only at other elements of the negligence enquiry, such as causation.[151] Is, then, reliance necessary for the existence of a duty based on an assumption of responsibility or not? The answer, unsurprisingly, depends on what we mean by 'reliance'. The term is rarely used consistently, and often used interchangeably with 'reasonable reliance' and 'detrimental reliance'. However, these terms mean entirely different things, some relevant to the existence of a duty, some irrelevant. Disputes about the appropriate role of reliance are therefore much the result of judges and commentators arguing at cross purposes.

For the most part, when courts and commentators speak of reliance they are referring to *actual* reliance by the claimant. Actual reliance is equivalent to *detrimental* reliance, as for the reliance to be detrimental, it must necessarily have been *actually* relied upon. This sense of reliance focusses on the claimant's subjective understanding of the defendant's representation, and conduct subsequent to it, rather than what the representation can be said to mean objectively. It is therefore clearly *not* relevant to whether the defendant can be said to have objectively

---

[151] See text accompanying (n 213) to (n 214) of ch 3.

assumed a responsibility to the claimant.[152] Indeed, as Barker notes, such an interpretation is 'illogical.'[153] Rather, this sense of reliance is more relevant to other elements of the negligence enquiry, and in particular the causation inquiry. It is this meaning of reliance that commentators have in mind when they say it is unnecessary to determine the existence of a duty.

Actual reliance can be contrasted with circumstances in which the defendant *induced* or *invited* the claimant to rely upon their representation, or made the representation in a way that suggested the claimant could rely on it. This sense of reliance focuses not on the claimant, but on the conduct of the defendant and the nature and apparent purpose of the representation made. It is this sense of reliance that commentators have in mind when they speak of *reasonable* reliance. This sense of reliance *is* necessary for the existence of a duty, as it is essentially equivalent to asking whether the defendant has objectively indicated to the claimant that they may be relied upon in some respect. Reasonable reliance and an objective assumption of responsibility are therefore flip sides of the same coin. Indeed, if a defendant objectively indicates that they can be relied upon, subsequent reliance will be reasonable, just as reliance on a representation will only be reasonable, if there has been some objective indication that it can be relied upon.[154]

Whether reliance is necessary for the existence of a duty therefore depends on what we mean by reliance. In the sense of actual or detrimental reliance it is unnecessary, but may nevertheless be useful in determining whether the defendant's carelessness caused the harm complained of. In its sense of reasonable reliance, however, it is necessary, as a finding that the reliance was reasonable is essentially equivalent to a finding that there was, objectively speaking, an assumption of responsibility.

IV. Putting it all Together: The Structure of the Notional Duty Enquiry

We have now seen that there are two *independent* ways to determine the existence of a notional duty. The first way is to show that the facts of the case fall within a specific inclusionary duty situation. Here a duty will exist because it is thought

---

[152] For a helpful analysis of why reliance (in this sense) is unnecessary, see Stevens, *Torts and Rights* (n 16) 14–15.

[153] Barker, 'Negligent Misstatement in Australia—Resolving the Uncertain Legacy of Esanda' (n 150) 328.

[154] Admittedly, this equivalence will depend on the term 'reasonable,' like assumption of responsibility, being construed narrowly. It would therefore preclude, for example, vulnerability justifying reliance, as being vulnerable would not make reliance on a representation 'reasonable' in the above sense. To some extent is it therefore artificial to describe reliance as 'necessary,' as it is only necessary if is defined synonymously with an 'assumption of responsibility,' but this understanding of reliance seems to be the most sensible way to explain judicial statements to that effect.

that such a situation ought to be subject to the laws of negligence. The second way is for the claimant to show that the defendant assumed a responsibility towards them. Here a duty will exist not because 'this category of case ought to be subject to the laws of negligence', but because, 'even though this category of case ought *not* to be subject to the laws of negligence, the defendant assumed a responsibility to the claimant and so ought to be bound by it'. To see how these discrete methods interact with one another, it is helpful to first focus on how they differ.

As we saw above, categorical notional duty determinations relate to situations, rather than to a specific set of facts. Situations can be either broad or narrow, as well as either inclusionary or exclusionary in nature. In particular, a small number of broad inclusionary and exclusionary situations are subject to a number of narrow exclusionary and inclusionary exceptions. The analogy drawn upon was seas and islets: three inclusionary seas (physical injuries, property damage, and psychiatric injury) subject to a number of exclusionary islets, and two exclusionary seas (omissions and purely economic loss) subject to a number of inclusionary islets. Where the facts of a case fall within a broad inclusionary situation, a duty will be held to exist unless the facts also fall within a narrow exclusionary situation. Similarly, where the facts fall within a broad exclusionary situation, a duty will be held *not* to exist unless they also fall within a narrow inclusionary situation.

A notional duty will also exist, however, if the defendant assumed a responsibility to the claimant. Notwithstanding that legitimate disagreement exists over where the line between assuming a responsibility and not assuming a responsibility should lie, it seems clear that the concept must be understood quite strictly if it is to have any meaning at all. In particular, it will depend on the exact nature of any representation made, and any words spoken, to the claimant by the defendant. Accordingly, unlike categorical duty determinations, a finding that there was an assumption of responsibility will be confined to the precise facts of the case; it will *not* apply to a broad situation, nor will it create any precedent. It is for this reason that cases like *White v Jone* and *Spring v Guardian Assurance plc*,[155] both of which were really justified on the basis that a notional duty *should* exist in the broad situation, and so clearly apply beyond their facts, are better understood as *categorical* determinations, rather than on the basis that the defendant assumed a responsibility to the claimant. Assumptions of responsibility are therefore an *exception* to the categorical nature of duty.[156]

How, then, do the two discrete justifications interact? As assumptions of responsibility can only justify the *imposition* of a duty, they will only ever be relevant in

---

[155] [1995] 2 AC 296 ('*Spring v Guardian*').

[156] Admittedly, on this understanding, it is arguable that the 'notional duty' terminology, which was defined above as concerning *categories* of case, is inappropriate. It will, however, continue to be used, as *both* the categorical and assumption of responsibility approaches to notional duty concern justifications for the imposition of the laws of negligence and so can logically dealt with together. In any event, provided it is clear that assumptions of responsibility form an *exception* to the categorical nature of duty, the introduction of new and potentially confusing terminology seems unnecessary.

exclusionary situations. The starting point in any notional duty determination is therefore to determine whether the facts of the case fall within a broad or narrow exclusionary situation. If they do not, and so fall within an inclusionary situation, a duty will exist, and so whether or not there was an assumption of responsibility is moot, there being no need to provide *another* basis for the existence of a duty. If, however, the facts of the case fall within an exclusionary situation, then there *will* be a need to determine whether there was an assumption of responsibility, as then, and only then, will there be any need to show why, despite the category of case not justifying the existence of the duty, the facts of the specific case do. Assumptions of responsibility are therefore best understood as a *secondary* method by which a notional duty may be established.

The structure of the notional duty enquiry is therefore as follows:

Diagram 1: The Structure of the Notional Duty Enquiry

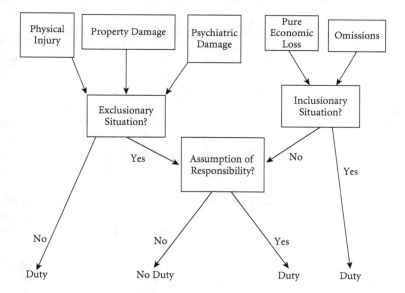

What we have, then, at least in most cases, is a two-to-three stage enquiry. First, the court must identify the broad category the facts fall within; secondly, they must determine whether the facts fall within a narrow exceptional category (or a narrow category that *should* be exceptional); and thirdly, assuming the enquiry is not over, they must determine whether there has there has been an assumption of responsibility.

There are numerous benefits to understanding notional duty enquiry in this way. First, it clearly explains how assumptions of responsibility interact with the general duty tests. As we saw in chapter three, this has given rise to much confusion in the past; some arguing that assumptions of responsibility are merely evidence of 'proximity', others arguing that assumptions of responsibility are an alternative test, though without being clear which test is to be preferred in which circumstances.[157] As we also saw, even *Customs and Excise Commissioners v Barclays Bank plc*,[158] though providing *some* guidance on the issue, only did so via a number of separate speeches, and ultimately left the issue unresolved.[159] Under the structure outlined above, the relationship is clear: the court begins by determining whether the broad situation ought to be subject to a notional duty, and only where that question is answered in the negative does the existence of an assumption of responsibility become relevant. Secondly, it discourages, and indeed makes unnecessary, fictitious uses of the assumption of responsibility concept. In particular, as the starting point in broad exclusionary situations is whether a narrow *categorical* exception ought to exist, cases like *White v Jones* and *Spring* are more likely to be (correctly) explained in categorical terms, rather than on the basis that there had been an assumption of responsibility; the need and opportunity for courts to explain the existence of a duty in such cases in terms of assumptions of responsibility will therefore no longer exist. Thirdly, it reduces the burden placed upon general duty tests, and simplifies them accordingly, as the tests will no longer be forced to justify the imposition of both consensual *and* non-consensual obligations under the same rubric, a futile mission that was abandoned in Roman times,[160] nor maintain that explicit undertakings are only enforceable if it is *also* 'fair, just, and reasonable' for them to be so. Fourthly, it clarifies that express disclaimers of liability, the relevance of which is not currently clear,[161] do indeed prevent a duty of care from arising (at least when based on an assumption of responsibility). In particular, if assumptions of responsibility are to be understood strictly, and on the basis of whether responsibility *was* assumed (albeit in an objective sense) rather than on the basis of whether responsibility *should* have been assumed (which would be a categorical duty issue), then an express disclaimer of responsibility is clearly incompatible with a finding that the conduct of the defendant objectively suggested that he or she was nevertheless assuming responsibility.[162] Finally, it clarifies the starting point of the duty enquiry. As we saw above, one of the main debates surrounding the duty enquiry is whether it is a 'control device' that limits the scope of liability for negligence, or something that defines our 'rights', which when infringed give rise to an action in negligence; that is whether the law of negligence is an ocean of liability with islands of non-liability, or an ocean of non-liability with islands of liability. Under the above structure, the position is clear: if the case concerns physical injury, psychiatric injury, or

---

[157] See ch 3, Section VII.

[158] [2007] 1 AC 181 (HL).

[159] See ch 3, Section VII.

[160] Gaius *Institutes* 3.88.

[161] Compare, for example, *Hedley Byrne* with *Smith v Eric S Bush*, particularly in light of *Customs and Excise Commissioners v Barclays Bank plc* [2007] 1 AC 181 (HL).

[162] The point was well made by Lord Devlin in *Hedley Byrne*, at 533: 'A man cannot be said voluntarily to be undertaking a responsibility if at the very moment when he is said to be accepting it he declares that in fact he is not.'

property damage, the starting point is that a duty exists, whilst if it concerns purely economic loss or omissions the starting point is that it does not.

Notwithstanding these benefits, it might nevertheless be objected that a narrow understanding of assumptions of responsibility proves too much, as even if it does result in a simpler understanding of the duty enquiry, it only does so by equating assumptions of responsibility with obligations based on consent, such that the real basis for the obligation lies in *contract* law, and so assumptions of responsibility ought not to create *tortious* obligations at all. There is certainly merit to this argument. This is why those who argue that assumptions of responsibility are a distinct type of justification tend to accept that this means they cannot belong in the law of negligence,[163] whilst those who believe they do belong in the law of negligence only do so on the basis that assumptions of responsibility are *not* a distinct type of justification,[164] but merely evidence of proximity, for example. Whilst the objection could easily be overcome if assumptions of responsibility were left to the law of contract, few appear to endorse such an approach, as it would mean that even explicit assumptions of responsibility could never form the basis of a legal obligation in the absence of consideration.[165] It also clearly does not represent the law; genuine assumptions of responsibility clearly *do* give rise to a duty of care in the law of negligence. Accordingly, given assumptions of responsibility *do* provide the basis for a tortious obligation, they need to be explained somehow. On the one hand, assumptions of responsibility could be understood fictitiously, or merely as evidence to be used in determining whether a more general test has been satisfied. We have seen that this approach is problematic; not only is it highly artificial and unconvincing, but explicit assumptions of responsibility tend to become sufficient justifications for the imposition of a duty in themselves in any event,[166] and so subject to the same objection—that such problems are more appropriately dealt with in the law of contract. On the other hand, as has been suggested, assumptions of responsibility could instead be understood strictly and as having real meaning, merely forming a *secondary* method by which a notional duty may be established. Such an approach, although endorsing a justification for

---

[163] See (n 124) and (n 125).

[164] See, eg, Barker, 'Negligent Misstatement in Australia—Resolving the Uncertain Legacy of Esanda' (n 150), Witting, 'What are We Doing Here? The Relationship Between Negligence in General and Misstatements in English Law' (n 140), and Robertson and Wang (n 122).

[165] Though this does not mean such a position is without merit. As Barker notes, by allowing assumptions of responsibility to create legal obligations, the law of negligence 'thus adopts an interstitial, gap-filling role to make good deficiencies in the law of contract, by rectifying damage caused by promises which the law of contract cannot enforce': Barker, 'Unreliable Assumptions in the Modern Law of Negligence' (n 122) 464. Indeed, it is difficult to see how one could support the doctrine of consideration whilst also believing that assumptions of responsibility, on even the clearest and most explicit foundation, ought to create legal obligations.

[166] See, eg, the comments of Lord Steyn in *Williams v Natural Life Health Foods Ltd* [1998] 1 WLR 830, 834 (HL): '[O]nce a case is identified as falling within the extended *Hedley Byrne* principle, there is no need to embark upon any further enquiry whether it is "fair, just and reasonable" to impose liability ...'

the existence of a duty of care that relies more on the law of contract than the law of tort, nevertheless provides a simpler, more convincing, and less artificial explanation of the law.

Notional duty is therefore best approached as a two-to-three stage enquiry. First, the court needs to determine which of five broad categories of case the facts fall within. Secondly, it must determine whether the facts also fall within a narrow inclusionary or exclusionary category. If they ultimately fall within an inclusionary category (whether broad or narrow) the enquiry is over and a duty exists. If, however, the facts fall within an exclusionary category (again, whether broad or narrow), the court must then ask whether there was an assumption of responsibility. If so, a duty exists; if not, a duty does not exist. As assumptions of responsibility depend on the precise facts of the case, rather than the broad situation generally, assumptions of responsibility are best understood as an exception to the generally categorical nature of notional duty determinations, as well as a secondary method by which to establish a notional duty. By approaching the notional duty enquiry in this structured manner, the interaction between assumptions of responsibility and general tests becomes clear, assumptions of responsibility are less likely to be fictitious, general tests will not have to do quite so much work, and the role of express disclaimers and the appropriate starting point of the duty enquiry is clarified.

V. A Suggested Approach to Resolving Notional Duty Problems

So far, so good. But the foregoing analysis has been almost exclusively structural in nature; it has identified the right questions to ask, but, at least in categorical cases, said little about how to answer them. In particular, little has been said about how to approach novel situations, being those categories of case that are floating in a sea rather than sitting on an islet, or categories of case that are subject to a rule the court wishes to reconsider. How do we determine whether such situations *ought* to give rise to a notional duty? This is indeed the single most difficult part of the notional duty enquiry.

As we saw in chapter three, courts tend to approach the ought aspect of the notional duty enquiry by relying on general duty tests, including looking at whether there are sufficient salient features, whether there is sufficient proximity, and whether the imposition of the duty would be fair, just, and reasonable. However, as we also saw, the difficulty with this approach is that, given the vast range of situations that do and do not give rise to a duty, such formulas inevitably descend into such a high level of abstraction that they end up having no prescriptive or analytical value at all. After all, whether an exception ought to be made to the general rule that physical injuries give rise to a duty, raises completely different considerations to whether an exception ought to be made to the general rule that damage that has resulted from an omission does not give rise to a duty. Yet this is precisely what general duty tests try to do. It is no wonder that the search for a general duty formula has been so spectacularly unsuccessful. The point is well made by Christie:

> the attempt to establish a single general principle of liability for all negligence cases—which run the gamut from physical injury to emotional distress to various kinds of economic loss—has shown itself to be as hopeless as it is unwise.[167]

That determining the existence of a notional duty in the different broad categories of case requires the examination of entirely different considerations ought to be explicitly recognised. The search for a general (notional duty) test should therefore be abandoned, and replaced with *different* sets of principles (or more focussed tests) in the five broad duty categories: one set for when a narrow exclusionary exception ought to exist to the general rule of recoverability in cases of physical injury, a second for when a narrow exclusionary exception ought to exist to the general rule of recoverability in cases of property damage, a third for when a narrow exclusionary exception ought to exist to the general rule of recoverability in cases of psychiatric injury, a fourth for when a narrow inclusionary exception ought to exist to the general rule of non-recoverability in cases of omissions, and a fifth for when a narrow inclusionary exception ought to exist to the general rule of non-recoverability in cases of purely economic loss. Such an approach would loosely resemble a combination of the pockets and general test approaches to duty; however, with broader and more discrete pockets, it would not be subject to the difficulties associated with overlapping pockets; and with five tests rather than one, and working from two rather than one starting point, nor would it be subject to the criticism that it was unable to deal with novel fact scenarios, or that the principles which governed the existence of a duty were too vague to offer any prescriptive or predictive value.

Approaching the notional duty enquiry in this way would allow the various and often discrete duty determinants (that is, reasons for and against the existence of a duty), many of which are currently grouped together under vague and unhelpful labels, to be separated out and considered only within the category of case in which they are relevant. The vague and unhelpful labels would therefore no longer be necessary. Proximity, for example, as we saw in chapter three, is generally little more than a label for a number of conceptually distinct reasons (or 'proximity factors') for the existence of a duty, and so ends up meaning completely different things in the different categories of case.[168] Whilst these discrete reasons are often highly relevant in determining the existence of a notional duty in the different

---

[167] George C Christie, 'The Uneasy Place of Principle in Tort Law' in D Owen (ed), *Philosophical Foundations of Tort Law* (Clarendon Press, 1995).

[168] Even Robertson agrees that 'considerations to be taken into account [under the proximity enquiry] will vary across different classes of case': A Robertson, 'Proximity: Divergence and Unity' in A Robertson and M Tilbury (eds), *Divergences in Private Law* (Hart, 2016) 12.

categories of case,[169] the attempt to unify them under the label of 'proximity' is unhelpful, as it tells us very little about what is *actually* required, and not required, for a duty to be established in individual categories of case. Approaching the five broad duty situations discretely, however, would identify precisely which 'proximity factors' needed to be considered in each category of case, and which proximity factors did not.[170] In cases of directly caused physical injury and property damage, for example, where proximity is treated synonymously with foreseeability, there would no additional factors to consider at all;[171] in cases involving omissions, or harm caused by a third party, the court would need to consider whether the defendant exercised any degree of control over the claimant, or third party wrongdoer;[172] whilst in cases of pure economic loss, the existence of a duty would depend on, among other things, whether the posited duty was inconsistent with the 'contractual relationship in which the parties interacted'.[173] In this way, the *substance* (or at least the intended substance) of the proximity requirement would continue to be influential, and indeed often determinative, but the proximity *label* would be redundant. The salient features test could be deconstructed in a similar way, so that rather than asking whether there are sufficient salient features *in all duty cases*, an approach that permits courts unfettered discretion in choosing which factors will be considered and how they will be weighed against one another, courts would instead consider only the salient features relevant to the broad category of case before it. This approach to notional duty problems would require the consideration of a far more circumscribed, focussed, and relevant list of considerations, leading to a simpler and more predictable enquiry.

Any suggestion to abandon general duty tests may be seen by some as radical. General duty tests are, after all, firmly embedded in the modern law and have been for many years, and sceptics are right to be apprehensive about potentially major changes to the law, as their consequences cannot always be easily predicted. The abandonment of general duty tests would not, however, at least in the manner suggested, be such a change. Indeed, aside from the fact that general duty tests were only really accepted as the appropriate way to determine the outcome of the duty enquiry in the 1970s in any event,[174] the application of different principles to different categories of

---

[169] The amount of work *actually* done under the proximity label is discussed further in ch 7, Section III(B).

[170] It might be objected here that this is what often occurs in practice anyway. But this is really a concession that proximity *is* merely an unhelpful label, precisely the problem the approach is trying to correct.

[171] Both Robertson and Witting agree that this is how proximity should be understood in cases of physical injury: Christian Witting, 'Physical Damage in Negligence' (2002) 61 CLJ 189, 189; Robertson (n 168) 25.

[172] Robertson lists this as a proximity factor: Robertson 13.

[173] ibid. For further proximity factors, according to Robertson, see ibid 11–13.

[174] As we saw in ch 2, notwithstanding that the *idea* of general duty tests can be dated back to *Heaven v Pender* (1883) 11 QB 503 (CA), and famously rose to prominence in *Donoghue v Stevenson* [1932] AC 562 (HL), it was not until the 1970s, and in particular *Home Office v Dorset Yacht Co Ltd* [1970] AC 1004 (HL) and *Anns v Merton LBC* [1978] AC 728 (HL), that they came to be accepted as *the* approach to resolving duty questions. Abandoning duty general tests would therefore *not* involve the abandonment of an idea deeply rooted in legal history, but only of an idea that is not even 50 years old.

case is *already*, to a large extent, orthodox, as the case law *already* treats the five broad categories of case discretely, and as subject to different principles. There is already, for example, considerable authority for the proposition that, subject to there being a good reason for not doing so, directly caused physical injury or property damage will generally give rise to a duty.[175] Similarly, negligently inflicted psychiatric injuries also tend to give rise to a duty,[176] notwithstanding a number of well-settled restrictions and exclusions,[177] many of which, at least in the UK, are openly acknowledged as 'arbitrary' and 'unprincipled'.[178] Where the damage is purely economic in nature,[179] or the result of an omission/failure to prevent harm caused by a third party,[180]

---

[175] See, eg: Lord Keith in *Alcock v Chief Constable of South Yorkshire* [1992] AC 310 (HL) at 396 ('In the ordinary case of direct physical injury suffered in an accident at work or elsewhere, reasonable foreseeability of the risk is indeed the only test that need be applied to determine liability'); Lord Oliver in *Caparo Industries plc v Dickman* [1990] 2 AC 605 (HL) at 632 ('in the context of loss caused by physical damage ... the nexus between the careless defendant and the injured plaintiff can rarely give rise to any difficulty'); Lord Oliver in *Murphy v Brentwood DC* [1991] 1 AC 398 (HL) at 486-87 ('The infliction of physical injury to the person or property of another universally requires to be justified'); and May LJ in *Sandhar v Department of Transport, Environment and the Regions* [2005] 1 WLR 1632 (CA) at 1644 [31] ('Personal or physical injury directly inflicted is the first building block of the law of negligence'); Lord Hoffmann in *Customs and Excise Commissioners v Barclays Bank plc* [2007] 1 AC 181 (HL) at [31] ('In the case of personal or physical injury, reasonable foreseeability of harm is usually enough ... to generate a duty of care'); and Hobhouse LJ in *Perrett v Collins* [1999] PNLR 77 (CA) at 91 ('[W]here the conduct would amount to a direct invasion of property or personal rights ... a special justification is required to negative liability').

[176] See, eg: *Page v Smith* [1996] 1 AC 155 (HL); *Tame v New South Wales, Annetts v Australian Stations Pty Ltd* (2002) 211 CLR 317. For further discussion, see Stevens, *Torts and Rights* (n 16) 54–56.

[177] *Alcock v Chief Constable of South Yorkshire* [1992] AC 310 (HL), *Greatorex v Greatorex* [2000] 1 WLR 1970, *Homsi v Homsi* [2016] VSC 354. Robertson characterises some of the restrictions, albeit not the aforementioned cases, as based on his concept of proximity: Robertson (n 168).

[178] See, eg: Lord Hoffmann in *Frost v Chief Constable of South Yorkshire Police* [1999] 2 AC 455 at 509 and 511 ('[the restrictions are] more or less arbitrary', and 'It seems to me that in this area of the law, the search for principle was called off in *Alcock v Chief Constable of South Yorkshire Police* ... No one can pretend that the existing law, which your Lordships have to accept, is founded upon principle'), and Lord Steyn in ibid at 500 ('[T]he law on the recovery of compensation for pure psychiatric harm is a patchwork quilt of distinctions which are difficult to justify').

[179] See, eg, Lord Oliver in *Murphy v Brentwood DC* [1991] 1 AC 398 (HL) at 486–87 ('The infliction of physical injury to the person or property of another universally requires to be justified. The causing of economic loss does not.'); McHugh J in *Perre v Apand Pty Ltd* (1999) 198 CLR 180 at 209 ('Denial of recovery for pure economic loss remains the rule, but, since *Hedley Byrne & Co Ltd v Heller & Partners Ltd* was decided in 1963, many exceptions to the rule have been recognised').

[180] See, eg, Lord Hoffmann in *Stovin v Wise* [1996] AC 923 (HL) at 949 ('The trend of authorities has been to discourage the assumption that anyone who suffers loss is prima facie entitled to compensation from a person (preferably insured or a public authority) whose act or omission can be said to have caused it. The default position is that he is not'); and Gummow, Hayne and Heydon JJ in *Stuart v Kirkland-Veenstra* (2009) 237 CLR 215 at [88] ('Personal autonomy is a value that informs much of the common law. It is a value that is reflected in the law of negligence. The co-existence of a knowledge of a risk of harm and power to avert or minimise that harm does not, without more, give rise to a duty of care at common law'); and Lord Toulson in *Michael v The Chief Constable of South Wales Police* [2015] AC 1732 (UKSC) [97] ('English law does not as a general rule impose liability on a defendant for injury or damage to the person or property of a claimant caused by the conduct of a third party ... The fundamental reason, as Lord Goff explained, is that the common law does not generally impose liability for pure omissions. It is one thing to require a person who embarks on action which may harm others to exercise care. It is another matter to hold a person liable in damages for failing to prevent harm caused by someone else.').

on the other hand, it is well recognised that the imposition of a duty will be exceptional; indeed, the former type of damage is often said to be subject to an 'exclusionary rule'.[181] A similar approach to the law is adopted by many leading tort law texts, which, after explaining that directly caused physical injuries and property damage rarely give rise to any duty issues, typically devote discrete sections (and sometimes chapters) to negligently caused psychiatric injury, omissions, and purely economic loss.[182] Recognising five discrete tests would therefore not be so much revolutionary, as an explicit recognition that this is, to a large extent, what is already done. The proposed change would therefore not be one of substance, but one of mere form.

None of this is to say that under this suggested approach determining the existence of notional duty will become a simple algorithm. It will not. Inevitably, the five sets of principles (or tests) will need to remain at a relatively high level of generality in order to retain flexibility and discretion in how those principles are applied. However, five separate and more precise sets of principles, specific to the actual type of harm suffered, and working from two different starting points, will be far *less* general than the existing general duty tests, and give rise to a far *more* focussed and predictable enquiry. As to what those tests and principles are, much guidance is offered by the existing law. A detailed exposition of these, however, including any general propositions they may give rise to, is beyond the scope of this book, and so left for another day.

VI. Conclusion

Notional duty performs an important normative function within the negligence enquiry; it determines which situations should be the subject of the laws of negligence, and which situations should not. Absent a notional duty, the defendant may carelessly cause harm to the claimant with impunity. A central feature of notional determinations is that they are categorical, and apply to situations rather than the precise facts of the case. As we have seen, these 'situations' can be inclusionary or exclusionary, as well as narrow or broad. When they are narrow, they ought to include references to the kind of harm incurred, the manner in which it occurred, as well as some reference to the parties' relationship to each other. Notional duty

---

[181] Peter Benson, 'The Basis for Excluding Liability for Economic Loss in Tort Law' in David G Owen (ed), *Philosophical Foundations of Tort Law* (OUP, 1995).

[182] M Lunney and K Oliphant, *Tort Law: Text and Materials*, 5th edn (OUP, 2013) 446; D Nolan and J Davies, 'Torts and Equitable Wrongs' in AS Burrows (ed), *English Private Law*, 3rd edn (OUP, 2013); Rachael Mulheron, *Principles of Tort Law* (Cambridge University Press, 2016). Public liability negligence is also usually considered discretely, though more because of the overlap with public law concepts (such as justiciability) than because special duty rules apply: *Gorringe v Calderdale Metropolitan Borough Council* [2004] 1 WLR 1057, *Michael v The Chief Constable of South Wales Police* [2015] AC 1732.

situations explained in terms of the relationship or kind of harm suffered only, are best avoided. They ought also not be formulated in overly narrow terms, nor in terms of a 'duty to do X'. Indeed, given that, as we saw in chapter four, the duty of care does not refer to a 'real' duty at all, arguably the 'duty' language is awkward and unnecessary: compare, for example, 'does the driver of a motor vehicle owe a duty to a passenger in relation to any physical damage that occurs to the passenger as a result of the driver's careless driving?' to 'can liability for negligence exist where a driver causes physical injury to a passenger as a direct result of their careless driving?' The 'scope' of the duty language is also potentially productive of confusion, given the multiple senses in which it is used, some of which are not only superfluous, but actively misleading.

Where a particular situation is deemed to not give rise to a notional duty, and so forms an exclusionary situation, the court may still find that a notional duty exists where the defendant has assumed a responsibility towards the claimant. This provides an entirely independent justification for why the defendant ought to have an obligation to compensate the claimant for any carelessly caused harm; it is not because everybody should have such an obligation in the particular situation, but because of the defendant's undertaking. Whilst assumptions of responsibility need not have been explicit, they nevertheless need to be sufficiently clear such that, as in contract law, the defendant can be said to have objectively consented to a legal obligation being imposed. Where the focus moves from whether the particular defendant *did* consent, to whether, given the circumstances, the defendant *should* have consented, the assumption of responsibility test becomes indistinguishable from general duty tests and loses all value as a duty determinant.

It has also been suggested that the determination of a notional duty ought to be achieved not via a single general duty test, but via five discrete sets of principles, being one for each of the five broad categories of case: physical injury, property damage, psychiatric injury, omissions, and purely economic loss. Such an approach would avoid many of the problems associated with general duty tests, and provide a more structured, tailored, and predictable method for determining the existence of a notional duty.

6

Notional Duty II: Theoretical Issues

I, for one, protest ... against arguing too strongly upon public policy;—it is a very unruly horse, and once you get astride it you never know where it will carry you.

Burrough J in *Richardson v Mellish* [1892] 130 ER 294, 303; 2 Bing 229, 252.

The duty to take care ... [is] an unnecessary fifth wheel on the coach, incapable of sound analysis and possibly productive of injustice.

WW Buckland, 'The Duty to Take Care' (1935) 51 LQR 637, 639.

I. Introduction

Chapter five concerned, among other things, the structure that should be adopted when identifying and expressing notional duty situations, as well as some broad guidance on how the notional duty enquiry should be resolved. The chapter was therefore mostly focussed on the more practical aspects, or general principles, of the enquiry. In this chapter, the focus shifts to more theoretical issues, being those that tend to attract more attention from academic circles than from the courts. In particular, the chapter will examine: first, the propriety of relying on policy considerations to determine the existence of a notional duty; and secondly, the necessity of notional duty in the first place—that is, whether notional duty is a necessary part of the negligence enquiry or merely an unnecessary 'fifth wheel on the coach', whose objects could be achieved via a method that does not depend on notional duty at all.

II. The Use of Policy Considerations

As we have seen, the existence of a notional duty is a normative issue; that is, the question for the court is whether a notional duty *ought* to exist. Whilst a clear assumption of responsibility tends to provide a justification for the existence of a notional duty in itself,[1] when determining whether a particular situation ought to

---

[1] That is, as we have seen, because the defendant consented to it.

be subject to a notional duty, courts frequently rely on considerations of 'policy', which, as we saw in chapter three, concern considerations of community welfare, as opposed to considerations of interpersonal justice. Indeed, this is hardly surprising, as whether the law of negligence ought to apply to a broad situation that transcends the particular facts of the case, will inevitably lend itself to consideration of factors that also transcend the particular facts of the case.[2]

The use of policy-based arguments in determining the outcome of notional duty issues is, however, highly controversial. Beever, for example, argues that it is impermissible and unnecessary,[3] and an 'admission of failure',[4] whilst Stevens claims that the attractions of policy-based arguments 'should be resisted', as, although they make 'the law of torts seem exciting and interesting ... The law of torts is much more boring than is commonly supposed.'[5] Courts should instead, according to critics, rely on considerations of 'principle'.[6] Others, however, believe the use of policy is perfectly acceptable. Stapleton, for example, argues that the use of policy lets 'daylight in on magic',[7] whilst Lord Edmund-Davies has stated that 'the proposition that "the policy issue ... is not justiciable" is as novel as it is startling ... [and] runs counter to well-established and wholly acceptable law.'[8] Whilst this debate about the appropriate role of policy-based reasoning is hardly new,[9] it has risen in prominence in recent years due to the increased influence of rights-based theories of private law, most of which tend to reject the use of policy-based reasoning.

---

[2] This is not to say that it will necessarily lend itself to *exclusive* consideration of policy. Non-policy reasons can also be relevant to the notional duty enquiry, as there is no reason why considerations of principle cannot also apply to broad situations. For example, that a notional duty exists in relation to physical injury directly caused to a passenger by a driver's careless driving could be justified on the basis of the close relationship of the parties as well as the parties' legitimate expectations, rather than simply because it is beneficial for society. Similarly, the general absence of a notional duty in relation to omissions can be, and usually is, explained on the basis that the recognition of a duty would impose too great an interference on individual's freedom of action, which is, again, a consideration of principle (see, eg, Lord Hoffmann in *Stovin v Wise* [1996] AC 923 (HL), 946).

[3] A Beever, *Rediscovering the Law of Negligence* (Hart, 2007) 29.

[4] A Beever, 'Policy in Private Law: An Admission of Failure' (2006) 25 UQLJ 287.

[5] R Stevens, *Torts and Rights* (OUP, 2007) 307. See also, EJ Weinrib, 'The Disintegration of Duty' in M Stuart Madden (ed), *Exploring Tort Law* (Cambridge University Press, 2005) and EJ Weinrib, *The Idea of Private Law* (rev edn, OUP, 2012).

[6] For the remainder of this book, the approach to resolving notional duty determinations that permits policy considerations will be called 'the policy based approach', whilst the approach that prohibits policy considerations will be called 'the principle based approach'.

[7] J Stapleton, 'The Golden Thread at the Heart of Tort Law: Protection of the Vulnerable' (2003) 24 Aust Bar Rev 135, 138.

[8] *McLoughlin v O'Brian* [1983] 1 AC 410 (HL).

[9] See, eg, the comments of Burrough J in *Richardson v Mellish* [1892] 2 Bing 229, 252; 130 ER 294, 303 ('I, for one, protest ... against arguing too strongly upon public policy;—it is a very unruly horse, and once you get astride it you never know where it will carry you') and Lord Mansfield in *Holman v Johnson* (1775) 1 Cowp 341, 343; 98 ER 1120, 1121 ('The objection, that a contract is immoral or illegal ... sounds at all times very ill in the mouth of the defendant. It is not for his sake, however, that the objection is ever allowed; but it is founded in general principles of policy, which the defendant has the advantage of, contrary to the real justice, as between him and the plaintiff, by accident, if I may say so'). See also the discussion in SM Waddams, *Principle and Policy in Contract law* (Cambridge University Press, 2011) Ch 5.

What, however, is it about policy-based reasoning that is thought to be so problematic? According to the critics of policy-based reasoning, there are four primary objections: first, judges are not qualified to rely on policy-based arguments; secondly, the use of policy-based arguments requires the balancing of incommensurables; thirdly, the use of policy-based arguments violates the rule of law; and fourthly, the use of policy-based arguments leads to a less coherent body of law. This section will examine these arguments in further detail.[10]

A. Judges are not Qualified to Rely on Policy Considerations

The most commonly advanced argument against the use of policy considerations is that judges are not qualified to rely on them. There appear to be three reasons for this belief: that judges lack political legitimacy, that judges lack technical competence, and that judges often lack sufficient evidence.

The argument that judges lack the political legitimacy to rely on policy considerations is based on the view that, in a liberal democracy such as ours, considerations of policy are most appropriately dealt with by a democratically elected Parliament, and not by the judiciary.[11] In particular, it is for the community to determine what is in its best interests and what policies it wishes for the law to reflect, and a democratically elected legislature is, at least in theory, the best way of achieving this. The judiciary, on the other hand, do not usually make their political views public and are not appointed on the basis of those views in any event (again, at least in theory). Accordingly, if judges are permitted to rely on policy considerations, there is no method of ensuring that such considerations in any way reflect the views of the public; indeed given the limited interaction of judges with members of the public, and the small section of the 'socio-economic elite' from which judges and the lawyers arguing before them are drawn, it is difficult to see how they could.[12] Judges are therefore thought to lack the political legitimacy to rely on, and thereby implement within the law, reasons of policy. None of this is to say, of course, that the judges are not well meaning, or even to deny that what they believe to be in the best interests of the community has a more rational basis than what the community believes to be in its best interests; it is, however, undemocratic, and to suggest otherwise is, according to Beever, 'incredible'.[13]

---

[10] Importantly, most of these arguments are advanced against the use of policy-based reasoning in private law, tort law, or the law of negligence *generally*, rather than the notional duty enquiry in particular. However, the notional duty falls within all these areas and is, in any event, the principal area of private law, tort law, and the law of negligence, in which these arguments are encountered.

[11] Beever, *Rediscovering the Law of Negligence* (n 3) 54; Stevens (n 5) 308; D Heydon, 'Judicial Activism and the Death of the Rule of Law' (2003) 23 ABR 110; Weinrib, *The Idea of Private Law* (n 5) 208–209; John Smillie, 'Who Wants Juristocracy?' (2005–2008) 11 Otago L Rev 183. See also the discussion in J Bell, *Policy Arguments in Judicial Decisions* (Clarendon Press, 1983) 9.

[12] Beever, *Rediscovering the Law of Negligence* (n 3) 54.

[13] ibid 54.

The argument that judges lack the technical competence to rely on policy-based reasons is based on the view that they do not have the necessary training or educational background to properly assess the legitimacy of policy-based concerns or how best to implement them. They should, therefore, not base a decision on, say, the potential economic consequences of that decision, as they are not only unqualified to determine whether such economic consequences are good or bad, but they are also often not qualified to determine the likely consequences of the decision in the first place; after all, judges, and the lawyers on whose arguments they rely, are trained in the law, not in social policy or economic theory.[14] Parliament, on the other hand, employs and is able to rely on specially trained policy advisers, with expertise in economics, social welfare, etc. As Beever notes:

> Why would [the public] be prepared to spend considerable effort and taxpayers' money setting up ministries containing expert policy analysts in order to ensure that ministers get the best advice possible, and yet be prepared to allow judges with little or no social policy training, advised by lawyers with little or no social policy training, to make social policy choices ...[15]

Without the necessary technical competence to assess policy concerns, it is thought that courts should therefore avoid relying on them altogether.

The argument that, even if judges did have the necessary political legitimacy and technical competence, they nevertheless often lack sufficient evidence to properly assess policy concerns, is principally based on the limitations of the forum. Indeed, courts are subject to significant institutional limitations, including the rules of evidence and the adversarial nature of proceedings—the advocate's role being to win his or her case rather than to present relevant facts or to find the truth.[16] Relevant evidence may also not be presented because it is too expensive for the parties to justify, too time consuming for a trial between two parties, or too complex for a single judge to consider. In the absence of such evidence, it is argued that courts may therefore resort to 'speculation',[17] which comes with the 'associated risk of errors'.[18] In *Hill v Chief Constable of West Yorkshire*,[19] for example, the claimant, acting on behalf of her daughter's estate, sued the police for their failure to apprehend the Yorkshire Ripper before he murdered her daughter. In finding that no duty of care existed, Lord Keith refused to exclude the possibility that a finding of liability could encourage 'detrimentally defensive' policing, despite no evidence

---

[14] Stevens (n 5) 309; Weinrib, 'The Disintegration of Duty' (n 5) 167; Weinrib, *The Idea of Private Law* (n 5) 208–209; C Witting, 'Tort Law, Policy and the High Court of Australia' (2007) 31 MULR 569, 580.

[15] Beever, *Rediscovering the Law of Negligence* (n 3) 173.

[16] Witting (n 14) 580.

[17] NJ McBride and R Bagshaw, *Tort Law*, 3rd edn (Pearson Longman, 2008) 202. See also, P Cane, 'Consequences in Judicial Reasoning' in J Horder (ed), *Oxford Essays in Jurisprudence* (OUP, 2000).

[18] C Witting, 'The House that Dr Beever Built: Corrective Justice, Principle and the Law of Negligence' (2008) 71 MLR 621, 633. See also K Burns, 'The Way the World is: Social Facts in High Court Negligence Cases' (2004) 12 TLJ 215, 232.

[19] [1989] AC 53 (HL).

being given on this point.[20] Similarly, in *Macfarlane v Tayside Health Board*,[21] a wrongful birth/conception case, despite all their Lordships disclaiming any reliance on policy, one of the reasons the court found that no duty existed was, at least according to Lord Bingham in a later case, that such a decision would 'offend the community's sense of how public resources should be allocated'.[22] Again, the court had heard no evidence on the consensus of public opinion, and so such a conclusion was merely the judge's best guess.[23] It goes without saying that courts should not be basing decisions on speculation as to the consequences of a decision for the community and, on the basis that courts often do not have sufficient evidence to do otherwise, advocates of the principle-based approach believe they should therefore avoid relying on considerations of policy altogether.

It would therefore seem that judges are neither politically legitimate nor technically competent to assess policy-based arguments, and, in any event, often lack sufficient evidence to properly assess such concerns. Yet, not everyone accepts these conclusions and numerous objections to the above arguments have been raised. As to the claim that judges lack the necessary political legitimacy, both Cane[24] and Dworkin[25] have questioned why the same objection is not raised to judicial consideration of questions of interpersonal justice. In particular, why is it undemocratic for unelected judges from a small and unrepresentative section of society to determine our legal rights based on their personal political views, but not undemocratic for those same judges to determine and prioritise our legal rights on the basis of their personal views on interpersonal justice? It might be objected here that it is because judges are experts in the latter but not in the former.[26] But, as Priel points out, this response simply begs the question; in particular, what is it that makes judges experts on questions of principle but not experts on questions of policy? It cannot be because they are exposed to the former and not the later because, not only *are* judges exposed to questions of policy in public law, but even if they were not, given there is apparently no objection to judges becoming experts to issues of interpersonal justice through exposure, the principal objection would be

---

[20] ibid 63 (Lord Keith). Similar concerns were expressed by Lords Carswell, Hope and Brown in *Van Colle v Chief Constable of the Hertfordshire Police; Smith v Chief Constable of Sussex Police* [2009] 1 AC 225 (HL) at [108], [76], and [132]. Compare the views of McLachlin CJ in *Hill v Hamilton-Wentworth Regional Police Services Board* (2007) 285 DLR (4th) 620 [57]–[58]. See also, Stevens (n 5) 309–10; A Robertson, 'Rights, Pluralism and the Duty of Care' in D Nolan and A Robertson (eds), *Rights and Private Law* (Hart, 2012) 454–55; Jonathan Morgan, 'Policy Reasoning in Tort Law: The Courts, the Law Commission and the Critics' (2009) 125 LQR 215, 215.

[21] [2000] 2 AC 59 (HL).

[22] *Rees v Darlington Memorial Hospital NHS Trust* [2004] 1 AC 309 (HL) 316 (Lord Bingham).

[23] Stevens (n 5) 311.

[24] P Cane, 'Rights in Private Law' in D Nolan and A Robertson (eds), *Rights and Private Law* (Hart, 2012), 55.

[25] Ronald Dworkin, *A Matter of Principle* (Harvard University Press, 1985) 23–28.

[26] See, eg, Allan Beever, *Forgotten Justice: The Forms of Justice in the History of Legal and Political Theory* (OUP, 2013) 306; P Birks, 'Equity in Modern Law: An Exercise in Taxonomy' (1996) 26 WALR 3, 97.

overcome by simply exposing judges to policy in the same way they are exposed to principle, thereby making them experts in questions of policy too.[27] The second claim, that judges are not technically competent, is also disputed. Robertson, for example, questions whether it is correct that policy decisions should only be made *by* experts rather than *on the advice of* experts.[28] Many members of Parliament, for example, have no training at all in matters of public policy, whilst those who do are invariably required to make decisions outside their individual areas of expertise, and so often have no choice but to rely on the advice of experts. If parliamentarians are able to rely on experts, despite not being experts themselves, then it is not clear why the judiciary cannot do the same (that is, when expert evidence is tendered). The third claim, that judges rarely have sufficient evidence on which to appropriately assess policy-based concerns, has also been questioned. First, it has been doubted how often this problem actually arises. As Robertson points out, matters of policy, such as the content of community values, can often be informed by readily available evidence, including reports of Royal Commissions and Law Reform Commissions.[29] Secondly, even if *some* cases exist in which judges lack sufficient evidence to appropriately assess policy-based concerns, it does not follow that judges should be prevented from assessing policy-based concerns in *all* cases, including those where sufficient evidence *is* available. Thirdly, as pointed out by Morgan, Law Commissions, Government and Parliament are *themselves* often required to undertake law reform on a 'speculative basis', because certain evidence may be too expensive to obtain (on a cost-benefit analysis);[30] again, it is not clear why this only becomes objectionable when done by the judiciary. It may be objected here that Parliament is nevertheless in a better position than courts to assess policy concerns because of their superior resources. Whilst it is certainly true that courts have fewer resources than Parliament, and so access to *less* evidence, it does not follow that they have access to *insufficient* evidence.

As well as the above responses to the specific claims made by advocates of the principle-based approach, numerous other, more general, objections have been made to the claim that the judiciary is unqualified to consider policy-based arguments. First, under the Human Rights Act 1998, judges are *required* to take policy considerations into account when determining the scope of certain rights and any limits that ought to be placed upon them.[31] Accordingly, as Morgan points out,

---

[27] Dan Priel, 'Private Law: Commutative or Distributive?' (2014) 77 MLR 308, 323–24.

[28] Robertson (n 20) 455–56.

[29] ibid 454.

[30] Morgan (n 20) 220.

[31] For example, the 'Right to respect for private and family life,' recognised in Article 8.1 of Schedule 1, may, by virtue of Article 8.2, be 'interfered with' where it is 'necessary in a democratic society in the interests of national security, public safety or the economic well-being of the country, for the prevention of disorder or crime, for the protection of health or morals, or for the protection of the rights and freedoms of others'; such considerations are clearly considerations of policy. The rights protected by Articles 9 to 11 of Schedule 1 are similarly limited (though the exact wording of the grounds for limiting the rights varies).

'If in such cases judges can be trusted to weigh the costs (to the individual) against the benefits (to society) of the challenged legislation, why should the same judges become incapable of a similar exercise when deciding tort cases?'[32] Secondly, the legislature often leaves the content of large areas of private law to be determined entirely by the courts, so that if considerations of community welfare are to be taken into account in these areas of law at all, it must *necessarily* be done by the courts.[33] Thirdly, even if courts do occasionally get it wrong, whether because the decision does not reflect the views of the wider community or because the court did not have the appropriate resources or evidence, ultimate control rests with the legislature anyway, and so the legislature can always substitute a court's decision with their own.[34] Fourthly, even if the problems with judicial use of policy-based arguments are conceded, it is debatable whether judges ignoring the potentially undesirable social consequences of their decisions is a better alternative;[35] indeed, as noted by Pollock LCB in *Egerton v Brownlow*:[36]

> My Lords, it may be that judges are no better able to discern what is for the public good than other experienced and enlightened members of the community; but that is no reason for their refusing to entertain the question, and declining to decide upon it.

The argument that judges are not qualified to rely on policy is therefore problematic, and, quite aside from these problems, there exist a number of arguments why judicial use of policy considerations is nevertheless desirable.

B. The Use of Policy Requires the Balancing of Incommensurables

A second, and very common, argument against the use of policy-based reasons is that it requires the balancing of 'incommensurables'. In particular, it is thought that, by allowing policy based reasons to be considered, judges may end up having to weigh considerations of interpersonal justice against considerations of community welfare, which are, according to critics, fundamentally different and so incommensurable. Weinrib, for example, argues that there is a 'disjunction between justice and policy considerations' and so queries how judges are:

> to determine whether in a given case the policy considerations are more important than the justice considerations that they can displace. How is this balancing of incommensurables to be done? ... [Requiring courts to balance such incommensurable

---

[32] Morgan (n 20) 221.
[33] S Waddams, 'Private Right and Public Interest' in M Bryan (ed), *Private Law in Theory and Practice* (Routledge, 2008) 19; P Cane, 'Taking Disagreement Seriously: Courts, Legislatures and the Reforms of Tort Law' (2005) 25 OJLS 393, 411.
[34] H Luntz and others, *Torts: Cases and Commentary*, 7th edn (Lexis Nexis, 2013) 148. Compare Dworkin (n 25) 18.
[35] Morgan (n 20) 221; Robertson (n 20) 456.
[36] (1853) 4 HLC 1, 151; 10 ER 359, 419.

considerations] puts into circulation two different normative currencies between which no rate of exchange exists.[37]

Stevens agrees, believing that asking courts to balance incommensurables is like asking a judge 'which is the greater of three kilos or six metres', or 'whether Mozart or chocolate is better. The goods are incommensurable'.[38] According to this argument, then, a court cannot determine that the public interest in allowing the police to investigate crimes in a non-defensive manner outweighs an individual's interest in their personal safety, as it would require the court to balance incommensurables.

Whilst it is clear that critics of policy based reasoning are against the balancing of incommensurables, it is not entirely clear whether this is because they believe incommensurables *cannot* be balanced, or that they *should not* be balanced. If the objection is that incommensurables *cannot* be balanced, then it is not clear why the same objection is not made to Parliament regularly doing exactly that.[39] In the absence of such an objection, the argument that incommensurables *cannot* be balanced is difficult to maintain. And, even if that is the objection, then, as Urbina notes, it does not follow that it is unreasonable or irrational to choose between the two in any event; just that one cannot commensurate them, and so must choose between them on other grounds.[40] If, on the other hand, the objection is that incommensurables *should* not be balanced, the similar absence of any objection to such balancing being undertaken by Parliament surely means that what is really being objected to is the balancing of incommensurables *by judges*, rather than the balancing of incommensurables *per se*. But, if this is the case, then the objection to the policy-based approach on the grounds that it requires the balancing of incommensurables is simply the objection about the competence of the judiciary in disguise.

The argument that the policy-based approach requires the balancing of incommensurables therefore appears to be little more than a re-wording of the argument that judges are unqualified to rely on policy considerations. Accordingly, it must also be subject to the same problems and limitations.

C. The Use of Policy Considerations Violates the Rule of Law

A third argument against the use of policy-based reasons is that their use violates one of the most fundamental tenets of the rule of law: that the law should be certain and predictable.[41] In particular, it is thought that the consequence of denying

---

[37] EJ Weinrib, 'Does Tort Law Have a Future?' (2000) 34 ValULRev 561, 567.

[38] Stevens (n 5) 310.

[39] The right to a fair trial, for example, is balanced against the public cost of providing such trials (in, say, increased expenditure on legal aid, funding for expert evidence, etc): Dworkin (n 25) 72–73.

[40] Francisco J Urbina, 'Incommensurability and Balancing' (2015) 35 OJLS 575, 581.

[41] 'Clarity of laws' is one of Fuller's eight requirements for a legal system: L Fuller, *The Morality of Law* (Yale University Press, 1964) 39, 63.

any distinction between principle and policy is that *no* type of argument becomes off limits and so *any* kind of consideration may be taken into account when determining the outcome of the notional duty enquiry. As Todd, for example, has written, when questions of policy are permitted, 'the question of responsibility for negligence may [therefore] be argued in an almost unlimited range of circumstances, and all kinds of considerations may be taken in to account in deciding how it ought be resolved.'[42] A policy-based argument may therefore be found to justify almost any conclusion.[43] After all, what type of argument could not be legitimately considered in determining whether the imposition of a duty was 'fair, just or reasonable'? In addition to the 'almost 'unlimited' number of potentially relevant arguments is the fact that, in a legal system where judges are not required to make their political views public,[44] and in which different judges have different conceptions of what is in the community's best interests,[45] parties have no way of knowing which arguments will appeal to judges and how much weight they will assign to them.[46] The combined effect of the 'unlimited' range of potentially relevant arguments and the inability to know how such arguments will be weighed means that predicting the method of determination of the notional duty enquiry becomes extremely difficult. As Beever notes, 'the problem with this … is that it is just not law. If judges are constrained only by their beliefs as to these and similar issues, then we have the rule of judges, not the rule of law.'[47]

There are, however, two difficulties with this argument. First, one might dispute that the policy-based approach allows consideration of an unlimited range of potential arguments at all. Certainly, the policy-based approach permits a *wider* range of arguments to be considered than the principle-based approach, but this does not mean the range of available arguments is *unlimited*. Robertson, for example, argues that there are numerous constraints on the use of policy-based arguments in resolving private law disputes, including: institutional constraints, which, by ensuring judges state their reasons publicly, prevent them from relying on unorthodox justifications, as such justifications risk being overturned on appeal;[48] common law method and convention, including the doctrine of precedent, which prevents judges from departing from the outcomes of previous cases;[49] consistency and coherence, which ensures consistency between related principles and bodies of law;[50] bipolarity and the need for justice to both parties,

---

[42] S Todd, 'Negligence: Duty of Care' in S Todd (ed), *The Law of Torts in New Zealand*, 3rd edn (Brookers, 2005) 151.

[43] Beever, *Rediscovering the Law of Negligence* (n 3) 28.

[44] Compare the position in the United States: Stevens (n 5) 312–13.

[45] McBride and Bagshaw (n 17) 191.

[46] R Bagshaw, 'Tort Law, Concepts and What Really Matters' in A Robertson and HW Tang (eds), *The Goals of Private Law* (Hart, 2009) 258.

[47] Beever, *Rediscovering the Law of Negligence* (n 3) 7.

[48] A Robertson, 'Constraints on Policy-Based Reasoning in Private Law' in A Robertson and HW Tang (eds), *The Goals of Private Law* (Hart, 2009) 268.

[49] ibid 269.

[50] ibid 271.

meaning that the judge's primary task is to do justice to both the claimant and the defendant, and not to give effect to their personal conception of the greater good by focusing *only* on considerations of community welfare.[51] HLA Hart, too, in one of his recently published 'lost' essays, has similarly observed that, regardless of a judge's personal beliefs, they are nevertheless always obliged to act judiciously, so that:

> [Even] if what officials are to do is not rigidly determined by specific rules but a choice is left to them, they will choose responsibly having regard to their office and not indulge fancy or mere whim, though it may of course be that the system fails to provide a remedy if they do indulge their whim.[52]

Such constraints place significant limits on the number of arguments able to be relied upon and so on a judge's ability to give effect to their personal views, thereby reducing the ostensible capriciousness of the policy-based approach. Accordingly, a judge could not, for example, refuse to impose a duty in relation to a psychiatric injury on the basis that he or she believed that recognising such injuries would unnecessarily increase insurance premiums, as such an argument would run counter to, and undermine, existing precedent.[53]

The second difficulty, or at least limitation, with the claim that the use of policy considerations violates the rule of law is that, even if this is accepted, it is not clear to what extent prohibiting policy-based arguments, and relying exclusively on principle-based arguments, would fare any better, as judges are only likely to resort to policy considerations in 'hard cases', where the outcome is uncertain and unpredictable in any event. In particular, whilst there may be a plethora of possible policy-based arguments at the court's disposal in novel cases, and so knowing which arguments a judge will rely on and how they will weigh them will be extremely difficult to predict, the fact that considerations of interpersonal justice can also be wide, varied, and potentially conflicting, will give rise to similar difficulties. As Cane notes, it is 'implausible to think that courts ... may not frequently be confronted by significant conflicts of rights that may be incommensurable.'[54] Whose interests are to be preferred when a person's tree branches hang over into their neighbour's property, for example, and whose interests are to be preferred when one person may be required to sacrifice another's life in order to save their own?[55] Although such questions do not raise matters of policy, they nevertheless do not give rise to obvious answers, as there is no 'mathematical formula or single yardstick'[56] for the ordering of considerations of interpersonal justice.

In response to these objections it could be argued that, whilst prohibiting policy-based reasons will not give rise to a simple algorithm that can be used to

---

[51]   ibid 272.

[52]   HLA Hart, 'Discretion' (2013) 127 Harv L Rev 652, 657.

[53]   See, eg, *Page v Smith* [1996] AC 155 (HL).

[54]   Cane, 'Rights in Private Law' (n 24) 49.

[55]   R Stevens, 'The Conflict of Rights' in A Robertson and HW Tang (eds), *The Goals of Private Law* (Hart, 2009), 142.

[56]   Stevens, *Torts and Rights* (n 5) 337. See also Stevens, 'The Conflict of Rights' (n 55) 141.

resolve notional duty issues, the task is nevertheless made *simpler*, and therefore *more* predictable, by virtue of the fact that the range of reasons in play is relatively restricted.[57] There are, however, three difficulties with this response. First, fewer reasons in play cannot necessarily be equated with greater certainty and predictability. In particular, whilst fewer reasons might mean that it is easier to predict *the reasons that will be relied on*, it does not follow that it will be easier to predict the *outcomes* of cases; judges will still have much discretion in how they will *apply* principles to facts, and predicting how they will do this will be far from straightforward. Indeed, given that principle-based reasons tend to be framed at a higher level of abstraction than policy-based reasons, predicting outcomes may actually be *more* difficult.[58] Secondly, even if we assume that the use of policy-based reasons does give rise to a higher degree of uncertainty than the exclusive use of principle-based reasons, to then conclude that using the former violates the rule of law whilst using the latter does not would involve arbitrary line drawing—that is, it assumes that one side of the line violates the rule of law whilst the other does not, but fails to explain why the line lies there rather than somewhere else. Thirdly, again assuming that the use of policy-based reasons gives rise to a higher degree of uncertainty than the use of principle-based reasons, to conclude that the use of policy-based reasons ought to therefore be prohibited outright presents a false choice. As Bagshaw notes:

> [One objection to the policy-based approach is that it carries] an unacceptably high risk of inconsistency and unpredictability. By contrast, approaches based on a number of tightly defined 'rights' [ie those that rely exclusively on principle] require few computations ... No doubt the concerns behind these criticisms are substantial, but it seems an overreaction to respond by insisting on reversion to a minimalist law of tort chiefly celebrated for the ease for which it can be explained. Such an overreaction misses the fact that there are legal techniques for *managing and controlling* such concerns, for seeking to steer and control innovation.[59]

The claim that the use of policy-based reasons violates the rule of law is therefore problematic. Not only is the use of policy-based reasons not as open-ended as is claimed, but the use of principle-based arguments give rise to similar uncertainty and unpredictability. Whilst it could be argued that the principle-based approach is nevertheless simpler, not only is such a claim debatable, but it does not imply that the outright prohibition of policy-based reasons is a preferable alternative in any event.

---

[57] Stevens, 'The Conflict of Rights' (n 55) 141. See also A Beever and C Rickett, 'Interpretive Legal Theory and the Academic Lawyer' (2005) 68 MLR 320; 332, and Beever, *Rediscovering the Law of Negligence* (n 3) 48–49.

[58] See, eg, J Gardner, 'Some Rule-of-Law Anxieties about Strict Liability in Private Law' in L Austin and D Klimchuk (eds), *Private Law and the Rule of Law* (OUP, 2014) 113–14, in relation to the abstractness of a number of principle-based concepts such as 'morality'.

[59] Bagshaw (n 46) 257 (emphasis in original).

D. The Use of Policy-Based Arguments Makes the Law Less Coherent

The final substantive argument advanced against the use of policy, and by far the most abstract, is that it produces a body of law that is less 'coherent' than the body of law produced by reliance on arguments of principle only. By this it is meant that the law will be more internally consistent and unified and so more able to 'sit comfortably alongside other basic private law principles'.[60] Coherence is clearly an ideal worth striving for, as the more coherent a set of rules, the easier they will be to understand and apply.

How coherent, then, is the law produced when considerations of policy are permitted? As we have seen, allowing policy-based arguments permits a wide variety of considerations to be taken into account when determining the outcome of a notional duty enquiry. The result of this is that different 'categories of case' are often justified on entirely independent bases. For example, some decisions rely on the desire to discourage free riding,[61] whilst others rely on the desire to avoid imposing a heavy financial or administrative burden on public bodies.[62] Despite, however, no single consideration explaining the outcome of *all* duty cases, when the different types of cases are looked at in isolation, the same types of arguments are consistently used to explain similar outcomes (that is, like cases are treated alike) and so form reasonably rational and coherent subsets.[63] According to Smith, a set of rules that rests on independent *but non-contradictory* bases is *weakly* coherent.[64] Allowing policy-based considerations, then, despite allowing judges to rely on different considerations in different types of cases, produces a body of law that is weakly coherent, because the different considerations that are used to justify decisions in different types of cases are non-contradictory and relatively rational when looked at in isolation from one another.

---

[60] JW Neyers, 'The Economic Torts as Corrective Justice' (2009) 17 TLJ 162, 167. See also Cane, 'Rights in Private Law' (n 24) 38; Weinrib, *The Idea of Private Law* (n 5) 12.

[61] J Stapleton, 'Duty of Care Factors: a Selection from the Judicial Menus' in Peter Cane and Jane Stapleton (eds), *The Law of Obligations: Essays in Celebration of John Fleming* (OUP, 1998), 'Convincing factor' 'countervailing to the recognition of a duty' number (11). See, eg: *Morgan Crucible Co v Hill v Samuel & Co* [1991] Ch 295 (CA), 303; *Esanda Finance Corporation Ltd v Peat Marwick Hungerfords (Reg)* (1997) 188 CLR 241, 283–90 (McHugh J).

[62] Ibid, 'Convincing factor' 'countervailing to the recognition of a duty' number (4). See, eg, *Hill v Chief Constable of West Yorkshire* [1989] AC 53 (HL); *Van Colle v Chief Constable of the Hertfordshire Police; Smith v Chief Constable of Sussex Police* 1 AC 225 (HL).

[63] This is, of course, not to say that irreconcilable cases do not exist with almost identical fact scenarios.

[64] SA Smith, *Contract Theory* (OUP, 2004) 11. Although Smith is using 'coherence' as a criterion by which to evaluate an 'interpretive legal theory,' as this is ultimately judged by reference to the body of law the theory would produce, his definitions of coherence are therefore equally appropriate to evaluate the body of law produced by prescriptive theories. The descriptor 'weak' is actually Beever's, Smith merely refers to a 'less-demanding' and 'more-demanding' version: Beever, *Rediscovering the Law of Negligence* (n 3) 21–22.

According to Beever, however, weak coherence is not enough, as we should also know why a particular consideration was relied upon in one case and not another.[65] We need to know why, for example, the fact that a claimant is a free rider is important in duty cases involving pure economic loss, but not important in duty cases involving personal injuries. A set of rules that lends itself to such an explanation, and so forms a unified system, is, according to Smith, *strongly* coherent.[66] The policy-based approach, however, by allowing conceptually independent reasons to explain different types of cases, *by definition* possesses no underlying structure or logic.[67] As Weinrib explains, again in relation to the duty of care:

> The invocation of such independent policies entails the disintegration of duty as a systematic and coherent concept. Given the heterogeneity of the available policies and different weightings of the various policies in the balancing process, a systematically unified conception of duty based on (in Lord Atkin's words) 'the element common to all cases in which [a duty] is found to exist' is out of the question. The variety of policies and the shifting balance among them leaves no place for a common element on which the various duties (again in Lord Atkin's words) 'must logically be based'. In these circumstances there can only be different specific kinds of duty, with each kind representing the particular policies or the particular balance among policies that are recognized as decisive in situations of that sort.[68]

The body of law produced by allowing policy considerations, then, by relying on a diverse range of independent considerations, despite being non-contradictory when looked at in isolated pockets and so able to be described as weakly coherent, lacks any underlying or unifying structure and so cannot be described as strongly coherent.

Where, however, policy-based reasons are prohibited, and considerations of principle are relied on exclusively, the body of law produced *can* be considered strongly coherent. Indeed, where the outcome of the notional duty enquiry is determined solely on the basis of the unified conception of interpersonal justice, the law will clearly be more coherent than where it is determined on the basis of a diverse range of independent policy concerns. Accordingly, Beever claims that when considerations of principle are relied upon exclusively, the law of negligence 'possesses a conceptually coherent, indeed conceptually *unified*, structure ... [and] the various stages of the negligence enquiry ... are seen as parts of a conceptually integrated whole ...'[69] Excluding considerations of policy, then, produces a simpler, more unified and more coherent body of law relating to the notional duty enquiry.

---

[65] Beever, *Rediscovering the Law of Negligence* (n 3) 24.

[66] Smith (n 64) 11. Note also (n 64) above.

[67] Weinrib, 'The Disintegration of Duty' (n 5) 145–46.

[68] Ibid 177 (footnotes omitted).

[69] Beever, *Rediscovering the Law of Negligence* (n 3) 30. See also Weinrib, 'The Disintegration of Duty' (n 5) 7.

Smith, however, at least in relation to contract law, questions whether such a high degree of coherence is actually necessary:

> [H]uman actions, including law-making actions, may be perfectly intelligible even when they are not unified in the sense just described ... Unless one assumes (as few people do) that all reasons for acting can, in the end, be reduced to a single master principle, it is accepted as perfectly intelligible, indeed appropriate, that people act for different reasons in different situations. Charity is an appropriate response to certain kinds of situations; in another situation, courage may be appropriate. Neither charity nor courage, however, seems reducible to the other, or to a third master value. The same must be true of legal systems ... I conclude, then, that a requirement of perfect unity seems not only unattainable in practice, but also inappropriate in theory.[70]

Accordingly, even if the prohibition of policy based reasons does produce a *more* coherent body of law, such a high degree of coherence is, at least according to Smith, unnecessary, such that the weak coherence of the policy-based approach is sufficient.

E. Is the Use of Policy Permissible?

Whilst the use of policy does indeed appear to give rise to a number of legitimate objections, the idea that the use of such considerations should therefore be prohibited *in their entirety* is not without its problems. In particular, even if policy-based reasons were prohibited, many of the problems attributed to such reasoning would remain, even if to a lesser degree. The case against the use of policy therefore seems to be less about *eliminating* the associated problems than *reducing* them. It is far from clear, however, whether the extent of that reduction justifies the prohibition of policy in its entirety given the costs involved in doing so.

III. The Need for Notional Duty

The need for a duty of care concept has been questioned for decades. As we saw in chapter four, as early as the 1930s the concept was being described as 'superfluous'[71] and 'an unnecessary fifth wheel on the coach',[72] on the basis that its function was already sufficiently performed elsewhere in the negligence enquiry. As we also saw, however, these criticisms were directed at the factual aspect of the duty enquiry only, and ignored the notional aspect entirely. Indeed, early commentary on the notional aspect of the duty enquiry described it as, far from being

---

[70] Smith (n 64) 12 (emphasis added). *cf* Beever, *Rediscovering the Law of Negligence* (n 3) 24.
[71] Percy Winfield, 'Duty in Tortious Negligence' (1934) Colum L Rev 41, 43, 66.
[72] WW Buckland, 'The Duty to Take Care' (1935) 51 LQR 637, 639.

a fifth wheel on the coach, both 'necessary'[73] and 'indispensable'.[74] Today, there continues to be widespread agreement that no legal system can allow *all* carelessly caused losses to be recoverable under the law of negligence,[75] and that notional duty plays an important role in achieving this.

A. Attacks on Notional Duty

Whilst the desirability of the *function* of notional duty is rarely called into question, the idea that this function needs to be achieved via an independent stage of the negligence enquiry (ie as part of the duty stage) has been. In particular, it has been suggested that the function of notional duty, like the function of factual duty, can be satisfactorily performed by the other elements of the negligence enquiry, thereby rendering the *entire* duty stage superfluous. Gibson, for example, in one of the earliest attempts to show that notional duty was superfluous, argued that, although duty performed a dual role,[76] 'nothing would be lost except a potential source of confusion if the "duty of care" notion were entirely discarded …'.[77] Yet in his duty-free alternative to the existing negligence enquiry, the first question the court needed to address was whether the 'type of conduct' or 'type of activity' is one in which the 'the law of negligence [ought to] exercise control'.[78] In other words, there was no 'notional duty' stage, but there was a stage that performed an almost identical, albeit narrower,[79] function. Some years later, Howarth also claimed that '[t]here is nothing in the concept of the duty-situation that cannot be dealt with adequately under the headings of fault, cause, and damage'[80] and that the concept is 'probably superfluous'.[81] Yet, whilst he, like Gibson, suggested (and sometimes convincingly demonstrated) that *some* of the traditionally notional duty issues could be dealt with at other stages of the negligence enquiry, he nevertheless concluded that there remained a role for notional duty in determining whether 'the type of case under discussion' should come within the purview of

---

[73] FH Lawson, 'The Duty of Care in Negligence: A Comparative Study' (1947) 22 TulLRev 111, 112.

[74] RWM Dias, 'The Duty Problem in Negligence' [1955] CLJ 198 204.

[75] See, eg, Prue Vines, Peter Hanford and Carol Harlow, 'Duty of Care' in Carolyn Sappideen and Prue Vines (eds), *Fleming's The Law of Torts*, 10th edn (Thomson Reuters (Professional) Australia Limited, 2011) 151–52; Stevens, *Torts and Rights* (n 5) 307.

[76] R Dale Gibson, 'A New Alphabet of Negligence' in Allen M Linden (ed), *Studies in Canadian Tort Law* (Butterworths, 1968) 190–91: 'The general test for determining whether a "duty of care" exists is, of course, reasonable foresight of unreasonable risk to the plaintiff …[yet] While recognising the general principle of responsibility to anyone within the range of reasonable foresight, the courts have chosen not to apply it in a few exceptional circumstances.'

[77] ibid 192.

[78] ibid 194–95.

[79] In particular, Gibson argues that questions about the kinds of harm that are recoverable, typically dealt with at a notional duty question, can be considered under the 'harm' (ie, actionable damage and causation) heading: ibid 202.

[80] D Howarth, 'Negligence After Murphy: Time to Re-Think' (1991) 50 CLJ 58, 68.

[81] D Howarth, *Textbook on Tort* (LexisNexis UK, 1995) 158.

the law of negligence, or whether the law should instead grant 'the defendant an immunity against liability in negligence'.[82] Again, a stage practically identical to the notional duty enquiry retained an important role in defining the limits of the law of negligence. Shortly after Howarth, Hepple, too, argued that the 'redundant and incoherent concept of notional duty' can be abandoned,[83] because:

> In the ordinary negligence action only three questions have to be asked: (1) was the defendant entitled to take the risk? (the fault issue); (2) if not, would the damage have occurred had the defendant acted without fault? (the factual causation issue); and (3) was the kind of damage to this class of plaintiff within the scope of the risk? (the remoteness issue). When it is sought to extend liability into new areas not covered by precedent, the starting point should be that loss lies where it falls, unless it can be shown that liability for negligence will empower individuals to acquire the information and knowledge which they need to control their situations, while at the same time distributing losses effectively and deterring harmful conduct.[84]

The final qualification, of course, even though not enumerated, is a clear equivalent to the notional duty enquiry.

In each of the above critiques, then, one of the elements in the reimagined formulas for determining liability for negligence closely resembles the notional duty enquiry, even if performing a more limited role and masquerading under a different name. It is therefore hardly surprising that none of the attempts to eradicate notional duty from the negligence enquiry have had any significant impact, and notional duty has never looked to be in any real danger of being abandoned.

A far more sophisticated attempt to attempt to 'loosen the grip'[85] of notional duty (and duty in general), however, has recently been provided by Nolan. Like the above critics, Nolan, too, argues that the various notional duty issues can be 'reallocated'[86] to the other stages of the negligence enquiry; though, unlike the above critics, Nolan details how this can be done, rather than merely suggesting that it is possible,[87] as well as advancing various reasons why it *should* be done. Immunities, for example, such as the combat and advocate's immunity, can be dealt with as defences;[88] liability for the deliberate actions of a third party, can be dealt with as matters of legal causation;[89] whilst the ostensibly notional duty issue of liability for secondary victims of psychiatric harm can, in fact, be resolved as

---

[82] Howarth (n 80) 93–94.

[83] B Hepple, 'Negligence: The Search for Coherence' (1997) 50 CLP 69, 93.

[84] ibid 93–94.

[85] D Nolan, 'Deconstructing the Duty of Care' (2013) 129 LQR 559, 560.

[86] ibid 567.

[87] Indeed, according to Nolan, one of the principal reasons earlier critiques of notional (and factual) duty have failed is because they have 'not been supported by a detailed demonstration of the way in which the issues currently considered under the duty umbrella could be accommodated within other stages of the negligence enquiry.' ibid 560.

[88] ibid 574. Indeed, all narrow exceptions to the broad inclusionary categories could be allocated in this way.

[89] ibid 570.

part of the remoteness enquiry.[90] Protected 'interests' (that is, the *kinds* of damage that are recoverable, such as physical injury and property damage, but not pure economic loss), 'the heartland of notional duty,'[91] Nolan argues, can be reallocated to the actionable damage element of the negligence enquiry.[92] Using this technique, categorical issues disappear from the notional duty enquiry almost entirely,[93] leaving only the question of notional duties that arise from assumptions of responsibility (or what Nolan terms 'acquired rights') remaining. Nolan concedes, however, that reclassifying obligations that arise from assumptions of responsibility is not so straightforward, and that there is a 'strong argument' that notional duty be retained for such questions.[94] Categorical exceptions to broad exclusionary categories, including cases such as *Spring v Guardian Assurance plc*[95] and *White v Jones*,[96] are similarly unable to be accounted for.[97] Accordingly, although Nolan is able to reduce notional duty to a considerably narrower enquiry, and provide a number of convincing reasons why it is desirable to do so,[98] *some* issues dealt with under the notional duty rubric nevertheless remain unallocated. In particular, his framework cannot account for circumstances that give rise to recovery for purely economic loss or the failure to provide a benefit; that is, when narrow inclusionary exceptions, whether categorical or based on assumptions of responsibility, can be made to broad exclusionary categories.

It seems, then, that whilst many of the issues presently dealt with at the notional duty stage can be reallocated to other parts of the negligence enquiry, *some* simply cannot be. A notional duty stage, in some sense, would therefore seem to be required. Of course, the conclusion that something resembling a notional duty cannot be *completely* abandoned, raises two interesting questions. First, given that many notional duty issues appear to be able to be reallocated to other stages of the negligence enquiry (immunities to defences, liability for deliberate acts of third parties to legal causation, etc), why is the notional duty enquiry so broad, and not simply confined to identifying exceptions to the general non-recoverability rule for pure economic loss and failures to provide a benefit? Secondly, if *some* notional duty element is required to be present in the negligence enquiry, then why is the (notional) duty stage unique to the common law?

---

[90]   ibid 571. *cf* Beever, *Rediscovering the Law of Negligence* (n 3) 407–409; JG Fleming, 'Remoteness and Duty: The Control Devices in Liability for Negligence' (1953) 31 Can Bar Rev 471, 492–93.

[91]   Nolan (n 85) 575.

[92]   ibid 575.

[93]   The 'almost' qualifier refers to the point made below about categorical exceptions to broad exclusionary categories, including cases such as *White v Jones* [1995] 2 AC 207 (HL) and *Spring v Guardian plc* [1995] 2 AC 296 (HL).

[94]   Nolan (n 85) 575, 587.

[95]   [1995] 2 AC 296 (HL).

[96]   [1995] 2 AC 207 (HL).

[97]   Again, this assumes that the cases are not able to be described as true assumptions of responsibility.

[98]   Nolan (n 85) 575–83.

B. Why is the Notional Duty Enquiry So Broad?

In relation to the first question, the wide variety of issues that are dealt with at the notional duty enquiry can, in large part, be put down to two reasons. First is the ease with which just about any question about the appropriate scope of liability for negligence can be framed as a notional duty question, including, as we have seen, questions about the kinds of damage that are recoverable, the way the harm occurred, and the status and nature of the relationship between the parties. Secondly is that framing issues about the scope of liability for negligence in terms of notional duty allows judges a wide degree of flexibility with respect to the types of reasons they rely on to justify their decisions. In particular, the notional duty stage allows courts to determine the boundaries of liability for negligence in accordance with what is 'fair, just, and reasonable', or by reference to a list of 'salient features' of indeterminate content and length. Such leeway is not, however, at least at the moment, given to judges in determining whether a new type of defence ought to be recognised, or whether a new kind of damage ought to be recognised, as such questions tend to be governed more by concrete rules than flexible general principles. Faced, then, with whether a new kind of damage *ought* to be recoverable, it is far easier to approach the issue on the basis of what is fair, just, and reasonable, than via the comparatively unchartered waters of what amounts to actionable damage. This is, of course, a result of the black letter law, and not any structural or doctrinal impediment; however, until that changes, and more guidance, or flexibility, is given to judges on when they can recognise new defences, kinds of actionable damage, etc, the preference to deal with such questions at the, arguably doctrinally inferior, duty stage, is unlikely to change.

C. Comparison to Other Legal Systems

Moving to the second question, if *some* notional duty element is required in the negligence enquiry, then why is the duty enquiry, and therefore notional duty, unique to the common law? The answer seems to be that, at least in some sense, it is not, as *functional* equivalents to notional duty can be found in numerous other legal systems. Indeed, Lawson, Oxford's first professor of Comparative Law, has written that 'a comparison with Roman law and a number of other legal systems ... proves that such a duty of care, or some other requirement substantially identical with it, can hardly be avoided.'[99] Under the Romans' *lex aquilia*, for example, which governed liability for wrongful damage to property (*damnum iniuria datum*), a defendant's liability was limited to the killing, burning, breaking, and, later, spoiling, (*occiderit, usserit, fregerit, ruperit*, and *corruperit*) of the claimant's property as a result of their bodily actions (*corpore corpori*); that is, liability

---

[99] Lawson (n 73) 113.

was limited to *physical* damage to the claimant's property caused by the defendant's *positive* conduct. Later Roman law, however, under the *actio in factum* and *actio utilis*,[100] *does* appear to have permitted recovery for indirectly caused non-physical damage, such as the facilitation of the escape of a slave or animal.[101] Despite such a rule ostensibly permitting recovery for loss caused by omissions and loss that is purely economic in nature, as Lawson also notes:

> [I]t has always been an accepted doctrine that Roman law gave an action for omissions in exceptional circumstances. Indeed, if we leave to one side obvious cases where a defendant failed to take precautions which his previous positive acts had necessitated, the only clear instance is the familiar case where one man lit a furnace and another, having taken over the job of watching it, negligently fell asleep and let the fire spread; and in that case it seems that the omissions must be coupled with an assumption of responsibility which, to use the terminology of the English law, raised a duty of care.[102]

Similarly, as we saw in chapter two, under the early common law liability for carelessly caused harm was restricted to a finite number of discrete situations (or 'forms of action'), including the negligent performance or non-performance of an undertaking, and the negligent loss of control of dangerous forces. Where the plaintiff suffered harm in a situation that was not covered by one of the existing forms of action, being the equivalent of not falling within an inclusionary notional duty situation, he was without a remedy.[103]

Functional equivalents of notional duty are also visible in modern civil systems. Section 823(1) of the German Civil Code, for example, also known as the *Bürgerliches Gesetzbuch*, or BGB, limits liability for carelessness to conduct that injures 'the life, body, health, freedom, property or another right'[104] of the claimant. Notably, the focus of section 823(1) is on acts rather than omissions, and the list of protected interests does not include a general economic interest. Liability for omissions and for purely economic loss nevertheless exists in specified circumstances: the former, where the defendant has breached an 'affirmative safety duty';[105] and the latter where the loss was caused by a public official's breach of an

---

[100] According to Zimmermann, although the difference between the actions was not clear, under the Digest they seem to have been treated interchangeably: Reinhard Zimmermann, *The Law of Obligations: Roman Foundations of the Civilian Tradition* (OUP, 1996) 993–96.

[101] Lawson (n 73) 113–16. See also WW Buckland, AD McNair and FH Lawson, *Roman Law and Common Law*, 2nd edn (Cambridge University Press, 1965) 367–70.

[102] Lawson (n 73) 115.

[103] As Winfield notes, 'The question was not "Is there a duty?" but, "Was the defendant in fact a bailee, common carrier, or the like and, if so, what excuse has he to offer for the harm that has occurred"': Winfield (n 71) 49.

[104] Section 823(1): 'A person who, intentionally or negligently, unlawfully injures the life, body, health, freedom, property or another right of another person is liable to make compensation to the other party for the damage arising from this.'

[105] Cees van Dam, *European Tort Law*, 2nd edn (OUP, 2013) 85, 252. See also, Gerhard Wagner, 'Comparative Tort Law' in Mathias Reimann and Reinhard Zimmermann (eds), *The Oxford Handbook of Comparative Law* (OUP, 2008) 1017–1020; Basil Markesinis and Hannes Unberath, *The German Law of Torts: A Comparative Treatise*, 4th edn (Hart, 2002) Ch 2.

official duty (section 839), where the loss was intentionally inflicted in a manner that was 'contrary to public policy' (section 826), where the loss was caused by the breach of a statute 'intended to protect another person' (section 823(2)), or where the loss was the result of an interference with the claimant's 'right to do business' (included as 'another right' in section 823(1)). The Principles of European Tort Law adopt a similar approach to the BGB, with Article 1.101 recognising a 'Basic Norm' of liability for damage caused by the fault of another, and Article 2:102 specifying that this protection only extends to certain 'interests,' and that 'protection of pure economic interests ... may be more limited in scope.'[106] Less obvious, however, is Article 1240 of the French Civil Code (formerly Article 1382, which was renamed following a complete reworking of the Code in February 2016), which provides that '*Any* act whatever of man, which causes damage to another, obliges the one by whose fault it occurred, to compensate it.' *Prima facie*, the scope of the section is unlimited and nothing resembling a notional duty is in sight. Behind the scenes, however, limits on liability for carelessly caused loss do exist. As Lawson explains:

> The typical code enunciating a general principle of liability for negligent damage is the French ... and it is from an examination of [this law], which I cannot help think has been unduly cursory, that an impression has been gained that a law can properly dispense with the duty of care or any analogous technique ... But it is common knowledge that the articles are too general to tell us much about the French law of civil responsibility, which must be found in the text-books and reports; and, on perusing these, we find that the actual solutions of particular cases are not so different from those of English, or, for that matter, German law.[107]

So, for example, the French courts limit the scope of the interests protected by the law of negligence through their interpretation of the word 'damage'.[108] Similarly, liability for purely economic loss, despite not being formally recognised as concerning a conceptually distinct kind of harm, seems to be the subject of an 'autonomous'[109] area of case law and subject to a generally more restrictive approach to recoverability; in particular, it is limited by, first, being judged by a higher standard of '*faute*' (that is, a higher standard of care) than liability for personal injury or property damage,[110] and, secondly, needing to be 'personal, certain, and legal' and 'immediately and directly' caused by the defendant's carelessness,[111]

---

[106] Article 2:102(4).

[107] Lawson (n 73) 118.

[108] van Dam (n 105) 169: 'French law does not provide an a priori limitation as to protected interests. It has been up to the courts to decide which interests are to be protected and which not, solely on the basis of the word *dommage* in article 1382 CC.'

[109] Christophe Radé and Laurent Bloch, 'Compensation for Pure Economic Loss Under French Law' in Willem H van Boom, Helmut Koziol and C Witting (eds), *Pure Economic Loss* (Springer, 2004) 44.

[110] van Dam (n 105) 210.

[111] As van Dam notes, these latter restrictions stem from the provisions in the Code relating to damages for contractual liability: ibid 319, 353. This hurdle is not unique to pure economic loss, but is more difficult to surmount for such loss.

obstacles that are often unable to be overcome when the loss is purely economic in nature.[112] And liability for omissions, despite seemingly being equated with liability for acts in Article 1241 (formerly Article 1383),[113] is restricted to situations where the defendant has breached an affirmative duty, these being established by the courts on the basis of what a reasonable person would do in the same circumstances.[114]

Functional equivalents of notional duty therefore appear to exist in a number of past and present legal systems. Can we conclude, however, as Lawson did, that 'a duty of care, or some other requirement substantially identical with it, can hardly be avoided'? To some extent, yes: but only if we are looking for *functional* equivalents, being some set of rules that prevents *all* carelessly caused harm being compensable. Such a conclusion is not, however, particularly surprising or remarkable; after all, *no* legal system could allow recovery for *all* carelessly caused loss, and so if we define 'notional duty' as simply the set of rules that prevent all carelessly caused loss from being compensable, then of course equivalents to 'notional duty' will be found in other legal systems. Even Nolan's duty-free version of the law of negligence has a *functional* equivalent to notional duty, albeit in the form of a set of rules that is redistributed throughout the other stages of the negligence enquiry; indeed, that is the entire point of his argument. Insofar as a singular notional duty *element* is concerned, however, nothing resembling it is apparent in the systems discussed above; the closest equivalent would appear to be section 823(1) of the BGB, but even that could arguably be described as defining the different kinds of actionable damage. Yet, whilst no equivalent of 'notional duty' as an *independent* element of the negligence enquiry appears to exist in any of the legal systems discussed above, it is particularly noteworthy that none of them has been able to limit recovery for purely economic loss or the failure to provide a benefit within a framework consisting of *singular* concepts of fault, causation, and damage; either an independent test or element is required, or alternative definitions of one of the primary elements are adopted.

D. Is Notional Duty Necessary?

Is, then, notional duty necessary? In its present form, the answer is surely no, as many of the issues presently dealt with under the notional duty banner are able

---

[112] For more on liability for pure economic loss under French law, see: ibid 210; Radé and Bloch (n 109); Mauro Bussani and Vernon Valentine Palmer, 'The Liability Regimes of Europe—their Façades and Interiors' in Mauro Bussani and Vernon Valentine Palmer (eds), *Pure Economic Loss in Europe* (Cambridge University Press, 2003) 126–31; Wagner (n 105) 1015–1017.

[113] The section reads: 'Everyone is liable for the damage he causes not only by his act, but also by his negligence or his imprudence.' See also van Dam (n 105) 57–57, 252–53.

[114] ibid 252. It is also notable that the reasonable person is judged according to a reasonable adult: ibid 272–73.

to be dealt with at other stages of the negligence enquiry. In a narrower sense, however, the answer appears to be yes, as, based on both Nolan's analysis *and* a comparison with a number of other legal systems, if recovery for purely economic loss and failures to provide a benefit are to be permitted at all, it must be done outside of singular concepts of fault, causation, and damage;[115] some *other* set of rules is therefore required, whether in the form of an additional element, as is done in the common law, or via the qualification of existing elements.

IV. Conclusion

In determining whether a particular situation *ought* to be subject to the law of negligence, considerations of policy can often be highly relevant. Reliance on such considerations, however, is highly controversial, as, according to some, judges are not qualified to rely on them, their use requires the balancing of incommensurables, their use violates the rule of law, and their use produces a body of law that is less coherent than the body of law that would exist if they were prohibited. Such arguments, however, are far from watertight, and are often subject to the same problems they are trying to overcome. Whilst they nevertheless seem to *lessen* a number of problems, the extent to which they do this is debatable, as is the issue of whether the cost of doing so is worth it.

The argument that notional duty is a 'fifth wheel on the coach' has been thrown around for decades. However, until recently, no-one has properly explained how this applied to notional duty. Nolan, however, has convincingly argued that many of the issues dealt with under the notional duty label can be 'redistributed' to other elements of the negligence enquiry. By doing so, Nolan argues that the negligence enquiry will be more structured, will treat like issues alike, will avoid the conflation of law with fact, and prevent confusion and incoherence; indeed, it was for similar reasons that it was argued in chapter four that factual duty was best left for the breach and remoteness enquiries. Yet even after deconstructing duty, there still remained the problem of explaining the circumstances in which carelessly caused purely economic loss and damage that had resulted from omissions were actionable. A comparison with other legal systems revealed that, despite them often approaching liability for negligence in entirely different ways, they, too, have had to invent special rules, outside of *singular* concepts of fault, causation, and damage, to allow recovery for purely economic loss and omissions, but in a way that was subject to some constraint. *Some* independent 'notional duty' question, albeit a potentially unrecognisable one, therefore seems inevitable. Though, until the courts develop more flexible and prescriptive rules on when, and in what

---

[115] Again, whilst the French *do* limit recovery for pure economic loss partially through the idea of 'fault', it is only by assigning it a different meaning to that used for other kinds of damage.

circumstances, the other elements of the law of negligence can expand, including when new defences and forms and damage may be recognised, a narrower version of notional duty seems unlikely.

Having now provided a detailed analysis of the structure of, and the various issues involved with, the duty enquiry, we will now explore how it is *actually* approached in practice.

7

Comparing the Duty Methodologies
of Australia, Canada and the UK

Social scientists and historians have long brought data to bear on the study of law and legal institutions. In ever-increasing numbers, legal academics throughout the world are following suit.

Lee Epstsein and Andrew Martin, *An Introduction to Empirical Legal Research*
(OUP, 2014) vii.

I. Introduction

The previous five chapters have provided a detailed overview of the duty of care enquiry, including some of the difficulties encountered within it. In particular, they have explored, *inter alia*, the development of the duty concept, the development and value of general duty tests, the dual nature of the duty enquiry, the need for factual duty, the categorical nature of notional duty, the role of assumptions of responsibility, and the controversy surrounding the use of policy considerations in determining the existence of a duty. For the most part, the principal focus of the book has therefore been on relatively high-level doctrinal matters. Chapter seven, however, shifts focus from the doctrinal to the empirical, and explores a study, involving both quantitative and qualitative aspects,[1] into how the courts *actually* approach duty questions, and the extent to which that approach differs in three important jurisdictions: Australia, Canada, and the UK. The study considers, in particular: (1) how frequently general duty tests are used; (2) how the courts determine the existence of a duty when they do not rely on general tests; (3) whether courts approach the duty enquiry in a 'categorical' or fact-specific manner; (4) the frequency with which policy-based reasons are used in duty

---

[1] The study was a 'content analysis'. For more on content analysis, see Mark A Hall and Ronald F Wright, 'Systematic Content Analysis of Judicial Opinions' (2008) 96 Cal L Rev 63.

determinations; and (5) the extent to which academic commentary appears to influence the courts.

An overview of the methodology that was relied upon is explained in Section II, including an explanation of how the cases included in the study were selected, and what conditions had to be met for the judicial opinions within those cases to be included in the data. Section III then explains how the cases and opinions were coded in accordance with the various methods and techniques being explored, before providing an overview and analysis of the quantitative and qualitative data obtained.

II. The Study

The study included 'duty' cases decided in the jurisdictions' ultimate appellate courts only; that is, the High Court of Australia, Supreme Court of Canada, and House of Lords and Supreme Court of the United Kingdom.[2] The study was restricted to ultimate courts of appeal for a number of reasons: first, with the constraints of precedent being lessened, courts were more likely to engage in a variety of different methodologies; secondly, the methodologies of the ultimate appellate courts have the most precedential value and so should reflect, at least in theory, what is occurring in lower courts; and finally, it kept the number of cases required to be read within reason—if trial and intermediate appellate courts were included in the study, the number of cases required to be read would have been in the thousands.[3] The cases included in the study were identified as 'duty' cases via searches on the various Westlaw databases: cases in the High Court of Australia were identified via WestlawAU by searching for cases where 'negligence' and 'duty of care' appear as 'catchwords;'[4] cases in the Supreme Court of Canada were identified via Westlaw International[5] by searching for at least *one* occurrence of the term 'negligence' and at least *three* occurrences of the term 'duty of care' anywhere in the text;[6] and cases in the House of Lords/UKSC were identified via

---

[2] For the remainder of the chapter, 'the House of Lords and Supreme Court of the United Kingdom' will be referred to singularly as 'the House of Lords/UKSC'.

[3] For example, in the period examined there were almost 2000 cases in the Court of Appeal of England and Wales alone that contained the terms 'duty of care' and 'negligence'. A similar number of cases could be expected in each of the State and Provincial courts of appeal of both Australia and Canada, and even more in the trial level courts.

[4] This produced 69 results, 41 of which were included in the final sample.

[5] Westlaw International was used because the Bodleian Law Library, where the study was undertaken, does not have a Westlaw Canada subscription.

[6] The exact search term was 'ADV: NEGLIGENCE & ATLEAST3("DUTY OF CARE") & CO (SUPREME COURT OF CANADA) & DA(aft 1/1/1985)'. This produced 73 results, 39 of which were

WestlawUK, by searching for cases where 'duty of care' and 'negligence' appeared anywhere in the text, *and* which were classified by WestlawUK as 'torts' cases.[7] Despite the searches identifying hundreds of cases in total, only cases where the existence of a duty was explicitly considered (that is, the opinion made a determination as to the existence of a duty or whether the case could be struck out on that basis) were included. Ultimately, this amounted to 121 cases in total: 41 from the High Court of Australia, 39 from the Supreme Court of Canada, and 41 from the House of Lords/UKSC. A full list of the cases included in the sample appears in the Appendix. The sample was also restricted to cases decided between 1 January 1985 and 31 December 2015. The 1985 start date was chosen because, as was seen in chapter three, it was only then that significant differences in the different jurisdictions' duty methodologies began to emerge: in particular, it was August 1984 that the High Court of Australia moved towards an understanding of duty based on Deane J's 'touchstone' of 'proximity',[8] October 1984 that *Anns v Merton LBC*[9] began its fall from grace in the House of Lords,[10] and July 1984 that the Supreme Court of Canada formally adopted the two-stage/*Anns* test in *City of Kamloops v Nielsen*.[11] December 2015 coincided with the last sensible endpoint prior to the study being undertaken.

Every individual judge's opinion[12] that considered the existence of a duty of care counted as one data point for quantitative purposes. A single opinion jointly written by three judges therefore counted as three data points, as did a single opinion written by one judge and supported by two single concurring opinions. Where a concurring opinion evidenced support for more than one opinion, each of those opinions was increased in weight proportionately; so, for example, if Judge A concurred with individual Judge B's opinion *and* individual

included in the final sample. The search was conducted 'anywhere in the text' as Westlaw International does not have a 'catchword' or 'Subject/Keyword' search function. At least three instances of the term 'duty of care' were required in order to keep the number of cases required to be read within reason (a search requiring only one instance of the term produced over 300 results). Since the search was conducted, the Westlaw International interface has changed, and the search (curiously) now produces a *shorter* list (*Fullowka v Royal Oak Ventures Inc* (2010) 315 DLR (4th) 577, for example, no longer appears on the list). I have been advised this is due to bugs in the software, though am unsure when they will be resolved.

[7] This produced 129 results, down from 235 as a result of confining the results to 'torts' cases, 41 of which were included in the final sample. For the avoidance of doubt, the study did not include cases heard in the Judicial Committee of the Privy Council.

[8] *Jaensch v Coffey* (1984) 155 CLR 549.

[9] [1978] AC 728 (HL) ('*Anns*').

[10] *Governors of the Peabody Donation Fund v Sir Lindsay Parkinson* [1985] AC 210 (HL). See especially Lord Keith at 240–41.

[11] (1984) 10 DLR (4th) 641.

[12] The neutral term 'opinion' will be used to refer to individual and joint judgments of the High Court of Australia, Supreme Court of Canada, and Supreme Court of the United Kingdom, as well as the individual speeches of the House of Lords.

Judge C's opinion, both Judge B and C's opinions counted as 1.5 data points.[13] As the focus of the study was on methodologies rather than outcomes, no distinction was drawn between majority and dissenting opinions. Where cases contained multiple parties, only where the individual claims raised substantially separate issues of law, *and* the existence of a duty was explicitly considered and determined in relation to each claim, were separate claimant/defendant combinations counted independently. This ensured that cases like *Sutradhar v Natural Environment Research Council*,[14] which involved over 700 claimants with essentially identical causes of action, did not distort, or water down, the data obtained from other cases.[15] Finally, where a number of independent bases were advanced to justify the existence of the same[16] duty, the individual bases were not counted separately, because, first, it was often not clear at which point an argument in support of the existence of the duty should count as an independent 'basis', and, secondly, in the rare cases in which different bases *were* explicitly considered, the methodology adopted for the consideration of each basis tended to be the same in any event. This methodology produced 742 data points in total: 223 in the High Court of Australia, 296 in the Supreme Court of Canada, and (coincidentally) 223 in the House of Lords/UKSC. The higher number of data points in the Supreme Court of Canada appeared to be the result of the Court frequently sitting with nine justices, compared to the five (and occasionally seven) member benches of the High Court of Australia and House of Lords/UKSC, as well as the Court's comparative infrequency of cases deemed to be 'duty' cases that included opinions that determined the outcome of the case on grounds other than the existence of a duty.[17]

III. The Competing Methodologies

A. A Brief Overview of the Data

Having identified the sources of the data, we can now explore how the opinions were coded in accordance with the various methodologies and techniques being

---

[13] See, eg, Lowry in *Alcock v Chief Constable of South Yorkshire* [1992] AC 310, 424 (HL), and Lord Nicholls in *Brooks v Commissioner of Police of the Metropolis* [2005] 1 WLR 1495 (HL).

[14] [2006] PNLR 36 (HL).

[15] Other examples of cases with multiple parties pursuing similar claims in law, albeit often based on slightly different facts, were *Alcock v Chief Constable of South Yorkshire* [1992] AC 310 (HL) and *Perre v Apand Pty Ltd* (1999) 198 CLR 180.

[16] Accordingly, the same case was counted more than once where discrete types of 'duties' were pursued; as, for example, in *Macfarlane v Tayside Health Board* [2000] 2 AC 59 (HL), where a duty was pursued in relation to the costs of raising a child, *and* for the mother's medical expenses.

[17] For example, in *Mulligan v Coffs Harbour City Council* (2005) 223 CLR 486, only one of seven opinions was decided on the basis of duty (the rest were on the basis of breach), and in *Macfarlane*

investigated, as well as the data produced. However, before we do so, it is worthwhile first providing a brief overview of the nature of the data obtained from the different jurisdictions.

i. Kinds of Damage

The cases included in the sample concerned a variety of different kinds of damage, and there appeared to be considerable variance in the different jurisdictions' interest in those different types of damage. In particular, whilst the High Court of Australia seemed principally concerned with the existence of a duty of care in personal injury cases, both the Supreme Court of Canada and House of Lords/ UKSC were considerably more concerned with damage that was purely economic in nature. A full breakdown of the different kinds of damage in the cases is presented below:[18]

Table 1: Kinds of damage

Kind of damage	HCA	SCC	HoL/UKSC
Physical injury	22	11	11
Property damage	2	3	2
Pure economic loss	10	20	18
Psychiatric injury	5	3	9
Other	2	2	6

ii. Nature of the Decision being Appealed

The nature of the decision being appealed varied considerably between the jurisdictions.[19] The High Court of Australia heard 43 appeals over 41 cases (two cases involved multiple appeals), 35 involving appeals from hearings on the merits of the case, and only eight against hearings not involving such hearings (eg strike outs, summary dismissals, etc). The Supreme Court of Canada had a similar split, hearing 40 appeals over 39 cases, 28 of those being appeals from trial determinations, and the remaining 12 from strike outs, etc. The UK, on the other hand,

---

v Tayside Heath Board [2000] 2 AC 59 only two of the five opinions were based on duty (the rest were on the basis of what amounted to actionable damage).

[18] Cases were counted more than once if they involved more than one kind of damage (eg the claim was for property damage *and* pure economic loss). Cases involving multiple parties pursuing claims for the same kind of damage were only counted only once. 'Other' included cases involving false imprisonment, wrongful birth/life, and a failure to provide an education.

[19] Where the case involved multiple appeals being heard together, each appeal was necessarily counted separately.

presented a very different split. From the 41 cases, the House of Lords/UKSC heard 54 appeals (six cases involved multiple appeals, some of which involved *more* than two appeals being heard together), 24 coming from trial decisions, and 30, representing a majority of the total appeals heard, coming from appeals of strike out applications, etc. Not only, then, was the House of Lords/UKSC more likely to hear conjoined appeals, they also demonstrated a much greater tendency to hear appeals from strike out applications, etc. A summary of the data is presented in the following table:

Table 2: Nature of the decision being appealed

Type of decision appealed	HCA	SCC	HoL/UKSC
Strike outs, etc	8	12	30
Trial	35	28	24

Whilst a comparison of the respective procedural rules governing permission to appeal would likely reveal why the House of Lords/UKSC heard so many more conjoined appeals than both the High Court of Australia and Supreme Court of Canada, such a comparison is beyond the scope of this book and so left for another day.

iii. *The Number of Independent Opinions per Case*

A comparison of the number of 'independent' opinions per case (that is, a discrete and non-concurring opinion, whether joint or individual, as to the existence of a duty of care), revealed that the level of (dis)agreement on duty issues within each jurisdiction varied considerably:

Table 3: The total number of 'independent' opinions

Type of opinion	HCA	SCC	HoL/UKSC
Independent	121	47	110
Concurring	16	11	91
Did not concern duty	24	8	6

By way of comparison, then, when the total number of independent opinions per jurisdiction is divided by the number of cases included in the sample, whilst the High Court of Australia and the House of Lords/UKSC had an average of 2.9 and 2.7 independent opinions per case respectively, the Supreme Court of Canada had an average of only 1.2 independent opinions per case.[20] Whilst this

---

[20] The reason for the large number of concurring opinions in the UK is that, prior to the formation of the Supreme Court, joint opinions were not given at all, and so *all* Law Lords sitting on a case gave *a* speech, whether 50 pages or one sentence.

statistic does not account for the weight of the independent opinions, it never-theless demonstrates that whereas the Supreme Court of Canada was typically united in its approach to duty questions, both the High Court of Australia and House of Lords/UKSC adopted almost three *discrete* methodologies per case. This contrast is further brought out by a comparison of the number of cases involving joint decisions of the entire court (that is, a single opinion authored or concurred with by the entire court). Whereas in the High Court of Australia only six of the 41 cases (five of which occurred since 2009) involved joint opinions, and 10 of 41 cases in the House of Lords/UKSC involved joint opinions, 24 of the 39 cases in the Supreme Court of Canada were joint opinions (20 of which have occurred in the 24 cases heard since 1995). The data also evidenced that opinions in cases identified as 'duty' cases were considerably more likely to rely on grounds other than duty in the High Court of Australia than in the Supreme Court of Canada or the House of Lords/UKSC.

iv. Success Rates of Claimants and Defendants

Finally, there was a noticeable difference in the success rates of claimants and defendants in the different jurisdictions. When multiple parties were taken into account,[21] of the 41 cases in the High Court of Australia, there were 228 determina-tions as to the existence of a duty of care. Of those, a decision was made in favour of the claimant on 91 occasions (89 of which followed appeals from trial decisions, whilst only two followed appeals from strike out decisions), and a duty was denied in the remaining 137 (93 from trial decisions, and 44 from strike out decisions). This is not especially encouraging data for claimants in general, and particularly for those hoping to appeal a decision to strike out their claim at first instance. In the Supreme Court of Canada, the split was slightly more encouraging for claimants; of the 296 duty determinations, 139 were made in favour of the claimant (117 fol-lowing trial and 22 following an appeal of a strike out decision), whilst 157 denied the existence of a duty (75 being appeals from trial decisions, and 82 upholding decisions to strike out the claim). Again, however, this is not particularly encourag-ing data for claimants hoping to successfully appeal a decision to strike out their claim at first instance. Of the 41 cases determined in the House of Lords/UKSC, there were 296 determinations as to the existence of the duty of care, and the news for claimants was more encouraging still: 148 of those decisions went in favour of the claimant (47 following trial decisions, and 101 following a decision to strike out the claim), and another 148 denied the existence of a duty (83 following an appeal of a trial decision, and 65 upholding decisions to strike out the claim), an

---

[21] Cases involving multiple parties where the court considered the existence of a duty independently in relation to each party were necessarily counted independently. If multiple parties were not taken into account, a case that, say, found a duty in relation to one claimant and no duty in relation to another could not have been meaningfully categorised. This essentially followed the methodology that was outlined in Section II, only claims that involved separate issues of fact, and so were considered by the court separately, were counted independently.

exact 50/50 split. Appeals from strike outs were, in contrast to the other two juris-dictions, in fact *more* likely to go in favour of the claimant. The above data are sum-marised in the following table:

Table 4: Success rates of claimants and defendants

Decision	HCA	SCC	HoL/UKSC
Decision in favour of claimant	91 (40%)	139 (47%)	148 (50%)
(After trial/After strike out)	(89/2)	(117/22)	(47/101)
Duty Denied	137 (60%)	157 (53%)	148 (50%)
(After trial/After strike out)	(93/44)	(75/82)	(83/65)

At first blush, the data appear to suggest that the High Court of Australia is the most pro-defendant (or anti-claimant) of the jurisdictions examined,[22] deciding the duty issue in favour of defendants 60% of the time, whilst the House of Lords/UKSC is the most pro-claimant, only finding for the defendant 50% of the time. However, before drawing any such inference from the data, a number of caveats must be added.

First, the imposition of a *duty* cannot be equated with the imposition of *liability*, as, whilst the denial of a duty was terminal to a claimant's claim, the imposition of a duty was no guarantee of success. Indeed, there were a number of cases where a duty was imposed but the claimant nevertheless failed on other grounds, usually by failing to show that the defendant acted carelessly.[23] Simi-larly, overturning a strike out of a claim on the basis that the defendant owed no duty, was not necessarily the same as a determination that a relevant duty existed; rather, it merely held that the existence of a duty was not 'unarguable', and so the claim ought not be struck out on that basis prior to a full hearing.[24] So even where the duty determination was made in favour of the claimant, a duty might never-theless have been denied at a later stage of the proceedings.

Secondly, a finding that no duty existed was not necessarily consistent with an anti-claimant mentality, at least insofar as 'claimant' is usually understood, in the sense of an injured individual. This is most clearly demonstrated in contri-bution proceedings, where the claim is being contested by multiple wrongdoers.

---

[22] Indeed, this observation has been made before. See, eg, Pam Stewart and Anita Stuhmcke, 'High Court Negligence Cases 2000–2010' (2014) 36 SydLR 585, 585; and H Luntz, 'A View from Abroad' [2008] NZLRev 97, 99.

[23] See, eg, McHugh J in *Brodie v Singleton Shire Council* (2001) 206 CLR 512, McHugh in *Romeo v Conservation Commission (NT)* (1998) 192 CLR 431, *Stewart v Pettie* (1995) 121 DLR (4th) 222, *Mustapha v Culligan of Canada Ltd* (2008) 293 DLR (4th) 29, and *Hill v Hamilton-Wentworth Regional Police Services Board* (2007) 285 DLR (4th) 620.

[24] For an example of comments to this effect, see Lord Slynn in *Barrett v Enfield* [2001] 2 AC 550 (HL).

In *British Columbia v Imperial Tobacco Canada Ltd*,[25] for example, one of the various claims before the court involved a large tobacco company (who was being sued by consumers) seeking a contribution from the Canadian government for misrepresenting and failing to communicate to them the health risks of cigarettes. Ultimately, the court held that no relevant duty existed, which, despite being a decision in favour of the defendant, would not normally be described as an anti-claimant type decision.

For what it is worth, however, the overall success rates of claimants and defendants in the cases included in the study, regardless of the grounds relied upon, were as follows:[26]

Table 5: The successful party

Successful party	HCA	SCC	HoL/UKSC
Claimant overall	36%	44%	44%
Claimant on duty question	40%	47%	50%
Defendant overall	64%	56%	56%
Defendant on duty question	60%	53%	50%

Unsurprisingly, the success rates of claimants *overall* were lower than the success rates of claimants when confined to the duty issue.

B. The Use of General Duty Tests

As we saw in chapter three, general duty tests play a significant role in modern duty jurisprudence, and, notwithstanding their limitations, today, Australia, Canada, and the UK all have relatively well-established tests for establishing the existence of a duty of care. In this section, we will explore how frequently these general duty tests are *actually* used in practice; that is, how frequently they are used in reaching conclusions about the existence of a duty of care.

i. Methodology

Whilst it is strongly arguable that many of the so-called duty tests are not 'tests' in any meaningful sense at all,[27] for the purposes of this section, which is to investigate

---

[25] (2011) 335 DLR (4th) 513.
[26] The success rates for the claimant/defendant on duty question are simply taken from Table 4.
[27] See the discussion in ch 3.

the courts' *use* of the so-called tests rather than the merits of the tests, general duty 'tests' will be understood broadly and so to include the following: Deane J's proximity test, the *Anns*/two-stage test, the *Caparo*[28]/three-stage test, the assumption of responsibility test, incrementalism, and the salient features test. Opinions were only counted as having relied on a test where it was made explicitly clear that the existence or denial of a duty depended on having satisfied or failed a test or a stage of a test. Reasoning that was consistent with, but not explicitly identified as, the application of a general test was therefore not counted as having relied on a general test. This relatively strict approach was adopted so as to minimise the use of discretion when coding the opinions, something that was especially important in the High Court of Australia, where almost *any* weighing of pro- and anti-duty arguments could legitimately be labelled as an application of the salient features test, but was also important in the UK and Canada when terms such as 'fair', 'just', and 'reasonable' were used outside the context of *Caparo* or *Anns*.

ii. The Results

A summary of the use of general duty tests in the three jurisdictions is provided in the following table:

Table 6: The use of different duty tests

Test	HCA	SCC	HoL/UKSC
Proximity	31(14%)	0	0
Anns/the two-stage test	1(<1%)	240(80%)	0
Caparo/the three-stage test	6(3%)	0	54(24%)
Assumption of responsibility	8(3%)	13(6%)	27(12%)
Incrementalism	1(<1%)	0	1.5(<1%)
Salient features	22(10%)	0	0
(Total tests)	(69)(31%)	(253)(86%)	(82.5)(37%)
No test	154(69%)	43(14%)	140.5(63%)

iii. Analysis

The three jurisdictions paint an entirely different picture of the use of general duty tests. At one end of the spectrum was the High Court of Australia, which relied on a general duty tests in only 31% of duty determinations. The House of Lords/ UKSC, though not quite to the same extent as the High Court of Australia, also

---

[28] *Caparo Industries plc v Dickman* [1990] 2 AC 605 (HL) ('*Caparo*').

assigned little role to general duty tests, using them only 37% of the time, despite being responsible for having invented not only the concept of general tests, but the majority of the tests themselves.[29] At the other end of the spectrum was the Supreme Court of Canada, whose reliance on general tests in determining the existence of a duty was almost universal, with 86% of all duty determinations analysed relying on some form of general test.

One might be tempted to explain away the comparatively infrequent use of tests in the High Court of Australia on the basis of the long period of uncertainty between the downfall of proximity and adoption of the salient features test. However, this explanation is not supported by the data, as, despite the salient features test ostensibly representing the law in Australia since *Sullivan v Moody*,[30] only 13% of the determination in 15 years since (that is, 14 of 114 opinions) have relied on the salient features approach,[31] the remaining 87% of all determinations being determined via alternative methods. One may therefore be forgiven for asking whether the 'disgraceful'[32] lack of guidance and 'doctrinal chaos'[33] that was thought to have existed prior to that time has actually been resolved at all.

a. The Most Popular Tests

The most popular tests in each jurisdiction were not particularly surprising. In the High Court of Australia, on those relatively rare occasions when general tests were used, Deane J's proximity test and the salient features test proved to be the most popular. Perhaps also unsurprisingly, on the occasions in which Deane's proximity test was used, 68% (21/31) of those times involved judgments of Deane J or judgments to which Deane J was a party, a further 16% (5/31) came from judgments handed down during Deane's time on the Court, whilst the remaining 16% (5/31) came from judgments delivered after Deane J's retirement from the Court.[34] This would certainly suggest that, even during the height of proximity's reign, the use of the test was driven principally by Deane J rather than the Court itself. In the Supreme Court of Canada, *Anns* dominated the Courts' approach to duty determinations, being used in 80% of all duty determinations made in the sample period,

---

[29] Indeed, even Deane J's proximity test was, according to Deane J himself, based on the dicta of Lord Atkin in *Donoghue v Stevenson* [1932] AC 562 (HL): *Jaensch v Coffey* (1984) 155 CLR 549, 579, 583–84; *Stevens v Brodribb Sawmilling Company Pty Ltd* (1986) 160 CLR 16, 51.

[30] (2001) 207 CLR 562 ('*Sullivan*').

[31] Note that this figure excludes the decision of *Sullivan* itself, as well as the pre-*Sullivan* opinion of Gummow J in *Perre v Apand Pty Ltd* (1999) 198 CLR 180, upon which the salient features test is based.

[32] *Metal Roofing & Cladding Pty Ltd v Eire Pty Ltd* (1999) 9 NTLR 82 (FC) (Bailey J) [24]. See ch 3, fn 245.

[33] Christian Witting, 'The Three Stage Test Abandoned in Australia—Or Not?' (2002) 118 LQR 214, 214. See ch 3, fn 246.

[34] For the sake of completeness, it should be noted that the proximity test has also been approved in a number of cases that did not fall within the sample, including *Burnie Port Authority v General Jones Pty Ltd* (1994) 179 CLR 520 (not a duty case); *Stevens v Brodribb Sawmilling Company Pty Ltd* (1986) 160 CLR 16 (not a duty case); and *Jaensch v Coffey* (1984) 155 CLR 549 (before 1985).

and 95% (178/187) of duty determinations made since 1995.[35] In the House of Lords/UKSC, *Caparo* was clearly the most frequently used test, though perhaps not as often as one might expect. In particular, the three-stage test only accounted for 24% of all duty determinations made since 1985, and 30% (54/179) of determinations made since *Caparo* was handed down in 1990;[36] accordingly, despite being the most popular test, its use is far from universal, suggesting that the reputation of Lord Bridge's dicta as the 'classic exposition of the modern approach to establishing a duty of care'[37] may not be deserved.

b. The Underrepresentation of Assumption of Responsibility and Incrementalism

Although the data show that neither the assumption of responsibility test nor incrementalism were used *in their own right* particularly often, both concepts were nevertheless regularly relied upon as part of the overall duty enquiry, and so the data somewhat misrepresents their actual influence. In particular, in a number of cases, assumption of responsibility was used to demonstrate the requisite degree of proximity as part of *Caparo*,[38] *Anns*,[39] and Deane J's proximity test,[40] whilst incrementalism was occasionally used as part of the salient features test,[41] and to show that the imposition of a duty would, or would not be, fair just, and reasonable under both *Caparo*[42] and *Anns*.[43]

c. Failure Rates of the Different Stages of *Caparo* and *Anns*

It is also worth noting that on the occasions on which *Caparo* and *Anns* were used, some 'stages' of the tests were more influential than others. Although it is true that *Anns* is generally thought of as involving *two* stages rather than three, as was made

---

[35] This is likely the result of *Hercules Managements Ltd v Ernst & Young* (1997) 146 DLR (4th) 577, which confirmed that the *Anns* test was to be used in *all* duty cases, even those involving purely economic loss which had previously tended to rely on the assumption of responsibility test. Indeed, *all* uses of the assumption of responsibility test occurred prior to 1995.

[36] Indeed, Lord Bridge himself did not appear to rely on the three-stage test to deny a duty in *Caparo*, instead relying on an absence of an assumption of responsibility.

[37] M Lunney and K Oliphant, *Tort Law: Text and Materials*, 5th edn (OUP, 2013) 137.

[38] *Customs and Excise Commissioners v Barclays Bank plc* [2007] 1 AC 181 (HL) (Lord Mance), *Phelps v Hillingdon London Borough Council* [2001] 2 AC 619 (HL) (Lord Clyde), *Smith v Eric S Bush* [1990] 1 AC 831 (HL) (Lord Griffiths).

[39] *Childs v Desormeaux* (2006) 266 DLR (4th) 257 (McLachlin J), *BCL Ltd v Hofstrand Farms Ltd* (1986) 26 DLR (4th) 1 (Estey).

[40] *Esanda Finance Corporation Ltd v Peat Marwick Hungerfords* (1997) 188 CLR 241, 254–5 (Dawson J), *Hawkins v Clayton* (1988) 164 CLR 539 (Mason CJ and Wilson J, and Deane J).

[41] *Harriton v Stephens* (2006) 226 CLR 52 (Crennan J).

[42] *Smith v Ministry of Defence* [2014] 1 AC 52 (HL) (Lord Carnwath), *Customs and Excise Commissioners v Barclays Bank plc* [2007] 1 AC 181 (HL) (Lords Bingham and Rodger), *Stovin v Wise* [1996] 1 AC 923 (HL) (Lord Nicholls).

[43] *Hall v Hebert* (1993) 101 DLR (4th) 129 (Sopinka J).

clear by McLachlin CJC in *Childs v Desormeaux*,[44] one of those 'stages' consists of two independent 'questions', so that foreseeability, proximity, and fairness, justice, and reasonableness are discrete requirements in any event, albeit as part of a slightly different hierarchy.[45]

A breakdown of the success rates of the various stages of the *Caparo* and *Anns* test is as follows:[46]

Table 7: Unsuccessful stages of *Caparo* and *Anns*

Stage(s) that failed	HCA	SCC	HoL/UKSC
Foreseeability	0	7(3%)	0
Proximity	0	89(37%)	9(15%)
FJ&R	0	77(32%)	23(42%)
None (ie all passed)	6(100%)	100(42%)	24(45%)

In both the House of Lords/UKSC and the Supreme Court of Canada, the success rates of claimants under *Caparo* and *Anns*, perhaps predictably, were similar to success rates overall. In the High Court of Australia, however, where Kirby J was responsible for all six uses of *Caparo*, due to the small sample size the data were not reflective of any overall trend.

d. 'Tests' were often Code for other Things

Notwithstanding the considerable variance in the use of general tests among the jurisdictions, the data clearly show that general tests play *a* role in a not insignificant number of duty determinations. But was that role a useful one? As we saw in chapter three, a common criticism of duty tests is that they perform little analytical work themselves, and merely act as a label for the conclusion that a duty of care exists, a conclusion often reached via some other more specific reasoning. Whilst quantitative data is limited in what it can tell us about the merits of duty tests, and so such issues are best explored qualitatively, there are nevertheless a number of features of the data worth highlighting.

---

[44] (2006) 266 DLR (4th) 257, 263 [12]. This largely echoed McLachlin CJ and Major J's comments in *Cooper v Hobart* (2001) 206 DLR (4th) 193.

[45] Indeed, Linden and Feldthusen have described the Canadian approach to *Anns* as 'remarkably similar' to *Caparo*: Allen M Linden and Bruce Feldthusen, *Canadian Tort Law*, 9th edn (LexisNexis, 2011) 299.

[46] Note that the data adds up to more than 100% because a small number decisions failed *multiple* stages of the *Caparo/Anns* tests. In particular, seven opinions (3%) in the Supreme Court of Canada failed the foreseeability *and* proximity stages, whilst 26 (11%) of opinions in the Supreme Court of Canada and one (1.8%) opinion in the House of Lords/UKSC failed the proximity *and* FJ&R stages. No decisions failed the foreseeability *and* FJ&R stages.

In the High Court of Australia, of the times that Deane J's proximity test was relied upon to determine the existence of a duty of care, a more specific test or concept was *explicitly* used to determine the presence of a sufficient degree of proximity on 68% of those occasions. In particular, the presence of 'proximity' was determined by an assumption of responsibility in 36% (11/31) of the opinions, 'reliance' in 16% (5/31) of the opinions, reasons of policy in 13% (4/31) of the opinions, and the presence of 'control' in 3% (1/31) of the opinions. On only 32% (10/31) of the occasions that proximity was used as a general test did the existence of a duty *actually* depend on some abstract notion of proximity. Indeed, in *Hawkins v Clayton*,[47] Deane J went so far as to *equate* proximity with assumption of responsibility in cases of pure economic loss, stating that, where:

> [T]he plaintiff's claim is for pure economic loss ... the categories of case in which the requisite relationship of proximity is to be found are properly to be seen as special in that they will be characterized by some additional element or elements which will commonly (but not necessarily) consist of known reliance (or dependence) or the assumption of responsibility or a combination of the two ...[48]

Mason CJ and Wilson J made similar comments, noting that '[regarding] the question of liability in tort, the relevant enquiry is whether the [relationship between the plaintiff and defendant] gave rise to a relationship of sufficient proximity *founded upon an assumption of responsibility* ...'[49] This deference to more specific concepts, depending on the facts of the case, strongly supports the various criticisms of Deane J's proximity test,[50] some of which we encountered in chapter three, and suggests that asking 'was there a sufficient degree of proximity?' is hardly any more helpful than asking 'was there a duty of care?'

In the Supreme Court of Canada and the House of Lords/UKSC, similar criticisms could be made of the use of *Anns* and *Caparo*, where, despite the ostensibly structured approach required by the two tests, the existence of a duty was often determined via a simple balancing of pro- and anti-duty arguments. First, as Table 7 indicates, the foreseeability stage played almost no role whatsoever in any court, failing on only 3% of duty determinations in the Supreme Court of Canada,[51] and on *no* occasion in the House of Lords/UKSC. Secondly, despite proximity playing a more significant role than the foreseeability stage, as was the case with Deane J's proximity test, its existence was often contingent on other,

---

[47] (1988) 164 CLR 539.
[48] ibid 576.
[49] ibid 545 (emphasis added).
[50] See, eg, Dawson J in *Hill v Van Erp* (1997) 188 CLR 159, 178; Brennan J in *Hawkins v Clayton* (1988) 164 CLR 539, 555–56; and McHugh J's extra-judicial comments in MH McHugh, 'Neighbourhood, Proximity and Reliance' in PD Finn (ed), *Essays on Torts* (Law Book Co Ltd, 1989) 36.
[51] Though note *Odhavji Estate v Woodhouse* (2003) 233 DLR (4th) 193, where the Supreme Court, although declining to rule on the issue of foreseeability, suggested that it may not have been satisfied if they had ruled on it. Note also that questions of foreseeability played a greater, albeit still marginal, role in cases where duty tests were not used. See Section III(C) below.

more specific tests, most notably an assumption of responsibility,[52] and, at least in the Supreme Court of Canada, considerations of policy.[53] By far the most important element of the enquiry was whether the imposition of a duty would be fair, just, and reasonable. In particular, on the occasions that *Caparo* or *Anns* were relied upon, this open-ended stage, where almost any pro- and anti-duty argument could be considered, was relevant in 74% of duty determinations in the Supreme Court of Canada, and 86% of duty determinations in the House of Lords/UKSC, not including those times in the Supreme Court of Canada where a similar enquiry was undertaken under the 'proximity' label. Accordingly, given the comparatively undemanding foreseeability and (at least in the UK) proximity stages, *Caparo* and *Anns* frequently reduced to the question of whether it was fair, just, and reasonable to impose a duty, suggesting that the guidance offered by the stages is often, as has been claimed, of limited analytical assistance.

C. Determining the Existence of a Duty without General Tests

The obvious question following the previous section is 'how do the courts determine the outcome of the duty enquiry when they do not rely on general duty tests?' The answer to this question is largely ignored by tort law courses and textbooks notwithstanding that, as we have just seen, in the *majority* of duty determinations in the High Court of Australia and House of Lords/UKSC, the courts determine the existence or absence of a duty *without* the aid of general tests. In this section, we will explore what methods they use instead.

i. Methodology

The various 'non-general test methodologies' were not identified prior to coding, and only emerged after coding had been completed. In particular, during the coding of the cases, where an opinion did not rely on a test to determine the outcome of the duty enquiry, a brief description of the methodology that *was* used was made, and these were classified at the completion of the coding into, ultimately, the following five broad categories: the foreseeability of the harm, the common law method,[54] experimental general duty tests, policy considerations, and a balancing of pro- and anti-duty arguments.

---

[52] See (n 38) and (n 39).

[53] *D(B) v Children's Aid Society* (2007) 284 DLR (4th) 682; *Hill v Hamilton-Wentworth Regional Police Services Board* (2007) 285 DLR (4th) 620. See also the discussion in *Cooper v Hobart* (2001) 206 DLR (4th) 193, 202–203 [29] (McLachlin CJC and Major J), where 'questions of policy' were explicitly recognised as relevant to the proximity stage.

[54] To some extent, of course, *all* judicial reasoning could be classified as following the 'common law method'. Here, however, by 'common law method' it is meant deference to existing principles and general analogical reasoning.

ii. The Results

An overview of the various methodologies relied on by the courts when they did not rely on duty tests is as follows:[55]

Table 8: Non-general test methodologies

Methodology	HCA	SCC	HoL/UKSC
No foreseeability	12(8%)	0%	17.5(12%)
Experimental duty tests	3(2%)	0%	10(7%)
Policy considerations	0%	0%	21(15%)
Common law method	62(40%)	43(100%)	69(49%)
The 'balancing approach'	77(50%)	0%	23(17%)

iii. Analysis

a. No Foreseeability

As Table 8 illustrates, a small number of opinions in both the High Court of Australia and the House of Lords/UKSC were determined on the basis that the harm suffered by the claimant was not foreseeable; in other words, there was no factual duty. No cases in the Supreme Court of Canada were determined solely on this basis. That foreseeability of harm to the claimant played such a minor role in ultimate appellate courts should not be surprising; ultimate appellate courts are generally reluctant to reconsider determinations of fact made in lower courts, as it is not in the public interest for those courts to spend their limited time and resources making rulings that will often be of limited application beyond the particular facts of the case before the court. Accordingly, when issues of foreseeability of harm were considered in ultimate appellate courts, it was usually to clarify the role played by foreseeability, and *what* precisely needs to be foreseeable, in certain types of cases, rather than merely to determine whether the foreseeability requirement was satisfied in that particular case.[56]

b. Experimental Duty Tests

In both the High Court of Australia and the House of Lords there were also a small number of opinions that determined the outcome of the duty enquiry on what could be best described as 'experimental' duty tests. In the High Court of Australia these alternative general duty determinants occurred during the period of uncertainty

---

[55] Percentages given are percentages of opinions that did not rely on general tests, rather than percentages of all opinions.

[56] For example, in *Page v Smith* [1996] 1 AC 155 (HL), the Court was not so much concerned with reconsidering the lower Court's factual findings, as with clarifying *what* exactly was required to be foreseeable in cases involving primary victims of psychiatric injury.

between the rejection of proximity as a general test and the rise of the salient features test, and included a concept of 'general reliance',[57] a somewhat open-ended and circular 'precise legal rights'-based approach,[58] and a 'control'-based test that examined the defendant's degree of control over the relevant risk.[59] In the House of Lords, also during a period of uncertainty, namely between the downfall of *Anns* and establishment of *Caparo* as the favoured replacement, a number of opinions, including several from Lord Jauncey, relied on what appeared to be a Deane J and Lord Atkin inspired concept of proximity as a general duty determinant.[60] In each case, the attempts were short lived and ultimately led to nothing, often following considerable criticism from other members of the court.[61]

c. Policy Considerations

In the House of Lords/UKSC, a number of opinions determined the outcome of the duty enquiry on the basis of considerations of policy. Whilst it is true that policy considerations play *a* role in many opinions, something that will be explored further shortly, in these opinions the role of policy was explicitly identified as the *principal* consideration. Significantly, all of the opinions that relied on this policy-based approach occurred in so-called 'immunity' cases,[62] where, according to Lord Dyson in *Jones v Kaney*,[63] 'The only question is whether there are sufficiently compelling policy reasons for according the [defendant] immunity from suit.'[64] The immunity cases concerned police immunity,[65] expert witness immunity,[66] combat immunity,[67] and advocate's immunity.[68]

---

[57] *Pyrenees Shire Council v Day* (1998) 192 CLR 332, 369–71 (McHugh J).

[58] *Perre v Apand Pty Ltd* (1999) 198 CLR 180, 201–202 (Gaudron J).

[59] *Pyrenees Shire Council v Day* (1998) 192 CLR 330, 389 (Gummow J).

[60] Including: all four substantive opinions in *Alcock v Chief Constable of South Yorkshire Police* [1992] 1 AC 310 (HL), Lord Keith (at 396), Lord Ackner (at 402), Lord Oliver (at 406), and Lord Jauncey (at 420); Lord Jauncey in *Smith v Eric S Bush* [1990] 1 AC 831, 871–72; and Lords Janucey and Oliver in *Caparo, passim*.

[61] For criticism of the 'general reliance' test, see *Pyrenees Shire Council v Day* (1998) 192 CLR 330, 389 (Brennan CJ). For criticism of the 'precise legal rights' test, see *Perre v Apand Pty Ltd* (1999) 198 CLR 180, 213–25 (McHugh J). For academic criticism of both concepts, see R Stevens, 'The Divergence of the Australian and English Law of Torts' in Simone Degeling, J Edelman and J Goudkamp (eds), *Torts in Commercial Law* (Thomson Reuters, 2011) 48–49.

[62] McBride and Bagshaw, for example, describe immunities as situations in which a claimant 'would *normally* be entitled to sue the defendant in negligence but in fact she is prevented from doing so by some special legal rule': Nicholas J McBride and Roderick Bagshaw, *Tort Law*, 4th edn (Pearson, 2012) 89. See also James Goudkamp, *Tort Law Defences* (Hart, 2013) 137 (fn 10).

[63] [2011] 2 AC 398.

[64] ibid 435.

[65] *Hill v Chief Constable of West Yorkshire* [1989] 1 AC 53 (HL) (Lord Templeman). Though note that, following *Michael v The Chief Constable of South Wales Police* [2015] AC 1732 (HL), it is arguably no-longer appropriate to describe the no-liability rule, at least as it applies to the police, as an 'immunity', given that the absence of a duty is now justified on the basis of there not having been an assumption of responsibility rather than on the basis of there being a special rule that applies to the police: see ibid [44]–[47], [116] (Lord Toulson). See also N McBride, 'Michael and the Future of Tort Law' (2016) 32 PN 14.

[66] *Jones v Kaney* [2011] 2 AC 398 (HL) (Lords Phillips, Collins and Dyson).

[67] *Smith v Ministry of Defence* [2014] 1 AC 52 (HL).

[68] *Arthur JS Hall & Co v Simons* [2002] 1 AC 615 (HL).

d. Common Law Method

The most popular non-general test methodology in both the Supreme Court of Canada and House of Lords/UKSC, and a close second in the High Court of Australia, was what can most conveniently be described as the common law method; that is, where the existence of a duty was determined by reference to existing principles of law and general analogical reasoning. That the common law method was used in so many duty determinations should not be surprising, as, according to conventional duty analysis, general tests are only to be used where the existing law offers no (or at least limited) guidance.[69] Cases that relied on the common law method did so in a variety of ways. At one end of the spectrum were cases that were determined on the basis that the facts of the case fell within an existing duty category.[70] Other opinions relied less on the explicit *outcome* of existing cases, or the duty situation recognised, and more on the *reasoning* from existing cases, usually in the form of guidance or tests.[71] Whilst at the other end of the spectrum, where no explicit guidance had been given in prior cases, were those opinions that relied on far more general guidance, or on high level general principles of law.[72]

e. The Balancing Approach

The fifth and final non-general test methodology identified was essentially an *ad hoc* balancing of pro- and anti-duty arguments ('the balancing approach'). This open-ended method was particularly popular in the High Court of Australia, accounting for 50% of duty determinations overall, but was also used in a small

---

[69] See, eg: *Caparo* 618 (Lord Bridge), 628 (Lord Roskill); *Perre v Apand Pty Ltd* (1999) 198 CLR 180, 217 (McHugh J); *Cooper v Hobart* (2001) 206 DLR (4th) 193 [41] (McLachlin J); *Childs v Desormeaux* (2006) 266 DLR (4th) 257 [15] (McLachlin CJ).

[70] See, eg: *Stuart v Kirkland-Veenstra* (2009) 237 CLR 215 (Gummow, Hayne and Heydon JJ); *Waller v James* (2006) 226 CLR 136 (Crennan J); *Van Colle v Chief Constable of the Hertfordshire Police; Smith v Chief Constable of Sussex Police* [2009] 1 AC 225 (HL) (Lords Brown and Phillips); and *Rees v Darlington Memorial Hospital NHS Trust* [2004] 1 AC 309 (HL) (Lords Bingham and Phillips).

[71] See, eg: French CJ in *Stuart v Kirkland-Veenstra* (2009) 237 CLR 215, at 239, who relied on the judgment of Gummow J in *Pyrenees Shire Council v Day* (1998) 192 CLR 332 to determine the circumstances in which a plaintiff will be owed a duty by a public authority; Wilson J in *Crocker v Sundance Northwest Resorts Ltd* (1988) 51 DLR (4th) 321, relying on *Jordan House Ltd v Menow* (1974) 38 DLR (3rd) 105, to determine the circumstances in which an occupier owes a duty to an intoxicated patron; and Lord Steyn in *Brooks v Commissioner of Police of the Metropolis* [2005] 1 WLR 1495 (HL), with whom the majority of the court agreed, who relied on the guidance in *Hill v Chief Constable of West Yorkshire Police* [1989] AC 53 (HL) to determine the extent of the duty owed by the police in the course of investigating an alleged crime;

[72] See, eg: Gummow, Hayne and Heydon JJ in *Stuart v Kirkland-Veenstra* (2009) 237 CLR 215, 248, who refused to impose a 'duty to rescue' on the grounds that it would conflict with the 'underlying value of the common law which gives primacy to personal autonomy'; Iacobucci J in *London Drugs Ltd v Kuehne & Nagel International Ltd* (1992) 97 DLR (4th) 261 [182]–[183], who relied on 'well established principles of tort law', including *Donoghue v Stevenson* [1932] AC 562; and Lord Keith in *Murphy v Brentwood* [1991] 1 AC 398, 471 (HL), who refused to impose a duty, on the basis that such a duty would be inconsistent with 'any basis of established principle … [in] the law of negligence'.

number of duty determinations in the House of Lords.[73] The essence of the open-ended balancing approach was, perhaps, best described in *Kuhl v Zurich Financial Services*,[74] where Heydon, Crennan, and Bell JJ stated that 'The existence of a duty of care depends on the circumstances of the case.'[75] The balancing approach shares much in common with the salient features test, which, ultimately, is little more than a formalised version of the balancing approach; indeed, in the High Court of Australia many of the opinions classified as relying on the balancing approach appeared to simply be undisclosed applications of the salient features test, in that the existence of a duty was determined on the basis of the presence or absence of well-established salient features, despite the test itself not being directly named.[76] Where opinions relied on the balancing approach, a wide range of pro- and anti-duty reasons were used. Mostly these reasons were orthodox and unsurprising; for example, whether the defendant exercised any control over the claimant,[77] whether there was the potential for indeterminate liability,[78] whether the claimant was vulnerable to the defendant,[79] whether the imposition of a duty would create a conflict with other laws[80] or competing duties,[81] and, in the case of public authorities, issues of justiciability[82] and whether the allegedly negligent decision was policy-based rather than operational.[83] In almost all opinions, the existing law was also considered as part of the balancing process.[84]

---

[73] No opinions in the Supreme Court of the UK were classified as having relied on this method.

[74] (2011) 243 CLR 361.

[75] ibid 390.

[76] It will be recalled that for opinions to be classified as applications of a general test the opinion had to be *explicit* that a general test was being applied. For example, in *CAL No 14 Pty Ltd v Motor Accidents Board* (2009) 239 CLR 390, at 404–11, Gummow, Heydon, and Crennan JJ, although not explicitly identifying the salient features test, denied the existence of a duty on the grounds that the claimant was not vulnerable, the imposition of a duty would interfere with the autonomy of the defendant, and the imposition of a duty would create incoherence in the law; in other words, on the presence or absence of well-established salient features. Similarly, in *Hunter and New England Local Health District v McKenna* (2014) 253 CLR 270, at [17]–[23], the majority, also without identifying the salient features test, denied the existence of a duty on the basis of the limited scope of the statutory power, potential problems of indeterminacy, and potential problems of incoherence in the law; again, on the basis of the absence of well-established salient features.

[77] See, eg, *Modbury Triangle Shopping Centre Pty Ltd v Anzil* (2000) 205 CLR 254 (Hayne J), and *Perre v Apand Pty Ltd* (1999) 198 CLR 180 (Gaudron J and Callinan J).

[78] *Perre v Apand Pty Ltd* (1999) 198 CLR 180 (Hayne J), and *Agar v Hyde* (2000) 201 CLR 552 (Gleeson CJ, and Gaudron, McHugh, Gummow and Hayne JJ).

[79] *Perre v Apand Pty Ltd* (1999) 198 CLR 180 (Hayne J).

[80] *Miller v Miller* (2011) 242 CLR 446 (French CJ, Gummow, Hayne, Crennan, Kiefel and Bell JJ); *Leighton Contractors Pty Ltd v Fox* (2009) 240 CLR 1 (French CJ, Gummow, Hayne, Heydon and Bell JJ); *Gala v Preston* (1991) 172 CLR 243 (Brennan J and Dawson J).

[81] *D v East Berkshire Community Health NHS Trust* [2005] 2 AC 373 (HL) (Lords Brown and Nicholls).

[82] *Stovin v Wise* [1996] 1 AC 923 (HL) (Lord Hoffmann).

[83] *Crimmins v Stevedoring Industry Finance Committee* (1999) 200 CLR 1 (Hayne J), and *Graham Barclay Oysters Pty Ltd v Ryan* (2002) 211 CLR 540 (Gleeson CJ).

[84] How much weight was placed on the existing law depended, of course, on its perceived merits as well as the extent to which it applied to the facts of the case. For what is perhaps the only exception, being an opinion that appeared to place almost *no* value in the existing law at all, see the judgment of Hayne J in *Perre v Apand Pty Ltd* (1999) 198 CLR 180.

Other opinions, however, particularly in the High Court of Australia, relied on extremely fact-specific considerations that were less orthodox and, arguably, inappropriate for the ostensibly categorical duty analysis,[85] including concerns that the risk that materialised was 'readily apparent',[86] a consideration conventionally dealt with under the fault stage or as evidence of contributory negligence, and concerns that the existence of a duty would impose an unreasonable burden on the defendant,[87] a consideration surely also more appropriate for the fault analysis.

iv. Some Additional Commentary

Having now seen an overview of the data, it is worth making some observations about the various non-general test methodologies. For the most part, the methodologies were orthodox and uncontroversial. The foreseeability requirement, for example, although more appropriately dealt with at the fault and remoteness stages, has nevertheless been a well-established element of the duty enquiry since the nineteenth century.[88] Experimental duty tests, too, are not particularly controversial, as all duty tests must start somewhere, and the fact that they were ultimately abandoned as general duty determinants says more about the tests themselves, than the propriety of relying on experimental tests in general. Reliance on the common law method, or general analogical reasoning, is, certainly, the most orthodox method of determining the duty enquiry of all, and an axiomatic aspect of common law legal systems generally. More controversial were those opinions that relied on policy considerations and the balancing approach. The debate surrounding the propriety of policy-based reasoning has already been explored in chapter six and so need not be repeated here. As for the balancing approach, whilst its open-endedness gives rise to many of the same criticisms directed at the policy-based approach, perhaps the major objection is that, without any structure to the analysis, it is difficult to know which arguments will be relied upon by the court and so predict the outcome of cases with any degree of certainty. Indeed, McHugh's criticisms of the salient features approach, which we encountered in chapter three, would appear to be equally applicable to the balancing approach:

> Left unchecked, this approach becomes nothing more than the exercise of a discretion— like the process of sentencing, where the final result is determined by the individual 'judge's instinctive synthesis of all the various aspects'. Different judges will apply different factors with different weightings. There will be no predictability or certainty in decision-making because each novel case will be decided by a selection of factors particular to itself. Because each factor is only one among many, few will be subject to rigorous scrutiny to determine whether they are in truth relevant or applicable.[89]

---

[85] The sense in which the duty enquiry is categorical is discussed further below.
[86] In *Mulligan v Coffs Harbour CC* (2005) 223 CLR 486, 499 (Gummow J).
[87] *Cole v South Tweed Heads Rugby League* (2004) 217 CLR 469, 476 (Gleeson CJ), 506 (Callinan J).
[88] *Heaven v Pender* (1883) 11 QB 503 (CA) (Brett MR).
[89] *Crimmins v Stevedoring Committee* (1999) 200 CLR 1 [77].

It could therefore be argued that, on this basis, the *ad hoc* nature of the balancing approach provides an inferior method for determining duty cases to general tests, as despite their defects, *some* guidance is better than *no* guidance. This certainly appears to be the essence of Kirby J's comments in support of general tests in *Pyrenees Shire Council v Day*:[90]

> [W]hatever the defects of the notions of 'foreseeability', 'proximity' and the imprecision of the policy evaluation inherent in measurement of 'fairness', 'justice' and 'reasonableness', some guidance must be given by the Court as to how the duty question is to be answered when it is contested in a particular case. Otherwise, confronted with a suggested new category, lawyers in their offices and courts in Australia would have no instruction for their task of reasoning by analogy from past categories ... the individual affected, the lawyer advising and the court deciding have a right to know at least the general approach which they should adopt in order to resolve the controversy.

Whilst it is no doubt true that some guidance is better than no guidance, this can only be an argument in favour of general tests to the extent that general tests *do* provide more guidance than the alternatives. The entire basis of the criticism of general tests, however, is that they do not; to argue in defence of general tests on this basis simply begs the question. Indeed, as we have seen, Deane J's proximity test was typically little more than a label for whatever consideration(s) seemed important on the facts, whilst under *Caparo* and *Anns*, not only does the proximity stage canvas a similarly wide range of considerations, but much of the analysis tends to be done under the open-ended fair, just, and reasonable stage, which often descends into a balancing of pro- and anti-duty arguments in any event. Similarly, the salient features test is essentially little more than a formal label for the balancing approach so as to give the method a semblance of jurisprudential legitimacy. So whilst the balancing approach is, *prima facie*, the antithesis of the structured and predictable approach to determining the duty enquiry sought to be achieved by general tests, in practice, the difference often appears to be little more than an illusion.

D. Do the Courts Approach the Duty Enquiry in a Categorical or Fact Specific Manner?

In chapter five we saw that one of the principal features of notional duty determinations is that they tend to be 'categorical' in nature; that is, they establish that a duty exists in a *situation* or *category of case*, rather than only on the particular facts of the case. It is the identification of this category of case that gives notional duty determinations their precedential value as well as making them questions of law rather than of fact. In this section, we will investigate the extent to which this understanding of notional duty is shared by the courts. In particular, we will

---

[90] (1998) 192 CLR 330, 415–16 (footnotes omitted).

explore whether the focus of the courts is on whether a duty exists in a particular *category of case*, or whether a duty exists on the *particular facts of the case*.

i. Methodology

For the purposes of this section, a 'categorical' duty determination was one that identified a particular situation, which both covered and applied beyond the facts of the case, in which a duty of care was held to either exist or not exist. Determining whether a duty determination was fact-based or categorical was informed by a number of considerations, including how the court worded its task (that is, 'to determine whether *the* defendant owe a duty to *the* claimant,' or whether '*a* defendant owed a duty to *a* claimant in this type of situation'), and the types of reasons relied upon by the court (that is, were they reasons that applied to the situation generally, or reasons that only applied to the particular fact-situation before the court?).[91] A considerable degree of judgment was, however, also required.

ii. The Results

The respective frequencies of categorical and fact-based duty determinations in the various courts is outlined in the following table.

Table 9: Whether notional duty determinations were categorical or fact-based

Type of notional duty determination	HCA	SCC	HoL/UKSC
Categorical	97(57%)	262(89%)	161.5(73%)
Fact-based	126(43%)	34(11%)	62.5(27%)

iii. Analysis

The data are clear that, at least for the most part, in all three jurisdictions duty is indeed understood as a mostly categorical issue. The next question, of course, is why are there still such a considerable number of fact-based determinations. Part of the explanation is that, as we have seen, there are at least two types of duty determinations that, notwithstanding the general categorical nature of duty decisions, are typically, and indeed often unobjectionably, confined to the facts of

---

[91] The former consideration was necessarily not conclusive. If, for example, an opinion specified its task as to determine when *a* defendant owes *a* duty for pure economic loss caused by negligent misstatement (ie in a categorical manner), but concluded that this will only be where the defendant assumes a responsibility towards the claimant, despite the task being framed in categorical terms, the fact that the existence of a duty depended on the exact facts of the case (ie whether the defendant assumed responsibility) meant the determination was not categorical.

the case: those based on foreseeability and those relating to purely economic loss or omissions.[92] In particular, whether or not something is foreseeable will depend on the precise facts of the case and the nature of the harm that materialises. Similarly, whether or not a duty is recognised in cases involving purely economic loss or omissions *tends to*[93] depend on whether there had been an assumption of responsibility, something that depends on the precise nature of any representation made by the defendant to the claimant, or, at least in Australia, whether the plaintiff was vulnerable or relied on the defendant,[94] factors that also depend on the precise facts of the case.[95] The above statistics ought therefore to take this into account, as the differences in the different jurisdictions' number of fact based duty determinations could simply reflect the differences in the number of cases involving issues of foreseeability or pure economic loss/omissions. What, then, does the data reveal when adjusted for this?

Table 10: Classification of fact-based notional duty determinations

Type of fact-based determination	HCA	SCC	HoL/UKSC
Categorical	97(57%)	262(89%)	161.5(73%)
Concerned foreseeability	12(5%)	0%	17.5(8%)
Concerned purely economic loss or omissions	62(27%)	21(7%)	39(17%)
Other fact-based determination	23(11%)	13(4%)	5(2%)

a. Analysis of New Data

Table 10 reveals a number of interesting findings. First, it reveals that, for the most part, outside of cases involving purely economic loss/omissions and issues of foreseeability, duty determinations are overwhelmingly categorical. Indeed, if we exclude the foreseeability and fact-based decisions involving pure economic loss/omissions cases from the data, then 81% (97/97+23) of opinions in the

---

[92] This is not true of *all* cases involving pure economic loss and omissions. Occasionally there are categorical determinations in such cases: see, eg, Lord Goff, in both *Spring v Guardian Assurance plc* [1995] 2 AC 296 (HL), and *White v Jones* [1995] 2 AC 207 (HL).

[93] Again, this is not always the case. See ibid.

[94] See, eg, *Brookfield Multiplex Ltd v Owners Corporation Strata Plan 61288* (2014) 254 CLR 185. (Hayne and Kiefel JJ); *Barclay v Penberthy* (2012) 246 CLR 258.

[95] Ideally the study would have excluded assumptions of responsibility only, given that it has been suggested duty determinations should not otherwise be fact-specific. However, outside of the UK, it was frequently difficult to distinguish between decisions based on assumptions of responsibility and those where it merely played a role (eg under the proximity label). Rather than incorporating further discretion into the study in order to distinguish between the two, the study instead focussed on fact-based determinations in broad *inclusionary* categories only.

High Court of Australia, 95% (262/262+13) of opinions in the Supreme Court of Canada, and 97% (161.5/161.5+5) of opinions in the House of Lords/UKSC were categorical in nature. Secondly, it showed that, outside of cases involving foreseeability and pure economic loss/omissions, the High Court of Australia was by far the most likely to confine a duty determination to the facts, doing so in 19% of opinions, compared to just 5% and 3% of opinions in the Supreme Court of Canada and House of Lords/UKSC respectively. Whilst a number of these cases could be explained on the basis that the High Court simply confused issues of duty and fault,[96] there can nevertheless be little doubt that the High Court of Australia simply *do* approach the duty issue with much greater emphasis on the facts of the case than the other two jurisdictions. Whilst this may not be overwhelmingly supported by the quantitative data, that it is nevertheless the case is suggested by a number of factors.

First, there have been a number of pronouncements in the High Court of Australia to the effect that the existence of a duty depends heavily on the precise facts of the case rather than the situation generally. In *Cole v South Tweed Heads Rugby League Football Club Limited*,[97] for example, Gleeson CJ made it clear that the duty enquiry is not to be considered at 'a high level of abstraction, divorced from the concrete facts [of the case];'[98] whilst in *Kenny & Good Pty Ltd v MGICA*,[99] Gummow J seemingly rejected the categorical nature of notional duty altogether, when he said:

> [I]n England, the duty has been formulated at some level of abstraction from any particular facts. In Australia, in accordance with authority in this Court, the determination ... of the existence and scope of a duty of care requires scrutiny of the precise relationship between the relevant parties.[100]

Secondly, as we saw in chapter five, the High Court of Australia is far more likely than the other jurisdictions to formulate the notional duty in terms of a 'duty to do x'. Such formulations are necessarily heavily influenced by the particular facts of the case, rather than the type of situation generally.

Thirdly, even where other jurisdictions have created categorical exceptions to the general exclusionary rules for purely economic losses and omissions, the High Court of Australia has tended to approach such problems in a fact-based manner. This is clearly illustrated in the competing approaches taken to defective

---

[96] For example, *Romeo v Conservation Commission (NT)* (1998) 192 CLR 431 (Gaudron J), and *Vairy v Wyong Shire Council* (2005) 223 CLR 422 (Gummow J). See also Section II(D) of ch 5. Note that, despite the claim that the opinions, in fact, concerned matters of fault, they were classified as notional duty determinations because *that is how they were identified by the court*, and this chapter is, after all, exploring how the courts *actually* approach the duty issue rather than how (it is argued) they *should* approach the duty issue.

[97] (2004) 217 CLR 469.

[98] ibid 472.

[99] (1999) 199 CLR 413.

[100] ibid 445.

building cases. Whereas both the House of Lords/UKSC[101] and Supreme Court of Canada[102] have dealt with such situations categorically, ruling that either *all* subsequent purchasers are or are not owed a duty, the High Court of Australia has not. In particular, the most recent pronouncement on the issue, *Brookfield Multiplex Ltd v Owners Corporation Strata Plan 61288*,[103] denied the existence of a duty on the grounds that the particular plaintiff lacked any vulnerability and on the basis of the particular wording of the contract between the plaintiff and the original owner.[104] As discussed in chapter five, the obvious problem with such reasoning is that the next defective building case that comes along, which will likely involve a slightly differently worded contract and slightly different degree of vulnerability, etc, will need to undergo a fresh duty evaluation. Perhaps, however, the majority opinion in *CAL No 14 Pty Ltd v Motor Accidents Insurance Board*[105] provides the clearest illustration of the High Court of Australia's fact-based approach to the duty enquiry. The plaintiff's husband, Mr Scott, was killed as he rode his motorcycle home from the defendant's hotel, following a lengthy drinking session at the hotel's bar. The accident was held to be a result of Mr Scott's intoxication. The plaintiff sued the defendant hotel on the grounds that they should not have let Mr Scott leave the hotel in his intoxicated state. Gummow, Heydon and Crennan JJ, with whom French CJ and Hayne J agreed, held that the defendant had not owed the plaintiff a 'duty to take reasonable care to prevent [the plaintiff] from riding the motorcycle while so affected by alcohol as to have a reduced capacity to ride it safely'.[106] Reasons for rejecting such a duty included a lack of vulnerability, and the exact nature of the arrangement between Mr Scott and the publican (that is, that the publican would keep Mr Scott's motorcycle keys until the following morning). Other more general considerations were also relied upon. However, it was only *after* the court determined that the particular defendant did not owe a duty to the particular claimant, on the exact facts of the case, that the court thought it desirable to offer some guidance on whether a duty was owed 'by publicans to customers: generally'.[107] Why the court did not deal with the issues the other way around is not at all clear.

E. To What Extent Do Courts Rely on Policy Considerations?

As we saw in chapter five, the use of policy considerations to determine the outcome of the duty enquiry is highly controversial. Whilst some believe that

---

[101] *D&F Estates Ltd v Church Commissioners for England and Wales* [1989] 1 AC 177 (HL).
[102] *Winnipeg Condominium Corp No 36 v Bird Construction Co* (1995) 121 DLR (4th) 193.
[103] (2014) 254 CLR 185.
[104] See especially, ibid [29] (French CJ), [56] (Hayne and Kiefel JJ).
[105] (2009) 239 CLR 390.
[106] ibid 404.
[107] ibid 411.

policy considerations are an essential part of any duty analysis, others believe that any use of policy is highly inappropriate and that such considerations should play no part in the duty enquiry whatsoever. Notwithstanding the controversy, there can be little doubt that the courts are generally more than happy for policy-based considerations to be taken into account as part of the duty analysis. Indeed, consideration of policy factors is explicitly *required* by the final stage of both the *Anns* and *Caparo* tests (and in the case of the former, the proximity stage too),[108] has featured in Deane J's proximity test,[109] and would certainly appear to be permissible under the salient features test too.[110]

Given that courts *can* rely on policy considerations, how often do they *actually* rely on policy considerations? For critics of policy-based reasoning, the answer to this is important. If, for example, the courts do not actually rely on policy, or at least only do so rarely, then the debate surrounding the propriety of policy-based reasoning would be of limited practical significance. On the other hand, if policy-based reasoning were universal, they might have greater cause for concern. The popular view seems to be that, at least in the ultimate appellate courts, policy does indeed play a crucial role in many duty determinations. Luntz, for example, has argued that, despite the High Court of Australia's ostensible distaste for policy-based arguments, such considerations nevertheless 'permeate many of their judgments';[111] Weinrib, too, has argued that policy is 'much invoked' in duty determinations;[112] whilst Beever, in perhaps the boldest statement of all, has said that, under the *Caparo* and *Anns* general duty tests, 'the duty of care is determined *entirely* by policy'.[113] In this section we will explore the accuracy of these claims further. In particular, we will investigate how frequently policy considerations were *actually* relied upon in the various courts.

i. Methodology

The first, and most obvious, difficulty in determining how frequently policy-based arguments are relied upon by the courts, is what we mean by 'policy'. 'Policy' is a slippery term, and is often used to refer to a wide variety of considerations.[114] The frequency with which courts rely on considerations of policy will therefore vary

---

[108] See (n 53) above.

[109] *Jaensch v Coffey* (1984) 155 CLR 549, 585 (Deane J), *Gala v Preston* (1991) 172 CLR 243, 260 (Brennan J), in *Bryan v Maloney* (1995) 182 CLR 609, 618 (Mason CJ, Dean and Gaudron JJ), and *Hill v Van Erp* (1997) 188 CLR 159, 176 (Dawson J).

[110] See, eg, *Sullivan v Moody* (2001) 207 CLR 562, [57], where, in applying the salient features test, the High Court referred to the potential for the recognition of a duty to lead to defensive policing as a factor to be considered when determining the existence of a duty of care—a clear policy-based consideration.

[111] H Luntz, 'The Use of Policy in Negligence Cases in the High Court of Australia' in M Bryan (ed), *Private Law in Theory and Practice* (Routledge-Cavendish, 2007) 83.

[112] EJ Weinrib, 'The Disintegration of Duty' in M Stuart Madden (ed), *Exploring Tort Law* (Cambridge University Press, 2005) 149.

[113] A Beever, *Rediscovering the Law of Negligence* (Hart, 2007) 187 (emphasis added).

[114] For more on the definition of 'policy' in the private law context, see James Plunkett, 'Principle and Policy in Private Law Reasoning' (2016) 75 CLJ 366, section II.

according to how we define 'policy'. If, for example, policy is understood broadly, as referring to broad considerations as to what is just between the parties, then 'policy' considerations would feature in almost every duty determination, a conclusion that, as Robertson notes, is accurate but 'unremarkable'.[115] It is for this reason that, in the duty context, policy tends to be understood more narrowly, referring to considerations of community welfare, as distinct from considerations of interpersonal justice.[116] Indeed, it is this understanding of policy that those who object to its use have in mind. Many common duty arguments can easily be classified in accordance with this definition. So, for example, arguments relating to the claimant's vulnerability, the degree of the defendant's control over the risk, the claimant's reliance on the defendant, and whether the duty would be inconsistent with an existing contract between the claimant and defendant, clearly relate to issues of interpersonal justice,[117] whilst arguments relating to the effect that recognising a duty would have on insurance policies, or the effect that recognising a duty would have on a class of persons including the defendant, clearly relate to considerations of community welfare.

Other arguments, however, do not so clearly lie on one side of the line or the other, and could conceivably be classified as arguments based on considerations of interpersonal justice *and* arguments based on considerations of community welfare.[118] The clearest examples of such arguments are those relating to fears of indeterminate liability and those relating to conflicting duties.[119] In the case of conflicting duties, Robertson, who has written extensively on the appropriate classification of duty-based arguments,[120] suggests focussing on whether the concern with conflicting duties is with the behavioural consequences of recognising the conflicting duty, in which case the argument relates to community welfare, or whether the concern is with how the defendant could be expected to reconcile and discharge the competing duties, in which case it relates to interpersonal justice. In relation to concerns with indeterminate liability, the solution is less obvious. On the one hand, the argument could be seen as based on fears that recognising liability will result in a flood of claims in the courts, causing delays in the legal system and requiring additional public resources, and so based on considerations of community welfare, whilst on the other hand, it could be understood as demonstrating a lack of any proximate relationship between the parties, or as creating an unduly onerous burden on the defendant (given the number of potential parties),

---

[115] A Robertson, 'Policy-Based Reasoning in Duty of Care Cases' (2012) 33 LS 119, 121.

[116] Plunkett (n 114) section II(B).

[117] Robertson (n 114) 122–23, 127.

[118] As Robertson, for example, notes, 'Like all legal dichotomies, the distinction between interpersonal justice and community welfare is at times difficult to draw': ibid 121.

[119] Ibid 122.

[120] See, eg, ibid; A Robertson, 'Constraints on Policy-Based Reasoning in Private Law' in A Robertson and HW Tang (eds), *The Goals of Private Law* (Hart, 2009); A Robertson, 'Justice, Community Welfare and the Duty of Care' (2011) 127 LQR 370; and A Robertson, 'Rights, Pluralism and the Duty of Care' in D Nolan and A Robertson (eds), *Rights and Private Law* (Hart, 2012).

and so based on considerations of interpersonal justice.[121] For the purposes of this section, however, arguments based on indeterminacy were classified as a policy consideration. A final type of argument that gives rise to difficulty relates to concerns over justiciability. Whilst this is often understood as a consideration of policy, according to Robertson, it is more convincingly understood as a question of whether the decision is suitable for judicial review, and so relating to neither community welfare nor interpersonal justice.[122] Nolan, too, argues issues of justiciability relate to neither community welfare nor interpersonal justice, and are better understood as relating to questions of fault.[123] Accordingly, for the purposes of this section, arguments based on justiciability were not classified as policy-based arguments.

The second difficulty with determining how often policy considerations were relied upon by the courts is what we mean by 'relied upon.' After all, there is a clear distinction between relying *solely* upon policy considerations, relying on policy considerations to support a conclusion already reached via other grounds, and stating that policy considerations would have been relevant, or even conclusive, were the facts different; yet all could be said to 'rely upon' policy considerations in some sense. Accordingly, for the purposes of this section, opinions were classified into the following four categories: policy considerations were not considered; policy considerations were considered but were held to be unconvincing or irrelevant on the facts; policy considerations supported the outcome of the duty enquiry *in addition to* non-policy considerations; policy considerations were determinative. When coding the data, a distinction was also drawn between pro-duty and anti-duty policy based arguments in order to determine whether such arguments were used primarily to support the imposition of a duty or to deny it.

ii. The Results

The number of duty determinations that relied upon considerations of policy is detailed in the following table:

Table 11: The use of policy in duty determinations

Did the opinion rely on policy?	HCA	SCC	HoL/UKSC
Yes	98 (44%)	164 (55%)	130 (58%)
No	125 (56%)	132 (45%)	93 (42%)

Of course, as it is only notional duty determinations that we would expect to rely upon policy, the differences in the use of policy could potentially be explained

---

[121] See, eg, the discussion in Beever (n 113) 233–39. See also Robertson, 'Policy-Based Reasoning in Duty of Care Cases' (n 115) 121.

[122] Robertson, 'Policy-Based Reasoning in Duty of Care Cases' (n 115) 124.

[123] D Nolan, 'Deconstructing the Duty of Care' (2013) 129 LQR 559, 566, 577.

by differences in the types of cases heard: the greater the number of cases involving issues of factual duty, the fewer the opportunities to consider questions of policy. Fewer cases relying on policy could therefore be the result of more cases involving issues of factual duty, than due to a reluctance of the court to rely upon it. If we therefore ignore opinions based on factual duty, and only consider opinions concerning notional duty issues, we get the following adjusted, though ultimately very similar, figures:

Table 12: The use of policy in notional duty determinations

Did the opinion rely on policy?	HCA	SCC	HoL/UKSC
Yes	98 (47%)	164 (55%)	130 (63%)
No	113 (53%)	132 (45%)	75.5 (37%)

Of those determinations that did 'rely upon' policy, whether for or against the imposition of a duty, the manner in which they did so (that is, whether the policy argument was relied upon to support the imposition of a duty, and so a 'pro-duty' argument, or to deny it, and so an 'anti-duty' argument) was as follows:[124]

Table 13: The manner in which policy was relied upon

Manner 'policy' relied upon	HCA		SCC		HoL/UKSC	
	Pro-duty	Anti-duty	Pro-duty	Anti-duty	Pro-duty	Anti-duty
Considered, but unconvincing or irrelevant on facts	4(4%)	48(49%)	11(7%)	67(40%)	10(8%)	38(30%)
Supported the conclusion in addition to non-policy reasons	14(14%)	32(33%)	32(20%)	52(32%)	16(13%)	67(53%)
Was determinative	0	17(17%)	4(3%)	41(25%)	6(5%)	17(14%)
(Total)	(18)(18%)	(97)(99%)	(47)(30%)	(160)(97%)	(32)(26%)	(122)(97%)

[124] Percentages are given as percentages of the total number of times policy was relied upon in the court, rather than the number of overall determinations.

iii. Analysis

The data demonstrate that the use of policy in notional duty determinations varied considerably across the different jurisdictions, ranging from only 47% of determinations in the High Court of Australia, to 63% of determinations in the House of Lords/UKSC. Falling exactly half-way in between was the Supreme Court of Canada, which relied on policy in 55% of determinations.

Yet, whilst the data clearly demonstrate that policy considerations were relied upon in a considerable number of duty determinations, they equally clearly demonstrate that the duty enquiry is far from determined 'entirely' by policy considerations. This is made even clearer still when we see *how* the policy considerations were relied upon. In particular, whilst a significant number of decisions 'relied upon' policy considerations in some sense, the majority of determinations that did so either dismissed such considerations as unconvincing or irrelevant on the facts, or only used them to support a determination that could be, or had already been, reached via grounds that did not depend on policy. Only in a minority of determinations were considerations of policy *solely* determinative of the outcome of the duty enquiry.

When policy-based arguments were relied upon, the data are also clear that it was predominantly in order to deny the existence of a duty rather than to support it. This was most clearly illustrated in the High Court of Australia where 99% of the opinions that relied on policy considered anti-duty policy arguments, whilst only 18% considered pro-duty policy arguments, none of which, incidentally, were determinative. The situation was similar in both the Supreme Court of Canada and House of Lords/UKSC, where policy-based arguments were also overwhelmingly anti-duty in nature; again, anti-duty policy arguments being considered in close to 100% of opinions that relied on policy, whilst less than one-third of those opinions considered pro-duty policy arguments. It is noteworthy that the limited role of pro-duty policy considerations calls into question the final stage of the *Caparo* and *Anns* tests. In particular, it is completely inconsistent with the idea that the imposition of a duty must be 'fair, just, and reasonable' in the circumstances. The true position, it seems, is that the imposition of a duty must *not* be *un*fair, *un*just and *un*reasonable. A similar imbalance in pro- and anti-duty policy considerations in trial and intermediate appellate level courts in Canada and England has previously been noted by Robertson.[125]

A further factor that became clear during coding was that there was a distinct lack of variety in policy-based arguments used in favour of imposing a duty.

---

[125] Robertson, 'Policy-Based Reasoning in Duty of Care Cases' (n 115) 131. Note also Robertson points out (at ibid) that this is inconsistent with Booth and Squires' claim that '[p]ost *Caparo*, the starting presumption is that a new category of duty will be recognised only when policy factors militate in favour of its recognition' (citing Cherie Booth and Daniel Squires, *The Negligence Liability of Public Authorities* (OUP, 2006) 3.06).

In particular, almost every pro-duty policy consideration was one of two arguments: that to impose a duty would encourage a higher standard of care,[126] or, particularly in the House of Lords/UKSC, that wrongs should be remedied.[127] In the High Court of Australia, the lack of variety was the most obvious, where of the determinations that relied on pro-duty policy considerations, 88% (16/18) of those relied on the argument that the imposition of a duty would result in a higher standard of care *only*, 6% (1/18) on the higher standard of care argument *in addition to* another pro-duty policy-based argument, and the remaining 6% (1/18) on other pro-duty policy arguments. In the Supreme Court of Canada, of the determinations that relied on pro-duty policy arguments, 81% (38/47) relied on the higher standard of care argument, either alone or in addition to another pro-duty policy argument, whilst the remaining 19% (9/47) relied on more general policy arguments. And in the House of Lords/UKSC, of the determinations that relied on pro-duty policy arguments, 81% (26/32) relied on either the higher standard of care argument or the wrongs should be remedied argument, or both, with the other 19% (8/32) relying on other pro-duty policy arguments. This homogeneity in relation to pro-duty policy based arguments stood in stark contrast to the wide variety of anti-duty policy-based arguments relied upon by the courts.

Finally, despite there being a much greater variety in the policy-based arguments that were used *against* the imposition of a duty, some arguments were nevertheless used much more frequently than others. The most commonly used anti-duty policy argument appeared to be that the imposition of a duty would potentially lead to indeterminate liability. As was noted above, for the purposes of this section, this was classified as a policy-based argument; however, as we also saw, many argue that it is, in fact, better understood as an argument based on interpersonal justice.[128] Accordingly, if we were to re-classify the argument as one

---

[126] This was classified as a policy argument because it aims to deter harm in *future* cases, and so is justified on the basis that it benefits the *community*, not the claimant before the court. It is curious that this argument was so influential when used to justify the imposition of a duty, when what is essentially the same argument is heavily criticised when used to justify the denial of a duty. For example, Lord Keith's comment in *Hill v Chief Constable of West Yorkshire* [1989] AC 53 (HL) that recognising a duty could encourage 'detrimentally defensive' policing, has been roundly criticised as speculative, yet the suggestion that recognising a duty would encourage a higher standard of care, which surely commits the same error, has attracted no criticism whatsoever.

[127] This is commonly described as a consideration of 'public policy.' See, eg, *X (Minors) v Bedfordshire County Council* [1995] 2 AC 633 (CA) 663 (Bingham MR); and *D v East Berkshire Community NHS Trust* [2005] 2 AC 373 (HL) [100] (Lord Roger). It must be noted, however, that the 'wrongs must be remedied' argument is highly problematic, and an almost perfect example of question begging, as it fails to explain *why* the careless causation of ham amounts to a wrong in the first place. For further criticism of this argument, see the comments of Lord Roger in *D v East Berkshire Community NHS Trust* [2005] 2 AC 373 (HL) [100], and McBride and Bagshaw (n 62) 118–9. *cf* Andrew Robertson, 'On the Function of the Law of Negligence' (2012) 33 OJLS 31, 37–38.

[128] See (n 121).

of interpersonal justice, the influence of 'policy' reduces considerably, as the following amended table demonstrates:[129]

Table 14: The use of policy considerations excluding those based on indeterminate liability

Did the court rely on 'policy'	HCA	SCC	HoL/UKSC
Yes (excl. indeterminate liability)	68(30%)	137(46%)	125(56%)
Yes (incl. indeterminate liability)	98(44%)	164(55%)	130(58%)
No (excl. indeterminate liability)	155(70%)	159(54%)	98(44%)
No (incl. indeterminate liability)	125(56%)	132(45%)	93(42%)

The change is most noticeable in the High Court of Australia, where the reclassification reduced the number of determinations that relied on considerations of policy from 44% to 30%, meaning almost one third of the occasions on which the court relied on policy, it was relying *solely* on the indeterminate liability argument. Similarly, in the Supreme Court of Canada, reclassifying concerns of indeterminacy reduced the number of determinations that relied on policy from 55% to 46%—again, a significant drop. In the House of Lords/UKSC, however, the reclassification was of only minimal effect, reducing the percentage of cases that relied on policy from 58% to 56%, meaning that only very rarely was the only policy argument considered by the court the argument that the recognition of liability could lead to indeterminate liability. Whilst it is also true that 93% (28/30) of the occasions on which the indeterminacy argument was 'relied upon' in the High Court of Australia it was dismissed as irrelevant or unconvincing on the facts, and 66% (18/27) of the time it was 'relied upon' in the Supreme Court of Canada it was only used in conjunction with another policy-based argument, the indeterminacy argument nevertheless clearly carries considerably more weight in the High Court of Australia and Supreme Court of Canada than in the House of Lords/UKSC. Although it is not immediately clear why, one possible explanation for the difference in the effect of arguments based on indeterminacy is the distinct approaches to pure economic loss taken by the courts. In particular, the House of Lords/UKSC generally approach pure economic loss cases (and omissions cases) on the basis that a general exclusionary rule exists,[130] a rule which can usually only be overcome where the claimant has assumed a responsibility towards the claimant or there is some convincing justification for a categorical exception. On this approach, there is little need for arguments based on indeterminacy; the exclusionary

---

[129] The data from Table 12, representing Yes and No 'incl. indeterminate liability,' are also included.
[130] See ch 5, fn 171.

rule is *already* taken to be justified, and so arguments based on indeterminacy are simply not necessary. In the High Court of Australia, on the other hand, there is a much greater tendency for each case to be approached on its facts. Where this occurs, there *is* a need for any determination to not give rise to indeterminacy, and so arguments based on indeterminacy must necessarily be considered.

F. To What Extent Do Courts Rely on Academic Literature?

Much ink has been spilled on the duty of care enquiry. Indeed, it typically takes up a considerable portion of tort law texts, and much has been written on it in academic journals and monographs, much of which has been explored in the course of this book. To what extent, however, does that commentary appear to have any influence on the courts? In particular, do the courts appear to take academic literature into account when reaching their decisions—and if so, how much—or do they ignore it entirely?

i. Methodology

Methodologically speaking, measuring the influence of *anything* on judicial opinions, from those opinions alone, is a notoriously difficult task. Opinions do not always state the full basis for their conclusions, and so any inferences about *why* a particular decision has been reached aside from the reasons given must be treated with caution.[131] At first glance, however, measuring the influence of academic literature seems simple: simply count the number of citations per opinion, and equate more citations with more influence. But such an approach has limits. First, there will be cases where academic literature was *in fact* influential, but its influence is nevertheless downplayed, or is not mentioned at all. As Stanton notes, 'There is ... no convention, equivalent to those which operate in the academic world, requiring a judge to attribute views drawn from another person's work. As a result, attributing the source of an idea is a matter of judicial taste.'[132] Secondly, opinions reached independently of academic literature might nevertheless cite literature in support of the conclusion in the hope of giving the conclusion added authority, particularly when that literature is by authors of eminence.

---

[131] Hall and Wright (n 1) 96, 99–100. For example, Patterson has hypothesised that the reason for Lord Brown's low rate of dissent in the House of Lords was his office's proximity to the coffee room, which had the effect of encouraging other Law Lords to visit his office (on their way to get a coffee), become better friends with Lord Brown, and thereby be more likely to agree with him on the outcome of cases. Whilst such a hypothesis is possible, and consistent with the data, whether or not that is the *actual* explanation, and so causative, is impossible to prove. See Alan Paterson, *Final Judgment: The Last Law Lords and the Supreme Court* (Hart, 2013) 158, 167–8.

[132] Keith Stanton, 'Use of Scholarship by the House of Lords in Tort cases' in James Lee (ed), *From House of Lords to Supreme Court: Judges, Jurists, and the Process of Judging* (Hart, 2011) 206.

As Stanton also notes, 'A judgment which did not consider the leading theoretical writing on the topic would be open to criticism and conversely, one which adopts the views of leading authors gains authority.'[133] Thirdly, academic literature is not only cited where it was ostensibly influential. On the contrary, it is often cited to illustrate an argument that the court is rejecting. Equating citations with 'influence' would therefore be misleading. Notwithstanding these limitations, however, provided that citations are distinguished on the basis of how they were used, the data would certainly give *some* approximation of the level of influence of academic literature on courts, even if not a perfect one. It is also questionable whether a more reliable alternative exists.[134] It is surely also safe to infer that, *at least on the whole*, more citations of ostensibly influential literature implies more influence, whilst fewer or no citations implies less influence.

To take into account the differing purposes of citations, opinions were classified into the following four categories: did not cite academic literature; cited academic literature incidentally or in a way that did not appear to influence the conclusion; cited academic literature in support of the actual state of the law or in support of the conclusion;[135] and, cited literature that conflicted with the conclusion as to the existence of a duty. Each opinion only counted once, regardless of the number of parties in the case.[136] Individual opinions were also able to cite academic literature in more than one way.[137] For the sake of clarity, academic literature included journal articles, textbooks, book chapters, and research papers, but did not include law reform commission reports (or the international equivalents) or unpublished extra-judicial speeches. Finally, the frequency of citations per opinion was not considered, as it was felt that it could potentially skew the data; in particular, it was felt that, say, nine opinions with no citations and one opinion with 10 citations, should not be equated with 10 opinions with one citation each, as the latter surely says more about the influence of academic literature *overall*, than the former.

---

[133] ibid 221.

[134] Interviews are the obvious alternative, but aside from the logistical difficulties in doing so (and indeed impossibility in the case of deceased judges), even interviews would not be an infallible method for determining the true influence of academic literature, as many judges would likely have forgotten many of the 'undisclosed' reasons for their opinions, other than those opinions given most recently, and even if they could remember, are unlikely to confess to presenting others' ideas as their own in any event.

[135] Whilst citations in support of the conclusion and citations in support of the existing state of the law are, arguably, distinguishable, the line between the two was frequently blurred (eg a conclusion that followed from a particular conclusion as to the state of the law) and so they were classified together.

[136] This avoided the difficulty of identifying which claimant/defendant combination the citation applied to, something that was rarely clear.

[137] For example, it could cite literature both for *and* against the conclusion reached.

ii. The Results

The manner in which the opinions of the various courts cited academic literature was as follows:[138]

Table 15: The use of academic literature in opinions

Manner academic literature cited	HCA	SCC	HoL/UKSC
Opinion did not cite	63%	42%	67%
Opinion cited incidentally	10%	11%	8%
Opinion cited as background or in support	33%	55%	29%
Opinion cited in conflict with conclusion	5%	5%	7%

iii. Analysis

Much of the data are unsurprising, as well as being relatively consistent across the different jurisdictions. In all jurisdictions, academic literature was predominantly cited to support the opinions' description of the law or the conclusion ultimately reached, including in more than half (55%) of all opinions in the Supreme Court of Canada. Academic literature was also only occasionally cited incidentally,[139] but was only rarely cited when it did not support the conclusion reached.[140] Despite much of the data being consistent across the jurisdictions, there was some variance in the number of opinions that did *not* cite any academic literature, accounting for 67% of opinions in the House of Lords/UKSC, 63% of opinions in the High Court of Australia, but only 42% opinions in the Supreme Court of Canada.

Whilst we have already noted the limits of measuring the influence of academic literature via the number of citations, a number of observations made during the coding appeared to suggest that, if anything, the true influence of academic literature is *under-represented* by the data. For example, in *Arthur JS Hall*

---

[138] The reason the percentages add to more than 100% is because many opinions cited academic literature for multiple purposes; for example, both for and against the conclusion. Percentages are given as a percent of total opinions per court.

[139] This was almost exclusively for historical purposes; for example, explaining how a doctrine of law emerged and developed over time.

[140] Stanton, somewhat cynically, suggests that the primary reason courts cite academic literature that conflicts with their conclusions is less to promote quality academic discourse on how the law should develop and more to address the possible objections of the counsel who cited it: Stanton (n 132) 214.

and Co v Simons,[141] Lord Hoffmann stated that 'in considering these questions I have been greatly assisted by a wealth of writing on the subject by judges, practitioners, and academics, in the United Kingdom and overseas. I hope that I will not be thought ungrateful if I do not encumber this speech with citations'.[142] In other words, academic literature *was* influential, yet no literature was cited. Accordingly, if we are measuring influence by citations, and the courts have explicitly said that they often do not cite academic work that has been influential, it seems safe to infer that the *actual* influence is greater than the *apparent* influence, based on a simple measure of the number of citations.

Academic literature therefore clearly has *an* influence on the courts. Quantifying that level influence, however, is extremely difficult and it is next to impossible to determine in any reliable way whether academic literature actually influences the *outcome* of cases, and if so, to what extent. Perhaps Stanton, despite writing about the House of Lords only, captures the true position best:

> The overall picture which emerges ... is of a senior judiciary which is prepared to be open about the material it uses to feed into its decisions, including the fact that it is considering and, at times, placing reliance on juristic writing. For academic jurists this holds out the possibility that their work may, albeit on rare occasions, have an impact on the development of the law, even though a precise assessment of the level of that impact is likely to be impossible.[143]

IV. Conclusion

This chapter explored a study of 121 duty decisions in the ultimate appellate courts of Australia, Canada, and the UK, over the 31-year period between 1985 and 2015. It has explored differences in the types of cases heard, the frequency with which the courts rely on general duty tests, what the courts rely on when they do not rely on general duty tests, whether the courts approach duty in a categorical manner, the extent to which the courts rely upon policy considerations, and the extent to which academic literature *appears to* influence the courts. The study has identified a number of differences in the methodological approaches of the different courts.

Of the 121 cases included in the study, 41 were from the High Court of Australia, 39 were from the Supreme Court of Canada, and 41 were from the House of Lords/UKSC. Perhaps the greatest difference in the nature of the cases heard concerned the number of appeals from trial determinations compared to

---

[141] [2002] 1 AC 615 (HL).
[142] ibid 688.
[143] Stanton (n 132) 224.

the number of appeals from strike outs and other pre-trial rulings. Whilst appeals from strike outs, etc, made up approximately 25% of the cases heard in both the High Court of Australia and the Supreme Court of Canada, they made up 55% of cases heard in the House of Lords/UKSC. And of the cases that were appealed from strike outs, etc, whilst they were almost invariably unsuccessful in both the High Court of Australia and the Supreme Court of Canada, in the House of Lords/UKSC, more often than not they *were* successful. The success rates of claimants also appeared to vary considerably, yet, due to the data's focus on the existence of a duty rather than the existence of liability, this particular data had to be viewed with caution.

The various courts approach to general duty tests also varied considerably. Whilst the High Court of Australia and the House of Lords/UKSC only relied on tests in a clear minority of cases, the use of general tests in the Supreme Court of Canada was almost universal. Though, upon closer analysis, general tests often appeared to be being often used at little more than labels for whatever arguments the court felt were appropriate for that particular category of case.

When duty tests were not used, a variety of other methodologies took their place. Unsurprisingly, what was described as the 'common law method' proved to be particularly popular in this regard. In the High Court of Australia, however, an *ad hoc* balancing approach also emerged as influential. Despite the balancing approach giving rise to a number of serious objections, there is nevertheless a strong argument that it does not result in an overly dissimilar method of determination than general tests; that is, the difference relates more to form than to substance. In any event, the data are clear that a considerable number of cases are resolved without reference to the more well-known duty methodologies; in particular, general duty tests and the common law method. Whilst the apparent ability of the courts to resolve so many cases without recourse to general duty tests might be seen to support the claims of those who criticise the value of duty tests, it also highlights a clear lacuna in the conventional understanding of the courts' approach to resolving duty problems.

The majority of duty determinations in all jurisdictions were also categorical in nature. Of those determinations that were based on the precise facts of the cases, in the House of Lords/UKSC and the Supreme Court of Canada, these were almost exclusively in cases involving issues of foreseeability, pure economic loss or omissions. In the High Court of Australia, however, fact-based determinations were not confined to such cases. This appeared to be explained on the basis that the High Court of Australia simply *is* more focussed on the particular facts of the case when approaching the notional duty issue.

Reliance upon policy considerations was also not as significant as some commentators have suggested. Despite courts generally seeing the use of policy considerations as perfectly appropriate, in many cases, including the majority of cases in the High Court of Australia, policy considerations were not mentioned at all, whilst in those cases that did consider policy-based arguments, the majority of such cases either dismissed them as irrelevant or unconvincing on the facts, or only used them to support a conclusion reached via means that did not depend on policy. Only in a small minority of cases were policy-considerations determinative of the outcome. Also of note was that policy considerations played an almost exclusively negative role, pointing *against* the existence of a duty rather than in *favour* of it; and of the occasions that they did point in favour of a duty, it was almost invariably on the basis that it would encourage a higher standard of care, or because wrongs should be remedied.

Finally, the influence of academic literature was examined. In both the High Court of Australia and House of Lords/UKSC, the majority of opinions cited no academic literature at all, and in the Supreme Court of Canada, it was not far from half of all opinions. Where academic literature was mentioned, it was predominantly for the purposes of supporting the opinion's overview of the law or conclusion reached. Only rarely was academic literature cited that conflicted with the conclusion reached by the opinion. Although inferring the *influence* of the literature on the basis of the number of citations is fraught with difficulties, there were nevertheless indications that, if anything, the influence of academic literature is greater than the number of citations would suggest. *How* much greater, or how best to describe this influence (significant, moderate, overwhelming, etc), is not something that can be sensibly concluded from the data alone.

As with all social science research, empirical legal research has limits, and the conclusions offered above, should not be equated with scientific fact. Much of the coding required considerable discretion and so it is unlikely that if the study were repeated the results would be perfectly replicable. Having said that, there is no expectation that *any* empirical legal research should be perfectly replicable, only that it be replicable *in principle*,[144] and it is hoped that the methodology has been described, and applied, well enough that if the study were repeated, substantially similar results would be obtained, and the same trends would be observed; in particular, that despite the three common law jurisdictions examined adopting similar high level approaches to duty (that is, the use of general tests, generally categorical determinations, not prohibiting the use of policy, etc), significant differences in their approach to duty problems nevertheless exist. The extent that these trends would be observed in lower level courts is not clear. On the one hand, lower level courts should follow guidance given by ultimate appellate courts; on the other hand, many of the trends observed have not been expressly encouraged (or even acknowledged) by the courts, and have really only emerged in the course of this study, and so are unlikely to be of much precedential value. Such a study, and a comparison with the results of this study, would nevertheless be of much value, and it is hoped it will one day be undertaken.

---

[144] See (n 1) 59.

8

Conclusion

Perhaps this is the ultimate lesson for legal theory in the attempted conceptualisation of the law of negligence and the expression of a universal formula for the existence, or absence, of a legal duty of care on the part of one person to another. The search for such a simple formula may indeed be a 'will-o'-the wisp'. It may send those who pursue it around in never-ending circles that ultimately bring the traveller back to the very point at which the journey began. Thus we seem to have returned to the fundamental test for imposing a duty of care, which arguably explains all the attempts made so far. That is, a duty of care will be imposed when it is reasonable in all the circumstances to do so ... So after 70 years the judicial wheel has, it seems, come full circle.

Kirby J in *Graham Barclay Oysters Pty Ltd v Ryan* 211 CLR 540, [244].

I. Introduction

The basic task of the duty of care enquiry is to determine the circumstances in which carelessly caused damage is recoverable. Where a duty of care exists, carelessly caused harm is compensable; absent a duty of care, carelessly caused harm may be inflicted with impunity. Today, negligence is the most commonly litigated of all the torts, and so understanding duty is more important than ever. Yet, so many discrete problems are now dealt with as part of the duty enquiry, that making sense of it has almost become an exercise in futility. Even the courts appear to have given up offering any sort of general guidance, and are seemingly only able to reconcile the various decisions by recourse to highly abstract concepts, such as what is 'fair, just, and reasonable'. Academic commentary, too, whilst often highly insightful, is typically of limited help, given the (inevitable) focus of the commentary on only discrete aspects of the enquiry. The sheer volume of commentary and cases also has the ironic effect of making the task of understanding duty even harder, given in the increased difficulty in identifying areas of agreement and disagreement. The duty of care enquiry is therefore a mess, and it has been the aim of this book to provide some much-needed clarity to the concept in the hope it will assist us in cleaning it up.

II. Moving Forward

Despite the confusion surrounding the duty concept, it is widely accepted that the function it performs is an important one. Whilst it seems that at least *some* of that function could be dealt with at other parts of the negligence enquiry, aside from the fact that this does not seem likely to occur any time soon, other parts of that function simply cannot be. Something akin to a duty enquiry therefore seems inevitable.

Much of the present difficulty surrounding the duty enquiry can be traced to the persistent belief, first proposed by Brett MR in *Heaven v Pender*,[1] but put more famously by Lord Atkin in *Donoghue v Stevenson*,[2] that 'in English law there must be, and is, some general conception [that is, a duty formula] of relations giving rise to a duty of care, of which the particular cases found in the books are but instances'[3]—in other words, that a general duty formula, capable of explaining *all* the duty cases, exists. This belief ultimately proved to be highly influential, and has shaped duty jurisprudence for the better part of a century. The search for a workable general test has, however, borne little fruit, and the various general duty tests that have been proposed have been subject to considerable limitations, generally due to their highly abstract nature. This is, for the most part, explicitly acknowledged by the courts. Indeed, as Kirby J notes in the quote at the start of the chapter, the search for *any* general conception, except in the most abstract (an unhelpful) of terms, is surely a 'will-o'-the wisp'.[4] Despite this, the belief that general duty tests are the way forward persists, and such tests continue to be widely used, even in ultimate appellate courts, and even though they often play little role in structuring the overall analysis.

There is therefore little to be gained from the blinkered view that the duty of care is best understood by reference to a general formula. Much *is* to be gained, however, by acknowledging that, as a result of its being forced to deal with such a wide range of problems, the duty enquiry, in fact, performs multiple functions, and is able to be greatly simplified if these are isolated and considered discretely. The two broadest of these functions are, first, determining whether the law of negligence *ought* to apply ('notional duty'), and, secondly, determining whether the particular defendant owed a duty to the particular claimant ('factual duty'). As factual duty is determined on the basis of whether harm to the particular claimant was foreseeable, the issue is able to be dealt with via the fault and remoteness enquiries. Factual duty is therefore functionally superfluous. Arguments that it should nevertheless remain as part of the duty enquiry in order to prevent

---

[1] (1883) 11 QB 503 (CA).

[2] *Donoghue v Stevenson* [1932] AC 562 (HL).

[3] ibid 580.

[4] Note that Kirby J was quoting Lord Oliver in *Caparo Industries plc v Dickman* [1990] 2 AC 605 (HL), 633.

negligence becoming an abstract enquiry are unconvincing, and so there is no theoretical justification for it to remain either. Removing the foreseeability element from the duty enquiry would be the first step towards simplifying the concept.

The notional element of the duty enquiry is also best understood as consisting of two discrete stages. The first stage requires the identification of a broad 'situation' or 'category of case' that the facts of the case fall within. We have seen that, at least for the most part, outside of cases involving purely economic loss and omissions, this is indeed how the courts approach the notional enquiry. In order to avoid confusion, the situations should reference the kind of harm suffered, the way it occurred, and the relationship of the parties to each other. They should also not be expressed in overly narrow nor overly broad terms. Formulations of notional duty as a 'duty to do X', which are becoming increasingly common in Australia, are awkward and focus the attention of the court on the wrong things, and so should be avoided altogether. Courts should also be mindful when speaking in terms of the 'scope' of the duty, given the confusion that can arise from the various, and completely inconsistent, meanings ascribed to the term.

The various duty situations are best understood as consisting of five broad categories, three inclusionary (physical injury, property damage, and psychiatric injury) and two exclusionary (omissions and pure economic loss), subject to a number of narrow exclusionary and inclusionary exceptions. Given that the considerations relevant to the existence of a notional duty will vary considerably depending on the broad category of case, it has been suggested that rather than determining whether an exception ought to exist by reference to the same general duty test, different principles ought to apply depending on the broad category of case. Whilst such an approach might seem radical at first blush, it is to a large extent already orthodox. Explicitly implementing/recognising such an approach would allow the development of far more tailored principles for each broad category of case, ultimately leading to a far more predictable duty enquiry, and providing a second step towards a simpler concept. Controversy surrounds whether policy considerations ought to be considered when determining whether a particular situation should or should not be subjected to a notional duty. We have seen that such considerations do indeed often play a role in determining the outcome of the duty enquiry, but also give rise to a number of objections; it is far from clear, however, whether any of these justify the prohibition of policy entirely.

If the court determines that the relevant situation does not give rise to a notional duty, it must still ascertain whether, despite reasons why the broad situation should not attract a notional duty, a notional duty should nevertheless exist because, on the facts of the case, the defendant assumed a responsibility towards the claimant. When determining whether the defendant assumed a responsibility to the claimant, courts must be careful not to conflate the normative issue of whether the defendant *should* have assumed a responsibility, with the factual issue of whether the defendant *did* (albeit in an objective sense) assume a responsibility towards the claimant. If the defendant did assume a responsibility towards the claimant, the claimant will overcome the otherwise exclusionary nature of the category and a notional duty will exist. Admittedly, this is not always the approach taken by the courts, but if it were, it would simplify the duty enquiry even further.

III. Conclusion

Making sense of the duty enquiry is no easy task. It is hoped, however, that this book has provided some guidance on what is wrong with the courts' current approach to duty, as well as provided a general framework through which the various debates and cases can be understood. It is also hoped that the proposed duty framework, consisting of five rather than one duty test, and completely independent from issues of whether the defendant assumed a responsibility, will assist future courts in tackling duty problems in a more structured way. This is not to say that determining when a duty does or does not exist is reduced to a simple algorithm; indeed, 'What is the relevant duty situation?', 'Should this broad situation be protected by the laws of negligence?', 'Is it appropriate to rely on policy considerations in this case?', and 'Can the defendant be said to have assumed a responsibility towards the claimant?', do not give rise to any easy answers. However, by isolating the discrete issues dealt with in the duty enquiry and dealing with them in a more logical manner, it is hoped that determining when a duty of care does and does not exist will at least be *easier*.

APPENDIX

Duty Cases from the High Court of Australia

1. *Sutherland Shire Council v Heyman* (1985) 157 CLR 424
2. *San Sebastian Pty Ltd v The Minister* (1986) 162 CLR 340
3. *Australian Safeway Stores Pty Ldt v Zaluzna* (1987) 162 CLR 479
4. *Hawkins v Clayton* (1988) 164 CLR 539
5. *Bus v Sydney County Council* (1989) 167 CLR 78
6. *Gala v Preston* (1991) 172 CLR 243
7. *Nagle v Rottnest Island Authority* (1993) 177 CLR 423
8. *Bryan v Maloney* (1995) 182 CLR 609
9. *Hill v Van Erp* (1997) 188 CLR 159
10. *Esanda Finance Corp Ltd v Peat Marwick Hungerfords* (1997) 188 CLR 241
11. *Pyrenees Shire Council v Day* (1998) 192 CLR 330
12. *Romeo v Conservation Commission (NT)* (1998) 192 CLR 431
13. *Crimmins v Stevedoring Industry Finance Committee* (1999) 200 CLR 1
14. *Perre v Apand* (1999) 198 CLR 180
15. *Agar v Hyde* (2000) 201 CLR 552
16. *Jones v Bartlett* (2000) 205 CLR 166
17. *Modbury Triangle Shopping Centre Pty Ltd v Anzil* (2000) 205 CLR 254
18. *Tepko Pty Ltd v Water Board* (2001) 206 CLR 1
19. *Brodie v Singleton Shire Council* (2001) 206 CLR 512
20. *Sullivan v Moody* (2001) 207 CLR 562
21. *Tame v New South Wales; Annetts v Australian Stations Pty Ltd* (2002) 211 CLR 317
22. *Graham Barclay Oysters Pty Ltd v Ryan* (2002) 211 CLR 540
23. *Gifford v Strang Patrick Stevedoring Pty Ltd* (2003) 214 CLR 269
24. *Woolcock Street Investments Pty Ltd v CDG Pty Ltd* (2004) 216 CLR 515
25. *Cole v South Tweed Heads Rugby League Football Club Limited* (2004) 217 CLR 469
26. *Neindorf v Junkovic* (2005) 222 ALR 631
27. *Vairy v Wyong Shire Council* (2005) 223 CLR 422
28. *Mulligan v Coffs Harbour City Council* (2005) 223 CLR 486
29. *Harriton v Stephens* (2006) 226 CLR 52
30. *Waller v James* (2006) 226 CLR 136
31. *Stuart v Kirkland-Veenstra* (2009) 237 CLR 215

32. *Sydney Water Corporation v Turano* (2009) 239 CLR 51
33. *CAL No 14 Pty Ltd v Motor Accidents Insurance Board* (2009) 239 CLR 390
34. *Adeels Palace Pty Ltd v Moubarak* (2009) 239 CLR 420
35. *Leighton Contractors Pty Ltd v Fox* (2009) 240 CLR 1
36. *Miller v Miller* (2011) 242 CLR 446
37. *Kuhl v Zurich Financial Services Australia Ltd* (2011) 243 CLR 361
38. *Barclay v Penberthy* (2012) 246 CLR 258
39. *Hunter and New England Local Health District v McKenna* (2014) 253 CLR 270
40. *Brookfield Multiplex Ltd v Owners Corporation Strata Plan 61288* (2014) 254 CLR 185
41. *King v Philcox* (2015) 255 CLR 304

Duty Cases from the Supreme Court of Canada

1. *BDC Ltd v Hofstrand Farms Ltd* (1986) 26 DLR (4th) 1
2. *Central Trust Co v Rafuse* (1986) 31 DLR (4th) 481
3. *Crocker v Sundance Northwest Resorts Ltd* (1988) 51 DLR (4th) 321
4. *Rothfield v Manolakos* (1989) 63 DLR (4th) 449
5. *Just v British Columbia* (1989) 64 DLR (4th) 689
6. *Fletcher v Manitoba Public Insurance Co* (1990) 74 DLR (4th) 636
7. *Canadian National Railway Co v Norsk Pacific Steamship Co* (1992) 91 DLR (4th) 289
8. *London Drugs Ltd v Kuehne & Nagel International Ltd* (1992) 97 DLR (4th) 261
9. *BG Checo International Ltd v British Columbia Hydro and Power Authority* (1993) 99 DLR (4th) 577
10. *Queen v Cognos Inc* (1993) 99 DLR (4th) 626
11. *Hall v Hebert* (1993) 101 DLR (4th) 129
12. *Edgeworth Construction Ltd v ND Lea & Associates Ltd* (1993) 107 DLR (4th) 169
13. *Brown v British Columbia (Minister of Transportation and Highways)* (1994) 112 DLR (4th) 1
14. *Swinamer v. Nova Scotia (Attorney-General)* (1994) 112 DLR (4th) 18
15. *Galaske v O'Donnell* (1994) 112 DLR (4th) 109
16. *Winnipeg Condominium Corp No 36 v Bird Construction Co* (1995) 121 DLR (4th) 193
17. *Stewart v Pettie* (1995) 121 DLR (4th) 222
18. *D'Amato v Badger* (1996) 137 DLR (4th) 129
19. *Hercules Managements Ltd v Ernst & Young* (1997) 146 DLR (4th) 577
20. *Bow Valley Husky (Bermuda) Ltd v Saint John Shipbuilding Ltd* (1997) 153 DLR (4th) 385

21. *Lewis (Guardian ad Litem of) v British Columbia* (1997) 153 DLR (4th) 594
22. *Ryan v Victoria (City)* (1999) 168 DLR (4th) 513
23. *Dobson (Litigation Guardian of) v Dobson* (1999) 174 DLR (4th) 1
24. *Ingles v Tutkaluk Construction Ltd* (2000) 183 DLR (4th) 193
25. *Martel Building Ltd v Canada* (2000) 193 DLR (4th) 1
26. *Cooper v Hobart* (2001) 206 DLR (4th) 193
27. *Edwards v Law Society of Upper Canada* (2001) 206 DLR (4th) 211
28. *Odhavji Estate v Woodhouse* (2003) 233 DLR (4th) 193
29. *Young v Bella* (2006) 261 DLR (4th) 516
30. *Childs v Desormeaux* (2006) 266 DLR (4th) 257
31. *D (B) v Halton Region Children's Aid Society* (2007) 284 DLR (4th) 682
32. *Hill v Hamilton-Wentworth Regional Police Services Board* (2007) 285 DLR (4th) 620
33. *Mustapha v Culligan of Canada Ltd* (2008) 293 DLR (4th) 29
34. *Design Services Ltd v Canada* (2008) 293 DLR (4th) 437
35. *Holland v Saskatchewan (Minister of Agriculture, Food and Rural Revitalization)* (2008) 294 DLR (4th) 193
36. *Fullowka v Royal Oak Ventures Inc* (2010) 315 DLR (4th) 577
37. *Broome v Prince Edward Island* (2010) 317 DLR (4th) 218
38. *Elder Advocates of Alberta Society v Alberta* 331 DLR (2011) (4th) 257
39. *British Columbia v Imperial Tobacco Canada Ltd; Knight v Imperial Tobacco Canada Ltd* (2011) 335 DLR (4th) 513

Duty Cases from the House of Lords and UKSC

1. *Leigh & Sillivan Ltd v Aliakmon Shipping Co Ltd (The Aliakmon)* [1986] 1 AC 785
2. *Smith v Littlewoods Organisation Ltd* [1987] 1 AC 241
3. *Curran v Northern Ireland Co-Ownership Housing Association* [1987] AC 718
4. *Ogwo v Taylor* [1988] 1 AC 431
5. *Hill v Chief Constable of West Yorkshire* [1989] 1 AC 53
6. *D&F Estates Ltd v Church Commissioners for England and Wales* [1989] 1 AC 177
7. *Calveley v Chief Constable of Merseyside Police* [1989] 1 AC 1228
8. *Smith v Eric S Bush* [1990] 1 AC 831
9. *Caparo Industries plc v Dickman* [1990] 2 AC 605
10. *Murphy v Brentwood District Council* [1991] 1 AC 398
11. *Department of the Environment v Thomas Bates & Son* [1991] 1 AC 499
12. *Alcock v Chief Constable of South Yorkshire* [1992] AC 310
13. *Henderson v Merrett Syndicates Ltd* [1995] 2 AC 145
14. *White v Jones* [1995] 2 AC 207

15. *Spring v Guardian Assurance plc* [1995] 2 AC 296
16. *X (Minors) v Bedfordshire County Council and Others* [1995] 2 AC 633
17. *Page v Smith* [1996] 1 AC 155
18. *Marc Rich & Co AG v Bishop Rock Marine Co Ltd (The Nicholas H)* [1996] 1 AC 211
19. *Stovin v Wise* [1996] 1 AC 923
20. *White v Chief Constable of South Yorkshire Police* [1998] 2 AC 455
21. *Williams v Natural Life Health Foods Ltd* [1998] 1 WLR 830
22. *Macfarlane v Tayside Health Board* [2000] 2 AC 59
23. *Waters v Commissioner of Police For The Metropolis* [2000] 1 WLR 1607
24. *Barrett v Enfield* [2001] 2 AC 550
25. *W v Essex County Council* [2001] 2 AC 592
26. *Phelps v Hillingdon London Borough Council* [2001] 2 AC 619
27. *Arthur JS Hall & Co v Simons* [2002] 1 AC 615
28. *Rees v Darlington Memorial Hospital NHS Trust* [2004] 1 AC 309
29. *Gorringe v Calderdale Metropolitan Borough Council* [2004] 1 WLR 1057
30. *Sutradhar v Natural Environment Research Council* [2004] PNLR 30
31. *D v East Berkshire Community Health NHS Trust* [2005] 2 AC 373
32. *Brooks v Commissioner of Police for the Metropolis* [2005] 1 WLR 1495
33. *Customs and Excise Commissioners v Barclays Bank plc* [2007] 1 AC 181
34. *Grieves v FT Everard & Sons Ltd* [2008] 1 AC 281
35. *Van Colle v Chief Constable of the Hertfordshire Police; Smith v Chief Constable of Sussex Police* [2009] 1 AC 225
36. *Jain v Trent Strategic Health Authority* [2009] 1 AC 853
37. *Mitchell v Glasgow City Council* [2009] 1 AC 874
38. *Jones v Kaney* [2011] 2 AC 398
39. *Smith v Ministry of Defence* [2014] 1 AC 52
40. *Cramaso LLP v Ogilvie-Grant* [2014] 1 AC 1093
41. *Michael v The Chief Constable of South Wales Police* [2015] 1 AC 1732

INDEX

CPSIA information can be obtained
at www.ICGtesting.com
Printed in the USA
LVHW021630150121
676579LV00006B/226